P9-DHS-819

SHOW ME THY GLORY

SARAH JEPSON COLEMAN

Ronald N. Haynes Publishers, Inc.

PALM SPRINGS CALIFORNIA

SHOW ME THY GLORY

Ronald N. Haynes Publishers, Inc.
Palm Springs, California 92263

Second Edition 1981

LIBRARY OF CONGRESS CATALOG CARD NUMBER: 81-83173
ISBN 0-88021-017-6

Printed in the United States of America

Originally published by
MOODY PRESS
2101 W. HOWARD ST.
CHICAGO, IL 60645

Preface

EARLY IN SCRIPTURE God's people were told to "hearken" and "do" that they might "live" and "possess." This principle was true for the nation of Israel and it is true for us in the twentieth century.

Throughout the pages of divinely inspired Scripture we see this principle. The Bible has been given to us not to speculate upon but to obey. When we keep God's Word we know the truth of His promise, "He that hath my commandments, and keepeth them, he it is that loveth me: and he that loveth me shall be loved of my Father, and I will love him, and will manifest myself to him" (John 14:21).

Such a privilege lies within the reach of all who would seek Him with diligent devotion, yet it is given only to the one who has the commands and keeps them.

It is sincerely hoped that this book, combined with His Word, will grant each reader new understanding of the continuity of God's message for us. Each day's thought carries a connection with the Bible reference, and the writings would indeed be barren without the accompanying sacred text. (The first reading given at the top of each page aims at helping the reader to complete the Bible in one year; the second and shorter one applies specifically to the devotional thought for the day.)

The Scripture says, "Blessed [happy] is he that readeth," and for those of us who are privileged to live in an age when God daily confirms His words, the blessings are inestimable!

May His words, illuminated by His Spirit, and these pages of simple illustration impress the message on individual hearts and cause each reader to hearken and do, that he may live and possess his inheritance, prepared for time and eternity.

SARAH ANNE JEPSON

Santa Ana, California

Acknowledgment

Grateful acknowledgment is made to the authors, publishers, and others who have so graciously made their works and stories available.

In some cases I do not know the authorship of the sayings, poems, and quotations used, and here no credit is given. However, any unacknowledged work will later be acknowledged if it is identified.

To each of you who helped make the book possible, a special thank-you. May our Lord continue to bless and enrich your life for His glory and honor.

January

GENESIS 1–2
GENESIS 1

> In the beginning God created the heaven and the earth.
> . . . The Lord thy God careth . . . from the beginning
> of the year, even unto the end of the year.[1]

THE PRESIDENT of a university once said that there are three
essentials to our happiness: (1) someone to love, (2) something to do, and (3) something for which to hope.

In the beginning, God created us. He has made provision for each of these basic needs for those who put their
faith and trust in Him.

Someone to love. Those who have been introduced to
Jesus Christ know beyond doubt that He loved us enough
to give His life for us. "Greater love hath no man than
this, that he lay down his life for his friends."[2] He, the
"altogether lovely" One, is interested in us as individuals
today. He made eternal life possible. He is both the Gift
and the Giver. Love begets love, hence "We love him, because he first loved us."[3] Besides His provision for our
eternal needs, He has given us His Word as a guide for
each day. Such love! And we can be the recipients. Yes,
He is Someone to love!

Something to do. As we begin a new year today, there
is much that we can do. God's first command was "Be fruitful, and multiply."[4] We can be fruitful only as we spend
time daily with Him in prayer and study. A life of devotion is essential. There is no substitute. This is the preparation necessary for building up the kingdom of God.

As Christians we are given a supreme task, and that is to communicate our faith to others. Those outside of Christ must realize that in Adam all men sinned and their fellowship was broken with their Creator. In Christ, men can be brought back into a living, vital relationship with God. To have close fellowship with God and then to share it with others produces spiritual fruit. There is much to do!

Something for which to hope. The Psalmist told us, "Hope thou in God." This will be another year of uncertainty, but we have the steadfast and sure hope that He will be with us. "The Lord thy God careth, from the beginning of the year, even unto the end of the year."[5] His guidance and protection are as real as the book you hold in your hand. We believe that He is the Source of "strength for today and bright hope for tomorrow." Tomorrow we can be forever with Him. "I will come again, and receive you unto myself; that where I am, there ye may be also."[6]

All beginnings must be in God—life and eternal life, creation and re-creation. As you begin to study the Bible, "as in physical creation, your heart and life may seem to be 'without form and void.' Do not be discouraged, the Spirit of God is within you, brooding amid the darkness, and presently His light will shine through."[7] Let His presence rule your life. And may He, who has given us every perfect gift, grant that our daily anticipation through this year will echo Moses' in Old Testament times: "I beseech thee, shew me thy glory."[8]

[1]Genesis 1:1; Deuteronomy 11:12.
[2]John 15:13.
[3]I John 4:19.
[4]Genesis 1:22.
[5]Deuteronomy 11:12.
[6]John 14:3.
[7]F. B. Meyer.
[8]Exodus 33:18.

❧ ❧ ❧

GENESIS 3–5
GENESIS 5

And Enoch walked with God. . . .[1]

ENOCH walked with God. Abraham was a friend of God. Throughout Scripture we have accounts of those who truly followed Him in faith and loving fellowship, "and it was counted . . . for righteousness."[2]

Many passersby stopped to ponder the meaning of a poster in a Rockefeller Center window: "Does only half of you travel abroad?" Its purpose was to advertise the study of a foreign language in preparation for a trip to another country. Without knowing another language an overseas experience could be disappointing.

The Christian could well ask himself a similar question in relation to his walk with God. If he is not experiencing daily fellowship and the true sweetness of His presence, something is sadly missing. It is essential to stop and take the time to "study to shew thyself approved unto God, . . . rightly dividing the word of truth."[3]

It has never been more vital to "rightly divide the word of truth" than it is today. As you begin reading Genesis, you may be well aware that there is a force at work to destroy faith in all that you believe. In the name of Christianity, many are questioning the literal interpretation of the early chapters of this book. In turning to the New Testament we find that the Apostle Paul accepted the story of creation and was convinced that it was true. His inspired writings made reference to early events when he wrote, "For God, who commanded the light to shine out of darkness, hath shined in our hearts, to give the light of the knowledge of the glory of God in the face of Jesus Christ."[4] It is in personally experiencing the miracle of re-creation that we come to understand and accept these beginnings. As one man said, "Our yardstick is not the changing ideas of men but the unchanging Word of God."

We are less than half living if we are not daily experiencing the power of prayer. Many of our yesterday's resolutions are broken today. In ourselves we are not adequate for a consistent Christian walk, but He meets us through prayer and meditation, speaks to us, and provides the path and power to journey in fullness of life. We become taller on our knees!

Walking and talking with God are the basis of gracious fellowship with Him. His promise is not for a life half complete or partially blessed but for one of total satisfaction—when we truly walk with Him.

The Psalmist witnessed to his walk with God. "Thou wilt shew me the path of life: in thy presence is fulness of joy: at thy right hand there are pleasures for evermore."[5]

[1]Genesis 5:22.
[2]Romans 4:3.
[3]II Timothy 2:15.
[4]II Corinthians 4:6.
[5]Psalm 16:11.

❧ ❧ ❧

GENESIS 6–9
GENESIS 6

> And God saw that the wickedness of man was great in
> the earth, . . . and it repented the Lord that he had
> made man on the earth, and it grieved him at his heart.[1]

IN A CLASS of youngsters we were trying to explain sin and
grace. For a while they could not see the connection between the two, then suddenly the light went on! It was
written all over one twelve-year-old's face. He had seen the
difference in the story of Noah. There was no time for him
to raise his hand, and the interruption was justified. Eagerness and enthusiasm almost crowded out clarity, but he
began his explanation of sin and grace.

"In the days of Noah there was a lot of wickedness and
wrong. God was getting tired of evil. He looked down and
in the middle of all this confusion He saw Noah and his
family. 'Noah found grace in the eyes of the Lord.'[2] Because of this God decided to save him in the time that
everyone else would be destroyed. He showed Noah how
to build an ark. It was not Noah's idea, it was God's. Noah
was not a boatbuilder."

And then he made his application. "All you kids know
we live in a world that needs judgment too. We sin, we
cheat on tests, and we try to get out of work. God looks
down on us and knows we have not done good, but here
is where grace comes in. He gives us a plan, just as He
gave Noah, for an 'ark,' but instead of one of wood it is an
'ark of salvation.' Jesus had not come in Old Testament
times, so His grace came another way. He has died for
us, and by grace we are saved today."[3]

As the youngster finished, I could not help thinking
of another Twelve-year-old who taught in the Temple one
day. Men were astonished at His wisdom and depth of

knowledge. Priests and teachers went away amazed, thinking about the things He said.

They were only a small class, but a child had led them. They could not forget that "where sin abounded, grace did much more abound."[4]

Each in his own way, we are guilty of building our own ships to escape judgment today. It may be with education or wealth. But our way is not God's way. Unless we follow His divine blueprints we are lost. Noah was saved because he "did . . . according to all that God commanded."[5]

I have often wished for a record of that young boy's simple but profound explanation. Yet, God has granted us His inspired record for our learning. Read, "and the Lord give thee understanding."[6]

[1] Genesis 6:5-6.
[2] Genesis 6:8.
[3] Ephesians 2:8.
[4] Romans 5:20.
[5] Genesis 6:22.
[6] II Timothy 2:7.

❦ ❦ ❦

January 4

GENESIS 10–12
GENESIS 12:1-8

> Now the Lord had said unto Abram, Get thee out of thy country, and from thy kindred, and from thy father's house,
>
> > . . . unto a land that I will shew thee
> > . . . I will make of thee a great nation
> > . . . I will bless thee
> > . . . [I will] make thy name great
> > . . . thou shalt be a blessing
> > . . . I will bless them that bless thee, and curse him that curseth thee
> > . . . in thee shall all families . . . be blessed.[1]

ABRAHAM SAID GOOD-BYE to his friends as he left Ur of the

Chaldees, equipped with the promises of God and eager to travel to a faith frontier. He could be called a spiritual pioneer. His journey would include unexplored places, he would cross burning deserts to unknown destinations. Yet he was not fearful. Friendships were left behind as he truly became "the Friend of God."

Why? His faith was in God, and God had given him these seven glorious promises. He knew that a future of serving God would well outweigh any temporary material blessings.

Abraham's willingness resulted in blessings, even for us today. "In thee shall all families . . . be blessed." Jesus Christ was a descendant of Abraham. Through Him these promises to Abraham have been made available to us. Our responsibility is to accept them by faith and to walk that pioneer trail.

It would be so easy if we could just look up and see that which is ahead. If only tomorrow could be clearer today! But this would not be pioneering and it would crowd out faith. "Without faith it is impossible to please him."[2] Abraham is an example to us. "He staggered not at the promise of God through unbelief; but was strong in faith, giving glory to God; and being fully persuaded that, what he had promised, he was able also to perform. And therefore it was imputed to him for righteousness."[3]

We go forward in the same assurance trusting God's promise of possessing the land. Our future is safe. He will bless us with His prosperity. The power of God is available, and its Source is immeasurable.

Danger ahead? Possibly, but we are promised protection, and our position, "hid with Christ in God,"[4] is eternally sealed.

[1]Genesis 12:1-3.
[2]Hebrews 11:6.
[3]Romans 4:20-22.
[4]Colossians 3:3.

❦ ❦ ❦

GENESIS 13–16
GENESIS 15

> And he [Abraham] believed in the Lord; and he counted
> it to him for righteousness.[1]

HOW EXCITING it is to find in the early part of the Bible,
tracing back to Abraham, the wonderful promise and fundamental truth of justification by faith alone. Abraham was
a living example of the divine declaration. Abraham taking God at His word, God imputed to him all of His righteousness. He will do the same for us.

An eighteenth century writer explained it like this, and
the careful reading of his words is most illuminating.

"Not that the faith of Abraham was, by a gracious estimation, accounted by God in the room of perfect obedience,
which the covenant of works required: but that, by his
faith, he laid hold on, and spiritually united or appropriated to himself the promised seed, by virtue of which union
all the righteousness of that seed was reputed to be his
righteousness. Thus in the book of God's accounts, the
great blessings of God are written on one page, as so many
talents bestowed on men: and the sins of men, not rendering to God the thanks due for so great benefits, as so many
debts: and lastly, the condemnatory sentence by which they
are declared guilty of eternal death. But as man's own
righteousness could not stand on the other page, the satisfaction and merits of Christ for the elect are inscribed, and
likewise their faith, as the gratuitous gift of God, and they
become partakers of all His righteousness. And thus upon
balancing the accounts, from their faith it appears that all
their debts are cancelled, and that they have sufficient to
give them a right to eternal life. Thus faith is imputed for
righteousness."[2]

One's heart leaps for joy at His eternal provision for us.
It also strengthens our faith to realize the great truths re-

corded by those prophets of old carry on into the New Testament. It has been said of the two testaments, "The New is in the Old contained, and the Old is in the New explained." There may be difficult moments of questioning, but there is depth of spiritual truth. We also have the reminder as we read God's Word, "Whatsoever things were written aforetime were written for our learning, that we through patience and comfort of the scriptures might have hope."[3]

[1]Genesis 15:6.
[2]From *Calvinistic Family Library* published by David Christy, 1835-36.
[3]Romans 15:4.

❧ ❧ ❧

GENESIS 17–18
GENESIS 18

January 6

> And when Abram was ninety years old and nine, the Lord appeared to Abram, and said unto him, I am the Almighty God; walk before me, and be thou perfect. . . .
> And Abram fell on his face: and God talked with him.[1]

GOD SO OFTEN SPEAKS to His children in moments of privacy when everything else is shut out and the sincere, seeking heart steps onto hallowed ground. Here the Almighty God reveals Himself.

In the journeyings of Abraham, it is significant to notice the many times he built an altar unto the Lord. He knew the dangers of constantly traveling from place to place without refreshing his soul in worship. Most often he sought God alone. It has been said that his pilgrimages were marked by the altars he built along the road.

As Christians we are called "pilgrims" and "strangers" in this land. We are only passing through. En route we too must take those special times at a private altar. Here

He meets us and shows us what Abraham experienced when "God talked with him." "He that dwelleth in the secret place of the most High shall abide under the shadow of the Almighty."[2] One must realize that "prayer is not a mechanical means of securing an automatic blessing." God knows our needs, and we pray because we are in need.

At the altar we become responsive to the needs of those around us when we as individuals are challenged by their needs. "Neither pray I for these alone, but for them also which shall believe on me through their word; that they all may be one; as thou, Father, art in me, and I in thee, that they also may be one in us: that the world may believe that thou hast sent me."[3]

Here also God burdens us, in private, as to our sacrificial giving of both self and resources. Giving to God at His altar is returning what has been given to us in sacred trust. Love for Him initiates giving, both of self and of means.

At this altar we learn, too, the cost of consecration—total surrender to Him and His will. General Gordon, a man of faith, once said, "I learned that to be consecrated to Christ we must not only have our will subordinated to His but we must be delighted to have it so." Consecration cannot be made reluctantly.

Altars are essential—personal, private, individual ones—built in your heart, with the love of Christ as the flame. At this place of worship God gives us strength to renew our vows and a burning desire to walk with Him.

[1] Genesis 17:1, 3.
[2] Psalm 91:1.
[3] John 17:20-21.

❧ ❧ ❧

16

GENESIS 19–20
GENESIS 19

THERE IS A STORY told of a man who visited the richest and the poorest homes in a certain city. In the rich man's dwelling he found elaborate architecture and costly furnishings. The owner welcomed his visitor and was proudly delighted to conduct him on a tour of his home. In the poor man's cottage the surroundings were very different. There were barely the essentials of life and scarcely enough bread for a guest. Yet again the visitor was welcome. At the second home he found the lack of furnishings unimportant because of a profound difference in the personalities of the cottage dwellers. Theirs was not a social concern for their guest but a spiritual one.

We have been reading in this first book of the Bible another contrast in homes. Three guests visited the tent of Abraham. He quickly made ready for their comfort. He welcomed them with thoughtfulness: "Let a little water, I pray you, be fetched, and wash your feet, and rest yourselves under the tree."[1] He quickly prepared a calf for supper and they ate. Little did Abraham know he was entertaining angels. Some have questioned Abraham's hospitality in not inviting the strangers in. One may note that it is not the interior comforts that make for good entertaining. It is the spirit with which one entertains and the warmth that is felt.

In the next chapter we have quite a contrast. Two angels came to visit Lot. Quickly the doors were opened so they could be impressed with what he had. Lot was wealthy in this world's goods. He depended on things to bring him happiness. His uncle Abraham looked to God for his peace and joy.

Is it not easy to take to heart the lesson here for each of us. We so often desire things: better cars, newer furniture, a better piece of property. When this is attained there is more to want, and then more, until we are striving and our desires end, as did Lot's, in destruction.

Looking to God for our sufficiency is so very different. I heard a mother explaining to another how she and her husband could afford to send their children to a Christian school. "You see, we are furnishing lives instead of homes. We think it is more valuable."

What are we doing to furnish our lives for God? Is the Holy Spirit welcome and at home in us? He wants a heart that is constantly ready to entertain angels unaware, to give a cup of cold water in His name, and to be a blessing.

[1]Genesis 18:4.

    ❧   ❧   ❧

January 8

GENESIS 21–23
GENESIS 22

> And Abraham stood up . . . and spake. . . . I am a stranger and sojourner with you.[1]

RECENTLY, while I was driving in a residential area, I noticed a little girl about five years old crying as if her heart would break. I stopped the car. "Honey, where do you live?" I asked, and through her tears she bashfully answered, "With my father." Then, she looked up and saw a man running down the street. At the sight of him her look brightened in an instant. It was her father, and she was going home.

Abraham often said he was a stranger, a pilgrim, or a sojourner. When asked where he lived, I am sure in his heart he felt his answer should be "With my Father God." There were great responsibilities as he was obedient and did the will of God, and his true address, with assurance of permanent residence, could only be said to be above.

18

In the New Testament we read of a certain day when John the Baptist was talking with a couple of men. Then a Man passed by. John pointed Him out and said, "Behold the Lamb of God!"[2] The Word tells us that at once the men left John and followed Christ. They must have felt a compulsion to know Him better. They may have been curious to see where He lived, but they learned that He was a Stranger and Sojourner. He was dedicated to His Father's business. One could surmise that Christ took the two men to a temporary residence. Some speculate it may have been on a hill; others, by the sea. It does not matter, because wherever He took them they found what they looked for. They went away with changed lives. One, Andrew, quickly became a missionary and brought his brother to Christ.

It is significant that in the short time they were with Jesus they and their life plans were changed. It was not by the surroundings; it was from being with Him.

"Where do you live?" The little girl was too young and frightened to remember. The confusion of being lost had dulled her memory. Then her father appeared and she knew all was well.

A young Christian may feel lost at times amid the confusion in which he lives, but the longer his experience with Christ, and the more maturity he gains, the closer and more constant is his touch with the Father. Moses said, "Lord, thou hast been our dwelling place."[3] Near to the heart of God is the place of true abiding. Where do you live? Christ graciously offers, "Abide in me."[4]

[1]Genesis 23:3-4.
[2]John 1:29.
[3]Psalm 90:1.
[4]John 15:4.

   ❧   ❧   ❧

I being in the way, the Lord led me.[1]

THIS IS ONE of the most beautiful stories of the goodness and guidance of God found in Scripture. Its simplicity and certainty lift the heart.

So many balk and chafe at the difficulty they experience in understanding and knowing the will of God. It is hard and impossible, they say. Hard? Impossible? The verse demonstrates the utmost clarity. The servant of Abraham was "in the way," therefore "the Lord led." Oversimplification? Not when you have experienced its living reality.

The late Dr. Norman Harrison advised his friends to read and study Scripture in the light of its two sides, God's side and man's side. Here one cannot miss the point. Man's side is merely to be "in the way." To be in the way he must have a prepared heart and open will to accept what is planned for him. He must be ready to carry through the job he is given to do. Some are too busy looking for a shorter way. "Sixty Seconds to a Better Christian Life" was the topic of a discussion. It took sixty minutes to explain the shortcuts to study, and no one felt enriched. If it is not the short way that is sought it is the roundabout one. Some individuals insist on delving into all the philosophies and teachings of those who wrote about Christ before seeing what He said for Himself. A combination is stimulating, but concentrating on that which surrounds the Object and not on the Object Himself is only frustrating.

"Being in the way" is for the one who puts himself where he can be led. It is then God's responsibility to lead. It is in seeking what God has for us ahead of schedule that brings confusion. If we keep our side, He surely will fulfill His promise. There may be doubts and wonderings such as the servant of Abraham possibly experienced. Yet his confidence in God was his direction and, in being obedient, he was shown God's faithfulness.

> "I being in the way" — that's my secret prayer,
> Knowing God's guidance waiteth for me there.
>
> "In paths of righteousness, for his name's sake,"
> I offer service, He my plans will make.
>
> Darkness overtakes me till faith lights the way,
> Trust keeps me unafraid, hope lifts the day.
>
> When I would wander from the way He planned,
> Let me be brought back by God's guiding hand.

[1]Genesis 24:27.

      ❧   ❧   ❧

January 10

GENESIS 25–27
GENESIS 26

THERE IS A WISE SAYING which makes one think: "Example is not just one way, it is the only way!" We see it in our daily lives, and for good or bad we use the common phrase "Like father, like son."

Bringing up children in the nurture and admonition of the Lord takes much more than a weekly trip to Sunday school and an occasional summer conference. Daily example and teaching in the home count far more. And remember, children do as their parents do.

In Old Testament times as well as New Testament times the God-ordained custom of worship brought people and families together around the Word of God. In Genesis 12 we read that Abraham built an altar to God. In our reading today, chapter 26 shows his son doing the same. Abraham could have told Isaac the benefits of such worship and sent him elsewhere to receive instruction, but he knew this was not enough. Isaac did what his father did. He had been trained by example in the blessed practice of worship.

It is awesome to realize that nearly 50 percent of today's young men who drop out of Sunday school give as their reason, "My dad doesn't go to church."

Communists admit, "The foe we most fear is Christianity." Yet this fear is cast aside as long as Christians fail to practice their faith daily and earnestly. A national magazine made this statement: "In America the family altar is secure against violation, but it is not secure against neglect!"

Today is a good day to take a long look at ourselves in the light of what God intends us to be. May we nurture, not neglect, true Christlikeness.

> Isaac learned from his father's ways
> Devotion to God is supreme, and praise.
>
> He followed the plan as he had been taught,
> And through his seed God's blessings were wrought.
>
> May we from our worship go forth to lead
> To the altar of God, those in need.
>
> Exemplifying in deed and word
> Our living, loving Saviour, Lord.

❧ ❧ ❧

GENESIS 28–30
GENESIS 29:1-20

> And Jacob served seven years for Rachel; and they
> seemed unto him but a few days, for the love he had to
> her.[1]

THE STORY of Jacob's great love for Rachel is a beautiful
illustration of what our love should be for our Lord. There
is no doubt that "those we love we love to please." Service
for them is done with a sense of the lightness of the duty
and with happiness of heart.

"Where love is queen time is too short, labor never hard,
distance never long, sacrifice unheard of."[2] Oh, that this
could give us a glimpse of what should be given to Him
because of His great love for us.

Time is often too short when it comes to preparing for
the visit of a loved one. It is easy to fly about the house
making ready and seeing to it that everything is perfect.
We Christians too seldom stop to realize we are called upon
to be in constant readiness for a return visit by the Altogether Lovely One. "Be ye also ready: for in such an hour
as ye think not the Son of man cometh."[3] This shortness of
time must make us swift to tell others of Him. We must be
busy making every possible contribution to the work of
God. Our hearts, daily prepared, must be kept pure and
filled with His grace and goodness.

Labor is not hard for those we love. Nor should labor
in His vineyard be painful. There may be days packed
with work: getting ready for a church dinner, pinch-hitting
in the Sunday school nursery when you had hoped to attend service. But count it all joy! It is for the Lord.

Our perspective is corrected when we learn to look out
into the distances of God. Sight is one thing; it takes in a
very small radius. Vision is quite another. It looks up and
beyond and finds ever so much more to do. The story is

told of a widowed mother living in Nebraska. Twice on Sundays and twice during the week she traveled fifty miles so that her family could worship in a sound church. There were heavy snows in winter and many obstacles, but she kept making the trip. Refreshment of soul always compensated for the wearisome drive. In thinking of Christ her soul soared, and distances for a purpose were accepted. Three sons faithfully serve the Lord today.

Thus Jacob's stay in Laban's home passed quickly because of the love that prompted it. May our love for the Lord show forth the same devotion and courage to do what is required, and more!

[1]Genesis 29:20.
[2] F. B. Meyer.
[3]Matthew 24:44.

❧ ❧ ❧

GENESIS 31–33
GENESIS 32

And Jacob called the name of the place Peniel: for I have seen God face to face, and my life is preserved.[1]

JACOB HAD BEEN TOLD by God to return to the land of his fathers, and with the command he was given a promise: "I will be with thee."[2] As he left we are told the angels were with him, so we know he was acting in obedience to God. Yet the path of obedience is often marked by testings. Jacob had recently escaped from the hand of Laban and now was about to meet his brother Esau. Why was he afraid of this meeting? The angels were with him: "This is God's host."[3] His prayer merits our attention. "And Jacob said, O God of my father Abraham, and God of my father Isaac, the Lord which saidst unto me, Return unto thy country, and to thy kindred, and I will deal well with thee: I am not worthy of the least of all the mercies. . . . Deliver me, I

24

pray thee, from the hand of my brother. . . ."[4] Here a saint is confessing his unworthiness. He is utterly casting himself on the word of God.

Then suddenly there is striking contrast. One might think it impossible for a man of Jacob's background and knowledge of God to rashly take things into his own hands. He had experienced deliverance. He actually was led with "hosts" before and behind. Mingled with his faith there was unbelief. Is it really so shocking? What about your own Christian experience? Has God not delivered you, guided you, and directed your way? Is it unthinkable that one day you got a bit frightened about certain circumstances and so did some private planning? There was nothing inherently wrong in Jacob's sending gifts to his brother, but the distrust in his heart was wrong. Clearly, Jacob feared Esau and cast away his confidence in God.

In rereading Jacob's prayer, it is hard to comprehend how he so suddenly lost his faith in God's sovereignty. But again it proves the presence in each of us of the "old man," or "the flesh." One must constantly be on guard against "the wiles of the devil."

Here is a picture of God's long-suffering and patience with us. Jacob wrestled and then there was victory. Jacob was renamed Israel, "prince with God." He saw God face to face. He called the place Peniel, which means "the face of God." May we each, from our disobedience, come back into perfect obedience and experience a personal Peniel.

[1]Genesis 32:30.
[2]Genesis 31:3.
[3]Genesis 32:2.
[4]Genesis 32:9-11.

❧ ❧ ❧

GENESIS 34–36
GENESIS 35:1-15

> And God said unto Jacob, Arise, go up to Bethel.[1]

HAVE YOU EVER BEEN at a crossroads? Have you been in a complete quandary as to where to go? It is not a pleasant experience, but it is a familiar one to most of us. It is one that Jacob faced.

He was eager to leave Shechem but the crossroads confused him. Traveling back to Laban was not the answer. He wanted to avoid Esau. The unhappy experience with the Shechemites made him anxious to leave quickly. Jacob had suffered adversity. No doubt he thought, *All these things are against me,* as he reviewed his past. He had traveled alone in strange lands. Yet over and over he had experienced the presence of Jehovah.

I am wondering if in Jacob's hour of great uncertainty the words of the Lord did not flash back to him: "Behold, I am with thee, and will keep thee in all places whither thou goest."[2]

In the darkest hour we are met by God. Such a time often proves that "man's extremities are God's opportunities." God spoke to Jacob and said, "Arise, go up to Bethel." He had been to Bethel before, and was familiar with its surroundings. On his previous visit he had thus given expression to his awareness of God's presence: "Surely the Lord is in this place."[3]

Jacob knew that returning to Bethel meant changing some of his past ways. To the entire household he said, "Put away the strange gods that are among you, and be clean, and change your garments."[4] The past had included sin and disobedience which he well recognized, and now he wanted for himself and his household a new beginning which would be marked by their return to Bethel. All were quick to put away the sin that had caused a broken rela-

26

tionship with their God, and on arrival at Bethel, an altar was built to the Lord.

It is significant that when originally leaving Bethel, Jacob started on a path which met with his own approval rather than God's. God often has us return to the place where we first lost the sweetness of His presence and real fellowship with Him. We must give up the strange gods and be willing to turn back for a forward start.

At Bethel, Jacob poured oil on the pillar he erected. It was a sign showing how God will pour His Holy Spirit upon us, when we in complete obedience turn back to Him. If your fellowship is impaired today, why not arise, and go to Bethel—wherever it may be for you—the place of loving communion with God. You will be restored and refreshed.

[1]Genesis 35:1.
[2]Genesis 28:15.
[3]Genesis 28:16.
[4]Genesis 35:2.

❧ ❧ ❧

January 14

Genesis 37–39
Genesis 37

> And it came to pass when Joseph was come unto his brethren, that they stripped Joseph out of his coat . . . and cast him into a pit. . . . Then there passed by Midianites merchantmen; and they drew and lifted up Joseph out of the pit . . . and they brought Joseph into Egypt.[1]

How often we do not understand God's dealing with us. Circumstances and problems make living turbulent. People and situations are difficult and disagreeable. Why? Why should God so deal with us?

No doubt Joseph, the beloved son of Jacob, had many times when he was at a complete loss to interpret the deal-

27

ings of God with him. Why should God allow his brothers so to mistreat him? Why should he be sold into slavery? And why should he be imprisoned in an Egyptian dungeon on a charge of which he was innocent? No doubt he felt forsaken.

One cannot help but think that even Elijah must have registered shock the day he went to Zarephath. God sent him to a widow after the brook Cherith had gone dry. Surely the widow would have means and she could provide for him. On arrival, Elijah found the woman preparing the last morsel of food for herself and her son. Humanly he might have felt that God had made a mistake. However, the circumstances prompted a miracle in which all three partook of God's gracious provision.

Jesus said, "In the world ye shall have tribulation: but be of good cheer; I have overcome the world."[2] This He is ready and willing to demonstrate. We may not understand His dealings with us and we may beseech Him, as did Paul, thrice and more to remove the thorn, but His grace and strength can prove sufficient.

It was not chance but Providence that brought those Midianites to find Joseph in his need. For the child of God everything is part of a plan. The very hairs of your head are numbered. You may feel you are in the deep pit of a problem, but God knows you are there and you need not be afraid. What a solemn but sacred thought—months before Joseph was cruelly cast into that pit, a caravan left a far country to arrive at the precise moment God had ordained.

Today we too receive this divine guidance. Sing praise in the darkness, for joy and deliverance will come in the morning!

[1]Genesis 37:23-24, 28.
[2]John 16:33.

❧   ❧   ❧

Genesis 40–42
Genesis 42

> And the famine waxed sore in the land. . . . And
> . . . [Jacob] said, I have heard that there is corn in Egypt.[1]

A MISSIONARY ORGANIZATION was suffering from financial famine. The home office became deeply concerned and sought God's direction. One of the staff members was reminded of her own savings. A small amount of stock had been left to her, and why should the missionaries suffer loss when she could help in her way? Going into the office the next morning she handed her superior an envelope containing the investments. Her comment was refreshing: "There is corn in Egypt!"

Everyone in the office had a warm smile. True, there was monetary famine, but how far had they gone to find out how much corn was in Egypt? Each in his own way "journeyed" out to seek substance for the mission. In two weeks the pressing debts were met. A letter to interested friends shared today's verse. The response it brought was overwhelming. Again it proved God has a granary and when He touches the hearts of His people, there is plenty for all.

After hearing the story I read again the account of Joseph and his family. It brought new assurance that God truly cares for His own. A storehouse of provision is available. It is inexhaustible and there will always be corn for those who trust in God. His promises are sure.

> Can the sun forget its rising?
> Can the stars forget to shine?
> Can the moon forget its duty?
> Then can God His will resign.
>
> Can the sea forget to roar?
> Can the waves cease and be still?
> Can the waters stop giving?
> Then can God forget His will.

Can the skies above be measured?
Can the foes of God prevail?
Can a man earth's structure fathom?
Then God's promises can fail![2]

[1]Genesis 41:56; 42:2.
[2]H. H. Savage.

❧　❧　❧

GENESIS 43–45
GENESIS 45

> And Joseph said unto his brethren, I am Joseph; . . .
> And God sent me before you to preserve you a posterity
> in the earth, and to save your lives by a great deliver-
> ance. So now it was not you that sent me hither, but
> God.[1]

HAPPY IS THE MAN who learns early to give thanks for all
things. There is no doubt that God deserves our praise
whether we feel like giving it or not. On dismal days particularly, it is good to look to the Psalms for examples of
praise and blessing.

Psalm 103 unfolds the story of a man who began blessing God in spite of himself and his feelings. He gave his
soul a command: "Bless the Lord, O my soul: and all that
is within me, bless his holy name."[2] It may be spiritual
speculation, but I do not believe he had a singing heart
when this incident was recorded. He knew it was right to
praise the Lord, and so to exercise his soul in obedience, he
repeated the command again. "Bless the Lord, O my soul,
and forget not all his benefits."[3] In reviewing the blessings
and benefits, his heart was lifted. A bit of interior reflection and his blessings multiplied. Continually he blessed
the Lord, and completed the psalm in desiring that "all
his works in all places of his dominion"[4] bless the Lord!

Joseph found that God overruled his unjust treatment,

and so he kept giving praise to God. He was able to look above self and beyond circumstance, trusting God to undertake for him. When exalted as Egypt's premier he found himself able to care for his brothers and father who came from a famine-ridden land. He told the family, "So now it was not you that sent me hither, but God." He remembered the cruel treatment his brothers had inflicted, but that was past, and he told them, "Ye thought evil against me; but God meant it unto good."[5]

Things today may seem unjust and at the straining point. Learn to look above and beyond. In cultivating the habit of thanks for all things, at all times, the wonderful secrets of joy are found. Love those that annoy, be patient with the impatient. The very act of praising God has freed many an enslaved soul from bondage to blessing.

[1]Genesis 45:3, 7-8.
[2]Psalm 103:1.
[3]Psalm 103:2.
[4]Psalm 103:22.
[5]Genesis 50:20.

❦ ❦ ❦

---

o be a good ambassador for his father. In talkin...
up of spectators, both believing and unbelieving,
"But now ye seek to kill me, a man that hath tol...
ruth."[2]

...th, in being obedient, became exalted: one in the h...
...haraoh in Egypt, the other at the right hand of (...
...ough their sufferings they were lifted up, and the...
...gs brought blessing to others.

...ur hearts should fill with joy when we recall that Jos...
Jesus each prepared a place for his own. In fami...
...ph brought his family to plenty. He provided for the...
...ry need. The Son of God has gone to prepare a plac...
His family, "that where I am, there ye may be also."...
...oseph was a great man, yet Jesus was still his Saviour...
... is our Saviour too, by simple faith and trust in Him....
...at He did was for all. How can we do less than truly...
...e Him our best and live completely for His praise and...
...ory?

[1]John 16:28.
[2]John 8:40.
[3]John 14:3.

❦ ❦ ❦

GENESIS 46–47
GENESIS 47

> "And God spake . . . "
>   One listened, heard
> The message
>   That was ministered.
> A call to Israel
>   In the night.
> "Go to Egypt,"
>   Joy's in sight!
> Jacob rose.
>   By chance? By choice?
> No! In obedience
>   To God's voice.

THE CATTLE were ready and the goods packed. The wagons began to move because God had spoken. A very old man longed to see his son and God had permitted it. There was a touching reunion. Then Joseph introduced his father to the Egyptian monarch, Pharaoh. Pharaoh asked the elderly gentleman a question which would be undiplomatic today, but was customary in eastern countries. "And Pharaoh said unto Jacob, How old art thou?"[1] Even kings were accustomed to bowing to old age.

The question is one to consider in our own Christian experiences. God speaks to us. How mature are we in our response? There are no doubt times when we resemble children, either shutting out all sound, or listening unmoved and forgetting soon.

Should not years of walking with God result in ability to listen? A trained ear comes with maturity. Do unpleasant conditions or temptations of life stifle the sound of heaven? How old are you in true Christian nurture and experience?

The response may be, "I am but a child. I have been fed with milk instead of meat, but I long to grow up in Him.

I want my eyes of spiritual understanding . . . I want the years to bring the Lord nearer . . . fellowship."

As a hymnwriter said, "The sands of time . . ." and one realizes that life is passing quickly. . . . important, then, that we spend each day in ga . . . itual maturity?

When God speaks, are you old enough to . . . voice and to agree with those people of Josh . . . said, "The Lord our God will we serve, and . . . we obey."[2]

[1] Genesis 47:8.
[2] Joshua 24:24.

❧ ❧ ❧

GENESIS 48–50
GENESIS 50

TODAY WE END the book of Genesis with a striki . . . between Joseph and Jesus Christ. Joseph is ofte . . . type of the Son of God. In reviewing Joseph we . . . clearer view of Christ and His great love for us.

Each for a time lived with his father. Said Jesus . . . forth from the Father, and am come into the . . . Joseph lived with his father and was greatly belove . . . God's Son.

Each was the object of great love and deep hate. . . . our Lord was greatly exalted as He came into Je . . . Shortly after, He was crucified between malefactors. . . . spit upon, He was wounded and bruised.

Joseph was sold for a few pieces of silver. Judas b . . . Jesus for a mere thirty coins. Each was plotted again . . . by his brothers, the other by His so-called friends. Th . . . no doubt that both were dishonored unjustly.

Amid the circumstances, however, neither lost oppo . . .

and so he kept giving praise to God. He was able to look above self and beyond circumstance, trusting God to undertake for him. When exalted as Egypt's premier he found himself able to care for his brothers and father who came from a famine-ridden land. He told the family, "So now it was not you that sent me hither, but God." He remembered the cruel treatment his brothers had inflicted, but that was past, and he told them, "Ye thought evil against me; but God meant it unto good."[5]

Things today may seem unjust and at the straining point. Learn to look above and beyond. In cultivating the habit of thanks for all things, at all times, the wonderful secrets of joy are found. Love those that annoy, be patient with the impatient. The very act of praising God has freed many an enslaved soul from bondage to blessing.

[1]Genesis 45:3, 7-8.
[2]Psalm 103:1.
[3]Psalm 103:2.
[4]Psalm 103:22.
[5]Genesis 50:20.

❧ ❧ ❧

> "And God spake . . . "
>   One listened, heard
> The message
>   That was ministered.
> A call to Israel
>   In the night.
> "Go to Egypt,"
>   Joy's in sight!
> Jacob rose.
>   By chance? By choice?
> No! In obedience
>   To God's voice.

THE CATTLE were ready and the goods packed. The wagons began to move because God had spoken. A very old man longed to see his son and God had permitted it. There was a touching reunion. Then Joseph introduced his father to the Egyptian monarch, Pharaoh. Pharaoh asked the elderly gentleman a question which would be undiplomatic today, but was customary in eastern countries. "And Pharaoh said unto Jacob, How old art thou?"[1] Even kings were accustomed to bowing to old age.

The question is one to consider in our own Christian experiences. God speaks to us. How mature are we in our response? There are no doubt times when we resemble children, either shutting out all sound, or listening unmoved and forgetting soon.

Should not years of walking with God result in ability to listen? A trained ear comes with maturity. Do unpleasant conditions or temptations of life stifle the sound of heaven? How old are you in true Christian nurture and experience?

The response may be, "I am but a child. I have been fed with milk instead of meat, but I long to grow up in Him.

I want my eyes of spiritual understanding enlightened. I want the years to bring the Lord nearer and dearer in fellowship."

As a hymnwriter said, "The sands of time are sinking," and one realizes that life is passing quickly. Is it not important, then, that we spend each day in gaining true spiritual maturity?

When God speaks, are you old enough to recognize His voice and to agree with those people of Joshua's time who said, "The Lord our God will we serve, and his voice will we obey."[2]

[1]Genesis 47:8.
[2]Joshua 24:24.

✿ ✿ ✿

January 18

GENESIS 48–50
GENESIS 50

TODAY WE END the book of Genesis with a striking parallel between Joseph and Jesus Christ. Joseph is often called a type of the Son of God. In reviewing Joseph we come to a clearer view of Christ and His great love for us.

Each for a time lived with his father. Said Jesus, "I came forth from the Father, and am come into the world."[1] Joseph lived with his father and was greatly beloved, as was God's Son.

Each was the object of great love and deep hate. One day our Lord was greatly exalted as He came into Jerusalem. Shortly after, He was crucified between malefactors. He was spit upon, He was wounded and bruised.

Joseph was sold for a few pieces of silver. Judas betrayed Jesus for a mere thirty coins. Each was plotted against, one by his brothers, the other by His so-called friends. There is no doubt that both were dishonored unjustly.

Amid the circumstances, however, neither lost opportunities to be a good ambassador for his father. In talking with a group of spectators, both believing and unbelieving, Jesus said, "But now ye seek to kill me, a man that hath told you the truth."[2]

Both, in being obedient, became exalted: one in the house of Pharaoh in Egypt, the other at the right hand of God. Through their sufferings they were lifted up, and the sufferings brought blessing to others.

Our hearts should fill with joy when we recall that Joseph and Jesus each prepared a place for his own. In famine Joseph brought his family to plenty. He provided for their every need. The Son of God has gone to prepare a place for His family, "that where I am, there ye may be also."[3]

Joseph was a great man, yet Jesus was still his Saviour. He is our Saviour too, by simple faith and trust in Him. What He did was for all. How can we do less than truly give Him our best and live completely for His praise and glory?

[1]John 16:28.
[2]John 8:40.
[3]John 14:3.

❧   ❧   ❧

Exodus 1–3
Exodus 3

> God called unto him out of the midst of the bush, and
> said, Moses, Moses. And he said, Here am I. And he
> said, Draw not nigh hither: put off thy shoes from off
> thy feet, for the place whereon thou standest is holy
> ground.[1]

A BABY WAS BORN, and God had wonderful plans for his life.
We are told that Moses was a beautiful child, but more than
that, he was born to be a deliverer. His parents hid him in
faith when the decree came that infant boys were to be
killed, knowing that God would protect him. Carefully his
mother, Jochebed, crafted a little ark for his safety. It was
made of bulrushes and the cracks were patched with pitch.
No doubt the mother carefully lined the inside with soft
padding. With Jochebed's confidence in God, the baby was
placed inside and taken to shallow water to be watched by
his sister Miriam.

Then the mother went to pray, and as she prayed she no
doubt reviewed the goodness of God in the past. Had he
not promised to bring them out of Egypt after four hundred
years? Surely the time was coming close! God had promised a deliverer, and each mother secretly hoped it would
be her son.

Faith is often shown at its best when the circumstances are
at their worst. It has been said that "faith looks impossibilities in the face and says, 'It shall be done!'" With Moses it
was done! God was at work as the daughter of Pharaoh
found the child and arranged for his own mother to raise
him until he could be taken to the princess' home. In due
season, Moses (meaning "drawn out") would draw his people out of oppression.

As Moses grew, the hand of God was upon him. He was
no ordinary child. He early learned he was not the son of

Pharaoh's daughter but one of the children of Israel. In facing his path in life there was no alternative: "Choosing rather to suffer affliction with the people of God, than to enjoy the pleasures of sin for a season; esteeming the reproach of Christ greater riches than the treasures in Egypt."³

Yes, God had plans for Moses, and He called to him one day in the fields. As all true believers, who sincerely love the Lord, Moses was quick to respond. God told him the ground he stood upon was hallowed. He told Moses He had seen the affliction of the people and that Moses would be used to deliver them. Moses' excuses then are familiar to us today. "Who am I that I should go?" God assured Moses, "Certainly I will be with thee."

In quietness before God, each believer is on hallowed ground. We too are surrounded by affliction and sin, by those in bondage and in need of a deliverer. As Moses was called from his flocks, Peter from his nets, Paul from a rabbi's school, so God calls us in our daily occupation to help free slaves of sin by introducing them to the true Deliverer, Jesus Christ. May we too respond, knowing He will be with us.

¹Exodus 3:4-5, 11-12.   ²Hebrews 11:25-26.

☙ ☙ ☙

Exodus 4–5
Exodus 4:10-17

> And Moses said unto the Lord, O my Lord, I am not eloquent, neither heretofore, nor since thou hast spoken unto thy servant: but I am slow of speech, and of a slow tongue.¹

THERE IS A SPEECH therapy center in a large western city. Many of the people who live there are trying desperately to overcome severe handicaps. One such young man was sixteen years old when he came to my attention. He was dark, had clean-cut features, and would have fit well into any high school, U.S.A. However, when he spoke my heart was saddened. Words took time to form and they came out, at best, lacking clarity and barely audible. For many years he had studied to obtain and maintain as much speech facility as he then had.

He was physically handicapped, but not the least hindered when it came to being a Christian. Early his mother had taught him Bible stories and about the goodness and guidance of God. She also had dedicated him to God to be used for His service. Used? With barely enough speech to be understood? The speech defect was not a deterrent. Marked boldly in his Bible were the words Moses gave to God in objection, "But I am slow of speech, and of a slow tongue." Then, carefully each letter was highlighted in the answer God gave to Moses: "And the Lord said unto him, Who hath made man's mouth? or who maketh the dumb, or deaf, or the seeing, or the blind? have not I the Lord? Now therefore go, and I will be with thy mouth, and teach thee what thou shalt say."[2]

With his slow speech and slow tongue, the young man has led many deaf children and handicapped adults to Jesus Christ. His first fruit was a boy named Aaron. The two make quite a pair as Aaron often helps his spiritual brother better communicate the message!

Somehow all the excuses of lack of eloquence, fear of people, inability to remember the words to say—all the little excuses we hide under in our plea for lack of witnessing—fade into insignificance as one thinks of this one boy in a speech and hearing center. Each sentence may take a full minute or more, but the message *is* being communicated, and people are being brought to know Jesus Christ.

We sing, "O for a thousand tongues to sing His praise." May we use the one God has given to us—today.

[1]Exodus 4:10.   [2]Exodus 4:11-12.

EXODUS 6–8
EXODUS 6:1-8

> Then Pharaoh called for Moses and Aaron, and said,
> Entreat the Lord, that he may take away the frogs from
> me, and from my people; and I will let the people go,
> that they may do sacrifice unto the Lord. And Moses
> said unto Pharaoh, Glory over me: when shall I intreat
> for thee . . . ? And he said, Tomorrow.[1]

TOMORROW is a word of futurity. It is a word of uncertainty. Tomorrow always remains a mystery. The wise man of Proverbs wrote, "Boast not thyself of tomorrow; for thou knowest not what a day may bring forth."[2]

Pharaoh was full of promises for tomorrow. Little did he realize that with each tomorrow his heart would become stony, and he would be beyond the reach of repentance.

Often delay is denial. Tomorrow you will speak to someone of Christ. Tomorrow you will start a regular time of devotion with the Lord. Yet, somehow tomorrow invites another tomorrow and another. Each day without Christ is another day lost. It can never be recaptured nor regained. No amount of wealth or position brings yesterday back, save as the memory of another day past.

Sin continues to increase, and the things that cannot become undone form a greater tangle and complication. Sin leaves its effect. True, sin can be forgiven, but the marks and scars are left. Just as primary Sunday school youngsters are shown this truth in the form of a board which has nails pounded in and then pulled out, so an adult recognizes the "impressions" are left, though the sin is taken away. The remaining scars bring no joy.

There is danger that, as with Pharaoh, facts will cease to convict, that all warnings and entreaties will strike on deaf ears. More than one individual has become gospel-hardened, and it is a fearful state of spiritual affairs.

Another warning comes—one of dread for the soul outside of Christ. It was spoken by David. "There is but a step between me and death."[3] Just a step, just a day—we do not know what the future holds—but it is of eternal import that we know of a certainty today, not tomorrow, who holds the future, and that we commit our future to Him.

A mother kept a list of chores for her children on a sheet of paper. Across from the duty was the time the task must be accomplished. One son continually wrote "tomorrow" on a job he did not relish. At last his mother made a special page and the assignment was written again. With indelible pencil and in block letters she inscribed "TODAY" as the time limit. In checking his jobs her son started to erase the today for a tomorrow, but found it was permanent. At once he started the job, and in ten minutes it was finished, much to his surprise. He had learned a lesson.

If you make a resolution to grow up in your faith, mark it indelibly "TODAY." Let us erase those tomorrows forever. "Now is the accepted time."[4]

[1]Exodus 8:8-10.
[2]Proverbs 27:1.
[3]I Samuel 20:3.
[4]II Corinthians 6:2.

❧ ❧ ❧

January 22

EXODUS 9–11
EXODUS 11

> And there was a thick darkness in all the land of Egypt three days: they saw not one another, neither rose any from his place for three days: but all the children of Israel had light in their dwellings.[1]

SCRIPTURE OFTEN SPEAKS to us in contrasts. Today we find a

striking one. The ninth plague was afflicting Egypt, a plague of darkness. Surely the people were filled with horror as the period stretched into the third day. Yet for the children of Israel there was light in their dwellings![1]

It gives us a picture of the world—apart from Christ—and the church—in Christ. Darkness surrounds us. Sin is darkness. Everyone is guilty before God. The state of condemnation exists. The outlook is only divine vengeance. Men are groping in darkness, afraid of the terrors of night and fearful of judgment and eternity.

In contrast is the church of Jesus Christ. It has been called the "light of the world."[2] Light amid the darkness!

We teach young children who constitutes the church. It is the spiritual seed of Abraham. It is those who fled like Noah, those who were faithful like Joseph and willing like Moses. Each was in the world, just as our story shows that Israel was in Egypt. In it, yes, but very separate from it. Light sheds its rays on the church. The light of the knowledge of God. Light sets the church apart as it shines against a dark world. Each member reflects its rays in his daily task. For a Christian everything is sacred. Each must walk in the light of God's holiness.

The illumination from the Sun of Righteousness should warm each heart and lift it heavenward. It should radiate into the darkness with a penetration that compels sinners to come to the Light.

God grant that together we can catch a glimpse of the gross darkness that is in the world away from God. Then let the light so shine that the words of Matthew will be a reality. "The people which sat in darkness saw great light; and to them which sat in the region and shadow of death light is sprung up"[3]—the light of the glorious gospel of Christ.

[1]Exodus 10:22-23. [3]Matthew 4:16.
[2]Matthew 5:14.

❧ ❧ ❧

40

Exodus 12–13
Exodus 13

> It came to pass, when Pharaoh had let the people go,
> that God led them not through the way of the land of
> the Philistines, although that was near; for God said,
> Lest peradventure the people repent when they see war,
> and they return to Egypt: but God led the people about,
> through the way of the wilderness of the Red sea: and
> the children of Israel went up harnessed out of the land
> of Egypt.[1]

"GOD REALLY LEADS ME in roundabout ways," exclaimed a
young missionary statesman. "It is usually the long way
around, but the day of arrival is always divinely scheduled!"

No doubt some of the children of Israel felt God was
leading them in a roundabout way too. A brief look at the
map verifies that the journey could have been completed
much more quickly if they had traveled the northern route.
But they had lessons to learn along the trip, and this de-
tour was appointed.

The missionary mentioned above shared a story that
bears this out. Preparing for his first term on the field he
was doing deputation work in his home state. Neither his
parents nor his wife was in complete accord with his choice
of service. He was very tired and toward the end of the
month decided to take a shortcut home, which would can-
cel some previously scheduled meetings. En route he developed a serious virus and was hospitalized for several
weeks in a small community. His wife came to be with him,
and they both had difficulty understanding the providence
of God. Yet, during these weeks of waiting great blessing
came to them. A Christian doctor was used to help the
couple better understand lessons in faith. The wife made a
new dedication to Christ. When released from the hospital
they traveled home and arrived at a God-appointed time.

A new neighbor had come to live in their block and was ministering to the missionary's parents. On the evening of their first day at home, both parents received Jesus Christ as Lord of their lives. The delay had at first been a disappointment but the arrival time proved that God is always on time!

God knew the children of Israel would suffer defeat, become discouraged, and turn back if they were too close to Egypt.

For the Christian, a roundabout way may be necessary. Possibly we are not equipped to face what is ahead in the journey to our land of promise. Though we may resist these delays, or deplore the fact that the journey will be lengthened, if we are in God's hands it means that ultimately we will safely reach our destination. If this is God's plan, let the delays of detours continue as we sing,

> All the way my Saviour leads me,
> Cheers each winding path I tread.[2]

[1]Exodus 13:17-18.
[2]Fanny Crosby.

❧   ❧   ❧

January 24

EXODUS 14–16
EXODUS 15:23-27

> And when they came to Marah, they could not drink of the waters of Marah, for they were bitter: therefore the name of it was called Marah. And the people murmured against Moses, saying, What shall we drink? And he cried unto the Lord; and the Lord shewed him a tree which when he had cast into the waters, the waters were made sweet.[1]

HAVE YOU HAD a "bitter cup" experience? Something that was to be wonderfully sweet, or some person who was everything you wanted him to be, until one day you were disillusioned? Surely, even God's people are not exempt from unpleasant experiences.

The incident we read today about the children of Israel is unusual. These people were on a journey directed by God. They followed a pillar of cloud by day and a pillar of fire by night. Was God punishing them? Were they not being obedient?

It is possible that we are being taught a most valuable lesson for our circumstances today. Disappointing and distasteful experiences may be in order because God wants us to taste of the bitter cup. Think of Job. It is true that sin causes calamity and suffering, but it is not always true that our "well" is bitter because we have sinned. Then why the accent on bitterness?

Each of us is guilty of praying, "Let this cup pass from me."[2] We want reprieve. Yet Jesus taught in vivid illustration that each such experience requires us to add, "Nevertheless, not as I will, but as Thou wilt." Though the taste be bitter, we may be required to drink to the bottom and, in so doing, find the ultimate purpose of God.

Yet our story does not end in this acid taste. It is well said that "God is not a prisoner of His own universe." He told Moses to cast a tree into the water, and it was made sweet. He can do as much for us, He teaches us, when we are obedient.

There is another lesson which parallels this. God in His mercy long ago provided another tree to sweeten the bitterness of life. It was formed into a cross. Jesus Christ, the Son of God, drank His cup of bitterness, turning that tree into a symbol of triumph that sweetens each bitter "well" of life.

Whatever your personal Marah may be, accept it as part of His plan for your life. Life is not all sweetness, but let the bitter make you better for His glory.

[1] Exodus 15:23-25.   [2] Matthew 26:39.

ჟ   ჟ   ჟ

Exodus 17–20
Exodus 18

> Hearken now unto my voice, I will give thee counsel,
> and God shall be with thee: Be thou for the people to
> God-ward, that thou mayest bring the causes unto God:
> and thou shalt teach them ordinances and laws, and
> shalt shew them the way wherein they must walk, and
> the work that they must do.[1]

IN THE SEATTLE, WASHINGTON AREA we have a mountain of
which we are very proud. On a clear day Mount Rainier is
visible at its more than 14,000 feet, and appears to stand
majestically alone. Yet such is not the case. Its heights are
approached only through the foothills and it is definitely
part of a range of mountains.

History has given us some mighty men who seem to tower
above others and stand alone. Careful study reveals that
most often they were surrounded with some "foothills" that
were a constant source of support and stability to them.

Such was the case with Moses. He had men around him
who were his pillars of strength and encouragement as together they served the God of Israel. The one we read
about today was his father-in-law, Jethro.

Jethro's introduction to Moses long before was through
his daughters when, at the close of day, they came to the
well to draw water. Moses was invited to be a guest in their
home. The visit extended forty years! Jethro gave Moses
his daughter Zipporah for his wife, and Scripture tells us
that a close bond grew between father and son-in-law.

Though Jethro was to be used as Moses' "foothill," he was
like our mountain; he stood alone. He was used to living
in solitary places. He knew God well. From his constant
communion with Him a godly wisdom grew. He lived
among people who had little moral conviction and were
primarily pagan, but we believe Jethro's family was true to

God. Often he would share his experiences with Moses. During these times he was unaware that Moses was the man upon whom God had His hand and that he was being used to mold him for service still unknown. True, Moses had been educated in the wisdom of Egypt, but he had some lessons to learn in practical living. Jethro taught him about the land, the very land that Moses would lead the Israelites through. The day would come when the two would be separated, and Moses would put to use what he had learned. Later, in reviewing God's goodness during their separation, "Jethro rejoiced for all the goodness which the Lord had done to Israel."[2]

As Moses grew into a mountain of strength, Jethro still faithfully assisted him from the foothills. He became concerned at his overwork and recommended some delegation of responsibility. He told Moses his job was "to be for the people to God-ward." Moses should leave the job of teaching ordinances and laws to others. Moses heeded his advice.

Today we may look at Jethro as an example of one who was willing to help lift the hands of another, one who was willing to help bring the ministry of another to unscaled heights, while standing by with prayer and encouragement. May we be faithful foothills.

[1]Exodus 18:19-20.
[2]Exodus 18:9.

❧ ❧ ❧

Exodus 21–24
Exodus 23

> Behold, I send an Angel before thee, to keep thee in the
> way, and to bring thee into the place which I have pre-
> pared. . . . I will be an enemy unto thine enemies, and
> an adversary unto thine adversaries. For mine Angel
> shall go before thee.[1]

A WONDERFUL SAINT of the Lord was talking with a group of
new Christians about the way a Christian should walk with
the Lord. He explained to them that in his youth as a
Christian he continually had compulsions to take all kinds
of matters into his own hands. If a friend were falsely accused he would rush to his defense. If he got a poor grade,
whether deserved or not, he would make a fuss. He did not
take these words of the Lord into account: "Vengeance is
mine; I will repay."[2]

Then one day while reading his Bible he started through
Exodus. His heart was moved as he read the twenty-third
chapter. He reread it earnestly. He meditated on the message and at last appropriated it to his own life. He now is
a living display of the riches in Christ. He does not fight
the battles, God does. He does not defend himself, God
does. The Lord's instructions for conquest are his instructions, by which the victory is consistently insured.

Notice how the angel of the Lord preceded and followed
God's people. Sure protection for those who put their
trust in Him is assured by the Author of such defense.

We may feel the frustration of trying to defend ourselves
in almost any area of life. We hear a story and know it to
be false, but how can we locate the source? Said a friend,
"It is like seeing the feather of a sparrow on your front
porch. How do you go about looking for the bird?" Well,
dear Christian, there is hope in this situation. If God sees
the sparrow fall, and if the very hairs of our heads are num-

46

bered, I believe He knows the sources of false words by those who would cause adversity to us, and when they are unjust, He will deal with it in His own way. Why defend ourselves when He is our rock and defense?

Isaiah wrote, "No weapon that is formed against thee shall prosper; and every tongue that shall rise against thee in judgment thou shalt condemn. This is the heritage of the servants of the Lord, and their righteousness is of me, saith the Lord."[3]

Dare we murmur and question God's place of service for us? No! Let us not forget He goes before and is behind, and murmuring prolongs our stay in the wilderness, which is no substitute for the Promised Land.

[1]Exodus 23:20, 22-23.
[2]Romans 12:19.
[3]Isaiah 54:17.

❧ ❧ ❧

January 27

EXODUS 25–27
EXODUS 25:1-9

And let them make me a sanctuary; that I may dwell among them.[1]

"WANDERERS" might be a good and appropriate title for mankind today. We wander from place to place, seeking for satisfaction in life, thirsting for truth, and searching for rest and happiness. Our picture in many ways parallels that of the children of Israel. They had been wandering, but they had a Guide. If they would listen to Him, they would be delivered.

Among His instructions was the order to build the Tabernacle. This would accompany them from place to place. Thus they could worship God on their journeyings. In the Tabernacle they could meet with Him.

In our unstable way of life and in our journeyings God

has provided instructions for us also in worshiping Him. Nothing is left to our own faulty planning. If His way is followed and heeded, we are safe in Him, and our worship of Him will be the joy of living.

The Lord is our Tabernacle, our Giver of life, Planner of our days, and our faithful Friend. In Him we find truth.

Many today are wandering in search of truth. Men have suffered death and martyrdom for that which they believed to be truth. The Israelites often questioned truth. Was God truly able to feed them on their long journey? Was it better to starve in the wilderness than to serve in Egypt? Would it not have been better to lose their children in bondage than to bury them in the wilderness? What was truth? We all resemble those who questioned Moses, and in doing so we question God. He had promised to make a way for the children of Israel. Today, Jesus Christ provides the way: "I am the way, the truth, and the life: no man cometh unto the Father, but by me."[2]

Think how much God offered to those who were wandering in the wilderness. A Tabernacle in their midst. Centuries later the Psalmist asked who could abide in the spiritual tabernacle of the Lord. The answer came, "He that walketh uprightly, and worketh righteousness, and speaketh the truth in his heart."[3]

Since Jesus Christ came, the Tabernacle of God is with men. Christ abides and rules in hearts cleansed by His blood and yielded to His Spirit. "Your life is hid with Christ in God."[4]

Have you sought and found Christ who alone is the way, the truth, and the life? Has your wandering soul found rest in Him? If not, may this be your experience.

[1]Exodus 25:8.
[2]John 14:6.
[3]Psalm 15:2.
[4]Colossians 3:3.

❧ ❧ ❧

Exodus 28–30
Exodus 27:20–28:3

> And thou shalt command the children of Israel, that
> they bring thee pure oil olive beaten for the light, to
> cause the lamp to burn always. . . . And thou shalt
> make holy garments.[1]

THROUGHOUT SCRIPTURE oil signifies the Holy Spirit. The
oil must be pure to accomplish its task in the Tabernacle.
The garments were specially made and symbolic of consecration.

Has God's Spirit been poured on you, today, like holy
oil? Are you ready to burn brightly, purely, in this world's
darkness? In your life and character, do you show forth
love? "Love is of God."[2] The light will be dimmed if you
do not practice love—love for those about you in the wilderness of life. Love to those who murmur (and there will
always be those who will). Love to that unlovely one who
complains and gossips, who belittles your actions, who is so
difficult to have around. Your attempts at love may be many
times beaten, as were the olives for the oil, but they will
make a brighter light!

Joy! Joy when the manna is all that God has given for
such a long time? Joy while toiling at the mundane things
of everyday life? Joy when there is an uphill climb and
weariness fills each part of your body? Yes, joy then.

Peace! In the human way of thinking it would seem
Moses had little peace. All those disobedient children for
whom he was responsible. All their pleas and quests, griev-
ings and gripings, must be met. Moses possessed a high level of toleration because God was His peace. He was to the
people "God-ward" and in bringing their causes and com-
plaints to Him, he found peace which passes understanding.

Patience! How we need it! I wonder if some of the work-
men on the Tabernacle did not have their moments of short-

ness of patience. All those minute instructions. The High Priest's garments too had to be perfect in every detail: the breastplate, the ephod, the robe, the embroidered coat, the bells.

Insignificant as those bells on the hem of the robe seemed, they had their purpose, as does everything in the plan of God. The bells announced to the people that their High Priest was alive and undertaking the work of atonement. They knew he was busy as they heard the bells ringing forth from the Holy of Holies.

May God's Spirit in us so shine forth that others will see us as real believers, God-anointed and equipped for carrying out the King's business.

¹Exodus 27:20; 28:2.
²I John 4:7.

❧   ❧   ❧

EXODUS 31–34
EXODUS 31

> And the Lord spake unto Moses, saying, See, I have called by name Bezaleel the son of Uri. . . . And I have filled him with the Spirit of God, in wisdom, and in understanding, and in knowledge, and in all manner of workmanship.¹

WHO EVER HEARD of Bezaleel? He surely was never in my roster of saints. David, Moses, Jabez, Paul—yes, they give us so much to consider and pattern our lives after. But Bezaleel!

Sometimes it is interesting to take a nobody, in human estimation, and start to study him, work with him, understand him. Much to our surprise he may emerge as a real somebody. After all, who are we to even speculate who is greatest in the kingdom of God?

Scripture tells us that the materials for the Tabernacle

50

were all ready. In fact, there was a surplus. The blueprints, the patterns, were all prepared, but there was no one who could provide the skill of a master craftsman. Moses sought the Lord. The Lord was as interested in providing the labor as the material. The answer came in Bezaleel.

It took some research to find out Bezaleel's background. Today's verse tells us that he was filled with the Spirit of God and had wisdom. No doubt he had learned his artisan skills in Egypt. Part of his early life was spent in slavery. Most likely when he began showing promise as a brickmaker, he was highly trained for the building of the treasure cities. Surely his days of slavery were filled with drudgery. (Building when your heart is not in it is wearisome.) Little did he know he was being prepared for a greater assignment. He would later have the opportunity to do immortal work.

The day came when Bezaleel was given his true place of service. God uses people where they best can serve. It has been said, "God could plan, Moses lead, and the people give, but Bezaleel could provide the necessary skill." And when he was called he was willing.

In the Body of Christ some are called to be ministers, some teachers, some housewives, and some Bezaleels. It is vital that we perform each task with all our hearts and for His glory. May we so be remembered:

> The skill of his hands,
> His spirit of heart
> Showed this man
> Was set apart.
>
> Ready and willing
> To build and be spent,
> He is remembered
> As heaven-sent.

[1]Exodus 31:1-3.

❧ ❧ ❧

Exodus 35–37
Exodus 35:1-21

> And they came, every one whose heart stirred him up,
> and every one whom his spirit made willing, and they
> brought the Lord's offering to the work of the taber-
> nacle of the congregation, and for all his service, and
> for the holy garments.[1]

MOSES GATHERED the family together. All were given an opportunity to bring the finest they had. Gold, silver, wood,
flax, oil—and so the list went on, and the hearts were
touched. He kept referring to the "willing heart," the "wise
heart," the "stirred heart." They must bring their gifts of
love to the house of God.

And they came! Can you not visualize that line—"both
men and women, as many as were willing hearted. . . ."[2]
One woman perhaps had a bracelet dear to her which she
had kept through the darkest days. She no doubt looked at
it longingly as she laid it on the altar, but certainly the joy
of being able to give something so special blessed her day.
There must have been another who was clever at spinning
flax, who brought her gifts. And down the line was perhaps another who deftly worked with the soft white wool
of sheep. Aholiab was surely in line. The Word tells us he
was "an engraver, and a cunning workman and an em-
broiderer in blue, and in purple, and in scarlet, and fine
linen."[3] His must have been a magnificent gift. Many
brought small things—their metal mirrors for instance—
which also had a place of use. I am sure some gave with
tears of joy, recalling the march through the Red Sea.
Others still recalled the rumble of the armies pursuing
them, and gave thanks they had not been consumed. They
remembered the manna, the bitter waters made sweet. Some
came in repentance for murmuring. All brought their gifts
—all that were willing in heart.

The work was started and completed, and God's plans had been fulfilled. "And Moses did look upon all the work, and, behold, they had done it as the Lord had commanded."[4]

We have a task in building the church of Jesus Christ. When we present our gifts, are they in great gratitude for His care and protection and love for us? Do we give more than enough? Is the work of God advanced because of our contribution by life and substance?

Let us look into our inner hearts today. Are we willing-hearted? The Hebrew phrase, we are told, signifies a heart driven by holy purpose. Let the love of Christ so constrain us that we too will be driven to give the best of self and service to the building of His church eternal.

[1]Exodus 35:21.   [3]Exodus 38:23.
[2]Exodus 35:22.   [4]Exodus 39:43.

❧   ❧   ❧

January 31

EXODUS 38–40
EXODUS 40

The glory of the Lord filled the tabernacle.[1]

THE OLD TESTAMENT tells us the glory of the Lord filled the Tabernacle. Today we end the first month of a new year. Our prayer has been that daily we would be shown His glory. In the New Testament era we know there is no such earthly tabernacle. The true Holy Place was found and fulfilled in Jesus Christ. Also, each believer becomes a tabernacle of God on earth.

The Apostle Paul reminds us that this tabernacle is also to house the Holy Spirit. "What? know ye not that your body is the temple of the Holy Spirit which is in you, which ye have of God, and ye are not your own? For ye are bought with a price: therefore glorify God in your body, and in your spirit, which are God's."[2]

53

Just as in the days of Moses a candle, lighted with oil, was placed in the Tabernacle, so today His Spirit is the candle placed in our hearts and also the oil that illuminates. How glorious to realize that while the Israelites only had a "type," and through faith had to believe God would fulfill His promises, we have the reality, daily at work in our lives!

We must realize the strength of this light and let it shine in a darkened world. God has indwelt us by His Spirit, and He longs to pour the Spirit on us continually. There is no magic formula for turning the lights on inside, nor can we work for that power. It is constant. It is indwelling. Its source is eternal and will never be depleted.

For what purpose do we have His glory filling our lives? Oh, that we would understand this and let this principle work in and through us! At one time that light was typified by the candlestick in the Tabernacle.

Today we as individual Christians have the glorious Light within. We are responsible before God to let that Light penetrate the darkness of sin in our world. May our attitudes never become passive but be accelerated and active to shine to those in need of His light. We have His promise: "The light shines on in the darkness, for the darkness has never overpowered it."[3] No matter how fierce the battle, the torch never goes out!

> Lead on, O King Eternal,
> We follow, not with fears;
> For gladness breaks like morning
> Where'er Thy face appears.
> Thy cross is lifted o'er us;
> We journey in its light:
> The crown awaits the conquest;
> Lead on, O God of might.[4]

[1]Exodus 40:34.
[2]I Corinthians 6:19-20.
[3]John 1:5, Amplified N. T.
[4]E. W. Shurtleff.

❧ ❧ ❧

54

February

LEVITICUS 1–4
LEVITICUS 1

> And the Lord called unto Moses, and spake unto him
> out of the tabernacle of the congregation.[1]

LEVITICUS must be approached with determination and expectation. Let us not yawn wearily but yield willingly to what lies below the surface of this book. God has something special for us within its pages. In Exodus we saw man not only outside of Eden but in the hands of a cruel and wicked enemy. He was a bondslave to the world. We saw his deliverance from Pharaoh. We saw how he, through the blood of a slain lamb, could be redeemed and justified. Here was God's answer to man's problem.

Leviticus unfolds God's provision for man's need. This provision comes through a sacrifice, a priest, and a place of worship. A careful reading of this book cannot help but bring us into closer fellowship with God. Divine repetition is instructive, thus we find much in review within these twenty-seven chapters. Fifty-six statements are similar to today's verse. Surely the Lord is reiterating for emphasis!

Sacrifice is the basis for worship. Acceptable worship is based on acceptable sacrifice. Man is guilty and unclean. He must be made fit for the holy presence of God. "Without shedding of blood is no remission."[3] Paul urged us to be exhibits of God's righteousness: "I beseech you therefore, brethren, by the mercies of God, that ye present your bodies a living sacrifice, holy, acceptable unto God, which is your reasonable service."[3] Let us never confuse going to a place of worship with worshiping God. God is holy and just, and there is but one way to approach Him.

In the burnt offering, which opens the book, we have another type of Christ. Here He is offering Himself without spot or blemish to God. Hebrews casts a clear light: "Lo, I come to do thy will, O God. He taketh away the first [the law], that he may establish the second [his will]. By the which will we are sanctified through the offering of the body of Jesus Christ once for all."[4]

Then we have the glorious provision of God's grace, the Lord Jesus as our High Priest in the presence of God for us. He ministers there. "We have such an high priest, who is set on the right hand of the throne of the Majesty in the heavens; a minister of the sanctuary, and of the true tabernacle, which the Lord pitched, and not man."[5]   As our High Priest He represents us. What a representative—the very Son of God!

The Christian's place of worship is "within the veil." Here we have joyous communion with our Lord. As His children we are granted "boldness to enter in."[6] We also have responsibility. Within the veil we are to "worship," and without the camp we must "witness."

[1]Leviticus 1:1.
[2]Hebrews 9:22.
[3]Romans 12:1.

[4]Hebrews 10:9-10.
[5]Hebrews 8:1-2.
[6]Hebrews 10:19.

❧ ❧ ❧

February 2

LEVITICUS 5–7
LEVITICUS 5

And if a soul sin . . .[1]

ANOTHER DAY in Leviticus! May our thoughts be composed and our hearts warmed as we search these truths to further understand the rich provision of grace for all our needs. Only His Spirit can awaken in our hearts a deep interest to delve into this book. He who inspired the words can surely expound their contents for each reader's blessing. "Thy word is a lamp unto my feet, and a light unto my path."[2]

In yesterday's and today's Scripture, five different kinds of offerings have been mentioned. Each is an illustration of what Jesus Christ has done for believers.

The burnt offering typifies His death for sin. The meal offering, with its components of oil, flour, salt, and frankincense portrays His perfect life. The peace offering pictures the Lord dying for us. He becomes our peace. The sin offering shows Him as our sin bearer, and the trespass offering clearly distinguishes sins—against God or against man.

In considering our sin and transgression, it is difficult to comprehend grace greater than all our sin. But grace He gives in abundance. Yet let us not be guilty of affirming the principles while denying the power and practice.

One of my favorite authors writes, "Grace not merely cuts up sin by the roots but transforms the sinner from a curse into a blessing, from a moral plague into a channel of divine mercy, from an emissary of Satan into a messenger of God, from a child of darkness into a son of light, from a slave of self into a willinghearted servant of Christ, from a cold, narrowhearted miser into a benevolent minister to the needs of his fellowmen. The blood of the trespass offering cleanses the conscience and sends the trespasser back to the one whom he has wronged with 'the principal' in his hand. Noble testimony this, both to the grace and righteousness of the God of Israel! Beauteous exhibition of the results of that marvelous scheme of redemption, whereby the injurer is forgiven and the injured becomes an actual gainer."[3]

May we view these offerings as types of His great sacrifice for us, that where sin abounded, grace may much more abound.

[1]Leviticus 5:1.   [3]C. H. Mackintosh.
[2]Psalm 119:105.

57

> And he brought the other ram, the ram of consecration:
> and Aaron and his sons laid their hands upon the head
> of the ram. And he slew it: and Moses took of the blood
> of it, and put it upon the tip of Aaron's right ear, and
> upon the thumb of his right hand, and upon the great
> toe of his right foot . . . and Moses sprinkled the blood
> upon the altar round about.[1]

EACH BELIEVER lives in awareness that he is not under Old
Testament law but New Testament grace. However, there
is much we can learn and better understand about our
Christian faith by studying these rituals given prior to
Christ's coming.

Today's portion speaks of the consecration of the priests.
It has much to say to us with regard to our consecration to
the Lord for His service. Real consecration, we know, is an
act of God, and its basis is the death of His Son, Jesus
Christ. Men and women are set apart when the blood of
Christ touches and cleanses them. When this happens we
become not our own but Christ's. How often we think of
His blood as that which cleanses and makes us different,
but how seldom we recognize that in so touching our lives
Christ possesses us. Through His atoning work for us,
Christ has a claim on us. We belong to Him by right of
purchase with His blood.

Notice the three places Moses put the blood of the sacrificial ram on Aaron when he was being consecrated.

First, he touched the ear. When our ears are open to
hear what God has to say, we go forth doing His work.
Christ was our example: "The words that I speak unto
you I speak not of myself: . . . for all things that I have
heard from my Father I have made known unto you."[2] It
is also written, "Whatsoever I command thee thou shalt
speak."[3]

Next Aaron's hands were touched with blood. Hands are a symbol of service. God seeks ready, willing, open hands to be filled with His tasks for His service. Like the Apostle Paul on the day he was converted, we should pray with outstretched, open hands, "Lord, what wilt thou have me to do?"[4]

Then came the feet. Feet symbolize action, walking, not standing still. Feet touched by the blood of Christ walk in the way of holiness. There is much in Scripture that tells us how to walk, and consecrated feet will walk honestly, in the Spirit, in love, in wisdom, pleasing to God. This means that we will walk in newness of life as children of light.

Let us give our ears that we may truly hear, our hands that we will faithfully serve, and our feet to walk even as He walked.

[1]Leviticus 8:22-24.   [3]Jeremiah 1:7.
[2]John 14:10; John 15:15.   [4]Acts 9:6.

❧   ❧   ❧

February 4

LEVITICUS 11–13
LEVITICUS 13

Ye shall therefore sanctify yourselves, and ye shall be holy; for I am holy: neither shall ye defile yourselves.[1]

LEVITICUS is also referred to as "the priest's guidebook." It has chapters that are full of guidance and instruction for those who would seek a close relationship with the true High Priest.

In the distinctions between clean and unclean food, surely God had the people's physical and spiritual health in mind. Here was a nation who had lived in Egypt. They had wandered and were about to settle down again. After their long days of weariness and exposure to the elements, God knew what was best for renewing body as well as soul. In making them separate, by this distinction, they were not to participate in heathen ceremonies and festivals. They were not even allowed to touch unclean things. Is this not easy to understand? It sometimes takes only a brush or a touch, and one soon becomes ensnared in the way of unrighteousness. God left no room for fancies or self-will. All was laid down with divine precision. The commanding authority of "Thus saith the Lord" meant these things were settled. The people's only obligation was to obey. It is true in the twentieth century as much as when the Scriptures were written, that "to obey is better than sacrifice."[2]

The instruction was also given for spiritual consecration. Carefully and specifically followed, the observance of these laws-to-live-by constantly reminded Israel that they were a separated people. Laws of things forbidden and permitted led to the best possible physical and spiritual health if followed.

Today, when so many people are concerned about mental health, how wonderful it would be if we would realize that God has provided for all our needs. He expects us to care for our bodies so that we can grow strong for the task to which we are assigned. Undernourished Christians cannot be fit for Christian battle. Likewise, spiritually we must have a steady diet of "feeding" on His Word, which allows us to grow in Him and keep ourselves pure for Him.

Lest the Christian become confused in reading these laws and wonder about applying them today, let us just remember that God in His wonderful grace, by giving His Son, showed that the "cloven hoof" was no longer to be the criterion. The standard is no longer ceremonial, but it is spiritual.

In these days of grace, "every creature of God is good, and nothing to be refused, if it be received with thanksgiving: for it is sanctified by the word of God and prayer."[3]

[1]Leviticus 11:44.   [3]I Timothy 4:4-5.
[2]I Samuel 15:22.

❧   ❧   ❧

LEVITICUS 14–15
LEVITICUS 14:1-20

A YOUNG MAN about two years out of college was working
into his father's business. Much of his time and energy was
spent learning and preparing for the profession his father
had prepared for him. One night in the office, burning the
midnight oil, he was reading some of the books that lined
the shelves of his father's office. One was a beautiful leather-
covered Bible. It had been a gift from a colleague but had
never been opened as far as the son knew. He opened it and
started reading at the fifteenth chapter of Leviticus.

Most of us would be surprised at his choice. Why Leviticus? Could not the Holy Spirit have directed him to John
or Romans or possibly the Psalms? What could the young
man possibly gain from these thirty-three verses about the
ceremonial laws of cleanliness which suddenly commanded
his attention and thought?

In our wondering, it may be well to remind ourselves
that "all scripture is given by inspiration of God, and is
profitable for doctrine, for reproof, for correction, for instruction in righteousness: that the man of God may be
perfect, throughly furnished unto all good works."[1] God
inspired every chapter, every verse, every line of His Book.

In his reading, the young man felt a sense of the divine
which in turn made him feel exceedingly defiled. Verse
thirty-one rang in his heart: "Thus shall ye separate the children of Israel from their uncleanness; that they die not in
their uncleanness."[2] As he pondered the early verses in the
chapter he recalled a statement his father had made: "That
which cometh out of the man, that defileth the man."[3] He
thought of his own mind. The wickedness of his past loomed
large. His deceitful methods of the past few years became
hateful. His pride, his conceit, his great desire to own the
business himself, appeared to him to be his death sentence.

With the Bible in his hand he cried out, "The God who spoke to Moses and Aaron, speak to me that I will be clean!"

How true are the words of Scripture. "And ye shall seek me, and find me, when ye shall search for me with all your heart."[4] The young man was sincerely seeking, and in the early morning hours he found cleansing in Christ.

It would be hard to doubt that this chapter was given its rightful place in divine canon. It has been well said, and here quite unusually demonstrated, "All Scripture teaches us the holiness of God, the vileness of nature, the efficacy of the blood, and the value of the Word."[5]

[1]II Timothy 3:16-17.
[2]Leviticus 15:31.
[3]Mark 7:20.
[4]Jeremiah 29:13.
[5]C. H. Mackintosh.

❧ ❧ ❧

February 6

LEVITICUS 16–18
LEVITICUS 17:1-16

> For the life of the flesh is in the blood: and I have given it to you upon the altar to make an atonement for your souls: for it is the blood that maketh an atonement for the soul.[1]

I WILL NEVER FORGET standing in a hospital emergency room when a young woman was brought in bleeding profusely. Within a few short minutes the doctor announced to her mother that she was dead. The words uttered by the stricken mother have caused me to reflect many times. "But only five minutes ago she was alive and perfect!" There were no broken bones, no bruises or injuries other than a small cut which had been inflicted by a knife the young woman had been sculpturing with. It was a vivid reminder. "The life of the flesh is in the blood."

The precious and vital doctrine of the blood seems to have lost its place in our modern study of theology. The blood of Christ is the foundation for every benefit in the spiritual realm, just as blood is essential to life in the physical realm.

It is the blood of Jesus Christ which cleanses from sin. We have read in the past weeks of the command to sprinkle blood on the doorposts, so that the firstborn of the children of Israel would be spared. The Scripture is familiar. "When I see the blood, I will pass over you."[2] The blood granted deliverance from bondage and from judgment. Yet the children of Israel were required to perform a specific act to avoid judgment. So we, with our hearts, our minds, and our wills, have to plead the blood of Jesus Christ to cleanse and cover our sins. God justifies us through His blood. Nothing less, nothing more, and nothing else than the blood makes atonement. It is gloriously all-conclusive. God's simple plan for the justification of simple man is set forth throughout His Word, from Genesis to Revelation. Throughout, the blood is the only ground for righteousness. Through the blood, peace and pardon and eternal life are obtained. Leviticus in its entirety—and especially today's chapter—gives us a real commentary on the doctrine of the blood.

It is precious in God's sight and makes atonement for the soul.

> What can wash away my sin?
> Nothing but the blood of Jesus;
> What can make me whole again?
> Nothing but the blood of Jesus.
>
> Oh, precious is the flow
> That makes me white as snow;
> No other fount I know,
> Nothing but the blood of Jesus.[3]

[1]Leviticus 17:11.   [3]Robert Lowry.
[2]Exodus 12:13.

❧ ❧ ❧

LEVITICUS 19–22
LEVITICUS 19

> Therefore shall ye observe all my statutes, and all my
> judgments, and do them: I am the Lord.[1]

CONTINUALLY God reminds us, "I am the Lord," and we cannot doubt that as the Lord, He was and is acquainted with all of man's ways and with all the capabilities of human nature. Since He is the holy Lord, He takes pains to work the principle of holiness in the lives of His children.

Clearly and precisely He commanded the children of Israel, "After the doings of the land of Egypt . . . shall ye not do: and after the doings of the land of Canaan, whither I bring you, shall ye not do. . . . Ye shall do my judgments, and keep mine ordinances, . . . I am the Lord your God."[2]

A Puritan of old wrote, "The Word of God must settle every question and govern every conscience: there must be no appeal from its solemn and weighty decision. When God speaks, every heart must bow. Men may form and hold opinions; they may adopt and defend their practices; but one of the finest traits in the character of 'the Israel of God' is profound reverence for, and implicit subjection to, 'every word that proceedeth out of the mouth of the Lord.' "

Many say they do not fully understand all the things a Christian must or must not do. What is essential to each child of God in relation to his conduct is that as a Christian, as one set apart, he has responsibilities. When one gives his allegiance to Jehovah God, his obedience must ensue.

The rules set forth by God through Moses were divided into two classes: first, those that were given because of the wickedness of man's heart; then, those that showed the tenderness and care of the God of Israel for His people. In regard to the latter, an illustration comes from California.

A family of new Christians moved into a fruit picker's shack for harvest months. They were destitute until the job became available and lived on two dollars a week. Payday was still another week away. In their morning devotions they were reading the Bible through. One day this verse touched their hearts: "Thou shalt not defraud thy neighbor, neither rob him: the wages of him that is hired shall not abide with thee all night until the morning."[3]

They were impressed with the thought that God understands the feelings that surge in the heart of a laborer about payment of a day's wages. God knows how the laborer counts on his pay, and how his family is dependent on him. While they read, in a house a few acres away, the owner's family was having devotions and read the same passage. They became concerned for their new hired hand, and felt compelled to take his week's wages to him in advance. Thus God made provision and all rejoiced.

This verse is a minute portion of God's precious and practical truth. May our hearts be receptive and sensitive to all of His Word and to its message and, as we apprehend its truths, may we influence others for God.

[1]Leviticus 19:37.
[2]Leviticus 18:3-5.
[3]Leviticus 19:13.

※　※　※

65

LEVITICUS 23–25
LEVITICUS 25

> And ye shall hallow the fiftieth year, and proclaim liberty throughout all the land unto all the inhabitants thereof: it shall be a jubilee unto you; and ye shall return every man unto his possession, and every man unto his family.[1]

THOSE WHO HAVE VISITED Philadelphia, Pennsylvania, cannot help but be touched by the Old Testament quotation and its association with the historic Liberty Bell: "Proclaim liberty throughout all the land unto all the inhabitants thereof." Truly the message is enshrined in the hearts of each patriot.

The significance of liberty was brought home to me through a friend who is a missionary in Nigeria. She was describing the feelings and thoughts of some of the thirty-five million Nigerians who experienced their independence on that special day in 1961. From every cult and belief, the educated and illiterate, friends and enemies, representing more than two hundred languages, all rejoiced together over a common achievement, the proclaiming of liberty.

The year of jubilee, recorded here in Leviticus, is significant. Every fifty years slaves were freed, debts canceled, and land returned to its original owners. One can envision the joy that resounded up and down the hills and through the valleys of the land of Canaan. The exiles were returned, the captives emancipated, and the debtors freed. Long lost relatives were returned to the family fold.

The Scriptures record, "And if thou sell ought unto thy neighbor, or buyest ought of thy neighbor's hand, ye shall not oppress one another: according to the number of years after the jubilee thou shalt buy of thy neighbor, and according unto the number of years of the fruits he shall sell unto thee."[2] Buyer and seller were reminded that all the land belonged to God. How significant! God declared this land to be His forever—a sacred trust for those to whom He promised it.

Here in Canaan the priests and the prophets ministered and testified. Here John the Baptist began his ministry. Here Christ was born and baptized. Here He preached and taught. Here he died, rose, and ascended to the right hand of the Father. Nations will continue in discord over the land, but Jehovah affirms, "The land is mine." The day will come when the trumpet of jubilee will be heard among these hills in Palestine. Isaiah referred to this when he said, "For thus saith the Lord, Behold, I will extend peace to her [Jerusalem] like a river."[3]

Oh, that our hearts would be united in proclaiming liberty to those who are enslaved by sin, that we might tell them that the Lord is at hand and that He will return on the true day of jubilee for those whose faith and trust are in Him. What a privilege is ours to live in an age when God is confirming His Word in our midst.

[1]Leviticus 25:10.
[2]Leviticus 25:14-15.
[3]Isaiah 66:12.

❧   ❧   ❧

LEVITICUS 26–27
LEVITICUS 26

> And I will walk among you, and will be your God, and
> ye shall be my people.[1]

LEVITICUS CLOSES with a solemn contrast—the blessings of
obedience and the consequences of disobedience. The first
thirteen verses of today's chapter are the conditions for
blessing. In our lives we may have the blessed rain of spiritual grace, the promise of increased spiritual fruit, and
peace of heart and mind. We may have abiding peace, for
the Scripture affirms, "None shall make you afraid."[2]

Then there is the quick contrast of failure. The people
forsook the Lord, they followed other gods—and they are
still suffering as a result. Walking contrary to God can
bring only desolation and captivity.

One writer has captioned this chapter "God's Government." Yet throughout it we see God's grace hovering. He
promised to remember His covenant with Jacob and Isaac
and Abraham. He declared, "I will not cast them away . . .
but I will for their sakes remember the covenant of their
ancestors, whom I brought forth out of the land of Egypt
in the sight of the heathen, that I might be their God: I am
the Lord."[3] Here sunshine breaks through the clouds of
despair. Man is unfaithful, but God is faithful!

Anew we recognize ourselves as debtors of His grace. In
ourselves we do not deserve to come to Christ, but we can
come in utter poverty and cast ourselves on Him. "It is
well to be poor, when the knowledge of our poverty serves
but to unfold to us the exhaustless riches of divine grace.
That grace can never suffer anyone to go away empty. It
can never tell anyone that he is too poor. It can meet the
very deepest human need: and not only so, but it is glorified
in meeting it. Grace is the basis of our salvation, the basis
of a life of practical godliness, and the basis of those im-

perishable hopes which animate us amid the trials and conflicts of this sin-stricken world. May we cherish a deeper sense of the grace, and a more ardent desire for the glory."[4]

> Oh, to grace how great a debtor
> Daily I'm constrained to be!
> Let that grace, Lord, like a fetter,
> Bind my wandering heart to Thee.
>
> Prone to wander, Lord, I feel it,
> Prone to leave the God I love:
> Here's my heart; Lord, take and seal it,
> Seal it for Thy courts above.[5]

[1]Leviticus 26:12.   [4]C. H. Mackintosh.
[2]Leviticus 26:6.   [5]Robert Robinson.
[3]Leviticus 26:44-45.

❦   ❦   ❦

February 10

NUMBERS: 1–2
NUMBERS 1

> And the Lord spake unto Moses in the wilderness of
> Sinai . . . , Take ye the sum of all the congregation of
> the children of Israel, after their families, by the house
> of their fathers, with the number of their names.[1]

NUMBERS is not just a historical document that traces Israel's journey from Mt. Sinai to Canaan's border; it is much more. The account continually exhibits the gracious and wonderful character of God: His wisdom, love, patience, and understanding. Though man's heart is rebellious and hard, God proves Himself faithful.

As the book begins we find the Israelites had been away from Egypt for more than a year. They had waited the forty days and nights while Moses was on the mount and God gave him the Ten Commandments. Then they disobediently worshiped the golden calf and had to wait another forty days. There was another wait while the Tabernacle was being built.

The time for the great census had arrived. The people were divided into large groups, each group consisting of the descendants from one of the sons of Jacob or Joseph. The tribe of Levi was separate. They were chosen to stay near the Tabernacle and care for its final preparation for the journey.

What a sight the children of Israel must have been as they completed the necessary task and once again were on their way. Covered wagons, oxen, carts, and about two million people. The pillar of cloud was over the Tabernacle. While it hovered close, they would remain, but when it lifted, they traveled on and followed it. This was their source of stop-and-go guidance and was unmistakable. The tribes were placed according to divine arrangement.

In considering the last tribe, the tribe of Dan, we note that the Lord said, "They shall go hindmost with their standards."[2] One cannot but wonder as to the feelings of those chosen to be last. The same situation is re-created in our lives today. Someone has to be last, and for some reason we do not esteem it a place of honor. However, all of the children of Israel had the promise that God was before and behind. Those very last Israelites were as much a part of the company as the first ones. The same pillar was theirs to follow. The same manna was theirs to eat. No matter the position, God has promised to go before. Being last may fulfill divine duty. The weary along the way must be encouraged, danger from the rear combated. The standard still must rise high.

God grant, as we follow the Israelites these days, that we will be challenged to walk closer with our God. His plan may call on us to lead or to follow, or even to be "hindmost." May we be willing to endure the perils which beset His pilgrims with joy in our hearts and dedication in our steps.

[1]Numbers 1:1-2.   [2]Numbers 2:31.

✿ ✿ ✿

Numbers 3–5
Numbers 5:1-10

A GROUP OF MISSIONARIES was about to sail on a large vessel
for a foreign port. Their leader admonished them as a peculiar people especially set apart to do the work of Christ.
He stressed the importance of their holiness to the Lord at
any cost. Nothing must separate them from God. They
must allow nothing to dissuade them from doing God's will,
nor should they even once look back toward home as the
ship sailed. He explained that adjustments and trials lay
ahead. Were they ready for spiritual combat? He talked to
them about any hidden resentments they might be harboring, and about the necessity of eliminating sin and guilt.
He ended with the question "Are you willing and eager
to serve our Saviour as a clean vessel?"

Those who had come to see them off were quite disturbed
by the challenge the leader had chosen. Should not these
people have been encouraged? Why had he not read a series of precious promises and encouragements to them?

Aboard ship it was a contrast. Here was an army of missionaries who were about to face hardship. In fact, one
of them was to face death. Among them there were some ill
feelings. A barrier had been raised between two families
years before. Steaming toward a common goal were people
separated to God but tragically alienated from each other.

The first night out, one family was reviewing these chapters from Numbers and the one following, which deals with
the separation of Nazarites. A message from Old Testament times spoke to them on a modern ocean liner. One by
one, problems were settled as the missionaries searched their
hearts and asked God to make them "clean vessels." Barriers were broken down and they debarked from that ship
in the knowledge that they would serve God in unity of
service.

How wise had been their leader who was himself directed by the true Leader of our lives. Today, just as yesterday, people must be right with God and with each other. The Israelites had to confess their trespasses for atonement to be made and restoration insured. Even so today we have One who is touched with the feeling of our weaknesses. When we confess to Him, atonement is made, and restoration brings His gracious benediction:

> The Lord bless thee, and keep thee:
> The Lord make his face shine upon thee, and be gracious unto thee:
> The Lord lift up His countenance upon thee, and give thee peace.[1]

Such a benediction as this from Numbers is a daily reminder of God's provision of peace for us and His daily presence with us.

[1]Numbers 6:24-26.

❧ ❧ ❧

NUMBERS 6–7
NUMBERS 6:1-8

> This is the law of the Nazarite who hath vowed, and
> of his offering unto the Lord for his separation, beside
> that that his hand shall get: according to the vow which
> he vowed, so he must do after the law of his separation.[1]

VOWS ARE ESTABLISHED to be unbroken. Those entering into
marriage in the true, solemn sense accept nuptial vows "until death us do part." There is a cult in India which binds
its children at an early age so the marks of its culture are
permanently impressed upon them. They have proved that
their tribespeople do not break the rules nor flee if they are
indelibly marked.

Many men in Scripture took vows. David wrote, "Thy
vows are upon me."[2] He was going on record as to the sacred contract he was entering with God. He wanted people
to know what he had done. Samson was another; and John
the Baptist.

The vows of the Nazarite are interesting to examine. Everything in the Old Testament is illuminated by illustration. That is why it can be called a picture book. Today's
verses picture one who felt he must separate himself from
others in a specific way. "He shall separate himself from wine
and strong drink."[3] This refers not only to abstinence from
wine and liquor but from partaking of anything that would
separate us from God. There is within all of us a craving.
It may be for evil, or for too much of something good. It
may be for pleasures which would take us away from the
Lord. What we must realize is that, as promised, "He satisfieth the longing soul."[4] It does not take indulgence to
make us happy. It takes Him!

"There shall no razor come upon his head."[5] How much
we would rather be conformed to the world than transformed. The Nazarite did not get a haircut. He was differ-

ent. Undoubtedly people made fun of him. A Christian is also different. He will experience mockery, but he knows his relationship with the Lord is more important, and he must be set apart, as was the Nazarite. Christians are to be in the world but not of it.

"All the days that he separateth himself unto the Lord he shall come at no dead body."[6] This is most significant. Before we knew Christ, we were "dead in trespasses and sins."[7] Now, in Him we are made alive. What is our relationship to death? Are we comfortable in the presence of those outside of Christ who are dead in sin? Comfortable, or concerned—concerned that those in the land of the dying find life everlasting? If we are compassionate we will act.

Let this chapter cause us to examine our hearts, to abstain from evil, and to be willing to be different for Him that those dead in sin will find life. Do not fear to take a vow and, with His gracious help, seek to fulfill its sacred contract.

[1]Numbers 6:21.
[2]Psalm 56:12.
[3]Numbers 6:3.
[4]Psalm 107:9.
[5]Numbers 6:5.
[6]Numbers 6:6.
[7]Ephesians 2:1.

❧ ❧ ❧

Numbers 8–11
Numbers 11:1-15

> And Moses said unto the Lord, Wherefore hast thou
> afflicted thy servant? and wherefore have I not found
> favour in thy sight, that thou layest the burden of all
> this people upon me?[1]

SUDDENLY and often we may experience a change of mood.
Things have been going well. The Bible has unfolded its
hidden treasures to us. Then, like sudden darkness in the
day, there is a violent change.

The Israelites had been given careful instructions for advance toward their destination, Palestine. They were su-
perbly organized and had experienced assurance and triumph. From the heights of hope they fell to the depths of
despair in just a moment, as they took their eyes off God
and focused them on self and the wilderness.

Amid this, Moses became discouraged. In utter helplessness and distress he sobbed to Jehovah, "Wherefore hast
thou afflicted thy servant?" Because His mercies are always
available God granted Moses an answer to his problem. He
provided seventy other men to help bear the load. He also
changed the diet of the murmuring people by graciously
providing quails instead of the manna.

Surely our heavenly Father has ways of trying our faith
too. In these times of superb organization and special planning, trials hit us hard. Do we really stand for what we
claim to believe? When those about us murmur and complain, are we steadfast and unmovable, ready to keep
abounding in the Lord's work? Or do we look up and bit-
terly lament our affliction?

It is well to check up on one's faith. It could be weakened by outside influences, just as the Hebrews were influenced by the multitudes that had joined them. How
worthless is a faith that cannot withstand a test! Paul said,

"We glory in tribulations also: knowing that tribulation worketh patience; and patience, experience; and experience, hope."[2]

It has been proved that "gilt is afraid of fire, but gold is not." How much faith do we exhibit when we look down, murmur, waver, and faint? How easy it is to speak for the Lord when health is flourishing, resources are competent, and the path of life is straight and clear. The test comes when illness strikes, the budget is strained, and guidance is uncertain.

God reaches out to an arm extended to Him. He will lift us up in our affliction, and make us aware of His victorious, abiding presence, our source of faith and comfort.

[1]Numbers 11:11.   [2]Romans 5:3-4.

❧   ❧   ❧

February 14

NUMBERS 12–14
NUMBERS 13:21-33

> Caleb stilled the people before Moses, and said, Let us go up at once, and possess it; for we are well able to overcome it. . . . But my servant Caleb, because he had another spirit with him, and hath followed me fully, him will I bring into the land whereinto he went; and his seed shall possess it.[1]

IT IS A SOBERING THOUGHT that of all the Israelites who journeyed out of Egypt, only two entered the land of promise. One was a man named Caleb. The Scripture does not give us a complete description of his background other than the fact that he was born in slavery and was a ruler within his tribe, the tribe of Judah. However, one specific thing set him apart, and surely kept him close to the heart of Moses. He had "another spirit." We think of Caleb when we read what was said of Daniel: "Then this Daniel was preferred above the presidents and princes, because an excellent spirit was in him."[2] Caleb possessed this kind of spirit.

76

"And the Lord spake unto Moses saying, Send thou men, that they may search the land of Canaan."[3] Twelve spies were sent to look over the situation which they were approaching. They returned and gave their reports. The majority affirmed it to be a land flowing with milk and honey, but with many obstacles. There was doubt in their report and they feared the mighty Amalekites. "They are stronger than we."[4] Caleb presented his minority report. True, he had seen the giants, the walled cities, and other obstacles, but he knew and worshiped a God greater than these. "And Caleb stilled the people before Moses, and said, Let us go up at once, and possess it; for we are well able to overcome it."[5]

How often a spirit of defeatism is prevalent in our own circles of service. It may be shown through a program of visitation evangelism in the church. A few become very concerned about those outside the family of God, and their minority report is one of faith. The majority, all too unconcerned, have doubts. They say people are too busy to be visited, and there is too much else to accomplish in the church. Thus it goes, and the work of God suffers.

We need more Calebs. They see the burdens and difficulties but they know from experience that "greater is he that is in you, than he that is in the world."[6]

A child playing with a pair of binoculars is always delighted to realize that when used properly, they will bring distant objects close. When turned around, the close objects seem far away. A true Caleb knows the proper way to look out into the distances of God. Why? Because he possesses "another spirit."

God grant that we may seek to early learn that the majority often ask, "Can God?" But the Calebs, the faithful believing minority, declare, "God can!"

[1]Numbers 13:30; 14:24. [4]Numbers 13:31.
[2]Daniel 6:3. [5]Numbers 13:30.
[3]Numbers 13:1-2. [6]I John 4:4.

NUMBERS 15–17
NUMBERS 16:36-50

> And remember all the commandments of the Lord, and
> do them . . . that ye may remember, and do all my com-
> mandments, and be holy unto your God.[1]

THERE ARE MANY PEOPLE still under the delusion that they
can be holy unto the Lord by keeping His commandments.
Theirs is a pride which displays itself in the fact that they
live good lives. They are good neighbors and occasionally
attend church. Surely God will richly reward them for their
goodness!

How erroneous this impression proves to be. One who
studies and understands God's Word knows that He says,
"If ye love me, keep my commandments."[2] In keeping these
commandments, we are not just following rules and regula-
tions for the sake of being good. We are patterning our
lives after His will *because* we love Him.

There is nothing an individual can do to become holy before God except place simple faith in Jesus Christ. "Therefore being justified by faith, we have peace with God
through our Lord Jesus Christ."[3] Then it is that we show
our love and obedience by keeping the commandments.

If we truly love Him, we will not murmur against Him,
or express our dissatisfaction with the way He has prepared
for us. In today's Bible reading, the Israelites were doing
just that. Their history tells of their consistent stubborn-
ness, complaining, and irreverence. But God's attitude to
them remains unchanged. It is one of goodness and mercy.
It is very easy to criticize the children of Israel, but they
only prove that man's nature today remains unchanged.
Before we can pass sentence on them, we must look deep
within the innermost recesses of our own hearts.

If we love God, we *will* keep His commandments. Recognizing the evilness of sin and the riches of His grace, one cannot help but earnestly seek His face and love Him more and more.

[1] Numbers 15:39-40.
[2] John 14:15.
[3] Romans 5:1.

❧ ❧ ❧

February 16

NUMBERS 18–21
NUMBERS 18

> Thou shalt have no inheritance in their land, neither shalt thou have any part among them: I am thy part and thine inheritance.[1]

A MIDDLE-AGED WOMAN was hospitalized with an incurable disease. Those who visited her often were amazed to find her spending much time studying the Old Testament books that deal with the history of the Israelites. When questioned, she answered that Numbers had been a particular blessing, and that the verse above had spoken specifically to her heart.

Although her position in life had been economically assured, and her possessions many, this was not the legacy she longed to leave her husband and sons. She was a new Christian, and meeting Jesus Christ had been the greatest experience of her life. In the days while she waited to join Him above, He proved to be everything she needed to make her happy. She wanted to share her inheritance in Him with her family.

Her Bible was well marked for one so young in the faith. The book of Numbers had been divided into three sections. The first ten chapters she called "God's provision for His people." The next fifteen were entitled "God's patience with His people." The section from chapter 26 to the end of the book was labeled "God's persistence."

Her joy overflowed as she related that just as God had organized those Israelites and given them the symbol of guidance, so He could make provision for the family she was leaving behind. She talked of the patience of God, first with herself as an individual who for many years had resisted coming to Him. She told how she had been disobedient to His call and grieved Him, but His mercies were new with each day while He called for her to become His. She knew He would be patient with the family, and that He would unceasingly and tenderly draw them to Himself.

She talked of divine persistence. By now she was aware that God usually works through ordinary men and in natural ways, but that He is not limited by His laws. What peace was hers to know that superordinary means could be used to fulfill His plans.

After her death, a pastor was faithful in following up the other members of the family. In time, each was individually introduced to the Saviour. This mother bequeathed her sons much more than wealth. Her testimony and love for the Lord showed them the true way, and they are now illustrating God's faithfulness and sufficiency in their own lives.

May His love be our daily portion, and may we in reality experience the treasure we have in Him. "I am thy part and thine inheritance."

[1]Numbers 18:20.

   ✤   ✤   ✤

Numbers 22–25
Numbers 23:13-30

> Surely there is no enchantment against Jacob, neither is
> there any divination against Israel: according to this
> time it shall be said of Jacob and of Israel, What hath
> God wrought![1]

"WHAT HATH GOD WROUGHT!" The expression is familiar
in testimonies of Christians, the recounting of miracles on
the mission field, or in the story of one who has experienced
God's unusual dealings in his life.

The story of Balak, king of the Moabites, and Balaam is
well known to most people with a Sunday school background. Balak was anxious to get rid of the Israelites, who
were pitching their tents above his plains. Balaam would
be his representative. Balak made several attempts to have
them cursed and brought low, but God placed hindrances
in his way. Here we see illustrated the fact that the coun-
sels of God are far greater than those of men. No amount
of planning or plotting could bring Balak's plan to fruition. When God stands in the way the foe is vanquished.
How true are the words of the Psalmist, "Let all the earth
fear the Lord: let all the inhabitants of the world stand in
awe of him. For he spake, and it was done; he commanded,
and it stood fast. The Lord bringeth the counsel of the
heathen to nought: he maketh the devices of the people of
none effect. The counsel of the Lord standeth for ever, the
thoughts of his heart to all generations."[2]

God will protect His people at all costs. They have been
called "the apple of his eye."[3] He told them through Isaiah,
"Behold, I have graven thee upon the palms of my hands."[4]
He has graciously covenanted to keep His own, and He
slumbers not nor sleeps. Is it not easy to understand then,
that "surely there is no enchantment against Jacob"?

What has God wrought? Daily His grace and mercy and

love are shown in the hearts of believers. Failing humans are not sufficient for the difficult things of life. Thus there is no question as to where the credit and honor go. It is God who delivers. It is God who is to be praised. It is God alone who deserves the glory. Everything is wrought by Him.

A writer of another day wrote, "Recognizing what God has wrought should be enough to always keep human nature in place!" It was not what Moses did, nor what Balak and Balaam didn't do. It is not what Martin Luther or any of the early reformers or martyrs did. It is always, and always will be, "What God hath wrought!"

May He ever be exalted for the blessings we enjoy, and for what has been accomplished in us and through us—all for His glory and praise.

[1]Numbers 23:23.
[2]Psalm 33:8-11.
[3]Deuteronomy 32:10.
[4]Isaiah 49:16.

❧   ❧   ❧

February 18

NUMBERS 26–28
NUMBERS 27

> And the Lord said unto Moses, Take thee Joshua the son of Nun, a man in whom is the spirit, and lay thine hand upon him.[1]

GOD CALLED for another census of the people. There remained only two, Caleb and Joshua, of those who had reached Kadesh forty years before. This was a new generation, and they were hopeful as they encamped near the Jordan River. Moses, their leader, was approaching death, but he had been allowed a glimpse into the land of promise. It is true he had been faithful, but some of the rewards were withheld because of his disobedience. Disobedience often blocks the path to the promised land. Yet he had been called upon to choose a successor.

There was probably little hesitation in the mind of Moses as to his choice. He must be a man of authority. One who, like Caleb, had a good spirit. He must have a capacity to guide and his relationship with the priests must be right. Moses' recommendation was made and approved by God, for the Lord spoke to him to take Joshua. "Joshua the son of Nun was full of the spirit of wisdom; for Moses had laid his hands upon him: and the children of Israel hearkened unto him, and did as the Lord commanded Moses."[2] Joshua had proved he was a man willing to stand for God, even in danger.

God gave a charge to Joshua also: "Be strong and of a good courage: for thou shalt bring the children of Israel into the land which I sware unto them: and I will be with thee."[3]

Throughout life, man is called upon to succeed man. Pastors will often confess that they rarely have the privilege of knowing their successors, but a faithful pastor will have laid a good foundation and sought the mind of God for the church in the choice of his successor. It is true also with lay people, as is evidenced on the high school and college campus, that when one leader must leave, the mantle falls on another.

May we be willing to continue God's work as others must step aside. May we also wisely prepare others to carry out His commission of telling the world about life in Christ. "Faithful is he that calleth you, who also will do it."[4]

[1]Numbers 27:18.
[2]Deuteronomy 34:9.
[3]Deuteronomy 31:23.
[4]I Thessalonians 5:24.

❧ ❧ ❧

83

NUMBERS 29–32
NUMBERS 30

> Everything that may abide the fire, ye shall make it go
> through the fire, and it shall be clean.[1]

I CAN REMEMBER as a small child going up the beach with
my father one day. Climbing over some old logs and trees,
I ran a sliver of wood into my finger. It was no crisis. On
arriving home Father lit a match and put the fire to a
needle's point, then with the fire-sterilized needle he soon
removed the source of irritation. His simple explanation to
me was this: "Fire makes the needle clean."

Throughout life, for every Christian there are times of
fire. I think of my father, long since gone to be with the
Lord, on this date, which was his birthday. In standing for
the pure faith of our fathers, he was put to many unpleasant
tests. Yet, through them all his life he was an example to
me of a true believer. His devotion to Christ was unques-
tioned. Every morning in the early hours of four and five
he was up spending time alone with his God. No doubt it
was during those times that he prayed for his children, that
they would grow into spiritual maturity and be able to
"abide the fire."

The children of Israel had their times of severe testing, as
did their leaders. It is a consolation to us today that these
tests are given by God to prove we can withstand their heat.
In our reading today it was said that things which could not
withstand fire were to be put in the water. Deep waters are
a test too! God in His great tenderness knows if His children can withstand fire or water.

I experienced in my own life a circumstance which put
me to a severe test. Could I withstand? No, not of myself,
but I remember thinking back to the illustration of years
gone by: "Fire makes the needle clean." The source of
irritation was not immediately removed, but the gradual

process taught this dependent child of God that "it is God which worketh in you both to will and to do of his good pleasure."[2]

Could it be that you are passing through fire or deep waters? For each there is a precious promise. Claim the one that fits your circumstance. "When thou passest through the waters, I will be with thee; and through the rivers, they shall not overflow thee: when thou walkest through the fire, thou shalt not be burned; neither shall the flame kindle upon thee. For I am the Lord thy God."[3]

[1]Numbers 31:23.
[2]Philippians 2:13.
[3]Isaiah 43:2-3.

❧ ❧ ❧

February 20

NUMBERS 33–36
NUMBERS 34:1-18

AS THE LORD SPOKE to Moses, and he commanded the children of Israel as to their boundaries and borders of the Promised Land, a great air of expectation must have passed over them. They were on the brink of inheritance!

Their position parallels the church of Christ today. As did those Israelites, the church has passed through many trials and difficulties. As from Kadesh-Barnea, so from here there are lands to be possessed and tribes who have never heard the message of salvation. The doors of opportunity are wide open, and the plan of God is clear. "Go ye into all the world, and preach the gospel to every creature."[1] As we look out, just what do we see? Walled cities, giants, difficulties? Or do we see men and women in bondage, lost and without hope? Do we advance, or do we retreat, in the way of God?

Today is a good day to take our spiritual temperature. It will take eyes of understanding, a clear vision of God

Himself, and a conquering faith, to step ahead. Are we spiritually prepared? The book of Numbers has shown us men like Caleb and Joshua who faced hindrance upon hindrance but were not hindered. Walled cities were a challenge to their faith in God alone.

We need more Apostle Pauls who steadfastly say, "I will tarry at Ephesus until Pentecost. For a great door and effectual is opened unto me, and there are many adversaries."[2] Paul's attitude toward the opportunity before him proved his attitude toward God. "Fear is born from lack of faith."

We stand on the threshold of fields white unto harvest. Laborers are needed. The rewards are great: new babes born into the family of God, for one. The joys of obedience and service could be likened to milk and honey. But then the offense of an unreceptive heart, or Satan's saying that "everyone should be responsible for himself," dims the horizon with doubt. We become paralyzed and retreat.

The promise is before us. "Ask of me, and I shall give thee the heathen for thine inheritance, and the uttermost parts of the earth for thy possession."[3] We are on the boundary of this great possession. G. Campbell Morgan wrote, "When the eye is single, the heart undivided, the love unified upon the one principle of winning God's victory, there is no halting and no turning back." What is our true purpose of heart? A door is open. God is ready. Are we?

[1]Mark 16:15.
[2]I Corinthians 16:8-9.
[3]Psalm 2:8.

❧   ❧   ❧

DEUTERONOMY 1–3
DEUTERONOMY 1

> The Lord your God which goeth before you, he shall
> fight for you, according to all that he did for you in
> Egypt before your eyes; and in the wilderness, where
> thou hast seen how that the Lord thy God bare thee, as
> a man doth bear his son, in all the way that ye went,
> until ye came into this place.[1]

PERHAPS this day finds a reader in the wilderness. Let him
take heart. From experience the Psalmist wrote, "Even
there shall thy hand lead me, and thy right hand shall hold
me. Yea, the darkness hideth not from thee; but the night
shineth as the day: the darkness and the light are both alike
to thee."[2]

We are surely not meant to wait long in this place of
desolation. Why are we here? Is it because of sin or lack
of faith? How amazed I was one day to learn that over-
tiredness is a quick route to the wilderness! Despair, depression, misunderstandings, all are wilderness experiences.

Often we confess there seems to be no way out! In ourselves it is true, we are most certainly hemmed in. But
there is a way out. A loving, merciful Father will bring us
through. What an act of condescension! What great love,
for Him to carry us out of the wilderness.

Christians must be discerning in understanding the difference between affliction, or trial, and wilderness experiences. One young woman told me of a series of temptations
she was battling. Rather brusquely she said it was her "personal wilderness." However, a more careful study of her
heart in the presence of God proved that she was being
tempted and, in passing the tests, going on to greater things
for God. Could the Apostle Paul say he was in the wilderness when he endured hardness and shipwreck? Were the
prison cells and the scourgings holding him back from the

promised reward? Not at all. They were steps forward in great devotion. A translator penned these words of Paul's that illustrate his position:

> We are hard pressed, yet never in absolute distress; perplexed, yet never utterly baffled; pursued, yet never left unsuccoured; struck to the ground, yet never slain.[3]

No matter the circumstances, when we in love and humility turn to God, He will never fail to bear us up all the way, carrying us out of the wilderness or through our afflictions. However, we will again be confronted with problems. But these are on the path that leads ahead, and the guidance keeps coming from above. In the growing process of daily piety there need be no setbacks. "Close followed by pursuers, yet not abandoned!"

[1]Deuteronomy 1:30-31.
[2]Psalm 139:10, 12.
[3]II Corinthians 4:8-9, Weymouth.

❧ ❧ ❧

February 22

Deuteronomy 4–7
Deuteronomy 4

> Behold, I have taught you statutes and judgments, even as the Lord my God commanded me, that ye should do so in the land whither ye go to possess it. Keep therefore and do them; for this is your wisdom and your understanding in the sight of the nations, which shall hear all these statutes, and say, Surely this great nation is a wise and understanding people.[1]

"Hearken" and "do," that you may "live" and "possess." This is the theme of Deuteronomy. God has given statutes and judgments, we must trust and obey. It was true in the days of Moses and Joshua and it is true in our twentieth century. This book truly exalts the Word of God and clearly portrays over and over the complete obedience that must be given.

A father told how he taught his child obedience. One day he instructed her not to go off the porch. Her quick response was, "Why?" His answer was simple but definite. "Because I told you not to." Some may question the theory used, but the father was primarily concerned that his daughter learn obedience—obedience without asking why! The same child might be in the middle of the street and the father shout, "Get out of the street!" If she stopped to ask why, she might be killed.

Obedience without question is what God demands. There are times, after we have learned, when we will see the reasoning or the discipline involved, but primarily the great lesson to be pressed into our hearts is to obey. Death is the alternative.

Understanding the divine statutes or their ramifications was not a matter of discussion among the children of Israel, not even in the Israelite "camp council." The wisdom was in the statutes given by God, not in the people who were affected by them. These statutes, when followed, were to illumine the character and behavior of these people so they would be a testimony to the neighboring people and to other nations.

Oh, that we could early learn the effects of obedience as compared with those of disobedience. God's powerful argument was: "For what nation is there so great, who hath God so nigh unto them, as the Lord our God is in all things that we call upon him for? And what nation is there so great, that hath statutes and judgments so righteous as all this law, which I set before you this day?"[2]

God graciously draws nigh to those who draw nigh to Him. Obedience for the sake of obedience is our privilege. Divine direction is our reward.

[1]Deuteronomy 4:5-6.   [2]Deuteronomy 4:7-8.

❧ ❧ ❧

DEUTERONOMY 8–12
DEUTERONOMY 8

> Therefore shall ye lay up these my words in your heart
> and in your soul, and bind them for a sign upon your
> hand, that they may be as frontlets between your eyes.
> And ye shall teach them your children, speaking of them
> when thou sittest in thine house, and when thou walkest
> by the way, when thou liest down, and when thou risest
> up. And thou shalt write them upon the door posts of
> thine house, and upon thy gates.[1]

UP THE FRONT STEPS came nine-year-old Kathi, bouncing
with her usual after-school enthusiasm. Her mother saw
her coming and went to open the door. "Thank you,"
Kathi said, and proceeded into her room to change into
playclothes. For her the experience and the thank-you
were quickly forgotten, but not for her mother. That evening when the children were tucked away, she related to her
husband the incident and the reflections that had been
hers since it happened. Together they talked of the glorious
privilege it is for parents to open doors for their children.
First, doors which lead to a saving knowledge of Jesus
Christ, and then doors that open up into a true knowledge
and deeper understanding of Him. That evening they
prayed that, in relation to their three youngsters, each
would be a more faithful parent and an alert doorkeeper in
the house of the Lord!

Israel was to be rewarded for her obedience in opening
the right doors for her children. First they must be taught
about Jehovah and His faithfulness. They must learn by
example. After seeing their parents storing in their hearts
the truths and statutes of God, the younger generation
would follow. Today we likewise are called upon to teach
and train our natural children, our adopted children, our
spiritual children. God asks us to make their young hearts

"libraries" where His truths and promises are stored through discussing, memorizing, and worshiping. His Word in the heart and home brings special illumination and blessing to all in the family: "That your days may be multiplied, and the days of your children, in the land which the Lord sware unto your fathers to give them, as the days of heaven upon the earth."[2]

General William Booth gave his daughter Evangeline some wise advice: "Progress is made by keeping pace with the stride of God." That is our business today, for ourselves and for those who follow in our steps.

[1]Deuteronomy 11:18-20.
[2]Deuteronomy 11:21.

❧ ❧ ❧

February 24

DEUTERONOMY 13–17
DEUTERONOMY 13

> Then shalt thou enquire, and make search, and ask diligently; and behold, if it be truth, and the thing certain, that such abomination is wrought among you; thou shalt surely smite the inhabitants . . . to do that which is right in the eyes of the Lord thy God.[1]

IT WILL EVER BE TRUE that a little leaven, when it is entertained, soon leavens the whole mass. This fact was proved in the case of the Israelites, whose downward trend started with a city slowly removing its allegiance from God and serving other gods. The church, or the city, or the individual, turning aside from the true God will be judged. Peter warned, "For it had been better for them not to have known the way of righteousness, than, after they have known it, to turn from the holy commandment delivered unto them."[2] It is a solemn statement.

The fact that these disobedient ones would dare suggest, "Let us go and serve other gods"[3] was an indication the children of wickedness were infiltrating among God's own. Instead of quick, drastic action, the cause of the trouble was to be ordered to a fair and honest trial. This would be carried out with the utmost care. "Shall not the Judge of all the earth do right?"[4]

We can learn a lesson today. In judging (and we are quick to judge and cast condemnation on those we hear have done wrong), would it not be wise for us to "enquire, and make search, and ask diligently"? Are there specific proofs of the truth of the gossip that spreads over the Women's Association, or the high school club, or the college campus?

God decreed that if the wrong was proved, "if it be truth and the thing certain," the city should be destroyed. The righteous would have their chance to be protected, but all else, families, houses, and goods, would be destroyed.

"Is this a God of love?" one may ask. "Would God destroy His own people?" His severity shows His love. It is dangerous to meddle in the things that He abhors. His glory will not be given to another. False gods must not be served. Yet His chastisement still allows for mercy, as Isaiah beautifully states: "For a small moment have I forsaken thee; but with great mercies will I gather thee. In a little wrath I hid my face from thee for a moment; but with everlasting kindness will I have mercy on thee, saith the Lord thy Redeemer."[5]

Let us be faithful when the time comes to faithfully "enquire" and "ask diligently." If our brother is to be disciplined by God, show him mercy. Who knows? But for the grace of God we could have been likewise tempted.

[1]Deuteronomy 13:14-15, 18.
[2]II Peter 2:21.
[3]Deuteronomy 13:6.
[4]Genesis 18:25.
[5]Isaiah 54:7-8.

❧ ❧ ❧

DEUTERONOMY 18–21
DEUTERONOMY 20

> What man is there that is fearful and fainthearted? Let
> him go and return unto his house, lest his brethren's
> heart faint as well as his heart.[1]

A GROUP OF "TENDERFOOT" SCOUTS were on their first hike.
Twelve of them were bravely pressing on, though signs of
fatigue were evident and the condition of their feet well
illustrated their name! There was only one mile to go
when suddenly one boy stepped out of the line and yelled,
"I've had it!" Their leader stopped the group and encouraged the boy to go on. He had been the one best equipped
for the trip, with hiking boots and canteen. Others only
wore tennis shoes, and one had heavy socks with rubber
galoshes over them. On they marched for about twenty
yards and another, spurred by the first, announced, "I'm
finished." The leader recognized the problem. One boy's
lack of determination and fortitude had infected all twelve
scouts. His brothers had been discouraged from reaching
their goal and weakened in their walk because one had
punctured the determination that had kept them marching
together, and had broken the team spirit.

How is it with your spirit today? Possibly you have a
sink full of dishes from last night, the house is in disarray
after a gathering, and the family were served their eggs
with an extra amount of spicy murmuring. Did they leave
home content or discontent? Who was the infectious one?

These rules in Deuteronomy make clear that some are
not ready for battle. It follows that they will weaken others.
If one will faint, let him return to his house.

The verse speaks to us today. Possibly you would rather
be doing anything except those dishes, or you are fretting
because you are unprepared for your Sunday school class.
Honesty before God is necessary. Tell Him about your

weariness. Tell Him the troubles of your heart. Tell Him, but spare those who would tend to be weakened by your complaint and confession of tiredness.

It may be that in your devotions you have struggled in the Word and sought to be persevering in prayer but the outcome was not as you expected and some need was not met. Again, tell the Lord about it. He may have the answer on the horizon or just around the corner. But don't hurt a new Christian with your doubt or faithlessness.

Let us never discourage others or dare to weaken their walk with the Lord. Let us claim His words, "My flesh and my heart faileth: but God is the strength of my heart, and my portion for ever."[2] Let the promise impress itself on your heart.

The Scotch have an old motto which has granted refreshment to many a heavy heart and tired body: "Pray and praise and peg away!" With God as the strength of your heart and your daily delight and portion, you cannot help but show grace and inspiration to all.

[1]Deuteronomy 20:8.
[2]Psalm 73:26.

❧ ❧ ❧

February 26

DEUTERONOMY 22–25
DEUTERONOMY 24:17-22

> And thou shalt remember that thou wast a bondman in the land of Egypt: therefore I command thee to do this thing.[1]

THE DAY Moses addressed his people thus he was doing some reminiscing. He reminded them that they had been hopelessly enslaved in Egypt, and then God in His mercy had broken the bonds of their oppression and effected their deliverance. Moses probably reviewed the Red Sea miracle, the times of trial for various families, the hardships, and some of the lighter moments. There was a hushed feeling, now that they approached the borders of the Promised Land. Lest they forget the God of Israel who had brought them this far, Moses recalled the past.

The people must not forget that they should never oppress a hired servant, whether a stranger or of their own people. Advantage must not be taken of widows or the fatherless. In harvesting, some grain must be left for the less fortunate. God had provided manna for them; they must share their increase. They must not cook a goat in its mother's milk. Each of these laws was given by a God of pure love.

The redemption of these Israelites gives us a clear picture of our redemption. Paul reminds us, "Wherefore remember, that ye being in time past Gentiles in the flesh . . . ye were without Christ, being aliens from the commonwealth of Israel, and strangers from the covenants of promise, having no hope, and without God in the world."[2] Their bondage was a type of ours outside of Christ. They were slaves to Egypt, and we were slaves to sin. The state was one of helplessness. Just as the children of Israel could not save themselves, neither can the sinner. Both were without hope.

In remembering bondage, redemption becomes more precious. Just as those fettered Israelites were freed by God's mighty arm, so are we. Israel looked to Moses, who interceded for them. We look to the very Son of God who came to "proclaim liberty to the captives."[3]

A slave in the days of Abraham Lincoln said, "No man can understand redemption until he has been set free." We have been set free, redeemed, not with silver or gold but with the precious blood of our Redeemer.

Lest we forget!

[1]Deuteronomy 24:22. [3]Isaiah 61:1.
[2]Ephesians 2:11-12.

❧ ❧ ❧

95

DEUTERONOMY 26–28
DEUTERONOMY 28

> And all these blessings shall come on thee, and overtake thee, if thou shalt hearken unto the voice of the Lord thy God.[1]

IT IS TRUE that we remember what we see much better than what we hear. The Israelites were given tangible things to remind them of the laws of God. There were specific objects that they could see. The tables of the law, which were preserved in the Ark, and the wearing of the Shema on their arms. Seeing was remembering.

God was now giving another sight on the horizon. There were two mountains. One was Ebal, which we are told was bare and rocky, and symbolized curses. The other was Gerizim, which was a mountain of blessing. Upon Mt. Ebal the law was to be written on stones. This would provide a monument that could be seen near and far. The law was before the people. The tribes were to be divided. Half of them would gather on Mt. Ebal and the others on Mt. Gerizim. Here the blessings and the curses would be read. It must have been an experience long remembered, hearing God's words echoing back and forth in a place known for its acoustics. If they would hearken, there would be blessing. If they disobeyed, there would be curses. The law served as a guide to show man his sin. Yet we are reminded, "By the deeds of the law there shall no flesh be justified . . . for by the law is the knowledge of sin."[2]

The people could look to the law and recognize their desperate need. The law points us to Calvary where Christ took our sins. We are "justified by his blood."[3]

The two mountains must have been spectacular at sunrise and sunset. One was the symbol of blessing contingent on total commitment and obedience. By following the law the people would prosper and victory was assured. Israel would be a "lending" and not a "borrowing" nation. But Mt. Ebal was a peaked reminder of calamity that would result if the curses must be given. It was a terrifying list: defeat, disease, and destruction; depression, scattering, and captivity.

The mountains taught a lesson, but Israel did not heed. They had the objects before them, but they ignored them. Seattle, Washington is surrounded by mountains. Often lifting up my eyes and seeing them, I am reminded of the blessings and the curses, of Ebal and Gerizim, and I pray I will be faithful.

[1]Deuteronomy 28:2.
[2]Romans 3:20.
[3]Romans 5:9.

❧ ❧ ❧

<h1 style="text-align:right">February 28</h1>

DEUTERONOMY 29–31
DEUTERONOMY 30

> Be strong and of a good courage, fear not, nor be afraid
> of them: for the Lord thy God, he it is that doth go
> with thee; he will not fail thee, nor forsake thee.[1]

THE QUESTION often is asked, "Do these Old Testament promises apply to me today?" Many are concerned, and sincerely so, whether or not they can claim such words today.

History shows us that the words were first spoken by Moses to the group of assembled Israelites. The enemies were many and powerful. We know there were as many as seven other nations who wanted to band together to combat the nation of Israel. The words first rang out to all the people. Again they were used by Moses to encourage Joshua, and later still, by God Himself, to exhort Joshua.

Our answer to the above question comes from the Apostle Paul. In writing to the entire church he said, "So that we may boldly say, The Lord is my helper, and I will not fear what man shall do unto me."[2]

We are apt to find ourselves more often than not in Moses' position. We have conflict with the world about us, and the power of Satan is strong. There is more against us than seven nations, and the odds are grim. But low odds are said to be high opportunities with God. Rather than turning aside from the enemy, we must engage in spiritual warfare. For it we have the promise of His presence with us: "For the Lord thy God, he it is that doth go with thee." His gracious, all-knowing presence is with us, surrounding us, yes, in us. This calms our fears. He is mighty. "If God be for us, who can be against us?"[3]

If we did not have this promise of His presence, we might cry like Moses, "If thy presence go not with me, carry us not up hence." But His presence is with us, lasting and abiding. "My presence shall go with thee, and I will give thee rest."[4]

Amid our weakness, His strength prevails. We can take heart when we recall that the wall of Jericho fell at the mere sound of rams' horns. Remember Midian. It was vanquished by a few broken pitchers and lamps. One small stone felled Goliath.

These are examples to encourage us, not just for biblical entertainment. Through other men of faith, our own faith is strengthened. Remembering them and the presence and power of their God and ours, we can be strong in the power of our Lord.

[1]Deuteronomy 31:6.
[2]Hebrews 13:6.
[3]Romans 8:31.
[4]Exodus 33:14-15.

❧　❧　❧

DEUTERONOMY 32–34
DEUTERONOMY 32

> The eternal God is thy refuge, and underneath are the everlasting arms.[1]

FROM THE GREAT ALASKA EARTHQUAKE comes the story of a little child who was found sleeping peacefully under a fallen beam in a little mission church. When awakened, the child told of his fears as the earth cracked, the buildings tumbled, and people were tossed about like toys on the sidewalks. "I remembered I'd be safe in Jesus," said the tiny tot," and I ran to get as close to Him as I could." The youngster took refuge in the church, itself mostly in shambles, but he knew he'd be "safe in Jesus."

As Moses addressed the tribes of Israel, he reminded them all that as long as they obeyed God they would be safe in Him. He would thrust the enemies out from before them. They would dwell in safety. "The eternal God is thy refuge, and underneath are the everlasting arms."

Everlasting arms mean the arms of all time—past, present and future. Early in Deuteronomy God promised, "The Lord thy God bare thee, as a man doth bear his son, in all the way that ye went, until ye came into this place."[2]

What of today, the present? Our reading pictures the wings of an eagle over the nest. "As an eagle stirreth up her nest, fluttereth over her young, spreadeth abroad her wings, taketh them, beareth them on her wings: so the Lord alone did lead."[3] He has led, and He will lead. Yesterday and today. Today we are told, "Casting all your care upon him; for he careth for you."[4] "He shall sustain thee."[5]

What of tomorrow? In the trinity of time, tomorrow is not forgotten. His arms truly are everlasting. "The Lord shall guide thee continually."[6] "Even to your old age I am he; and even to hoar hairs will I carry you."[7] The Psalmist expressed this state of continually feeling those everlasting arms when he wrote, "O God, thou hast taught me from my youth: and hitherto have I declared thy wondrous works. Now also when I am old and greyheaded, O God, forsake me not; until I have shewed thy strength unto this generation, and thy power to every one that is to come."[8]

As we close another month may we feel those everlasting arms girding us, strengthening us, and enabling us in a more perfect way to know we have felt His glory.

[1]Deuteronomy 33:27.
[2]Deuteronomy 1:31.
[3]Deuteronomy 32:11-12.
[4]I Peter 5:7.
[5]Psalm 55:22.
[6]Isaiah 58:11.
[7]Isaiah 46:4.
[8]Psalm 71:17-18.

❧ ❧ ❧

March

JOSHUA 1–5
JOSHUA 1

> This book of the law shall not depart out of thy mouth;
> but thou shalt meditate therein day and night, that thou
> mayest observe to do according to all that is written
> therein: for then thou shalt make thy way prosperous,
> and then thou shalt have good success. Have not I com-
> manded thee? Be strong and of a good courage; be not
> afraid, neither be thou dismayed: for the Lord thy God
> is with thee whithersoever thou goest.[1]

A STALWART CHRISTIAN of yesterday who accomplished great
things in the kingdom of God used to advise new believers,
"Put your foot on God's promises!" Joshua was an example
of one who did just this. He had this advice from God just
as he was on the verge of accomplishing God's true purpose
for him. If he had dared to look ahead he might have been
discouraged by the difficulties. But in the past, Joshua had
learned to "step" on each promise, to claim it for his very
own, and this habit gave him the courage and confidence
for his tomorrows.

He well knew what was required for true spiritual conquest. "Have not I commanded thee? Be strong." Strength
is essential. Think of the years he cultivated this strength.
He had hiked in the wilderness. The way had been hot
and rugged and wearying, and surely he must have been
tried at times, but through the testing he developed endurance.

Joshua meditated in the law. This was his source of

spiritual strength and courage. With the task of leading more than three million people into the Promised Land, Joshua must have spent much of his time in meditation and prayer, so that the way would be prosperous.

The story is told of a professor, formerly at Harvard, who was greatly beloved of his students. The seniors would always admonish the freshmen, "Stay close to this man, and he will show you something wonderful every minute."

In studying Joshua, we see what we would like to be in the kingdom of God. Strong, courageous, learned in the Lord! So many complain that even after years of church attendance they are still "weak in the faith." Do not blame the surroundings. Look into your heart. Are you cultivating true friendship with Jesus Christ? If time is spent with Him, He will "show you something wonderful every minute." If He is to be real, we must live in His presence, and step on His promises. As a result we will have the reward of Joshua: "Every place that the sole of your foot shall tread upon, that have I given unto you."[2]

[1] Joshua 1:8-9.
[2] Joshua 1:3.

❧　❧　❧

Joshua 6–9
Joshua 6

> And the Lord said unto Joshua, See, I have given into
> thine hand Jericho. . . . Shout; for the Lord hath given
> you the city. . . . Get thee up; wherefore liest thou thus
> upon thy face?[1]

Is IT POSSIBLE for there to be a time when one should not
pray repeatedly but instead advance and possess what God
already has waiting for us? God said to Joshua, "Get thee
up." Undoubtedly he had been asking God for directions,
sincerely seeking His face. When Jericho was conquered,
he knew it was not the shout which brought down those
walls but the faith behind the shout. The shout was the
action needed to prove to God that they believed Him.
The victory followed.

Bobby lived in an orphanage. As his twelfth birthday was
nearing, how he prayed for the things he needed! His
mother always remembered, and so did an aunt in Pitts-
burgh, and an uncle in Detroit. Birthdays and Christmases
were very special events to him, and he had never been forgotten.

The birthday arrived but no presents. Not wanting to
show his overanxious feelings, he stayed away from the
orphanage post office. He kept the disappointment to himself and kept talking to the Lord about it.

Almost a week passed, and Bobby was discouraged. Then
one of his friends came tearing into his dormitory. The
friend had a package slip which had been put in his box
by mistake. Since he had been in the infirmary the slip
had just waited for a week. At once the two took off to get
Bobby's package. Not one but several waited for him. The
postmistress apologized for the mistake but asked Bobby
why he hadn't come as he usually did, to claim what was
his. Bobby had learned a lesson, and later he told the

same friend, "You know, sometimes a guy has to act on his prayers!"

Bobby's lesson was the one learned by Joshua, and we need to learn it today. There comes a time to act on our prayers. Does this mean we stop praying? No, we must continue, but we must recognize that the real answer to asking is receiving. Too many fail to appropriate answers to their prayers and thus miss out on the blessing God is waiting to give.

It has been said, "God's anteroom of heaven is full of unclaimed packages." Through our eyes of unbelief this may seem impossible, but belief is willing to shout when all looks lost. Then the walls come down, and victory is won. "Ask, and ye shall receive, that your joy may be full."[2]

[1]Joshua 6:2, 16; 7:10.
[2]John 16:24.

❧ ❧ ❧

March 3

Joshua 10–12
Joshua 10

> Therefore the five kings . . . gathered themselves together, and went up, they and all their hosts, and encamped before Gibeon, and made war against it. . . . And the Lord said unto Joshua, Fear them not: for I have delivered them into thine hand.[1]

As we look at Joshua, we see that there must be no standing still if one is to advance in the Christian life. After Joshua took command of the Israelites there was one battle after another: "Joshua had taken Ai, and had utterly destroyed it; as he had done to Jericho and her kings, so he had done to Ai and her king; and . . . the inhabitants of Gibeon had made peace with Israel, and were among them."[2] As God led, they went forward and there was victory.

Standing still is no way to make progress. In fact it can be a means of retreat. One need only look at a bicycle to recognize that it must be moving to be upright. It will not stand still by itself without falling. Too many in the family of God today are standing still. Their faith is dormant, and because it is not used it grows weak.

God has a plan. It may be one which looks like retrogression, but if it is the plan of God, going backward is going forward! Obedience to Him means progress.

Notice that along the way Joshua was careful to root out anything that would hinder his people or cause them to stand still. This is illustrated in the story of the five kings. These kings banded together to declare war on the Israelites. God promised His people victory. When the battle was over the kings had hidden in caves. Joshua had determined that they would not escape, and part of the mop-up exercise was to reckon with these men. Joshua said, "Open the mouth of the cave, and bring out those five kings unto me."[3] The kings were brought out and put to death. He used the five kings as an object lesson to show the captains and men of war that the Lord would so smite all their enemies if they would fear Him and be of good courage.

Joshua dealt with the wicked kings and experienced a victory. The kings must be put to death or they would continue to cause trouble. We too must deal ruthlessly with whatever comes into our lives that would bring evil. Sin must be put away. Then we too will realize continued Christian conquest. "Faith is the victory that overcomes the world."

[1]Joshua 10:5, 8.
[2]Joshua 10:1.
[3]Joshua 10:22.

❧   ❧   ❧

JOSHUA 13–15
JOSHUA 15:13-19

> Give me also springs of water. And he gave her the
> upper springs, and the nether springs.[1]

WHILE VISITING in a nursing home, I was introduced to a
precious lady well into her eighties. Her real name was
given, but the director warmly told me that they called her
"Achsah." He quickly brought to my remembrance the
story of today's reading, and then explained, "This dear
person truly lives from the upper springs!"

In the book of Joshua, we are told that Achsah was the
daughter of Caleb. Her father and Joshua had been faithful
in the time of Moses and were remembered for their favorable minority report regarding the land about to be possessed. When the land had been divided, Caleb had given
a certain portion to his daughter. However, she knew this
was land severely parched in the heat of summer and asked
her father for springs of water. Her request was granted.
Thus in the arid season, when the land dried up and was
thirsty, she and her family could draw from the upper
springs and their land would be truly refreshed.

"Achsah" in the nursing home had learned early that
when her soul became parched and dry and her thirst cried
out for the living God, she could draw from "streams of
living waters." Oh, the bounty of God's rich provision of
grace and love and mercy. When most of the pleasures of
earth had passed and there were lonely hours, her soul could
still be nourished from an everlasting supply.

For a true child of God to have those "upper springs" is
common throughout Scripture. God does not leave us barren. Remember, Abraham drank from springs up on Mt.
Moriah. Moses went up to drink in the hills of Midian.
David learned that refreshment was always available to a

weary heart. In drinking from God's springs, his soul was often refreshed and benefited.

Many a believer has learned to drink from the wells of faith. Think of Isaiah, who sang while drawing from these springs. Even Paul and Silas, in prison and shut off from the world, drew deeply, and their souls overflowed with the water from those streams which still flow for us today.

No matter what the circumstance, the "upper springs" and "nether springs" are ever available. Drink, that you may truly live!

[1]Joshua 15:19.

❧ ❧ ❧

March 5

JOSHUA 16–20
JOSHUA 20

> The Lord . . . spake unto Joshua, saying, Speak to the children of Israel, saying, Appoint out for you cities of refuge, whereof I spake unto you by the hand of Moses.[1]

THE CITIES OF REFUGE make an interesting study. There were six, and they were provided for those who killed someone unintentionally. The River Jordan separated the cities, with three on one side and three on the other side. Each was accessible and we are told that any fugitive might reach his destination within half a day.

In his study on the cities of refuge, Charles Spurgeon tells us that the roads were strictly cared for, that the path might be clear and unobstructed. He also tells us that annually the elders would check each road and remove any hindrance or obstacle that would deter a person on the road to refuge.

The one being falsely accused of crime could come to the gates of one of these cities, state his case, and be safe until the people tried him. According to law, if his story was found to be correct he would remain, protected, until the death of the high priest. Then he was free to return to his home with no sentence against him.

The writer of Hebrews tells us, "We . . . have a strong consolation, who have fled for refuge to lay hold upon the hope set before us."[2] Our refuge is in Jesus Christ. "The name of the Lord is a strong tower: the righteous runneth into it, and is safe."[3]

Those who would flee sin have a way cleared for them. "The way of the cross leads home!" Each stumbling block has been removed by the one who clearly says, "I am the way, the truth, and the life: no man cometh unto the Father, but by me."[4] All along the road to Christ, our refuge, there are guideposts pointing toward Him. And He said, "Him that cometh to me I will in no wise cast out."[5]

Just as the fugitive found safety by entering within the walls of the city, so the one outside of Christ can be safe in Him.

When the high priest died, the refugee was set free. So our High Priest died that in every sense we could be free. "God is our refuge and strength, a very present help in trouble. . . . The Lord of hosts is with us; the God of Jacob is our refuge."[6]

[1]Joshua 20:1-2.
[2]Hebrews 6:18.
[3]Proverbs 18:10.
[4]John 14:6.
[5]John 6:37.
[6]Psalm 46:1, 11.

❧ ❧ ❧

Joshua 21–24
Joshua 24

> Choose you this day whom ye will serve; . . . but as for
> me and my house, we will serve the Lord.[1]

WE LEAVE JOSHUA knowing that he was one of the great
hearts of the Old Testament and of the world. He was every
inch the hero. Whether leading the spies into the Promised
Land and making with Caleb the immortal minority report, or leading Israel across Jordan's flood, or in battle
with Jericho and the bristling fortresses and hostile tribes
of Canaan, or on his knees before the angel of the Lord,
Joshua is a man who wins our admiration. Loyal, obedient,
courageous, faithful, and above all, a man of decision and
of immediate action."[2]

Joshua called together all the tribes of Israel with all the
elders for some final words. He reminded them of the past
and warned them of the future: "Now therefore fear the
Lord, and serve him in sincerity and in truth: and put away
the gods which your fathers served on the other side of the
flood, and in Egypt; and serve ye the Lord."[3] The choice
was before them but each must decide for himself. The
pressure from others, the temptations of evil, all must be
reckoned with in individual hearts. Within man's heart is
a place of solitude where all else is shut out. Here decisions
are made.

For Joshua and his family the choice was certain. They
would serve the Lord. The choice cost something then even
as it does today. To the disciples it was written, "If any
man will come after me, let him deny himself, and take up
his cross daily, and follow me."[4] Crossbearing is not easy.
Renouncing sin is difficult, but no man can serve two
masters.

The family of Joshua were with their father in his decision. They had seen his life of faith and surely it drew

them closer together as well as to the Lord. As a family unit they faced the obstacles together and shared the blessings and the disappointments.

Abraham Lincoln once made it clear that no nation could endure while half slave and half free. How that truth can be demonstrated in the lives of individuals! One cannot walk with one foot in the world and one foot separated from the world. It is as impossible as it would have been for Israel to have one foot in Egypt and one in the Promised Land.

Is the statement of Joshua for his family true at your address? May the light of God's presence truly shine to enlighten those who now believe and to penetrate the darkness of those who have not made the eternal choice. May the day be hastened, because of your faithfulness, when the declaration will resound up your block and into the world: "We will serve the Lord!"

[1] Joshua 24:15.
[2] C. E. Macartney.
[3] Joshua 24:14.
[4] Luke 9:23.

❧ ❧ ❧

JUDGES 1–3
JUDGES 3:1-11

> And when the children of Israel cried unto the Lord,
> the Lord raised up a deliverer to the children of Israel,
> who delivered them, even Othniel the son of Kenaz,
> Caleb's younger brother. And the Spirit of the Lord
> came upon him.[1]

"IF YOU WANT TO READ unvarnished history," said a Bible
scholar, "then study the book of Judges." It certainly glosses
over nothing. Some of the stories are incredibly shocking,
but rich and deep truths are also manifest.

The book covers the period between Joshua and Samson
and the story is one of repeated sin, punishment, repentance, and deliverance. The book also gives us further insight into the continuing message of justification by faith.
This came only through accepting God's way of holiness,
and in His strength alone.

God's special messenger, the first judge, is introduced today. His name was Othniel. He was a nephew to Caleb
and, like his uncle, was a true warrior of the faith. His
name accurately describes him, a "powerful man of God."

It is significant that we are told, "The Spirit of the Lord
came upon him." Often we associate the Spirit only with
individuals who lived after the coming of Christ. Yet, even
in these Old Testament days He came upon them for special work. He "breathed" upon many to help accomplish
the work of Jehovah. During the history of Israel, there
were many men who, like Othniel, were equipped for special tasks. Joseph was "a man in whom the Spirit of God
is."[2] When God had Moses appoint the seventy elders He
said, "I will take of the spirit which is upon thee, and will
put it upon them; and they shall bear the burden of the
people with thee, that thou bear it not thyself alone."[3] In

reference to Joshua we are told, "He was full of the spirit of wisdom."[4]

The Spirit came upon specific people for special tasks. When Jesus was about to leave the earth after His resurrection, He told His followers, the early group of believers, "The Father . . . shall give you another Comforter, that he may abide with you for ever."[5] He then bequeathed the Holy Spirit to them, not just to "come upon" them but to "dwell within." Christ's ministry on earth was ending, but the Holy Spirit would abide with, be close beside, actually be within each of God's own, to accomplish His work on earth.

This gives each believer a responsibility. Men mighty for God, like Othniel, had the Spirit upon them, but we have the inestimable privilege of having Him within us. May His residence be kept cleansed and yielded to Him.

[1]Judges 3:9-10.
[2]Genesis 41:38.
[3]Numbers 11:17.
[4]Deuteronomy 34:9.
[5]John 14:16.

❧ ❧ ❧

Judges 4–6
Judges 5

> But Zebulun . . . risked life and death with Naphtali
> out in the open field.[1]

RECENTLY I READ the biography of a parachutist. From his
early childhood he wanted thrills and excitement. He was
always good for a dare and usually took the extra step to
prove that the hazardous was no hardship, only a challenge.

When he began sky-diving, he kept searching for better
stunts and more spectacular achievements. He would coast
for hundreds of feet before pulling the rip cord. He tried
somersaults out of the plane. Then one day he went a bit
too far in taking a risk, and plunged to his death. The
crowd watching was small. Many afterward asked why he
had been so foolhardy. It was not for scientific accomplishment. As for wealth, he had obtained none, nor was it on
the horizon. As the crowd broke up, a few heads were shak-
ing. I doubt that anyone really answered the question. The
man who lost his life had said on another occasion, "I would
risk all for a moment of satisfaction."

History is full of those who have devoted themselves to
causes—many with good results and achievements. Others
lived just for the moment, for a fleeting joy. Few worked
for eternal results.

Zebulun and Naphtali in today's story were willing to
risk their lives for God. The brunt of the battle fell on
Zebulun. Liberation was on his shoulders. A cause? Yes, he
had a cause and was willing to take that extra step, knowing that God would be with him. "Let all thine enemies
perish, O Lord: but let them that love him be as the sun
when he goeth forth in his might."[2]

Do you lack the enthusiasm and vision today to answer
Christ's call to respond, to go forward? It has been two

thousand years since Christ came. Many have been willing to take risks for self but few for the Saviour. There may be a war on poverty, but few take up the banner to abolish poverty of man's soul.

Think what Jesus Christ did for you, how He lived and died and conquered death and promised to be with us in His risen life in all our ways.

Barnabas and Paul were enthusiasts for the Lord. "It seemed good unto us . . . to send chosen men unto you with our beloved Barnabas and Paul, men that have hazarded their lives for the name of our Lord Jesus Christ."[3] The book of Acts is full of dedicated and devoted men who were willing to take that extra step to turn the world to Christ. Scores even died a martyr's death.

What has happened to the deep desires and willing hearts that one day were given to Christ? If we have taken them back in self-interest, let us renew our love today by losing ourselves in Him and daring to hazard our lives in His service.

[1]Judges 5:18, Moffatt.
[2]Judges 5:31.
[3]Acts 15:25-26.

❧   ❧   ❧

Whosoever is fearful and afraid, let him return and
depart early.[1]

THE NARRATIVE OF GIDEON is a favorite of mine. Here was
a young man, full of life and zest, called specifically by God
to help his people. Prior to the story, the Israelites for
twenty years had been under King Jabin the Canaanite,
who oppressed them. God graciously subdued this enemy
and there was peace for forty years. Then the Israelites began to doubt and to sin again. The Midianites attacked
them and they were defeated. They were driven from their
homes and had to survive in dens and caves. Their grain
was taken as were their oxen. In their distress they remembered God, and in His mercy He heard their prayers.

In calling Gideon, God chose a man who would show the
Israelites their wickedness and who would deliver them
from the Midianites. Gideon was busy in the fields threshing wheat when the angel came to him to tell him he had
been called to set the people free. His dialogue with the
angel proved Gideon's humility. He explained that he was
from a poor family and was the least of his father's house.
The angel explained that God would be with him. At once
Gideon offered a sacrifice to the Lord. He then put away
the false god his father had erected, setting aside this obstacle in the way of serving the true God. It was then that
the Spirit of the Lord truly came upon him.

As the Midianites set up camp in the valley of Jezreel,
Gideon blew the trumpet that called his men together.
Many heeded the call. After receiving further reassurance
from the Lord by his "fleece of wool," Gideon was ready to
go to battle. God, however, made him pause en route.
This victory was to be God-planned and God-glorifying.
To this end God had to reduce the army.

This involved trimming down the army from 32,000 to 300. "Whosoever is fearful or afraid, let him return and depart early." Any doubtful motivations must be eliminated. When only twenty-two thousand were left, Gideon told more of what God expected, and more thousands turned away. Again the remainder were tested and only three hundred were left—three hundred chosen by God for a special job.

In the United States we had a somewhat similar situation in our search for the first astronauts. The number started in the thousands, was trimmed to five hundred, then to three hundred men, from whom seven were finally chosen. Quality, not quantity was required.

Napoleon said to a soldier, "In war, men are nothing; the man is everything." So it is in the warfare of the Cross. God needs those who will sacrifice beyond self-gratification and convenience. He must sift His army for soldiers who will endure in the name of Jesus Christ!

¹Judges 7:3.

❧ ❧ ❧

JUDGES 10–13
JUDGES 11:1-13, 30-31

Now Jephthah . . . was a mighty man of valour.[1]

JEPHTHAH has been called the "man of the hour." In God's hall of fame, his name is inscribed with the names of others who were faithful. Of them it is well said, "Who through faith subdued kingdoms, wrought righteousness, obtained promises, stopped the mouths of lions, quenched the violence of fire, escaped the edge of the sword, out of weakness were made strong, waxed valiant in fight, turned to flight the armies of the aliens."[2] What a memorial!

Jephthah's early life had not been easy. He was despised by his half brothers as an illegitimate son, and had become an outcast. When given an opportunity for the Lord's service, he was so eager for victory that he "vowed a vow unto the Lord." If God would help him triumph over Ammon, he would give the Lord whatever would greet him on his return from battle.

Vows are solemn things before God. I wonder what was in Jephthah's heart when the victory was won and he returned home. Who greeted him first? His much beloved only daughter. When her father told her of his vow, she accepted it in obedience saying, "My father, if thou hast opened thy mouth unto the Lord, do to me according to that which hath proceeded out of thy mouth."[3] It was a great sacrifice for them both. It ultimately meant she could not take her place in the history of Israel as a mother of Israel. Both had learned obedience and it was counted to them as excellent service in the sight of God.

How many parents face the crisis of Jephthah when it comes to giving a child, possibly an only child, to Jesus Christ. Theirs is true victory when they vow the vow and fulfill it in their willingness to send the loved one to a foreign field or some other place of service. It is truly a test of love and obedience. Do you love the Lord more than the one you love best? The question was put to Peter many years after Jephthah's time. Said Christ to him, "Lovest thou me?" to which he replied, "Yes, Lord, you know that I do." He was asked again, then again, and at last Christ said, "Feed my sheep."[4]

"All we like sheep have gone astray; we have turned every one to his own way; and the Lord hath laid on him the iniquity of us all."[5] God made a vow to send His only begotten Son to first save and then feed the sheep of His pasture.

May such love and compassion as was extended to us be ours to share, in perfect obedience, in our "vows" to Him.

[1]Judges 11:1.
[2]Hebrews 11:33-34.
[3]Judges 11:36.
[4]John 21:15-17.
[5]Isaiah 53:6.

❧ ❧ ❧

JUDGES 14–17
JUDGES 16

SAMSON'S STORY is most extraordinary. His birth was foretold by an angel and he was singularly set apart, by Nazarite vows, for service. For this reason the heights and depths of his life are so significant.

Scripture portrays him as an outstanding personality. He was greatly gifted. He was a champion and a born leader. How could Samson miss with all these benefits? We must beware, lest the very thing that causes us to rise becomes the cause of our ultimate downfall.

While Samson was a judge over Israel, he was greatly feared and the Philistines feared to attack him. His unbelievable strength foiled many of their plans, as when one night he picked up the gates of Gaza and freed himself despite their plot to apprehend and kill him.

Surely the Philistines knew that there must be some weakness that would cause Samson's fall. It was found in Delilah. Consistently she tried to discover the secret of his strength. Little by little she penetrated his resistance and at last he told her. During this period, Samson did not realize that the anger of the Lord was kindled against him and "he wist not that the Lord was departed from him."[1]

Again the three-letter question arises: why? One can understand that it was not a situation which suddenly appeared from nowhere. Continued disobedience in Samson's heart was reaping its harvest, though outwardly it may have remained unnoticed. Christians today are apt to maintain their outward appearance, but the inner life is the testing ground. Samson had not neglected his outward testimony of the Nazarite vows, but his soul had become barren. How well we understand why God looks on the heart rather than at the exterior life. Samson's inner lack was daily weakening him and his fall was inevitable.

Beware, dear one, of such a thing in your own life. It is not difficult to attend church on Sunday, to keep certain religious exercises, but these are not enough. You may find yourself like Samson, gradually declining spiritually and not knowing that the Lord is withholding His blessing and power. "The cares of this world, and the deceitfulness of riches, and the lusts of other things entering in, choke the word, and it becometh unfruitful."[2]

God had a promise to keep. He had told the Israelites they would be delivered. In death, Samson was used to release the people from bondage. Yet he died with his enemies.

The closing picture is a vivid reminder of what sin does. It is blinding and binding. Samson died far from being the man God intended him to be. May the tragedy of Samson not be ours, and may we resolve to serve our God in life and death.

[1]Judges 16:20.   [2]Mark 4:19.

> In those days there was no king in Israel: every man
> did that which was right in his own eyes.[1]

A GREAT WALL held back the water at the site of a most in-
tricately constructed dam in another country. It was the
pride of its engineers. One day it developed minor water
seepage. It was temporarily overlooked, though some contended that it should be watched. The continual seepage
weakened the cement and soon a stream of water flowed
through. There was more delay to study the cause and its
remedy. As the days passed into weeks, the seepage grew
worse and temporary measures were taken to patch it. However, it had been left too long, and one day the dam tragically collapsed with disastrous results.

The Christian living close to the Lord has a wall of divine defense about him. Jesus Christ will gird and protect,
but we should beware of any slight departure in our lives.
It may be just a small sin, or something of a peripheral nature, but it starts to weaken the soul and, if left, or if only
temporary measures are used to deal with it, there will be
rapid deterioration with sad results.

Such was the case in the time of the judges. Again and
again the people let sin grow and disobedience go unnoticed
until God became angry and grieved and their downfall was
certain. Temporary patches would not hold back the force
of sin's tragic results. The book of Judges gives us warning
that "the wages of sin is death,"[2] a fact true not only for
Israel but for our own nation. Man cannot go on doing
what is right in his own eyes, without a crumbling of the
spiritual life.

No sin is small when we realize that it is against God.
Man cannot say he is compelled to do what is right in his
own eyes, for doing it proves his consent to the action. It is

the little breaks with God that rob men of their power and usefulness.

We must take inventory and reckon with sin. Think of the case of Saul. Had he destroyed all the Amalekites, no Amalekites could have retaliated. It proves that no toleration can be shown even to little sins.

May we seek to do that which is right in God's eyes, and walk openly before Him.

[1]Judges 21:25.
[2]Romans 6:23.

❧   ❧   ❧

March 13

RUTH
RUTH 1:1-17

> And Ruth said, Intreat me not to leave thee . . . for whither thou goest, I will go . . . thy people shall be my people, and thy God my God.[1]

AN ELDERLY LIBRARIAN said one day, "Never measure the value of a book by its bulk!" This principle may be applied as we open the book of Ruth and see its rare, living message. Ruth, the picture of faith and trust and loyalty. Ruth, who was redeemed by Boaz, and whose story of love is one of the most beautiful idylls in literature. Ruth, an ancestor of our blessed Lord.

Ruth is often extolled for her great love and concern for Naomi, her mother-in-law. Yet we may learn much of Naomi's character from the farewell scene in today's verse. Ruth had been taught the ways of the Lord by Naomi, and in adversity Naomi had not only spoken her faith but had lived it. Ruth had a godly teacher who taught well.

Oh, that we would daily live so that others would forsake the gods of their choice and, from being with us and seeing our walk, want our God for their God!

Ruth's piety was clearly shown and demonstrated to

121

Boaz. "It hath fully been shewed me, all that thou hast done unto thy mother in law since the death of thine husband: and how thou hast left thy father and thy mother, and the land of thy nativity, and art come unto a people which thou knewest not heretofore."[2]

In Boaz and Ruth we see a crystal-clear picture of true saints, ones separated for special service. They were true to God no matter how trying the circumstances. Their sufficiency was found in God alone. Though Boaz is pictured as a great landowner, he had known hardships, and his testimony had not been easy to maintain in a time when men were turning away from God. It is said of true saints that circumstances never make a difference. Devotion to God is supreme. They were both living object lessons of faith.

Neither could foresee the closing sequence of the book: "And Salmon begat Boaz, and Boaz begat Obed, and Obed begat Jesse, and Jesse begat David."[3] The infant son of Boaz became the grandfather of David, and the story does not end with David. Later the prophet sang, "Thou, Bethlehem Ephratah, though thou be little among the thousands of Judah, yet out of thee shall he come forth unto me that is to be ruler in Israel."[4]

The centuries rolled on to reveal the birth of Jesus Christ, a descendant of Boaz and Ruth. They did not know the ultimate result of their faith and trust. Nor are we often given a glimpse of what our service may accomplish. However, we too may go forth faithfully and loyally to serve our Redeemer and propagate the faith of which He is Author and Finisher.

[1]Ruth 1:16.
[2]Ruth 2:11.
[3]Ruth 4:21-22.
[4]Micah 5:2.

❧　❧　❧

122

I Samuel 1–2
I Samuel 2

> Now the sons of Eli were sons of Belial; they knew not
> the Lord.[1]

I REMEMBER hearing a woman completely broken in heart
pour out a tragic story in a counseling room one evening.
She was the mother of four sons and related how frequently
people said, "Those boys surely are chips off the old block!"
In every way, she said, they resembled their father, and her
heart was burdened because her husband was a man of
divided allegiance. On Sunday he was often in church and
practicing piety. On leaving the sanctuary, the church cloak
was thrown aside until the next visit.

How well this dear mother could identify with the story
of Eli and his sons, recorded in these opening chapters of
First Samuel. Hophni and Phinehas, though acknowledged
sons of the priest, lived dishonestly and immorally. God
visited Eli with a warning: "Honourest [thou] thy sons
above me? . . . them that honour me I will honour, and they
that despise me shall be lightly esteemed."[2] The priestly
mantle would not fall on them but on another chosen, faithful priest.

How could the sons of Eli serve Belial? The answer comes
in Christ's words, "Ye cannot serve God and mammon."[3] It
is not just a command, it is a fact. It is impossible to live
both in sin and in Christ. Only frustration results. Total
allegiance must be given to one or the other.

The grieved mother in the counseling room knew that
her children could not watch their father's motions of serving God and his conflicting actions without soon knowing
what he really was. She dreaded the day of their understanding.

There is a parable of a man who caught a great eagle.
He carefully made it an elegant nest and a fence many

stories high. He obtained plenty of good food and thought the eagle would be happy in its "ideal" situation. But the eagle died in an attempt for freedom. He had been born to soar unhindered and he could not be satisfied with even comfortable captivity.

Man is made to have fellowship with God, to soar upward with Him in daily fellowship and communion. It was never intended that he be placed in the confines of sin and Satan, and under bondage.

The disconsolate mother earnestly sought the Lord. Her tears ceased to flow when she remembered another story. It was of the prodigal. He had experienced divided loyalties but came to himself saying, "I will arise and go to my father." When he did so, he was received.

No matter what conflicts divide the home, each family member, in seeking the solution, must take a step toward the heavenly Father. "As many as received him, to them gave he power to become the sons of God."[4] May we be obedient to our Father, and seek to live consistent lives for His glory.

[1] I Samuel 2:12.
[2] I Samuel 2:29-30.
[3] Luke 16:13.
[4] John 1:12.

❧ ❧ ❧

I Samuel 3–7
I Samuel 3

The Lord called Samuel: and he answered, Here am I.[1]

THE STORY of Samuel's birth shows another one of God's gracious visitations to people. One can easily visualize Hannah with her husband Elkanah annually going to sacrifice and pray. How much her prayers must have been centered on God giving her children. How frustrating it must have been for her to see her husband's other wife with a flock of children following her.

The conflicts of her heart compelled Hannah to do a very wise thing. She sought out a place alone with her God, and did some prevailing praying. When she prayed she concluded with a vow to God that if He would give her a son, she would give him back to God. Then her prayer was answered.

Is it not a lesson for our contemporary benefit? Many of us have experienced spiritual barrenness. We have pleaded to be used in bringing people to God. Hannah only asked for *one* son whom she would give back. We have but *one* life and we must be willing to give it back, completely, to God. Then He will visit us and the barren soul will be fruitful.

Hannah's son was a real gift from God. From earliest childhood he was taught the importance of communicating with God. He must learn to speak, to feel, and to listen. Listening is quite often the most difficult lesson. Yet the ear can be trained to be receptive.

A mother complains, "My children never listen to me." God could express the same concern and say, "My children will not take time to listen." Eli the priest taught the boy Samuel the importance of listening. "If he call thee, thou shalt say, Speak, Lord; for thy servant heareth."[2]

Listening was a way of learning the ways of the Lord.

"Prepare your hearts unto the Lord, and serve him only."[3] Samuel must learn to do this.

How often on Sunday mornings do we sincerely pray, as the message comes forth through song and word, "Speak, Lord; I'm listening"? If we did we would be much better prepared to face each day. In preparing for each day let us remember we are responsible also for each tomorrow.

Henry Drummond wrote:

> It is for active service soldiers are drilled, and trained, and fed, and armed. That is why you and I are in the world, not to prepare to go out of it some day, but to serve God in it NOW.

May our ears be receptive as we prepare to serve God TODAY.

[1] I Samuel 3:4.
[2] I Samuel 3:9.
[3] I Samuel 7:3.

※　※　※

March 16

I Samuel 8–11
I Samuel 10

> And let it be, when these signs are come unto thee, that thou do as occasion serve thee; for God is with thee.[1]

FLEXIBILITY is needed in the kingdom of God. No one knows what one day will bring forth. It may be a continuation of the routine of months, or it may be a sudden change. However, we are all expected to be faithful and willing, if called from one task, to assume another in God's total program.

Saul had no idea what was to take place in his life. Then drastic, new demands were made on him. With the demands were given spiritual and physical provisions.

When God calls, He has made advance preparations. There is always spiritual provision: "As thy days, so shall thy strength be."[2] There is the promise of guidance: "I will instruct thee and teach thee in the way which thou shalt go."[3] There is the promise of His presence: "My presence shall go with thee, and I will give thee rest."[4]

Saul made a good beginning. The Spirit of God was upon him and his army was an instrument of deliverance. His early characteristics were commendable, but he later allowed a form of sin to grip his heart. He put aside the fact that God was with him and was not faithful in all things.

Faithfulness and flexibility are essential to "do as occasion serve thee." This is well illustrated in the story of a family who were active in church. Father was Sunday school superintendent, Mother taught junior girls. Both children were officers in their youth groups. To many they were a perfect example of obedient Christians serving the Lord. Abruptly they were transferred to another city. In the new situation the "stalwarts" could not "find" themselves. A new church did not provide the opportunities that they had before and all of them were discouraged. Their responsibilities in the new church seemed small and unimportant. Then came a letter from their pastor: "Do as occasion serve thee, for God is with thee."

Each member of the family was quick to take inventory. They had made good beginnings when the circumstances were right, but had been too easily discouraged by change. Their vision had become tarnished and they had forgotten how essential little things are in the work of the Lord. Now they served not for the sake of service but out of devotion for the Lord.

The change in their lives resulted in much blessing. When people seek God things happen. Their ministry was enlarged and today their family's chief aim is to serve God well, knowing that He is with them.

[1] I Samuel 10:7.   [3] Psalm 32:8.
[2] Deuteronomy 33:25.   [4] Exodus 33:14.

❧ ❧ ❧

I Samuel 12–14
I Samuel 12

> And Jonathan said to the young man that bare his
> armour, Come, and let us go over unto the garrison of
> these . . . : it may be that the Lord will work for us:
> for there is no restraint to the Lord to save by many or
> by few. And his armourbearer said unto him, Do all
> that is in thine heart: turn thee; behold, I am with thee
> according to thy heart.[1]

THE STORY of John Paton and his life service of bringing
Christ to those in the New Hebrides Islands is well known.
He left home with only his wife and with complete trust
in God that those cannibal tribes would be evangelized.
He was barely into his ministry when his wife died, and he
was left alone. Alone? No, nor was he afraid. He put himself in most vulnerable positions to preach the unsearchable
riches of Christ. The Saviour he proclaimed transformed
the savage people into a nation which now names the name
of Christ and whose culture is Christian. He often said that
he had proved that with God one man constitutes a majority.

Such was the feeling of Jonathan. He had but one armor-
bearer but he knew that with God they were a force stronger
than all the Philistines. Joshua had proved it, Gideon's
small army knew it, and multitudes of the faithful have experienced it.

Picture Israel. Again they were both oppressed and depressed. They were surrounded by enemy armies and they
had no way to escape. How complacent were those Philistines. They had not allowed a blacksmith among the Israelites lest he make arms for them. They had heavily gar-
risoned and fortified the vulnerable spots. Their position
was strong. Yet one man had courage and faith to launch
out. He experienced victory.

The story must stir our hearts, particularly in the days in which we live. One cannot scan the newspaper without feeling grief. The forces of evil are great and the darkness lowers. Satan is at work with increasing intensity. Can a few Christians conquer such forces? Yes! How? With God we are the majority.

When He ascended into heaven, Jesus left behind only a few believers to stand against an insurmountable force. About one hundred twenty Christians against the entire Roman Empire. But with God there was victory. The church, the Body of Christ, grew and flourished.

God is still all-powerful. We are challenged, "Only fear the Lord, and serve him in truth with all your heart: for consider how great things he hath done for you."[2]

Consider what He has done, and then recognize that with Him you are a majority. With such power within and put to work, victory is assured.

[1] I Samuel 14:6-7.
[2] I Samuel 12:24.

❧ ❧ ❧

March 18

I SAMUEL 15–17
I SAMUEL 16

> But the Lord said unto Samuel, Look not on his countenance, or on the height of his stature; because I have refused him: for the Lord seeth not as man seeth; for man looketh on the outward appearance, but the Lord looketh on the heart.[1]

THE SETTING for the statement "Man looketh on the outward appearance, but the Lord looketh on the heart" was the time of Saul's rejection by God from being king over all Israel. Samuel was told to take a "horn of oil" and to anoint one of the sons of Jesse to this office. One by one they passed by, some that were no doubt tall and of fine physique.

129

When all had passed, Samuel asked Jesse, "Are here all thy children?" and he explained that the youngest was out keeping sheep. At once David was called, "and the Lord said, Arise, anoint him, for this is he."[2]

God is not limited by the vision we possess. Surely these other men were older and Samuel felt they should be considered, but God looked into their hearts. In David He found a man after His own heart. It was his internal qualities which set David apart.

When God calls a man, He first looks into the heart. "The eyes of the Lord are in every place, beholding the evil and the good."[3] He does not slumber nor sleep and all things are open before Him. He searches the heart of man, ponders the heart, and weighs the spirit. Surely this is what prompted Solomon to say, "Give to every man according to his ways, whose heart thou knowest (for thou, even thou only, knowest the hearts of all the children of men)."[4]

God knows what our future before Him will be. In hearing that God looks on the heart a youngster said, "I wonder what He sees." Most of us know what He sees—whether our hearts are divided, or fixed upon Him.

In the days of Noah, many hearts were filled with guilt and lust. In the times of Jeremiah, conditions were the same. "The heart is deceitful above all things, and desperately wicked."[5] When Christ was on earth, He found the heart of man in the same condition, without God and without hope.

Today it is the same. We may shine to a luster the outside of a beautiful red apple, only to cut it open and find that a worm has corrupted the heart. Our exterior may be impeccable but God looks right through. I wonder what He sees.

[1] I Samuel 16:7.
[2] I Samuel 16:11-12.
[3] Proverbs 15:3.
[4] I Kings 8:39.
[5] Jeremiah 17:9.

❧ ❧ ❧

130

I Samuel 18–20
I Samuel 18

The soul of Jonathan was knit with the soul of David.[1]

THE FRIENDSHIP of David and Jonathan is a continuing symbol of mutual love and trust. Their hearts were knit together.

What brought these two together? It was their faith in God. This is the divine cement which sanctifies any relationship and makes it beautiful and bountiful. They belonged to God, so they belonged together. Believing is belonging, and the family of God is a great host called together in unity.

Together David and Jonathan could talk of the Lord and enjoy the fellowship of sitting down and sharing their precious faith. Whether in joy or sadness the sharing of a mutual Saviour is the basis for abiding friendship. Here two can walk together on the path of faith.

David and Jonathan could pray together, committing their needs to God. Two hearts knit together can richly fellowship in prayer. Someone has said that "friendships at best are fragile things and require as much care in handling as any other fragile and precious thing. Care and prayer strengthen and enrich." David and Jonathan experienced the blessing of being agreed in prayer, before the Lord.

Their friendship pictures our friendship with Jesus Christ. He is One who sticks closer than a brother. It is possible for human beings to have companionship with the divine Saviour who strengthens us in our weakness, understands our needs, and makes intercession for us.

May our friendships with fellow believers be strengthened as we read of David and Jonathan. And may we remember that we have a true, abiding Friend in Christ.

By friendship you mean the greatest love, the greatest usefulness, the most open communication, the noblest sufferings, the severest truth, the heartiest counsel, and the greatest union of minds of which brave men and women are capable.[2]

A true friend is the gift of God, and He only who made hearts can unite them.[3]

[1]I Samuel 18:1.
[2]Jeremy Taylor.
[3]Robert South.

❧ ❧ ❧

I SAMUEL 21–24
I SAMUEL 23

And Jonathan Saul's son arose, and went to David into the wood, and strengthened his hand in God.[1]

THE FRIENDSHIP OF David and Jonathan was not just dependent on good fellowship and mutual agreement. It survived times of adversity.

David had fled to the woods knowing that Saul was after his life. Jonathan knew that his father was out to destroy David, but he was not afraid of his father or the palace officials. He went to seek his friend. "And he said unto him, Fear not: for the hand of Saul my father shall not find thee; and thou shalt be king over Israel, and I shall be next unto thee; and that also Saul my father knoweth. And they two made a covenant before the Lord: and David abode in the wood, and Jonathan went to his house."[2]

Here we see the greatness of Jonathan again. His relationship with David stood in the way of his succession to the throne. If his father destroyed David, he would be next in line. The father was the enemy to David, his son the friend. God had surely done some preparation in Jonathan's heart. He was human. What happened to his natural spirit of rivalry? What prompted his love for an obscure outsider? God alone had warmed Jonathan's heart for David.

David was in great peril. His conflicts had been with more than lions and bears, or even Goliaths, as God had prepared him for true warfare. His heart had been broken. But a broken heart is the opening to true friendship with God and with those who know Him. How David valued Jonathan's unselfish love. Surely the sight of Jonathan coming to his place of hiding was like seeing light in darkness.

Jesus Christ does not leave us in our times of personal crisis. He is right there as the "light of the world," ready to refresh and lead us beside still waters. He is always there to restore our souls.

What of the one you may know today who is in need, one who may be held in your heart as a friend? Has this one grieved you? He may be going through a personal problem and needs someone to minister to the need—one who is kind and has a heart filled with understanding and tenderness.

Jonathan strengthened David's hand in God. May we too seek to lift the arms of those about us needing help who may be, as David, "in the woods," but who may be refreshed with streams of living waters through us.

"Even as the Son of man came not to be ministered unto, but to minister,"[3] so may we fulfill our responsibility of Christian friendship.

[1] I Samuel 23:16.
[2] I Samuel 23:17-18.
[3] Matthew 20:28.

❧ ❧ ❧

I Samuel 25–27
I Samuel 25

> Abigail: . . . a woman of good understanding.[1]

Abigail has been referred to as the most understanding woman in the Old Testament. Her true character was in sharp contrast with that of her husband. He was arrogant and insolent. She was tender and gracious and faithful.

David and his men had been protecting the flocks of Nabal and in return David asked that his troops be provided for. The answer came as quite a shock: "Shall I then take my bread, and my water . . . and give it unto men, whom I know not whence they be?"[2] David was angry and ready to take up the sword against him when Abigail entered the picture. She took the place of a mediator and quickly provided bread and food. Her wisdom, humility, and thoughtfulness are described in this chapter.

David was impressed, and took Abigail's advice. How grateful he was for her wisdom which spared him a tragic mistake. Not once but three times he blessed her and his God for sending her. "And David said to Abigail, Blessed be the Lord God of Israel, which sent thee this day to meet me: and blessed be thy advice, and blessed be thou, which hast kept me this day from coming to shed blood, and from avenging myself with mine own hand."[3]

Abigail was one who never forgot her dignity. No doubt she was greatly beloved in her own household and provided well for those about her. She understood human nature and took into account the ill behavior of others. Her tolerance had often been tested, but it only added to her nobility.

On finishing her mission to David and providing for his men, Abigail immediately returned home. She knew where she belonged. Within a few days her husband fell ill and died. When David heard this, he remembered the woman of "beautiful countenance" who had ministered to him. He did not forget the way she had foretold God's continuing love and care. David did not hesitate to send for her to become his wife. Carefully she must have pondered the message. She well knew he was chosen of God for a special task. Could she help in some way? Her beautiful humility shows again in her reply to David: "Behold, let thine handmaid be a servant to wash the feet of the servants of my lord."[4]

God knew what David needed. He was impetuous at times, as when he wanted to fight Nabal, and he was willful. Undoubtedly Abigail lovingly taught him patience and inspired great confidence. Together they lived at Gath and then at Hebron, where a son, Chileab, was born. David thanked Abigail more than once for her understanding and blessed advice.

May we be set apart as those of "good understanding."

[1] I Samuel 25:3.
[2] I Samuel 25:11.
[3] I Samuel 25:32-33.
[4] I Samuel 25:41.

❧ ❧ ❧

March 22

I Samuel 28–31
I Samuel 30

David encouraged himself in the Lord his God.[1]

Wave after wave lashes over man's soul.
Hindrances keep his eye from the goal.
Distress and discomfort vie to o'ertake
The blessings of hurt, incurred for His sake.
Know ye not that the wilderness sand
Can be a step toward the Promised Land?
Low valleys lead to mountains high;
Darkness reminds that dawning is nigh.
Defeat prepares for what may be
The final step toward victory!

WHAT MUST DAVID have thought in his heart as he returned to Ziklag and found the city destroyed? Distress upon distress, for the goods were stolen and the wives and children carried off. David was unpopular with the troops. Where could he turn? In his distress "he encouraged himself in the Lord." Here was a situation of utter defeat and impossibility. Yet he chose the way of God's encouragement and the result was the defeat of the enemy and the total recovery of that which had been stolen.

How often in the Christian life there are times when wave after wave of distress sweeps over the soul. One may feel, as David did, that all has been carried off. This is a place of choice. Some may take the way of discouragement. Others, like David, will encourage themselves in the Lord.

In days past we have talked about the time when the Israelites were about to go up to possess the Promised Land. Spies were sent out and on their return the majority gave a dark, grim picture. God had promised victory, but the people chose to accept the message of human beings. And those few men infected the great majority of the Israelites with gross discouragement. To those who were trusting in themselves, the cities did look big, the walls thick, and the people giant-size. When one sees with his natural eyes, this is the result. The faithful spies, looking through the eyes of God, said that His power could overcome. They were encouragers.

Anyone can follow the wide road that is well marked. Few can abide the strait and narrow. Here the encouragement must come from the Lord. In His power and promise there is advance. Retreat is self-inflicted.

Christians are called to be encouragers. There are too many in our own circle who succumb to Satan's most effective weapon, discouragement. May we, as David, encourage ourselves and others in the Lord our God.

[1] I Samuel 30:6.

❧   ❧   ❧

II Samuel 1–2
II Samuel 1

IN FIRST SAMUEL we were introduced to David and saw the
preparations for his appointed task. In Second Samuel we
see him in the place where God put him, carrying out the
purposes of God. He reigned over Judah. His attitude toward God set him apart and these words of his will stir the
heart:

> Therefore the Lord hath recompensed me according to
>   my righteousness;
> According to my cleanness in His eye sight.
> With the merciful thou wilt shew thyself merciful,
> With the upright man thou wilt shew thyself upright.
> With the pure thou wilt shew thyself pure;
> And with the froward thou wilt shew thyself unsavoury.
> And the afflicted people thou wilt save: but thine eyes
>   are upon the haughty, that thou mayest bring them
>   down.
> For thou art my lamp, O Lord:
> And the Lord will lighten my darkness.
> For by thee I have run through a troop:
> By my God have I leaped over a wall . . .
> For who is God, save the Lord?
> And who is a rock, save our God?
> God is my strength and power:
> He maketh my way perfect.[1]

David recognized the greatness of God and His complete
righteousness. He also had tasted of His mercy. At times
he faltered, but the God of His faith never faltered. The
problems came when he trusted in himself and not in Jehovah.

It is a merciful and wonderful God who has chosen to
judge us, not by our most recent sin but by our attitude
of soul toward Him. David wrote, "Thou art my lamp, and
the Lord will lighten my darkness." If along the way there

is temptation, our God will shed light on it, and show us what is right if we are willing to seek His counsel.

The following words of G. Campbell Morgan were written of David but are applicable to us. It may be well to ponder them in the quietness of being alone before God and in the intimacy of one's personal sanctuary:

> David was a man after God's own heart, because of the posture of his soul; and God at last fulfilled the underlying desire of his heart. The triumph of a man is the triumph of God over him, and man only wins when he yields to Him.

[1]II Samuel 22:25-33.

❧ ❧ ❧

March 24

II Samuel 3–5
II Samuel 5

> And David went on, and grew great, and the Lord God of hosts was with him.[1]

IN MISSIONARY ANNALS there is a story about a young man who went to Africa after reading in the quietness of his bedroom one evening of the needs there and of the great commission to every Christian. No board supported him, and few at home knew why he was selling his few possessions and going abroad. Those who did had banded together for regular prayer that the Lord would be with him and help him.

The years passed and another missionary joined him. It was a great day when he could fellowship with someone from home. Yet the full story never came from the senior missionary to his new helper. It came from one of his first converts to Christ. Said the national to the new man on the field, "This God-man had many problems when he came here, but he went on. He faced death many times, but he went on. We saw him sick lots of times, but he went on." He closed his recap of the past years by saying, "God is with him."

The story finds a parallel in the life of David. His days in the fields were not easy, but he went on. In the palace there were great griefs, but he went on. He was exiled and outcast, and attempts were made on his life. Was he deterred? No, he went on.

It is no wonder that the verse continues, "and grew great." One cannot experience the continuing guidance or staying hand of God, or His presence and provision, without growing up in Him. David gave the Lord credit for victory at a certain place by naming it "Baal-perazim," meaning "Lord of the breakings-through."

Many times the Lord had broken through difficulties for David, and in this knowledge he went on. It was vital reassurance to know that "the Lord of the breakings-through" was with him.

Possibly next door to you is a neighbor who closes the door to the gospel. Or maybe at your place of work or even at home, for years you have sought for the key to open the door of a certain heart but in defeat you have been turned away. On your side is the Lord of hosts, the "Lord of the breakings-through." You must do as David did—go on. Obstacles may not diminish, but go on in His strength. Inconvenience? Locked doors? No conceivable way? "And David went on, and grew great, and the . . . ['Lord of the breakings-through'] was with him."

¹II Samuel 5:10.

❧ ❧ ❧

II Samuel 6–9
II Samuel 7

> And now, O Lord God, the word that thou hast spoken
> concerning thy servant, and concerning his house, estab-
> lish it for ever, and do as thou hast said.[1]

A CHILD HAD BEEN BUSY preparing a special birthday present
for her mother. She had worked on it for days and could
hardly wait to present the gift. When the day came she
handed her mother a loosely wrapped package which contained three promises. Each was simply stated: "I will
always love you." "I will obey you." "I will help you."
The mother loved the little promise box and asked her
daughter if she really meant each one. The reply was in
simple sincerity. "Each is a promise I promise to keep!"

God has given us untold promises and each is a promise
He has promised to keep. How clearly and wonderfully
He assures us, "I have loved thee with an everlasting love:
therefore with lovingkindness have I drawn thee."[2] He
has given us promises for guidance and instruction. He
has given rest for the weary, compassion, tenderness and,
above all, the blessing of communion with Him. Each is
wrapped up in the Bible and may be found through simply
opening and reading the Book.

God never intended that the promises be cast aside but
that they be used every day and in every circumstance. He
delights in having His children use and possess them.

On several occasions the mother in our story had to remind her daughter of her promise to help. Her little heart
had forgotten, but she took up the job with joy, remembering what she had said: "Each is a promise I promise to
keep."

David went into the presence of the Lord for a special
time with Him. He came in humility and lowliness. He
thanked God for the promises He had kept and recounted

the things which God had done for him and revealed to him. He poured out his heart: "Wherefore thou art great, O Lord God: for there is none like thee, neither is there any God beside thee, according to all that we have heard with our ears."[3] He gave God the glory for everything, then continued, "Do as thou hast said."

God always does what He says. His promises are never broken. This is one of life's few certainties. Our promises to Him are sometimes broken, but not His to us. They are immutable.

When God promises forgiveness, He grants it. In one of his psalms David assures us, "As far as the east is from the west, so far hath he removed our transgressions from us."[4] Mercy is given in abundance. His compassions fail not.

God will not be poorer for giving you the riches He has promised. He is ready and willing to give, and give, and give again!

[1]II Samuel 7:25.
[2]Jeremiah 31:3.
[3]II Samuel 7:22.
[4]Psalm 103:12.

❧ ❧ ❧

II Samuel 10–12
II Samuel 12

> And it came to pass in an eveningtide, that David arose
> from off his bed, and walked upon the roof of the
> king's house.[1]

A WELL-KNOWN Christian counselor was lecturing on temptation and sin. He used the tragic story of David and Bathsheba as an illustration the like of which I had never heard
before.

The counselor said that on the particular evening when
David rose to go to the rooftop, in all possibility he was
going out to meditate or to pray. It may have been that he
was rethinking and reflecting on his actions. Should he not
be out fighting battles rather than being in Jerusalem? His
thoughts at the moment are not known, but what we do
know is that he saw Bathsheba.

David's sin is known, and the length of time that it took
him to come to repentance. Some are quick to use the story
for personal consolation. If David, the king and a man after God's own heart, fell, who then is safe? Others take it
as an example to them of this truth: "Let him that thinketh
he standeth take heed lest he fall."[2]

We should indeed take heed as we are tempted on every
side. We may feel there is complete safety in the quiet
hours of night, but beware, the evil one may approach at
any hour. Even in our times of devotion, we are not
exempt from sin. It is something to think about before the
Lord.

The repentance of David, the counsel of Nathan, and the
boundless forgiveness of God build up to a monument of
mercy. We must be willing to confess and acknowledge
transgression. "Only acknowledge thine iniquity, that thou
hast transgressed against the Lord thy God. . . . Turn, O
backsliding children, saith the Lord."[3]

There may be one who has harbored or cherished sin in his heart for a long time. It is hard to understand why. Thus sin is covered with sin and more sin. We must not become hardened but confess to Him who is gracious to those of a contrite spirit. He said, "I have seen his ways, and will heal him: . . . But the wicked are like the troubled sea, when it cannot rest."[4]

The storm will pass by as we trust in the goodness of God. In His forgiveness we will find rest. From past experience we realize that our guard must constantly be up against those who would seek to destroy our faith, whether in the busy day or the quiet night. There is no security without the true Watchman of both day and night.

[1]II Samuel 11:2.
[2]I Corinthians 10:12.
[3]Jeremiah 3:13-14.
[4]Isaiah 57:18, 20.

❧   ❧   ❧

March 27

II SAMUEL 13–15
II SAMUEL 15

> But if he thus say, I have no delight in thee; behold, here am I, let him do to me as seemeth good unto me.[1]

HOW MANY OF US are sincerely willing to make this statement? "Let him do to me as seemeth good unto him." It is a blessed attitude of heart and soul that accepts what He gives and trusts even when He withholds. It is living in complete submission to the fact that He does all things well, that He will truly perfect that which concerns His own.

God often leads in difficult ways. There may be a long stretch of barrenness and then an oasis where for a moment we are refreshed. How many dread going to work each morning. There is little challenge in their employment.

There are many problems, and the route to and from work is uninspiring. Yet, it is only by passing through the day that we may approach the evening, usually a time of joy, with its refreshing and relaxing hours.

Often we long for the easy way or the shortcut. This would bring peace and rest so much sooner. But the pilgrim will be first to admit that the short way may cause us to relax our vigilance, and soon we become unfit for the work of the day. It is by way of the long, hard path that our muscles are trained and disciplines learned. There pressure and pain prepare and shape us for true service, and valuable lessons are learned.

The following lines were written more than a century ago, but they show how the perilous ways, difficult paths, and hardships were endured by multitudes before us who also had the sure knowledge, here unusually expressed, that our God knows what we need. "Let him do to me as seemeth good unto him."

> O wherefore thus, apart with drooping wings,
> Thou stillest, saddest angel,
> With hidden face, as if but bitter things
> Thou hadst, and no evangel of good tidings?
>
> Thou knowest that through our tears
> Of hasty, selfish weeping,
> Comes surer sun; and for our petty fears
> Of loss, thou hast in keeping
> A greater gain than that of which we dreamed.
>
> Thou knowest that in grasping
> The bright possessions which so precious seemed,
> We lose them, but if clasping thy faithful hand
> We tread with steadfast feet the path of thy appointing
> There waits for us a treasury of sweet
> Delight: royal anointing.[2]

[1] II Samuel 15:26.
[2] Helen Hunt Jackson.

❧ ❧ ❧

144

II Samuel 16–18
II Samuel 18

> And the king was much moved, and went up to the
> chamber over the gate, and wept: and as he went, thus
> he said, O my son Absalom, my son, my son Absalom!
> would God I had died for thee, O Absalom, my son, my
> son![1]

DAVID'S LIFE was like a checkerboard. There were the trials
and the joys, the continual ups and downs, the sunshine
and the shadow. The problems were related to him not
only in a personal way but on a national level. Yet one of
the greatest heartbreaks was his son Absalom. To parents
and children the story unfolds the great responsibility of
each one.

There is no doubt that God has placed in the hearts of
all parents a great love for those who are their own. Many
will confess that love seems greater for one who has caused
trouble or has been afflicted. One parent expressed it thus:
"I have seven lovely, obedient children. The eighth is
wayward. He is never repentant nor sorry for his actions.
Yet, I hold him in my heart in a way no other child is held."
In later years this mother recognized it was wrong to indulge this youngster more than the others. However, it
was almost too late to give those who were a joy and blessing in the home what they needed because of her overwhelming feeling for the weaker one.

Throughout Scripture we are told that children are a
loan rather than a gift. God has granted them to us for
upbringing in His nurture and admonition, that they will
entrust their hearts and lives to Him.

No doubt the day that David waited between those inner and outer gates, his mind was busy. He may have used,
in his own way, the words that so often come into our
thoughts: *If only I had it to do over again.* Why, he must

have wondered, had he neglected to warn and discipline and instruct his son? It was one thing to lose a life, still another to lose a son, but his greatest grief was the rebellion of his son. No wonder he wished to God he could have died in his son's stead.

In seeing David's broken heart for his son, we can see the heart of God as He looked on lost and wayward mankind. Man's heart has always been rebellious, yet we can see His manifest love which sent His Son to die for those who were sinners.

He is Judge, but He is also Redeemer, and those that seek Him will find Him and obtain His most gracious mercy and pardon.

[1]II Samuel 18:33.

❧ ❧ ❧

II Samuel 19–20
II Samuel 19:31-40

> And Barzillai said unto the king, How long have I to live . . . ?[1]

Meet Barzillai! At eighty years old he was as full of generosity and courage, kindness and truth, as he was full of years. He knew the ways of the Lord. He had lived through the times of Eli, Samuel, Saul, David, Jonathan, and even Absalom. To those in need of refreshment or lodging, his home must have been a haven of hospitality. David was a recipient of much kindness from Barzillai.

The time had come when David, wanting to show his gratitude, entreated Barzillai to spend the rest of his days in the king's house. Here there would be rest after the past busy years and refreshment in reward for the scores of times he had uplifted others.

Barzillai declined! His reason is found in his words:

"How long have I to live?" How graciously unselfish he was at a time when most people become concerned for their own welfare. He felt he would be a burden to his lord, David, and chose to turn back.

As David blessed him, David's heart must have been warm and loving toward this wonderful elderly man. David could not forget Barzillai's loyalty to him at a time when the outcome was uncertain in the conflict between the forces of David and Absalom. There was no middle of the road for the aged friend as God had shown him what to do. He did it regardless of the consequences. It has been said, "David's adversity was Barzillai's opportunity." We have all been given similar opportunities.

If this dear person could have lived today, he would have been a profound illustration of the New Testament principles: "Be kindly affectioned one to another with brotherly love; in honour preferring one another."[2] "Submitting yourselves one to another in the fear of God."[3] "Yea, all of you be . . . clothed with humility: for God resisteth the proud, and giveth grace to the humble."[4] It is said, "Humility and courtesy are court manners in the kingdom of heaven."

It is not just the aged who should follow Barzillai's example of how to accept the coming years. The young and the more mature also should cultivate these God-given virtues in the knowledge that no one knows what a day may bring forth. Each day we should ponder, *How long have I to live?* Each day we should live unselfishly in His fullness of life for His glory and praise.

Barzillai is remembered for his imprint on the world in calm and in crisis. May we pray, "Teach us to number our days, that we may apply our hearts unto wisdom."[5]

[1]II Samuel 19:34.   [4]I Peter 5:5.
[2]Romans 12:10.   [5]Psalm 90:12.
[3]Ephesians 5:21.

II Samuel 21–22
II Samuel 22

> God is my strength and power: and he maketh my way
> perfect.[1]

THE FOLLOWING STATEMENT is food for thought:

> If we have been doing our best, the failure of our work
> is the success of God's work in us. If we have done our
> full duty as prayer discloses it to us, then failure was
> part of our duty. God sometimes sets tasks in order that
> they may not be done, for the lessons of failure are far
> more precious than the teachings of success and far
> more difficult to learn.[2]

What lessons of failure would God, who has strength for
every need and power for any occasion, give the Christian
to learn? What does it take to make our way perfect?

In falling we often rise, and at times we must go backward to start forward. The humiliation of anything less
than success is hard to take. Perhaps we have worked very
hard on a Sunday school lesson which we know is our best
yet. Hours are spent in study, meditation, and time with
the Lord about the results. Presentation time comes and
the lesson seemingly falls on the deaf ears of a disinterested
Sunday school class. What was wrong? If we were truly
doing our best, there is no doubt about the statement above:
"Our failure is the success of God's work in us." It is easy
to be proud when all goes well. When the class is eager
and receptive a pride of accomplishment comes, and naturally so, but it is unusual if this brings us to our knees. It
is incidents in which we cannot understand the results that
force our cry to God. Here we realize that our nothingness
can be used only when it is put into His almighty hands.
Thus we learn humility.

Patience is another lesson. To perfect our way there may
be necessary stops along the route. Intervals of marking

time, when it would be much more agreeable to be making time. If all went well, and there were no delays and denials along the way, would we truly learn to trust in God's strength and power to lead us along? "Let patience have her perfect work."[3]

Trust is a lesson that can only be learned as we completely rest in Him. We must present our labors, our deeds, and our lives to Him for safekeeping and trust Him for the fruit and blessing. We must trust as much on dark days as when we bask in His sunlight.

The failures, the successes, must all be given to Him. Through both, lessons are learned. There is no doubt that God is working to make the way—your way, my way—perfect.

[1]II Samuel 22:33.
[2]Amos Wells.
[3]James 1:4.

❧ ❧ ❧

March 31

II Samuel 23–24
II Samuel 24

> Neither will I offer burnt-offerings unto the Lord my
> God of that which doth cost me nothing.[1]

As we close the books of Samuel we come across these profound words which stir our hearts. God has graciously revealed His glory. Do we have the right to hold back our gifts of love to Him?

St. Ambrose wrote, "One coin out of a little is better than a great treasure out of much; for it is not considered how much is given, but how much remains behind."

One cannot help but think of Mary the day that she was selecting a special gift for the Lord. No doubt there were perfumes and spices of every price. The cheaper common ones would be in large containers, and the more expensive, rare ones in small flasks. She must have handled many and wondered what would please the Master. Put yourself in her place, remembering how on some occasion you carefully chose a gift for someone dear to you. Nothing seemed quite good enough. Then the storekeeper brought out the alabaster box! How Mary's eyes must have lit up, for it was just the right thing. Expensive? Yes, three hundred pence. "I will not offer unto the Lord my God of that which doth cost me nothing."

Think of the Magi bringing their gifts to the Saviour, gifts of gold, frankincense and myrrh. Again nothing was too good for the Lord. The record of their gifts is an example for us today.

A missionary conference was closed with the story of a young African girl who brought a very special gift. Her background had been bondage and slavery. Then she heard of redemption and received the gift of eternal life. On that particular mission station, each Christmas they celebrated the Lord's birthday by bringing something special to Him. Maybe it was a bouquet of flowers, possibly some excellent fruit from the crop. The people were very poor and their gifts represented sacrifice, no matter how small. One particular year, this young girl came, not with her usual cent but with a coin worth eighty-five cents, and gave it to God. At once she was questioned, for the amount was huge, but she sweetly explained that she had sold herself for that sum. For the rest of her life she had obtained eighty-five cents. Only her entirety would satisfy her desire to give Him all she could for her redemption.

How much do we give that costs us anything? "No coin of earth is current except those that have on them the image of Christ stamped in Christian service in a needy and sinful world."[2] May we give until it costs, and withhold nothing that belongs to Him.

[1] II Samuel 24:24.
[2] I. W. Gowen.

April

I Kings 1–2
I Kings 2

> Now the days of David drew nigh that he should die;
> and he charged Solomon his son, saying, I go the way of
> all the earth: be thou strong therefore, and shew thyself
> a man; and keep the charge of the Lord thy God, to
> walk in his ways, to keep his statutes.[1]

DAVID'S DAYS from the time he held a shepherd's crook to
the time he wielded the scepter of Israel portray a most remarkable man. After a series of wonderful and tragic events,
he faced eternity. In charging his son, who would take his
place, he counseled him to manly strength and complete
obedience to God.

David had experienced the powers and perils that would
confront young Solomon. His brother, Adonijah, felt sure
that he would be king, and had desperately worked toward
that end. He was the logical successor, well groomed and
kingly. Again, God looked on the heart and found Solomon,
not Adonijah, one who could show himself a man. The
future would indeed be treacherous. The book of I Kings
tells of a nation starting in great prosperity and falling to
gross poverty. It tells of a succession of kings, and shows the
failure of human government. The significance is evident.
In a failing world there is still an unfailing God. Govern-
ments may rise and fall, but of His kingdom there shall be
no end. The charge He would give to us is the same, to
be strong and of good courage, to walk in the ways of the
Lord. "Keep his statutes, and his commandments, and his

judgments, and his testimonies, as it is written in the law of Moses, that thou mayest prosper in all that thou doest, and whithersoever thou turnest thyself: that the Lord may continue his word which he spake . . . If thy children take heed to their way, to walk before me in truth with all their heart and with all their soul, there shall not fail thee . . . a man on the throne of Israel."[2]

What a charge! Can we keep it? A charge to recognize God and keep His commandments. A charge to be true to our trust as Christian citizens. Our influence must be extended through adherence to Christlike principles, as duty and devotion to Him demand.

> God give us men. A time like this demands
> Clear minds, pure hearts, true faith, and ready hands:
> Men who possess opinions and a will,
> Men whom desire for office does not kill,
> Men whom the spoils of office cannot buy,
> Men who have honor, men who will not lie,
> Tall men, sun-crowned men, who live above the fog
> In public duty and in private thinking.
> God give us men.[3]

[1] I Kings 2:1-3.
[2] I Kings 2:3-4.
[3] Oliver Wendell Holmes.

❧   ❧   ❧

I Kings 3–5
I Kings 3

> In Gibeon the Lord appeared to Solomon in a dream by
> night: and God said, Ask what I shall give thee. And
> Solomon said, . . . Give therefore thy servant an under-
> standing heart.[1]

IN LOOKING AT THE TASK before him, the onerous job of
welding together a nation which had been chosen to be a
great people "that cannot be . . . counted for multitude,"[2]
Solomon prayed for a wise and discerning heart. The prayer
pleased God and his request was granted.

What a prayer for us today in a time when things are as
topsy-turvy as they were in the days of Israel! What a motto
this would be to take on entering any new position or purpose! What a blessing it would be to have a heart big
enough to see the full, clear picture of what surrounds us!
It would make such a difference in everything if we took
time to consult the Lord in every decision and seek His wisdom alone.

A minister wrote to a friend asking that he would pray
for him. The friend wrote back and said he would appreciate specific requests. That way he could do real business
with God. The minister replied. His specific request was
for wisdom. He stood in need of an understanding heart.
The friend posted another letter. "Specifically, what kind
of wisdom, and for what situation do you want it?" The
minister answered, "Specifically, wisdom."

By now the message was getting across to the clergyman's
friend. Too often we are prone to want something definite
surrounded with detail on every side, and it is possible for
details to obscure the true concern. Solomon's prayer came
from the fullness and sincerity of his heart. It was simple
and unenhanced, not smothered with vain repetitions. "And
the speech pleased the Lord."[3]

His circumstances were much like those of the church today. The people about us are a great multitude. Visitation surveys barely estimate the unreached masses. We need hearts of understanding to discern their need, to reach them, and to evangelize them.

Solomon knew that his prayer ascended to God who rules the world and who also rules man individually. In his knowledge of God, he knew he could count on Him to delight in answering prayer.

Let us ask God specifically for wisdom. "If any of you lack wisdom, let him ask of God, that giveth to all men liberally, and upbraideth not."[4]

A discerning heart inwardly possessed and outwardly expressed is a true gift from God.

[1] I Kings 3:5-9.
[2] I Kings 3:8.
[3] I Kings 3:10.
[4] James 1:5.

* * *

I KINGS 6–7
I KINGS 6

April 3

> And the house, when it was in building, was built of stone made ready before it was brought thither: so that there was neither hammer no axe nor any tool of iron heard in the house, while it was in building.[1]

IT IS EXHILARATING to note the precision with which God builds. The description of the Temple shows the planning of a Master Architect who designed in infinite wisdom. Its elegance and grandeur were without compare.

David had longed to be the one to erect the Temple, but God had made it clear to him that he could not. He had been through wars and battles and he had himself shed blood. It was thus passed on to his son Solomon to do what was denied the father. David planned and Solomon constructed. It took seven years.

So minute were the details that we are told the stones were ready before they were brought to the Temple site. It was not necessary to use hammers or experience the usual loud noises of building. The perfection of God's design was so complete that even the great Temple could be built in quietness and dignity. Solomon was pleased with this wonderful preparation and delighted at the responsibility that was his. It must have been thrilling to watch the pieces brought one by one, and fitted together perfectly. Nothing needed changing, and no repair nor refining was necessary. In Proverbs, Solomon left a record of this fantastic method of building when he said, "Prepare thy work without, and make it fit for thyself in the field; and afterwards build thine house."[2]

In building individual lives, we can learn much from the blueprints of the Temple. True piety is not built in a life filled with noise and strife and confusion. This takes careful consideration, quiet dedication, and solemn stillness before God. It is not just in saying a vocal "Lord, Lord" but in doing the will of our Father that we become fit and prepared for the total will of God. Rough edges have to be removed in the process, or they would cause imperfections in the completed building. Christians should be so heart-and-soul-prepared that as living stones, solid with purpose, and completely polished and finished, they can take their place as a part in the whole of God's structure. Paul described this high calling when he wrote, "That we henceforth . . . speaking the truth in love, may grow up into him in all things, which is the head, even Christ: from whom the whole body fitly joined together and compacted by that which every joint supplieth, according to the effectual working in the measure of every part, maketh increase of the body unto the edifying of itself in love."[3] May we so build.

[1] I Kings 6:7.
[2] Proverbs 24:27.
[3] Ephesians 4:14-16.

155

I Kings 8–9
I Kings 8:38-66

> What prayer and supplication soever be made by any
> man, or by all thy people Israel, which shall know every
> man the plague of his own heart, and spread forth his
> hands toward this house: then hear thou in heaven thy
> dwelling place, and forgive, and do, and give to every
> man according to his ways, whose heart thou knowest.[1]

Prayer, to be acceptable to God, must meet specific conditions. Here Solomon, as he dedicated the Temple to God,
gave instructions by his example of true devotion. The people were not just to pray for themselves but for the generations to come.

Scores of years ago, I am told, a missionary began praying for his family and for the unborn generations to come.
It has been more than fifty years since his intercessory prayer
began on behalf of his sons' sons and their children, but the
great-grandfather has seen a continuing line of stalwarts in
the faith.

Such prayer must come from a heart that is fervent, one
that sincerely believes in God. Complete obedience and
submission to the plan of God constitute the true approach
to the throne of grace. Solomon spoke of every man knowing the "plague" of his heart. Sin consistently besets the
believer, and he must know whence it comes. It must be
definitely and severely dealt with in the helplessness of
knowing one cannot do battle against it without God's help
and mercy. We depend on Him.

The personal approach to God, through Jesus Christ, is
the glorious privilege of each believer. "And this is the
confidence that we have in him, that, if we ask anything
according to his will, he heareth us: and if we know that he
hear us, whatsoever we ask, we know that we have the petitions that we desired of him."[2]

God knows the sins and grants forgiveness when they are confessed. He knows the problems and trials and stands ready to help and deliver us. Victory is available for every crisis. When the Apostle Paul had afflictions and suffered, he was reminded, as we are, "My grace is sufficient for thee: for my strength is made perfect in weakness. Most gladly therefore will I rather glory in my infirmities, that the power of Christ may rest upon me."[3]

Nothing less than fervent prayer from cleansed hearts should be offered up to Him who has offered up everything for us.

[1]I Kings 8:38-39.
[2]I John 5:14-15.
[3]II Corinthians 12:9.

       ❧ ❧ ❧

April 5

I KINGS 10–12
I KINGS 10

> And when the queen of Sheba heard of the fame of Solomon concerning the name of the Lord, she came to prove him with hard questions.[1]

THE MISSION of the Queen of Sheba's visit to Solomon is summed up in a single statement: "She came to prove." She had heard of his marvelous wisdom. A representative could not give her the whole picture, so she came in person. Her object was to receive personal knowledge of a man who had spoken more than three thousand proverbs and who was said to have composed more than a thousand songs. The perfection of his laws and the wise administration of his political affairs were known abroad.

There was more to her searching! As her camel caravan began the journey from southern Arabia to Jerusalem, a distance of almost twelve hundred miles, she must have been pondering on the God of Solomon. She "heard of the fame of Solomon concerning the name of the Lord," and she wanted to "prove him with hard questions."

When she arrived, her heart must have leaped within her. The half had not been told! The riches and splendor and magnificence of his palace and other possessions surpassed her imagination. "I believed not the words, until I came, and mine eyes had seen it: and, behold, the half was not told me."[2]

We are sure Solomon took the opportunity to tell the queen of the God of Israel. What a great delight it must have been for him to take her through the Temple and explain each object and its significance. She may have inquired about sacrifices. Solomon could well explain what God required of His people. His magnificent kingdom would not be the focal point in Solomon's mind. Rather, he would be eager for the opportunity to commend her to the God of Israel.

The Old Testament Solomon had a New Testament counterpart. Matthew tells us, "The queen of the south . . . came . . . to hear the wisdom of Solomon; and, behold, a greater than Solomon is here."[3]

Many may have heard what Jesus Christ has done and that He is the ultimate in wisdom, and possesses the richest of understanding. Yet they may be guilty of what some did in Solomon's time, sending only a representative to hear.

Those who will make the effort to approach "the greater than Solomon" or to ask the "hard questions" come away and say, "The half has not been told." God's word through Jeremiah is still relevant: "And ye shall seek me, and find me, when ye shall search for me with all your heart."[4]

[1] I Kings 10:1.
[2] I Kings 10:7.
[3] Matthew 12:42.
[4] Jeremiah 29:13.

❧ ❧ ❧

158

I Kings 13–15
I Kings 13:1-32

> And when the prophet that brought him back from the
> way heard thereof, he said, It is the man of God, who
> was disobedient unto the word of the Lord: therefore
> the Lord hath delivered him unto the lion.[1]

OH, THE HONESTY of Scripture! As God instructed Moses
concerning the Israelites, "Shew them the way wherein they
must walk, and the work that they must do,"[2] so are we
shown our duty plainly. In the story of the disobedient
prophet, we have an illustration of a man who was cut off
because of his disobedience. In this case God chose an example for our warning, one that will give us a vivid illustration. Through this we must clearly see that disobedience
is folly. We must seek to walk in the way of true obedience,
leading others in the same upright path.

In the Bible we have stories of men like Noah, who in
difficult circumstances stood singularly fast for God. He was
an overcomer when it was not popular to do what God said.
He was a godly man in an ungodly age. In time of pressure
he was exemplary. But when the pressure let up, Noah fell.
Lot and this unnamed prophet are other examples of those
whose obedience did not carry through.

No doubt at one time this prophet was used of God. Beware. No command or word of God is to be taken lightly.
His pure Word must be "the only rule to direct us how we
may glorify and enjoy Him."[3]

We recognize that our service is hindered by disobedience.
Service and worship are high privileges of the Christian, but
what tragedy it is for them to be cut off. Paul wrote, "But I
keep under my body, and bring it into subjection: lest that
by any means, when I have preached to others, I myself
should be a castaway."[4] He reminded his charges that "with
many of them God was not well pleased: for they were over-

thrown in the wilderness."[5] Paul stressed the importance of not lusting after evil things, which could be power, or acclaim, or idolatry, or tampering with the world. The believer has a great responsibility to know the will of God and to heed it.

A lying prophet is a dangerous person. How much damage can be done by an unfaithful or dishonest witness? Others can be led astray and ensnared. Had this prophet been true to God he could have been used by God to rebuke Jeroboam and he might have had a record of honor rather than dishonor.

Those who fail must take heed and see the error of their way. There may not be the danger of being cut off, but there is a danger of becoming a dead branch and not bearing fruit. Oh, the grief of being withered and cast aside from service and communion with Him. Let us never be weary in our well doing. He has promised that we will reap if we faint not.

[1] I Kings 13:26.
[2] Exodus 18:20.
[3] Westminster Catechism.
[4] I Corinthians 9:27.
[5] I Corinthians 10:5.

❧ ❧ ❧

I KINGS 16–18
I KINGS 18

> And [he] said to his servant, Go up now, look toward
> the sea. And he went up, and looked, and said, There is
> nothing. And he said, Go again seven times. And . . .
> he said, Behold, there ariseth a little cloud out of the
> sea, like a man's hand.[1]

THE PRAYER OF ELIJAH which is found in this chapter is one of the truly great prayers of Scripture. Elijah mentions himself only once, and that was to ask God to hear him. How he longed for the ear of God, to present the petitions of his heavy heart, a heart full of concern for others. Many carry the burden of a family, ministers bear a burden for their parishes, but this man bore the burden of a nation. How earnestly he spoke to God: "Hear me, O Lord, hear me, that this people may know that thou art the Lord God, and that thou hast turned their heart back again."[2]

Drought had parched Israel for more than three years. The springs were dry and the greenery ceased to grow. Like the widow of Zarephath, many prepared their last meal before waiting for death. Now a man arose and announced that there would be an abundance of rain! Many must have looked up, but disbelieved when there was no sign of a cloud. The sun beat heavily on them. But Elijah knew God and trusted Him implicitly. He told his servant to go look toward the sea. The report came back, "Nothing." "Look again." Seven times, Elijah gave the order. How the servant must have rushed back when the small but real cloud, about the size of a man's hand, arrived on the horizon! It was enough. Little is much when God is in it. The cloud grew and the rain revived Israel. Elijah, being a real man of God, rightly related to Him, could interpret the sign on the horizon.

Clouds in Scripture are often significant. Think of the

one that led the children of Israel. It took them on their way. Moses, the man of God, could interpret its significance. If it hovered, they stayed; if it ascended, they progressed on their journey.

Clouds from the devastating bombs of our day may be symbols of destruction. Man would do well to realize that at any moment his soul may pass into eternity.

Christ's return will be in a cloud, we are told. "Be ye therefore ready also."[3] Possibly on the horizon today there seems little that is distinguishable, yet look again, and again. The more we search Scripture the more evident it becomes that His appearing will be soon. The signs of the times may not be too discernible, but the child of God will be able to interpret them as he searches the Word.

Let us all prepare ourselves, as men of God would do, by earnest, unselfish prayer. Then we will fear neither the sun nor the shadow, when we realize that He formed both.

[1]I Kings 18:43-44.
[2]I Kings 18:37.
[3]Luke 12:40.

❦   ❦   ❦

April 8

I Kings 19–20
I Kings 19:1-18

What doest thou here, Elijah?[1]

ELIJAH WAS DISCOURAGED. He had experienced failure. "The children of Israel have forsaken thy covenant, thrown down thine altars, and slain thy prophets,"[2] he told the Lord. He was tired and dejected, and even requested of the Lord that he might die!

Elijah, the mighty man who had defied the king, fled for his life in fear of a wicked queen. Under the juniper tree, God dealt with him tenderly, knowing, as God always does, the need for refreshment and sleep.

162

On the mount, however, God rebuked Elijah. "What doest thou here?"¹ He had chosen his own way and turned aside from God. He had left his post with no one to take his place. He, who had experienced the goodness of God on Carmel, and known His divine favor, had become a deserter.

No doubt Elijah had felt Mt. Horeb would bring him closer to God. On an adjoining mountain, Moses had been given the Ten Commandments. Possibly he felt the elevation would help lift his soul heavenward. Whatever the reasoning, he was far away from the demands of life.

Does it not sound somewhat familiar? In our everyday living, we Christians experience failure. It is not that we have not seen God's glory manifest in countless ways, for we have. Yet, sometimes an eclipse of faith occurs, and our impulse is to flee—in search of a mountaintop experience. Here, if we will stop and listen, God will appear with His voice of correction: "What doest thou here?"

To Elijah God said, "Go, return." It was a divine call back to duty. Elijah was prepared to answer, as was Samuel, "Speak, Lord; for thy servant heareth."³ In obedience he went forth, and did as he had been told.

Life is uncertain and often discouraging. With Elijah there were seven thousand who had not bowed to Baal. We wonder just how many are with us. But God is faithful! Each new morning presents an opportunity to go forth to the ministry He has assigned. God meets us in our moments of tribulation as well as triumph, in our weakness as well as our strength. Our failures may be preparing us for greater usefulness in God's service.

¹I Kings 19:9.
²I Kings 19:10.
³I Samuel 3:9.

❧   ❧   ❧

I Kings 21–22
I Kings 22

> Jehoshaphat made ships of Tharshish to go to Ophir
> for gold: but they went not; for the ships were broken.[1]

IN THE HEART of India, a young missionary couple waited
on the Lord for guidance as to their future. They had met
with problems and adversities. The fruits of their labor
had not been evident, and they prayed while they wrote
the home office for advice. Their letter arrived at head-
quarters as the founder of the mission was about to depart
on a trip. He quickly read it and determined to spend time,
while traveling, praying and seeking an answer for them.
His secretary, after his departure, did not realize he had
seen the letter and brought it to the attention of a new
board member who was sincere and very businesslike. At
once he suggested the couple return and be reassigned to
another post. Their health and lack of penetration pointed
to one thing in his mind: a change of duty. The air letter
was mailed.

In the interim, the missionary founder, a real man of
God, sought out Scripture with which he could encourage
the couple, and wrote that they should consider complet-
ing a half term. This way they would better understand
the field and could seek for the key which would unlock the
field. It was not unbelievable that the defeat could be
turned into victory. His letter was postmarked about a week
after the first one.

The latter letter arrived first. The husband and wife
agreed that this would be the will of God for them and
ascertained how best they could serve the remaining half
term. They prayed more and studied and worked as never
before. Just as they had experienced the blessing of their
first convert to Christ, the second letter arrived from the

board member. On it was a notation that the plane which carried the mail to the continent had been downed. The mail had been recovered but this accounted for the long delay. How grateful the missionaries were that the letter mailed first had reached them last. Some would speculate whether this was coincidence or Providence. The growth of those two and the extent of their fruitful service have proved the latter to be the answer.

The missionary telling the story referred to today's Scripture. She pointed out that Solomon's ships had made the route safely and prosperously, but Jehoshaphat's shipbuilding had proved a failure. As he sought to reestablish trade, the ships were wrecked while they were in harbor. The cause of his loss is plainly told in Scripture: "Because thou hast joined thyself with [wicked] Ahaziah, the Lord hath broken thy works."[2]

Let us remember the same God who prospers one can break another. Jehoshaphat walked in the ways of the Lord, but the Lord checked up on his plans! Coincidence or Providence? "Shall not the Judge of all the earth do right?"[3]

[1] I Kings 22:48.
[2] II Chronicles 20:37.
[3] Genesis 18:25.

❧ ❧ ❧

II KINGS 1–3
II KINGS 2

> And it came to pass, when they were gone over, that
> Elijah said unto Elisha, Ask what I shall do for thee,
> . . . And Elisha said, I pray thee, let a double portion of
> thy spirit be upon me. . . . The spirit of Elijah doth
> rest on Elisha.[1]

WHEN ELIJAH was caught up into heaven, his mantle fell
on Elisha. How eager the latter was for the blessing of God
upon him, and his great desire was expressed in his request
for "a double portion of thy spirit." He was sincerely seeking to be a true prophet of Jehovah.

We are told that the word *prophet* in its root meaning is
"one who speaks for another." Here it indicates one who
speaks for God. The spirit which was of Elijah had now
come to Elisha, not just as a symbol, or a so-called clerical
outfit, though there were external signs of an internal experience.

Would to God, today, that we would have more who earnestly covet the power of the Spirit of God in their lives.
"The supply of the Spirit of Jesus Christ"[2] is readily available. "How much more shall your heavenly Father give
the Holy Spirit to them that ask him?"[3]

The Source of power and His ministrations are often confused or the latter emphasized out of proportion. Some feel
that the Spirit is evidenced in "great arrows of fire." Others
feel "it" is a "liquid" or even an "element." The Holy
Spirit is a person. Our identification with Him is based on
the solid foundation of union with Christ.

Elisha did not ask for a double portion of the Spirit as a
means of power alone. He sought the true Source of power, the all-powerful God. He had seen Him work through
Elijah, and wished to partake of the same experience. Believers can take a lesson here. We pray for the Spirit to

come upon us so we can become a Moody or a Finney, yet we are not willing to overcome by His power in the place where we stand. "The power of the Holy Spirit is granted not to make us famous, but fruitful. It is given to us to make us effective for His service, not popular with our fellowman."[4]

A man filled with the Spirit of God has abandoned himself. He does not proudly say, "I have something which you have not." But his life gives witness and evidence of the Spirit's fruit. More joy, love, peace, patience, meekness, are demonstrations that the Spirit lives within. "We cannot be filled by deciding to claim it by faith. Neither are we filled by praying for it; and once filled there is no guarantee that we will be in the same blessed state tomorrow. We are only filled with the Spirit as we yield ourselves to God and walk in obedience to His Word. . . . If the Word dwells in us richly, it is being filled with the Spirit."[5] Elisha did not seek the outward signs but the inward grace. When God takes charge, the difference is well known within and without to His glory and praise.

[1] II Kings 2:9, 15.
[2] Philippians 1:19.
[3] Luke 11:13.
[4] Harry Ironside.
[5] Harry Ironside.

❧ ❧ ❧

167

II Kings 4–6
II Kings 4

> And there came a man from Baal-shalisha, and brought
> the man of God bread of the firstfruits, twenty loaves
> of barley, and full ears of corn in the husk thereof. And
> he said, Give unto the people, that they may eat. And
> his servitor said, What, should I set this before an hun-
> dred men? He said . . . , Give . . . for thus saith the
> Lord, They shall eat, and shall leave thereof.[1]

THE PARABLE of Elisha and the man who came with ears of
corn and twenty loaves of barley bread has always been a
source of encouragement to me. Here was a man bringing
his tithe to the prophet, the firstfruits of his harvest, and he
was pleased and proud of it. Elisha asked his servant to
give the barley bread and the corn to the people for them
to eat. The servant looked at the gift, small in contrast to
the one hundred people, and was puzzled. Should he set
this before them? Surely it was not enough. Elisha told him
to give it to the people and there would be some left over!

Notice how God multiplied the gift which was given to
Elisha. The true secret of getting is giving. It is in giving
that we receive. What a blessing that tither must have had
in seeing all those people eat until they were filled. Giving
makes life worthwhile. How startling it must have been to
the man to see God multiply the gift, but he would never
forget, and it would be an encouragement in all his future
giving.

Hearing accounts of miracles can stir our imaginations.
The ancient Hebrews learned, "Cast thy bread upon the
waters: for thou shalt find it after many days."[2] In the
natural it is foolish to toss bread into a rushing river or
great ocean, but someone said, "To see only the sheer logic
of life is to miss the significance of life's unseen realities
such as the Spirit of God, who magnifies the gift and re-

plenishes the giver, not with bread that perishes but with the bread from heaven."

We cast a small amount of service into the kingdom of God. Either our imaginations are dull, or we are blind as to what can happen through the unlimited resources of God. Elisha knew God and relied on His unmeasurable capacity for doing the impossible.

You may say, "I would cast my bread upon the waters, but I have so little that it wouldn't count." It does count, every little bit. Christ asks that you give what you have. No matter how small or how insignificant, the important thing is to "cast," to give! It may be a batch of cookies to a new family next door. It may be giving your last six cents in an offering, or sharing a book; but take the step, for ultimately you are sharing Jesus Christ and your faith.

"Cast your bread," the bread of simple things, upon the waters of life, and the return, after many days, will be far-reaching and eternal.

¹II Kings 4:42-43.
²Ecclesiastes 11:1.

❧ ❧ ❧

II Kings 7–9
II Kings 8

> And the king talked with Gehazi the servant of the
> man of God, saying, Tell me, I pray thee, all the great
> things that Elisha hath done.[1]

IN A BUSY BLOCK of a housing project for dependents at a
naval air station, two housewives were hanging out their
family wash. Both were mothers of very large families. The
similarity ended here. One was brought up to love and
serve the Lord. Her faith and service were extended when
she married a young theological student who became a
chaplain. They had served at home and abroad and loved
their mission for Christ. The other lady came from a home
where she never heard the name of Christ except in irreverence. She was quite impressed with the chaplain's wife, her
poise, her concern for others, and the unusually good behavior of her large family. On this particular day, the unchurched woman put down her clothes basket and called
over the fence to the Christian, "Tell me, what makes you
different? Is it church or something?"

Who would not be thrilled with such an opportunity?
It was a joy for the chaplain's wife to set her laundry basket
down, and on the back steps tell about Jesus Christ and
the great things He had done for her and her family.

We see a similar situation in today's reading. King Je-
horam was talking with Gehazi, Elisha's servant. Possibly
he had been deep in thought over the question he posed, or
perhaps it came suddenly upon him. "Tell me . . . all the
great things that Elisha hath done."

What an opportunity for Gehazi. He traced the history
of some of the things the man of God had been allowed to
accomplish. He probably detailed stories such as the one
about the well of Jericho. The water was "naught" and
the ground "barren."[2] Then the miracle occurred. Elisha

simply suggested the addition of salt, and "the waters were healed."[3] Surely Gehazi also related to the king the story of the poor widow. Elisha had told her to collect containers from all the neighbors and then pour out her small supply of oil. All the vessels were filled. Another miracle! And he must have told about the twenty barley loaves that fed one hundred hungry men! The king was moved by the stories, even by the one of the raising from the dead of the Shunammite woman's son—a story verified by the mother herself. And the glory was given to Elisha's God.

With the chaplain's wife, we have a wonderful story to share with the world. The God of Elisha sent His Son. He performed untold miracles, but the greatest was His overcoming death to provide eternal life for all who will believe in Him.

May we be ever faithful in sharing all the great things He has done.

[1]II Kings 8:4.
[2]II Kings 2:19.
[3]II Kings 2:22.

❧ ❧ ❧

II Kings 10–12
II Kings 10

> And he said, Come with me, and see my zeal for the Lord.[1]

A MISSIONARY STATESMAN took a congregation on a verbal trip viewing foreign missions in Korea. "Too often," he said, "foreign missions become a faceless picture." Vividly he brought into focus the true needs of men and women around the world: a starving child, a leprous woman, a man dying without God and without hope. These questions faced each individual: Do you really care? Are you in any way concerned that while you live in plenty, the masses go to bed hungry? Are you moved at all to pray for the salvation of those who are without Christ, those who have not heard the good news of the gospel? This missionary was a true example of one who could say, "Come with me, and see my zeal for the Lord."

Where is our zeal today? If the picture is out of focus it is because we are not willing to take the time or the trouble to look about us. Few magazines are published without the needs of man boldly portrayed on their pages. We look, but do we really see?

The example is given of Jesus Christ, who was moved with great compassion for the multitudes which followed Him. At times there would be those who would rebuke Him by saying, "Lord, they follow You because You make provision for them. Send them away." The choice before the Master was the one that confronts us—today and every day. Will we give to them, provide for them, feed them, or will we merely send them away hungry and in dire need?

It has been well said that "no work is as wearisome as doing nothing" and that "no self-sacrifice is as costly as self-indulgence." We need inspiration and zeal to look, and see, and pray the Lord of the harvest to send forth laborers into His harvest. He is looking to you. You are required to be up and doing. The labor may be that of prayer or that of giving, but every opportunity faces you with the choice that was Jesus Christ's—to give and to feed, or to send the needy and dying away.

It is well said, "The royalty of democracy are the people who care."[2] As Christians we need a resurgence of people who care. Too few exercise true Christian concern. Too few are willing to give generously and liberally, to do more when they have already done much, and to pray without ceasing!

> Up! Awake! And let my prayer
> Be offered up because I care.
> The world's heartbeat I'm called to share,
> And this I know, God meets me there.

[1]II Kings 10:16.
[2]Harold Voelkel.

❧   ❧   ❧

II Kings 13–15
II Kings 14

Why shouldest thou meddle to thy hurt . . . ?[1]

IN THE MIDST of the account of Israel and Judah at war we have this statement which stops us and makes us think.

Why is it that in the family of God there are often those who choose to delve into the affairs of others uninvited and unnecessarily? Possibly an unhappy occurrence has taken place in your circle of Christian friends. It is true that we must be helpful to one another, but let us pray for discernment when it comes to probing into the lives of others, making sure that it is concern and not curiosity which prompts us.

This point was made by a mother of a large family of teen-agers. They were continually prying into each other's affairs—as sometimes even a happy family can do. But at times this caused hard feelings. The mother explained that some things are sacred, and that no one can live another's life. On the back door of her large home she had a small sign reading, "Peddlers forbidden." One day, as the family came to dinner, they noted that the sign from the kitchen door had been removed and transferred inside. One letter was changed, and they got the message: "Meddlers forbidden!"

This may seem petty, and one would be quick to come to the rescue, affirming that if a family cannot share life's problems, who can? Yet this godly mother wanted her family to learn the lesson of true concern and compassion, and yet develop a sensitivity to the areas where one member chose to walk alone. Their inquiries, even in the home, must be helpful and loving, and around her table they must learn discernment and seek for the understanding heart God intended for His own.

Today, believers need to develop hearts that are willing

to stop, to listen, to understand, and to be slow to pass judgment on another. We may hear that a brother has fallen, investigate with Christian concern, if led, and then learn that he hasn't fallen at all! Eyebrows can be raised at a seeming lack of spiritual insight in those about us. A mistaken impression is often formed in haste in our own minds and we too easily condemn others without even seeking divine understanding.

Too often, as the Scripture states, meddling can be to hurt. What good does it do us to know unhappy details? After all, how much better are we than the one whose affairs we have chosen to delve into? "Why do you stare . . . at the very small particle that is in your brother's eye, but do not become aware of and consider the beam of timber that is in your own eye?"[2]

There is much burden-bearing to be done, but let us do it with concern and not with curiosity. This Old Testament question is asked of us today: "Why shouldest thou meddle?" Should we not discuss the question and its principle with Him?

[1]II Kings 14:10.
[2]Matthew 7:3, Amplified New Testament.

❧ ❧ ❧

175

II Kings 16–17
II Kings 17

They feared the Lord, and served their own gods.[1]

IT IS NOT UNCOMMON to meet those who fit the description above. All too many feel a sort of obligation to pay their respects to something religious. It may be attendance at a form of worship, or ministering to the poor to appease a guilty conscience. Whatever the motive, it is exterior service unless the heart is really involved.

The text refers to some of the inhabitants of Samaria. In subduing the tribes of Israel, the king of Assyria had taken the people and placed them throughout his own dominion. His idea was to scatter Israel among the others and in doing so, break their former ties. When all did not go well for some of the reassigned people, they sent to the king of Assyria to return to them a priest who had been there before to instruct them in the ways of Jehovah. Thus they combined their worship of Jehovah with worship of the gods brought from Babylon and other places. Their religious standards were shown in the words, "Howbeit every nation made gods of their own, and put them in the houses of the high places which the Samaritans had made, every nation in their cities wherein they dwelt."[2]

We are told that the Jewish people despised these Samaritans. In John we read an account which shows their dislike of mixing with them: "Then saith the woman of Samaria unto him, How is it that thou, being a Jew, askest drink of me, which am a woman of Samaria? for the Jews have no dealings with the Samaritans. Jesus answered and said unto her, If thou knewest the gift of God, and who it is that saith to thee, Give me to drink, thou wouldest have asked of him, and he would have given thee living water."[3] The story is familiar. Jesus explained that the water He gave quenched spiritual thirst. It was not a mixture, nor a combination of this religion and that, but it was pure, unde-filed life everlasting. "The woman then left her waterpot, and went her way into the city, and saith to the men, Come, see a man, which told me all things that ever I did: is not this the Christ?"[4]

There are those who fear the Lord, and serve their gods, and prefer a mixture, like the inhabitants of Samaria, to the pure gospel. They may have been brought up to love Jesus Christ, but the gods of this world have blinded their minds. Theirs is an unsatisfying form of religion. How graciously Christ made clear His love and great mercy, in extending His grace to the woman of Samaria. He says to-day, "Him that cometh to me I will in no wise cast out."[5] True faith in God has God alone for its object. Let us serve only Him.

[1] II Kings 17:33.
[2] II Kings 17:29.
[3] John 4:9-10.
[4] John 4:28-29.
[5] John 6:37.

❧   ❧   ❧

II Kings 18–19
II Kings 18:13-16; 19:1-37

> That which thou hast prayed to me against Sennacherib
> king of Assyria I have heard.[1]

HEZEKIAH TRUSTED GOD and brought about a revival of
righteousness. He was strong in the Lord, and though only
twenty-five years old when he ascended to his father's throne,
he was a dedicated man, determined that the degeneration
of his father's wicked reign would turn to regeneration in
years to come. God delivered Hezekiah from the mighty
Sennacherib, king of Assyria. Trust in the Lord is never in
vain.

Picture Hezekiah receiving a letter from Rabshakeh: "Let
not thy God in whom thou trusteth deceive thee, saying,
Jerusalem shall not be delivered into the hand of the king
of Assyria."[2] Carefully Hezekiah takes the letter and spreads
it before the Lord in the house of the Lord. Humbly he
beseeches the God he trusts, "O Lord God of Israel, . . .
thou art the God, even thou alone, of all the kingdoms of
the earth. . . . Bow down thine ear and hear: open, Lord,
thine eyes and see: and hear the words of Sennacherib,
which hath sent him to reproach the living God . . . Now
therefore, O Lord our God, . . . save thou us . . . that all
the kingdoms of the earth may know that thou art the Lord
God, even thou only."[3] The word comes back to Hezekiah
that God has heard and He will defend the city. And Sennacherib is destroyed with his army.

Let us grasp a lesson today from Hezekiah. God will
not be mocked. "He that sitteth in the heavens shall laugh:
the Lord shall have them in derision."[4] Yet His mercy is
still in evidence, and after the lessons are learned, He will
restore.

Hezekiah proved that "faith's opportunity is in the day of
trouble." And in the trouble he sought God. No problem is

too great for Him. Hezekiah simply took the problem, spread it out before the Lord, and received His answer.

This account about Hezekiah gives us an idea about what to do with difficult letters. We too may spread them out before Him, seek His wisdom, and apply for His counsel.

The enemy army was destroyed in the providence of God. Hezekiah's faith was rewarded. God honors faith because faith must honor God. "He that hath received his testimony hath set to his seal that God is true."[5] God made a covenant and He does not go back on His Word.

God says He will hear "that which thou hast prayed to me" if the praying hearts are right before Him. There is no problem so grave nor circumstance so impossible that it cannot be spread before Him. He can be trusted. Happy is the man that trusts in the Lord.

[1] II Kings 19:20.
[2] II Kings 19:10.
[3] II Kings 19:15-19.
[4] Psalm 2:4.
[5] John 3:33.

❧ ❧ ❧

II Kings 20–22
II Kings 22

> And Hilkiah the high priest said unto Shaphan the
> scribe, I have found the book of the law in the house
> of the Lord. And Hilkiah gave the book to Shaphan,
> and he read it.[1]

WHAT A DAY OF REJOICING—the law of the Lord was redis-
covered! During the repairing of the Temple no doubt the
renovation uncovered a copy of the book of the law. The
priests had passed down notations and phrases from it, but
here a complete copy was found. Hilkiah, who was close to
young King Josiah, read to him from it. Some scholars feel
it may have been chapters from Deuteronomy that had great
influence on Josiah. The sin and havoc that Manasseh had
wrought and the failure of his subjects to obey God had
taken its toll. The law, which had been ordered destroyed,
was now before them, and how it delighted Josiah to hear
it read. "Because thine heart was tender, and thou hast
humbled thyself before the Lord, when thou heardest what
I spake against this place, and against the inhabitants thereof, that they should become a desolation and a curse, and
hast rent thy clothes, and wept before me; I also have
heard thee, saith the Lord."[2]

Those who would seek to destroy God's law were not all
confined to this time. Think of those who ordered the Bible
to be burned in Tyndale's time. Think of the Communist
rulers who would do anything to destroy the Bible today.
And many of us are guilty too. In our lives it is evident at
times that the "book of the law" is missing.

We hear parts of it read and enjoy listening to those
who expound the blessings and eliminate the cursings. It
is available, but we let it stand unopened on our shelves for
future discovery! Oh, that today we would repair the temples in our hearts and find God's Word anew. The Psalmist

wrote, "I delight to do thy will, O my God: yea, thy law is within my heart."[3] How much of the law is in our hearts? Are our hearts tender toward things of the Word and toward its Author?

Those whose minds are darkened toward the whole of Scripture are forerunners of those who would seek to destroy or steal it. Robbery most often is committed at night when the sin will not be discovered. Our darkened minds may also be in league with the thieves who seek to break through and steal His word from us. It is only as we walk in the light that we have true fellowship.

May we seek out the Word of the Lord and be receptive to its teaching.

[1]II Kings 22:8.
[2]II Kings 22:19.
[3]Psalm 40:8.

❧ ❧ ❧

April 18

II KINGS 23–25
II KINGS 23

> And the king stood by a pillar, and made a covenant before the Lord, to walk after the Lord, and to keep his commandments and his testimonies and his statutes with all their heart and all their soul, to perform the words of this covenant that were written in this book. And all the people stood to the covenant.[1]

MAKING A COVENANT with God is a solemn and sacred transaction. In our story today it was not done hastily, but Josiah's heart had been touched by the discovery of the law. One theme throughout its pages was that of the judgment and doom that follow disobedience. Josiah was quick to warn the people in order to avert what seemed inevitable if they did not walk in the ways of the Lord God of Israel. Josiah's integrity and devotion set him above other kings.

"And like unto him was there no king before him, that turned to the Lord with all his heart, and with all his soul, and with all his might, according to all the law of Moses; neither after him arose there any like him."[2] His reformations will not be forgotten.

Of Hezekiah it had been said that "he trusted in the Lord . . . so that after him was none like him."[3] People are quick to say that this is a contradiction! Both men had specific excellencies which set them apart: Hezekiah, his great confidence in God and Josiah, his zeal in rebuilding and reestablishing the way of the Lord, and his personal piety. From both we can take example!

Josiah's covenant with God was not made in haste, nor was it for himself alone. He strove to bring all the priests and the prophets and the people of Jerusalem into covenant with God. He exercised his influence for good. In reflecting on the past history of God's people he knew there was but one way to escape from future judgment, and that was by serving God and being obedient to Him.

Josiah's action should be our action. Does our influence stir those with whom we work or live? Is ours an influence for good or for evil? Possibly we have no influence at all! That is a tragedy too.

Josiah's zeal and diligence were incredible for such a young man. He broke the idols into pieces and he traveled throughout the land to make sure that the people were worshiping God. It was not an armchair war on wrong, it was getting up and fighting and working for the right with all his might and soul. In all this he adhered to the Word of God that was now in his possession. His example helped others make their covenant with God. Ours is the same mission.

[1] II Kings 23:3.
[2] II Kings 23:25.
[3] II Kings 18:5.

❧ ❧ ❧

182

> All scripture is given by inspiration of God, and is prof-
> itable for doctrine, for reproof, for correction, for in-
> struction in righteousness: that the man of God may be
> perfect, throughly furnished unto all good works.[1]

THE QUESTION has been asked me in all seriousness, "Do you
honestly believe that every word from Genesis 1 to the end
of Revelation is inspired?" More than once I have seen
shock registered on the face of a genuine seeker on hearing
my reply: "Yes, every line." If we yield a word our foundations are insecure. The opening chapters of First Chronicles have often been the target of questions. What can be
learned from names and more names? Is it really possible
that these genealogical tables are written for our learning
too?

My heart was greatly warmed at hearing a man of God
expound genealogical records. Since then when I have been
tempted to speed up my reading of the "begats," I slow
down. In them is a precious and wonderful lesson about
God's great concern and His untiring care for the people
of Israel, His own people. Just because they are scattered
is no reason to think that He has lost track of His own.
"The very hairs of your head are all numbered."[2] He is
aware of the sparrow's fall. He really loves and cares for
His own. In His time He will pick up the ones who are far
from home today and put them in their Promised Land—
and all according to His promise to Abraham, to Isaac,
and to Jacob.

Doesn't this make you want to look up to Him and say,
"Thank You, thank You"? When you read that "he careth
for you,"[3] you know it is not just a temporary promise. He
extends His care over the past, the present, and the future.

Generation after generation are in the center of His vigilance.

Someone has expressed it like this: "Now, is not all this full of blessed instruction for us? Is it not full of comfort for our souls? Is it not most confirmatory of our faith to mark the gracious painstaking of our God? Most assuredly it is. And ought not our hearts to be interested in all that interests the heart of the Father? Are we not to take an interest in anything save what directly concerns ourselves? Where is there a loving child who would not take an interest in all his father's concerns, and delight to read every line that drops from his father's pen?"

Today is a good time to start reading the Word of God. Never doubt that He, the Author, can illuminate the difficult portions and show Himself even more precious through these words.

The third name in this first chapter is significant: Enosh, meaning "Inquire of the Lord!"

[1]II Timothy 3:16-17.
[2]Matthew 10:30.
[3]I Peter 5:7.

❧ ❧ ❧

I Chronicles 3–4
I Chronicles 4

> And Jabez called on the God of Israel, saying, Oh that
> thou wouldest bless me indeed, and enlarge my coast,
> and that thine hand might be with me, and that thou
> wouldest keep me from evil, that it may not grieve me!
> And God granted him that which he requested.[1]

IN TODAY'S READING there is an interruption in the genealogical tables. A man called Jabez is recognized though his father's name is not mentioned. "Jabez was more honourable than his brethren,"[2] because he exalted God. His prayer is further evidence of God's promise that "them that honour me I will honour."[3]

Two of the areas of his life which distinguished him were his honor and his devoted prayer life. As for his prayer life, he gave himself to definite, specific prayer. "And God granted him that which he requested."

Jabez' life must have been a true channel of blessing! Such blessing from God would surge in and through a man like a river. Only its relation to the Source of eternal springs could cause it to overflow into the lives of those about. "Freely ye have received, freely give."[4] We know the "blessing of the Lord, it maketh rich."[5] God's blessings are riches untold.

"The effectual fervent prayer of a righteous man availeth much."[6] Think back over the months we have read and considered the prayers of God's people. Abraham prayed, and God heard and blessed his seed exceedingly. Abraham's servant prayed, and Rebekah appeared, just as he had asked. Moses cried to God for a fleeing group of Israelites as they faced the Red Sea, and the sea became dry land! Remember the gracious, persevering prayer of Hannah. Oh, how she prayed! "And the child Samuel grew on and was in favour both with the Lord, and also with men."[7] David prayed, and his prayers have touched and searched hearts over the centuries. He saw specific answers to definite prayer. Remember Elijah, who prayed in the midst of the three-year drought and was not surprised when the black cloud began to form on the horizon.

Jabez prayed! He wanted the blessing of God. He wanted an enlarged opportunity to be of service. He wanted protection from the evil one so that he would not grieve his God. Jabez prayed, and his prayer was answered. "Prayer is the key to all the treasure of heaven, but faith is the hand that turns the key!"

[1]I Chronicles 4:10.
[2]I Chronicles 4:9.
[3]I Samuel 2:30.
[4]Matthew 10:8.
[5]Proverbs 10:22.
[6]James 5:16.
[7]I Samuel 2:26.

❧ ❧ ❧

April 21

I Chronicles 5–6
I Chronicles 5

> For there fell down many slain, because the war was of God. And they dwelt in their steads until the captivity.[1]

WHEN WILL THE ISRAELITES learn the secret of conquest? When will we, who also have seen the great Deliverer at work in our midst, learn the secret? "And they were helped against them, and the Hagarites were delivered into their hand, and all that were with them: for they cried to God in the battle, and he was intreated of them; because they put their trust in him."[2] The Israelites were now acting as they should. They followed the example of their previous leaders. Their armies were strong, but they did not put their confidence in manpower. They put their trust where it belonged—in God.

In their distress they fled to Him. "God is our refuge and strength, a very present help in trouble,"[3] and He answered their entreaty, for He has never failed one who put his trust in Him.

The victory was won and they shared in the spoils. Their army was not as great as the enemy but this was inconsequential for "the war was of God." When the battle is His, He delivers the foe into our hands.

Have you experienced a recent battle? It may be with sin. The lust or love for it constantly reappears. There are days when you wonder if you really love the Lord or belong to Him. Verses of assurance are earmarked and underlined, but for some reason you do what you don't want to do: you sin, even though you hate sin. I heard a young college man say with saddened heart and dejected countenance, "You'll never understand how deeply I am involved. It is too great. I'm in too deep for help." The story of the victory of Reuben, Gad and half of Manasseh was a source of strength to him. Was it possible that his God, the God of Israel too, could slay the monsters of evil in his life? Could the foes that were crippling him be overcome? In utter helplessness he confessed to the Lord that the battle was not his but God's. How to defeat the enemy he did not know, but he longed for victory over the awful oppression in his soul.

Today, his testimony is radiant. "For there fell down many slain, because the war was of God." The sin was reckoned with and brought into captivity. He is victorious.

> To him that overcometh,
> A crown of life shall be;
> He with the King of glory
> Shall reign eternally.[4]

[1] I Chronicles 5:22.
[2] I Chronicles 5:20.
[3] Psalm 46:1.
[4] George Duffield.

✤ ✤ ✤

187

I Chronicles 7:8
I Chronicles 7

> All these were the children of Asher, heads of their
> father's house, choice and mighty men of valour.[1]

HAVE YOU EVER VISITED old friends and found yourself deep
in reminiscing? "How is Mrs. Jones? What is her daughter
doing? Did her children grow up to love the Lord?" The
questions are asked eagerly, and you rejoice to hear a good
report.

In today's chapter we have the genealogies of those in
each tribe who were "mighty men of valour": Issachar, Benjamin, Naphtali, the divided tribes of Manasseh and Ephraim. The final mention is of Asher. Here for a few moments
we stop and inquire about a group which was valiant but
small in number. What of their descendants?

More than fifteen centuries later we would have a good
report of Anna, the daughter of Phanuel, of the tribe of
Asher. She truly belonged to the godly remnant. In Luke
we have a brief history of her. "And there was one Anna,
a prophetess, the daughter of Phanuel, of the tribe of Asher:
she was of a great age, and had lived with an husband seven
years from her virginity; and she was a widow of about
fourscore and four years, which departed not from the
temple, but served God with fastings and prayers night and
day. And she coming in that instant gave thanks likewise
unto the Lord, and spake of him to all them that looked for
redemption in Jerusalem."[2]

Certainly Phanuel prayed for his family and their descendants. If he could have looked into the future his
heart would have been warmed to see his daughter, humble in spirit, living in the Temple and possessing expectant
faith. Possibly Anna may have seen the brilliant star that
special night when Christ was born. She had heard the
ancient scrolls read. The prophecies were as familiar to her

as the Temple where she lived. When she saw the Baby Jesus she recognized her Redeemer.

What greater joy could there be than that of seeing our children, and their children's children, walk in the ways of God, seeing Jesus and recognizing Him as their Redeemer.

[1]I Chronicles 7:40.
[2]Luke 2:36-38.

❧ ❧ ❧

April 23

I Chronicles 9–11
I Chronicles 9

> And these are the singers, chief of the fathers of the Levites, who remaining in the chambers were free: for they were employed in that work day and night.[1]

I REGRETFULLY REMEMBER awakening one morning without a song in my heart. All the great joys of the past—and they had been multiplied—seemed to be quenched in deep heaviness. I turned on the radio for an early edition of news and heard the strains of a familiar song:

> When morning gilds the skies
> My heart awaking cries,
> May Jesus Christ be praised.
> Alike at work and prayer
> To Jesus I repair:
> May Jesus Christ be praised.

Praise in the midst of problems? A song when there was so much sadness? Was this required?

How gracious God is to His children. He well knows that despair and despondency are unhealthy and also displeasing. If the hymn was not enough to gladden my heart, the morning devotional reading was. The verse was today's, along with the following comments:

> Well was it so ordered in the temple that the sacred

189

chant never ceased: for evermore did the singers praise the Lord, whose mercy endureth forever. As mercy did not cease to rule either by day or by night, so neither did music hush its holy ministry. My heart, there is a lesson sweetly taught to thee in the ceaseless song of Zion's temple. Thou too art a constant debtor, and see thou to it that thy gratitude, like charity, never faileth. God's praise is constant in heaven, which is to be thy final dwelling place. Learn thou to practice the eternal halle- lujah. Around the earth as the sun scatters his light, His beams awaken grateful believers to tune this morn- ing hymn, so that by the priesthood of the saints, per- petual praise is kept up at all hours.[2]

Nothing to sing about after a double portion of His pro- vision for my own intimate needs? Somewhere a song must be born, and possibly those from the depths of hurt and an- guish are received as a true sacrifice of praise.

> Be this, while life is mine
> My canticle divine,
> May Jesus Christ be praised:
> Be this th' eternal song
> Through all the ages long,
> May Jesus Christ be praised.

[1] I Chronicles 9:33.
[2] C. H. Spurgeon, *Morning and Evening*.

❧   ❧   ❧

I Chronicles 12–14
I Chronicles 12

> Then the spirit came upon Amasai, who was chief of
> the captains, and he said, Thine are we, David, and on
> thy side, thou son of Jesse: peace, peace be unto thee,
> and peace be to thine helpers; for thy God helpeth thee.
> Then David received them, and made them captains of
> the band.[1]

In yesterday's chapters were recorded Saul's death and the accession of David to the throne as king over Israel. There is no doubt that David had some mighty men with him. Today we read how more approached him, in particular the children of Benjamin and Judah. "And David went out to meet them, and answered and said unto them, If ye be come peaceably unto me to help me, mine heart shall be kind unto you; but if ye come to betray me to mine enemies, seeing there is no wrong in mine hands, the God of our fathers look thereon, and rebuke it."[2]

What David was saying had been spoken before in Exodus: "Who is on the Lord's side? let him come unto me."[3] It is significant for us to take special note and see if we can answer with Amasai, "Thine are we." David was not asking for a quick, impulsive answer. He wanted them to reason and consider if they would be willing to surrender to his claims.

The pattern David followed in asking these men to ponder the question is echoed in the New Testament. Remember how the Apostle Paul, writing in Romans, filled eleven chapters with reasoning and good logic, all to be contemplated before his urging, "I beseech you therefore, brethren, by the mercies of God, that ye present your bodies a living sacrifice, holy, acceptable unto God, which is your reasonable service."[4] After due consideration, one must admit that such sacrifice is "reasonable."

It is important that each child of God seriously ponder the question when it comes to taking up the banner of the cross. Some cults and associations have secret followers or underground groups. But a true Christian is willing to identify himself with his Captain and follow where He leads.

Demonstrating our love for Him and specifically choosing His side will bring joy to Him and to us and knit our hearts more closely with His. There is no middle road nor neutral ground. God grant that through searching and reasoning, our choice will be a glad one and our decision definite: "Thine are we."

[1]I Chronicles 12:18.
[2]I Chronicles 12:17.
[3]Exodus 32:26.
[4]Romans 12:1.

    🍀   🍀   🍀

April 25

I CHRONICLES 15–16
I CHRONICLES 16

> So he left there before the ark of the covenant of the Lord Asaph and his brethren, to minister before the ark continually, as every day's work required.[1]

IT IS INTERESTING to note the various tasks given to those who ministered before the Ark. There were porters and priests. There were musicians and caretakers. Each did the job to which he was called and for which he had special responsibility before God.

In the Body of Christ, the ministry in our churches and other places of service is performed by varied people with many different talents. Each fits together to make up the whole.

My heart was warmed one Sunday on hearing an associate minister point out the various ways his congregation blended together. The organist had a wonderful gift of music, but surgery had taken her voice. She could offer no vocal praise, but her music was a dedicated gift. The Sunday school superintendent who had tried for years to teach felt unable to communicate with the children, yet he was a master of organization and had found his place. The janitor had never been given the opportunity for education, but his floors were waxed and pews polished to the glory of God. The nursery staff were gifted in handling youngsters, and on through the building were other individuals working together, each doing his own job.

Emerson said, "Nature arms each man with some faculty which enables him to do easily some feat impossible to any other." We all have seen the truth of this in our daily experience. One can speak, another can cook. One can manicure the lawns and care for the shrubs, while another delves deeply into the "hidden meanings and treasured thoughts" that come only with study. But the one who speaks must be fed physically, and the one who cooks must be fed spiritually. The man who trims the yard and delights in the beauty of God's universe can also profit from the soul-refreshing gift of the one who lives within four walls. The important thing is that we all need each other. And we must recognize that the task of one is as vital as that of another.

Who is greater, he who gives a dime or he who gives a dollar? The one who builds props for a Christmas program or the one who has the lead in the cast? How unfortunate it would be if we all were called to be "arms" in the Body of Christ, or all "mouths" for Him. How out of proportion His kingdom would be! It is true that in the world there are no two souls alike. It is essential, however, that each freely offers acceptable gifts to the Saviour.

[1] I Chronicles 16:37.

❧   ❧   ❧

I Chronicles 17–21
I Chronicles 17

> Now therefore thus shalt thou say unto my servant
> David, Thus saith the Lord of hosts, I took thee from
> the sheepcote, even from following the sheep, that thou
> shouldest be ruler over my people Israel: and I have
> been with thee whithersoever thou hast walked, and
> have cut off all thine enemies from before thee, and
> have made thee a name like the name of the great men
> that are in the earth.[1]

How eager the true believer is to know God's will for his
life. We know that for everyone there is a plan. The Scriptures dwell on the subject, but often the message is missed.
Those who have turned to the sacred pages for the promised
instructions and plan will be quick to testify that therein is
found the true science of guidance.

Men of faith have found the path divinely appointed.
Abraham learned that he must leave the complacency and
luxury of his home in the city of Ur of the Chaldees and
"go out into a place which he should after receive for an inheritance . . . and he went out, not knowing whither he
went. For he looked for a city which hath foundations,
whose builder and maker is God."[2] Moses had the choice of
the riches of Egypt or a life of wilderness wanderings,
"choosing rather to suffer affliction with the people of God,
than to enjoy the pleasures of sin for a season; esteeming
the reproach of Christ greater riches than the treasures of
Egypt."[3] Today's verse recalls the call of David when a
boy wearing a shepherd's coat and following the sheep, to a
path which led to the king's throne in Israel.

God's plan is a very personal thing. "As personal as your
own signature," said a handwriting expert. And that is personal; no two are alike. Surely God knows all about us.
He made us and He follows our movements. Our thoughts

and plans and deeds are before Him and nothing is hid from His sight. To individuals He says, "Wherefore be ye not unwise, but understanding what the will of the Lord is."[4] As Christians we are entitled to know what His will is for us.

The steps are simple but specific. First there must be a relationship to Jesus Christ. He must be our Saviour to be our Guide. Next we must live in fellowship with Him. "Let the word of Christ dwell in you richly."[5] His teachings must abide in us. Then we must have willing and responsive hearts. The promise follows: "Thine ears shall hear a word behind thee, saying, This is the way, walk ye in it."[6]

A God-planned life is the only happy one. "Blessed is the man that walketh not in the counsel of the ungodly . . . But his delight is in the law of the Lord . . . and whatsoever he doeth shall prosper."[7]

[1] I Chronicles 17:7-8.
[2] Hebrews 11:8, 10.
[3] Hebrews 11:25-26.
[4] Ephesians 5:17.
[5] Colossians 3:16.
[6] Isaiah 30:21.
[7] Psalm 1:1-3.

❧ ❧ ❧

I Chronicles 22–23
I Chronicles 22

> And David said, Solomon my son is young and tender,
> and the house that is to be builded for the Lord must
> be exceeding magnifical, of fame and of glory through-
> out all countries: I will therefore now make preparation
> for it. So David prepared abundantly before his death.[1]

EACH CHILD OF GOD is given the wonderful opportunity of
building every day for the kingdom of God, and "the house
. . . must be exceeding magnifical."

David's death was approaching and his son was young,
so he must make preparations for the house of the Lord.
The young are full of ideas, but wisdom most often comes
with age. The building must be so special that its fame
would spread throughout the world as a testimony to the
God of Israel. There could be no mistakes. Second best is
not good enough for the Lord.

What kind of building are we constructing? The United
States has recently taken inventory in the design, manufac-
ture and export of scores of products. When standards fail,
even in a small way, the total reputation of the fifty-one
states is impaired. Builders abroad may complain that products arrive with joints that do not fit, and that others are
made of inferior materials. Everyone suffers somewhat if a
faucet shipped to another country, marked "Made in USA,"
drips, or if a representative dishonestly depicts a product.

In the kingdom of God the same is true. A Christian who
offers inferior service is hurting Christendom around the
world. If precision and care are not consistent the divine
product we teach will soon be known only as "second best."
The statement has come to my hearing, "I don't like dealing with Christians. They rely on their Christianity rather
than on true character." What a stinging indictment, and
what a tragedy. A Christian is one in whom Christ lives.

Our bodies are temples of His Spirit. Does it not behoove us to build wisely, to add prayerfully to the inward beauties and graces that show what a believer is meant to be—one transformed by His power, a new creation?

As did David, so do we have a responsibility to help blueprint for those young and tender ones about us. In our church there is a father whose son made just a few dollars over the stipulated six hundred dollars one year. When it came to paying income tax it would have been so easy to alter the records, just minutely, but not this father. Though not a man of means, he said he would rather pay the full amount than have his son see him alter the record by one cent. Here is a wise father, building well for himself and for his family.

May we so build that the house of the Lord will be "exceeding magnifical."

[1] I Chronicles 22:5.

❧ ❧ ❧

I CHRONICLES 24–25
I CHRONICLES 25

> Moreover David and the captains of the host separated to the service of the sons of Asaph, and of Heman, and of Jeduthun, who should prophesy with harps, with psalteries, and with cymbals.[1]

LET US NEVER UNDERESTIMATE the value of music. In the Temple David had set apart musicians and had designated them for service. Each was consecrated to fulfill a sacred responsibility in the family of God. Their gifts, ministered in the Temple, brought them closer to God.

It is said that there is truly no division between the secular and the sacred. All employment should be usable in the kingdom of God. There were prophets in the Temple with their harps. They would help reveal the will of God to many through their music. Music has a special way of stimulating us to do a better job in a more dedicated way. The United States Army Recruiting Service made a survey in small towns. When the recruiters were preceded by a band, the interest was greater and the appeal much stronger than when they came in unnoticed. Few can hear a rousing march without wanting to respond! Music can also soothe the mind and bring calm. Undoubtedly these prophets sometimes played when tensions were high and adversities numerous, and the people were relaxed and refreshed.

But why the emphasis on music? It was for the glory of God. We are told there were about four thousand musicians in the Temple choirs and musical groups "to give thanks and to praise the Lord."[2]

Each can partake in this ministry of music. God is the reason for music within. "The Lord is my strength and song, and is become my salvation."[3]

> Singing I go, along life's road,
> Praising the Lord, praising the Lord,
> Singing I go, along life's road,
> For Jesus has lifted my load.[4]

"Let the word of Christ dwell in you richly in all wisdom; teaching and admonishing one another in psalms and hymns and spiritual songs, singing with grace in your hearts to the Lord."[5]

[1] I Chronicles 25:1.
[2] I Chronicles 25:3.
[3] Psalm 118:14.
[4] E. E. Hewitt.
[5] Colossians 3:16.

❧ ❧ ❧

I Chronicles 26–27
I Chronicles 26

> And of the Levites, Ahijah was over the treasures of
> the house of God, and over the treasures of the dedi-
> cated things.[1]

THE CHARGE of the treasurers of the Temple was important.
They were given the trust of receiving gifts to the Lord, and
"out of the spoils won in battles did they dedicate to maintain the house of the Lord."[2]

These men were made stewards in God's house, a position
in which each Christian finds himself. "Every good gift and
every perfect gift is from above."[3] We are not mere deposi-
tories of God's gifts; we are called to be wise dispensers,
making full use of our resources and talents. To the Corinthian church Paul wrote, "Let a man so account of us, as of
the ministers of Christ, and stewards of the mysteries of
God. Moreover it is required in stewards, that a man be
found faithful."[4]

"To maintain" the house of the Lord is more accurately
translated "to strengthen" the house of the Lord. This applies not just to the exterior of the building but to each
effort for God, and to the encouragement of those who come
to worship and serve. When funds are depleted, they must
be replenished.

Someone posed this provocative question: "As a treasurer
of your individual life, what is your present condition in relation to your potential in the kingdom of God?" By careful study of the Word, you can see if you are what you
ought to be. The Scripture calls us stewards. Webster de-
fines the duties of stewards thus: "An officer or employee in
a large family, or on a large estate, to manage the domestic
concerns, supervise servants, collect income, and keep accounts . . ."

We are members of the very large family of God in the

estate of mankind. There are many domestic concerns. Affairs at home and at work all must glorify the Master. With the supervision of the Holy Spirit, the areas may be conquered which would be displeasing to the One who called us to be stewards.

Collect income and keep accounts! That is a tall order but also a blessed privilege. A child of God caring is one sharing. "Bring ye all the tithes into the storehouse . . . and prove me now . . . if I will not open you the windows of heaven, and pour you out a blessing, that there shall not be room enough to receive it."[5] Keep accounts! We are completely accountable to God for everything. If He checks you up in your life, mind those checks and you'll be victorious.

Yesterday has been likened to a canceled check, tomorrow, a promissory note. Today must be wisely spent as a sacred trust to God.

[1]I Chronicles 26:20.　　　[4]I Corinthians 4:1-2.
[2]I Chronicles 26:27.　　　[5]Malachi 3:10.
[3]James 1:17.

❧　❧　❧

I CHRONICLES 28–29
I CHRONICLES 29

> For we are strangers before thee, and sojourners, as
> were all our fathers: our days on the earth are as a
> shadow, and there is none abiding.[1]

WE ALL ARE SOJOURNERS. We are born, we pass through life, and we die. It is not a pleasant thought for those who do not know Jesus Christ and have no hope of spending eternity with Him.

Our days are as a shadow. Job wrote, "Man . . . fleeth also as a shadow, and continueth not."[2] Swiftness, uncertainty, darkness! Said an old man who had seen life in its rawest form, "Shadows were my career." Solomon did some

200

deep thinking before he wrote, "For who knoweth what is good for man in this life, all the days of his vain life which he spendeth as a shadow? for who can tell a man what shall be after him under the sun?"[3]

Without Christ and without hope, life would be vain. But our Lord penetrated the darkness with light. The Psalmist lost his fear of shadows: "Yea, though I walk through the valley of the shadow of death, I will fear no evil, for thou art with me."[4]

David charged Solomon, "And thou, Solomon my son, know thou the God of thy father, and serve him with a perfect heart and with a willing mind."[5] David knew shadows would pursue his son and his days would quickly pass. He wanted to instill in his heart strength and courage in the Lord in order to abolish fear and forestall dismay. "The Lord God, even my God, will be with thee; he will not fail thee, nor forsake thee, until thou hast finished all the work for the service of the house of the Lord."[6] Solomon need not fear shadows.

The shadows of yesterday can be forgotten. We place all regrets and losses of the past in our Father's hand, and trust Him to blot out the transgressions with His blood. He remembers them no more! They are removed as far as east is from west, a distance never spanned.

Peace, joy, and blessing bring sunlight into the shadows, light reflected from the Son of Righteousness. We are grateful that our stay here is temporary and we long for eternity in the city of God.

> Show me Thy glory in shadows, I pray.
> My sojourn on earth swiftly passes away.
> In darkness give light; let Thy peace be mine;
> And forever, Lord, the praise will be Thine.

[1] I Chronicles 29:15.
[2] Job 14:1-2.
[3] Ecclesiastes 6:12.

[4] Psalm 23:4.
[5] I Chronicles 28:9.
[6] I Chronicles 28:20.

❧ ❧ ❧

May

II Chronicles 1–5
II Chronicles 2

> I build an house to the name of the Lord my God, to
> dedicate it to him.[1]

Second Chronicles begins with a review of and a reempha-
sis on Solomon's established kingdom and the building and
furnishing of the Temple. Solomon's wisdom was given
for practical purposes, to build and to govern and to do the
work of the Lord. In considering these chapters, we may
well survey our own homes. Have we built "to the name of
the Lord"?

In California there is a contractor who specializes in building rich and elegant homes. He is known in his profession
as a wise and brilliant builder. With his prosperity, however, he experienced poverty of soul. One evening he was
reading a magazine of his trade, and four lines were the
means of changing his life:

> They go to the forest for palm or pine,
>   the stuff for the humbler homes;
> The mountain gives up its valued gifts,
>   for the stately spires and domes:
> But whether they work with marble or sod,
> The builder is hand in hand with God.[2]

The contractor recognized he was not "hand in hand with
God," and the foundations on which he had established his
life and home were far from solid. He gathered his family
that very night and together they prayed for cleansing, then
asked God to take their hands in His. God did!

At once they determined their home would be Christian, and each dedicated himself to be a temple in which Christ could live. The outlook of former days was marvelously changed and their barrenness was transformed to fruitfulness.

In surveying our homes and our lives, are we building "to the name of the Lord"? It depends on where we focus our sight. Some see the dust of their feet, while others see the stars. Many see only a seed, while the perceptive see the flower wrapped within it. Some face shadows alone and in despair, while others face the sun, letting even their own shadows fall behind. Once the contractor had a futilitarian point of view. Then he focused upward and "built" and "dedicated" his all to Christ. In so doing he experienced that Christ is all and in all.

[1]II Chronicles 2:4.
[2]William Dunbar.

❦   ❦   ❦

II Chronicles 6–8
II Chronicles 7:12-22

> If my people, which are called by my name, shall humble themselves, and pray, and seek my face, and turn from their wicked ways; then will I hear from heaven, and will forgive their sin, and will heal their land.[1]

A TEACHER OFFERED a reward to any child who would complete a fourfold assignment. At the given time several of the youngsters brought the work in half completed. A couple did three of the four parts, but only one fulfilled all the requirements and received the award. Some considered the teacher unfair, feeling their work should also be acknowledged. Those who almost completed the work were unhappy that the reward was given only to the one who had done all. But the requirements could not be changed.

Today's verse has been called God's assignment for revival. It also is fourfold. As did the little children, some will partially complete the "duties," others may be willing to go a step farther. But God settles for nothing short of the total requirements. His reward is revival.

"If my people, which are called by my name, shall humble themselves." The Scripture tells us that "God resisteth the proud, but giveth grace to the humble."[2] Self is excluded when His true Spirit is included in every detail of the life, and that makes all the difference. Humility! He requires us to bow in subjection to His plan, not ours, and to seek direction as a yielded servant. It is said that those who build high must first dig deep. James said, "Humble yourselves in the sight of the Lord, and he shall lift you up."[3]

Prayer is the next requirement. When opportunity knocks, it is prayer that opens the door and lets the blessing in. "With men it is impossible, but not with God: for with God all things are possible."[4] To a young person who claimed the inefficiency of prayer a wise minister put the question, "Is prayer a habit or an emergency measure with you?" Develop the habit of regular, effectual, fervent prayer. Multitudes have learned that God is only a prayer away!

"Seek my face." A life of devotion is part of the program for revival. The personal devotion of men who have known revival or unusual evangelistic outreach towers high above others. Devotion ignited their zeal to make them torch-bearers of the true faith.

Repentance. True repentance means not only a heart broken for sin but a heart broken from sin. Throughout the history of Israel and that of Judah, God blessed those who not only sought Him but turned from their wicked ways.

One may be willing to pray, but prayer is not enough. God requires all four things to merit His reward, a "healed land."

[1]II Chronicles 7:14.
[2]James 4:6.
[3]James 4:10.
[4]Mark 10:27.

II Chronicles 9–12
II Chronicles 12

> And he did evil, because he prepared not his heart to
> seek the Lord.[1]

THERE IS DANGER in rendering lip service from a heart that is cold and unconcerned toward God. When King Rehoboam ascended the throne he had shown evidence that he would follow the steps of Solomon and of his father, David. However, when he was well established and strong, "he forsook the law of the Lord, and all of Israel with him."[2]

The reason for his evildoing is outlined. He acted as he did because his heart was not prepared. David knew the importance of heart preparation before the Lord. He had written, "Early will I seek thee."[3] To seek the Lord means to look for Him, and find Him, and listen to His voice. The search is not in vain, for our lives are changed by time spent with Him. "And ye shall seek me, and find me, when ye shall search for me with all your heart."[4] The search does not just involve the lip service that King Rehoboam gave, or a few scattered and unfulfilled intentions. Seeking involves the whole heart—a broken and contrite heart—which is completely open to Him. This is the beginning and price of godliness. "My son, forget not my law; but let thine heart keep my commandments. Trust in the Lord with all thine heart; and lean not unto thine own understanding. In all thy ways acknowledge him, and he shall direct thy paths."[5]

A resolved heart is a prepared heart, and glorifies the Lord. The consequence of a vacillating, unprepared heart is grave. Only evil can come from a heart that is not rightly related to God. One Puritan writer said, "External reformation only drives the heart further from God. Christian profession without possession is to none avail." St. Augustine said, "If you must flee from God, flee to Him!"

How seldom we acknowledge the fact that every step of our lives is either to Him or away from Him. Each action is for His glory or hurt. Every day the distance lessens or widens between us and Him.

What joy it is to have a heart prepared to love God's law and to meditate on it! When one with such a heart calls, He answers. When he seeks, he also finds; when he knocks, the door is opened.

God grant that none of us will "play church" or go through the motions of make-believe, as did King Rehoboam. May we lift our hearts toward the Lord—preparing to seek Him, to do good, and to depart from evil.

[1]II Chronicles 12:14.
[2]II Chronicles 12:1.
[3]Psalm 63:1.
[4]Jeremiah 29:13.
[5]Proverbs 3:1, 5-6.

❧ ❧ ❧

II Chronicles 13–16
II Chronicles 14

> And Asa did that which was good and right in the eyes
> of the Lord his God. And Asa cried unto the Lord his
> God, and said, Lord, it is nothing with thee to help,
> whether with many or with them that have no power:
> help us, O Lord our God; for we rest on thee, and in thy
> name we go against this multitude. O Lord, thou art our
> God; let not man prevail against thee.[1]

HOW MANY TIMES I have told the Lord that if circumstances
had been just a bit different, I was sure that He could have
worked out my situation. What immaturity! What folly
to "tell" Him anything. How well He knows us. "For the
eyes of the Lord run to and fro throughout the whole earth,
to shew himself strong in the behalf of them whose heart is
perfect toward him."[2] He not only knows the circumstances,
He has made them. More wonderful still, He can remove
them or improve them.

I remember a young athlete picturing God as the great
Talent Scout. He portrayed Him as searching the earth
for those who could do various jobs. It was a good picture
of a talent scout, but not of my God. He does not look for
achievement or attainment in us. We are not measured or
wanted because of our strength or our gifts. He looks for
those who will put His strength in the place of their weakness. Those who know that they have no power must rely
on Him. He does not expect us to show ourselves well. Instead He wants to show Himself strong on our behalf.
There is a difference!

God will make Himself strong on behalf of those whose
hearts have faith in Him. His strength and power are available, although too often they remain unused. The story
is told of a woman who for years had operated a power ma-
chine in a clothing company. She had always done piece-

work and was paid a small amount hourly plus a bonus for so much extra work. One day she was looking dismayed and a neighbor asked her why. She explained that she was looking for a new job. The neighbor wondered why a person so efficient would resign a job she had held for so long. The power operator explained that it was not lack of work or equipment. The problem was that the circuits were overloaded, so the company could allow only a few of their employees to work at a time. She was losing so much time waiting for her turn with the power that she felt the job was no longer worthwhile.

The problem in the factory is similar to the problem of many Christians. There is adequate machinery but not adequate power, though all the while the Lord is waiting to show Himself strong, to exert His power. All the qualifications we have and all the materials available are not enough without His power. God's "circuits" are never overloaded. He is readily available and knows no insufficiency. Let us appropriate these divine resources and live and work for His glory.

[1]II Chronicles 14:2, 11.
[2]II Chronicles 16:9.

❧ ❧ ❧

II CHRONICLES 17–19
II CHRONICLES 17

> And his heart was lifted up in the ways of the Lord:
> moreover he took away the high places and groves out
> of Judah.[1]

JEHOSHAPHAT made a sincere and wise beginning. Immediately he "strengthened himself against Israel."[2] He walked in the ways of his father David, which fact gives him a good reputation. The surrounding nations had their various gods and Baals, but Jehoshaphat sought the Lord God. Thus the Lord allowed him to establish his kingdom.

This verse warms the heart. Here was a man who lifted up his heart in the ways of the Lord. As one minister put it, "His heart was really in his work, and his work was the work of the Lord!" A heart in the Lord's work is an enlarged heart and an encouraged heart.

We have a friend who never feels she can do enough for the Lord or for her friends. She is "fervent in spirit; serving the Lord."[3] She constantly bubbles. Her cup runs over. Joy and blessing are constantly flowing from an abundant reserve. She has a happy, affectionate relationship with Jesus Christ and it stems from an enlarged heart in the ways of the Lord. She is not exempt from problems, but she is above them. Her burdens are multiplied, but they are carried on wings of prayer. Disappointments? I've never heard of one with so many. But she accepts them as God's appointments and in so doing looks up to give thanks in the midst of adversity. She is an example of a genuine Christian.

Jehoshaphat was not only a wise man with a good heart but he was also a man of accomplishment. "Moreover he took away the high places and groves out of Judah." He removed the idols. He replaced the false teachers with true men of God. The infiltration of evil was exchanged for the infiltration of good. Those in the cities of Judah were to be taught in the right way—in the ways of the Lord.

God's blessing comes with obedience, but it can quickly be lost by disobedience. Jehoshaphat's riches increased, but not his wisdom. We are warned to take heed while we stand, lest we fall. Unfortunately, Jehoshaphat became enamored with material things, and his wise beginnings were not continued.

May we take solemn note and resolve not only to begin with the Lord but to daily continue in His ways.

¹II Chronicles 17:6.
²II Chronicles 17:1.
³Romans 12:11.

❧ ❧ ❧

May 6

II Chronicles 20–23
II Chronicles 20

Neither know we what to do: but our eyes are upon thee.¹

THE STORY OF JEHOSHAPHAT can find a parallel in our lives today. "And Jehoshaphat feared, and set himself to seek the Lord."² Have you not often been afraid? Afraid of what tomorrow would bring, or afraid of the future for a loved one? Fears concerning the provision of the needs of the family both physically and spiritually are often expressed.

Jehoshaphat had his days of being tied in those fear knots. But fear led him to prayer: "O Lord God of our fathers, art not thou God in heaven? and rulest not thou over all the kingdoms of the heathen? and in thine hand is there not power and might, so that none is able to withstand thee?"³ He reminded God of His promises. Have we not done this also? Many a night I have written down promise after promise and inserted my own name. It may have been for guidance, or growing faith, or just for courage. Personalizing makes the impression deeper in our hearts, and reminds us that His promises are meant for our individual needs.

In his dilemma of fear Jehoshaphat's only resource was to look up. There is much evidence that man is taller on his knees! It is from hallowed prayer ground that we look up and see One who is acquainted with our needs and who directs the battle before us.

A national park ranger tells the story of a little six-year-old boy whom he found in the dawn hours in the forest. He was fast asleep in an upright position, with his little head resting on a rock and tilted slightly upward. The child and parents later disclosed this story: After the boy had become separated from the family, he had seen an animal and set off to chase it. The mother thought he was with the father, and the father was certain the son was with the mother. Thus many hours went by before they discovered that the child was lost. They searched in many directions until dark. When the boy had been found and his position noted by the ranger, the explanation was quite simple. The boy had been told, "When you don't know what to do, look up." He had kept looking up. The tops of the trees had been fascinating, and when dusk came, the twinkling stars were even more so. However, above them all, he knew, was Someone called Jesus. He had sung under the stars that night:

> Jesus loves me! This I know,
> For the Bible tells me so.
> Little ones to Him belong.
> They are weak but He is strong.

Jehoshaphat was lost and surrounded but not baffled when he wrote these words in Scripture, for he looked up!

[1]II Chronicles 20:12.   [3]II Chronicles 20:6.
[2]II Chronicles 20:3.

II CHRONICLES 24–26
II CHRONICLES 25

> Amaziah was twenty and five years old when he began
> to reign, . . . And he did that which was right in the
> sight of the Lord, but not with a perfect heart. And
> Amaziah said to the man of God, But what shall we do
> for the hundred talents which I have given to the army
> of Israel? And the man of God answered, The Lord is
> able to give thee much more than this.[1]

WE ARE NOT ABOVE seeking human help at times when there
is a crisis, even though we well know that the battle is the
Lord's. Sometimes we feel that a few extras can be held
aside and victory will be more certain. Why are we finite
creatures given to such rationalization when superhuman
strength is available from One greater than any opposition?

As with so many other kings and judges, Amaziah served
the Lord but not with all his heart. He was paying for an
army when the Lord was able to give much more!

As a very young child I remember hearing Gypsy Smith.
One of his stories was kept alive in my mind by reading his
book, and it illustrates the great provision of God for this
unusual evangelist while he was young.

His father and mother had always followed the gypsy way
of life. The father played his fiddle in saloons or public
places to make a living. Then one day he was wonderfully
converted to Jesus Christ. How true is the scripture "Therefore if any man be in Christ he is a new creature: old things
are passed away; behold, all things are become new."[2] To
the father, the "old things" meant fiddle-playing in ques-
tionable places. However, he had a grave problem. The
mother had passed away and he had several small children
to provide for in the "new" way.

One Christmas season the little caravan was sadly lacking
in supplies. One of the children asked, "What will we have

for Christmas dinner?" The father replied that he did not know but would talk to the Lord about it. What a temptation it was to look up on the wall of the gypsy wagon and see the fiddle. By taking things into his own hands he could surely have raised the money needed for provisions. However, old things had passed away, and he must live the new way. He prayed again, and after the prayer announced to the children that they would sing, and sing they did until a knock came at the door. A missionary brought information that an abundance of food and supplies was waiting for them at a certain shop in town. There was so much that it took a wheelbarrow to carry it back to the gypsy wagon.

The Lord provides for His children, and His giving is ever-increasing—in life and in death. Did not the Apostle Paul write, "For to me to live is Christ, and to die is gain"?[3]

[1] II Chronicles 25:1-2, 9.
[2] II Corinthians 5:17.
[3] Philippians 1:21.

❦ ❦ ❦

II Chronicles 27–29
II Chronicles 29

> My sons, be not now negligent: for the Lord hath
> chosen you to stand before him, to serve him, and that
> ye should minister unto him, and burn incense.[1]

OH, THE DANGER of being negligent—even just a little negligent. How well one mother realized this after leaving some
sleeping pills within reach of her two-year-old. It was an
oversight, but she lost her son.

A simple cold persists, but there is so much to do, so we
work on. Neglect, yes, but we shrug and say, "It always gets
better." This time things are different, and a long siege
with pneumonia results from a "little" cold.

The Levites were chosen to stand before the Lord and to
serve Him. They must not be negligent, even in the smallest tasks. Remember Ahaz the king? He had neglected his
heart. The little sins grew, and he drove out the workers
in the Temple. He cut up the gold vessels and closed the
Temple. The judgment of God fell on the nation. It was
inevitable.

Then the son of Ahaz came to the throne. Hezekiah
might have been hindered by the memory of his father who
was gravely negligent. Instead, he took heed to the things
that were most important. He opened the Temple that had
been closed for years, and he instructed the priests to clean
out and renovate it. There was not much to encourage
Hezekiah, for the Scriptures tell us that the Temple had
been shut for sixteen years. Think of the cobwebs, the dust
and deterioration, that would characterize the place after
such disuse.

Some rural missionaries told of going into a little coastal
village where the people had neglected the church for a
long time. First had come the little sins, such as lack of
attendance and decreased giving. But little by little neglect

grew until the building was closed and boarded up. Into the neighborhood came Christians. Their hearts were heavy that the "temple was closed" and they began to work to prepare for the time when a minister would come. How their hearts rejoiced on the day the church was reopened, scrubbed, polished, and readied for worship. How they praised God when the song of worship ascended again in that house of the Lord.

This modern illustration gives us a picture of the day described in today's reading. The Temple was prepared for worship. The cymbals, the harps, the trumpets were all ready. "And Hezekiah commanded to offer the burnt-offering upon the altar. And when the burnt-offering began, the song of the Lord began."[2]

The negligence was put away, the repairs were made, and the once-silent Temple was filled with song. May we never neglect the work God has assigned us. Faithfully let us minister in our daily tasks with a glad, unceasing song of praise.

[1]II Chronicles 29:11.
[2]II Chronicles 29:27.

❧ ❧ ❧

May 9

II Chronicles 30–32
II Chronicles 32

> Be strong and courageous, be not afraid nor dismayed for the king of Assyria, nor for all the multitude that is with him: for there be more with us than with him: with him is an arm of flesh; but with us is the Lord our God to help us, and to fight our battles. And the people rested themselves upon the words of Hezekiah king of Judah.[1]

Think of the encouragement Hezekiah gave to his people. They listened and learned. They rested in the Lord. What a position! Amid the confusion and terror caused by the strong enemy—to rest. The king's words made the difference.

"In the world ye shall have tribulation: but be of good cheer; I have overcome the world."[2] These are words spoken to us by the King of kings. No matter what the circumstances, He has promised, "Lo, I am with you alway."[3] How essential that we pause to listen and, in hearing, find rest.

Consider the turmoil that would have prevailed among the people of Judah if Hezekiah had not shown his unfailing faith in God. He made careful preparations, as a good soldier will do, thus putting feet to his faith. But his assurance was not in the cutoff water supply nor in the fortifications. It was in the God he trusted. Here alone was rest.

When we as Christians become upset inside and find rest a less-than-frequent reality, it is time to check and see if we are really paying attention to our King. Restlessness comes from neglecting what He has been trying to say to us. It comes from decreased devotion. He speaks, but we do not hear. We become restless.

As we read and study the Word, let us take time to pause and let God speak to us. In so doing there is rest and refreshment. His strength is just as available at times of crisis as when all is calm. Shut out the noise without and let Him speak within. Here is the source of the encouragement, strength, courage, and rest that the arm of flesh cannot give. "With us is the Lord our God to help us, and to fight our battles. And the people rested themselves upon the words of . . . [the] king."

> We rest on Thee, our Shield and our Defender.
> We go not forth alone against the foe.
> Strong in Thy strength, safe in Thy keeping tender,
> We rest on Thee, and in Thy name we go.[4]

[1]II Chronicles 32:7-8. [3]Matthew 28:20.
[2]John 16:33. [4]Edith Gilling Cherry.

🍂 🍂 🍂

217

> Because thine heart was tender, and thou didst humble thyself before God, . . . I have even heard thee also, saith the Lord.[1]

IN THIS CHAPTER we read of a young king's noble guidance of his people. Josiah's heart was toward the Lord. He sought to fulfill the law, not with any individual interpretation but by submitting himself fully to it.

Today it is so easy to say, "Everybody's doing it—even Christians," and to engage in something which Scripture forbids, because others have lowered the barriers. The law has been given as a mirror that we may see ourselves as we are in God's sight. It takes a tender heart and a humble spirit to subject oneself to such scrutiny.

How much we stand in need of humble hearts and feelings tender toward others. It is said that everyone has a heartache, and the longer we live the more we realize this. We Christians need a new sensitivity toward loneliness and the needs of others. We need empathy and understanding.

In your own circle of friends there are no doubt many who have specific needs which they hesitate to share. One may have a child who is away from home and far from the Lord. Only a mother knows the anguish that comes from uncertainty about her children. How quickly an outsider may say, "Commit it to the Lord." True, but God gave us friends to share burdens. "Bear ye one another's burdens, and so fulfill the law of Christ."[2]

I have a precious friend who continually ministers to a blind woman. Her time is no longer her own, for her compassion has been so imparted that the sightless one has become dependent. Many admire the stalwart Christian for her service, but amazingly few have shared the load. We are told to minister to the widows, the orphans, the fatherless, the blind, and the afflicted—and there is reward. "Inasmuch as ye have done it unto one of the least of these my brethren, ye have done it unto me."[3] It may be lack of tenderness that stops us from fulfilling the law of love.

Pastors, those ministering to us spiritually, often have needs of their own. So often, as shepherds of the flock, they sit in ivory towers, but we forget that the shepherd as well as the sheep needs refreshing and restoring. Are we unaware or untender toward these? How much time is spent praying for their physical and spiritual renewing?

The Lord heard Josiah and was with him because his heart was open and responsive to the needs of those about him. He not only prayed but he was sensitive, and his response strengthened the nation.

May we have tender hearts, open and responsive to what God commands.

[1] II Chronicles 34:27.
[2] Galatians 6:2.
[3] Matthew 25:40.

❧ ❧ ❧

May 11

Ezra 1–2
Ezra 1

> Then rose up the chief of the fathers of Judah and Benjamin, and the priests, and the Levites, with all them whose spirit God had raised, to go up to build the house of the Lord which is in Jerusalem. And all they that were about them strengthened their hands.[1]

IN THIS BOOK of Ezra, we have a continuation of the story of the Jewish people which we read in Chronicles, which ended with their being taken into captivity. But God delivered them by moving the heart of the king of Persia to allow them to go and rebuild their Temple in Jerusalem and worship God. It was Ezra, a child of captivity, an unusual scribe and student, who taught the people and helped them rebuild their Temple. He was fitted for this work by his prepared heart and his great knowledge of the law of God. Some call him the first real preacher in Israel. How he loved books and, above all, the book of the law!

In church history, Ezra's parallel is found in men like John Calvin. Amid great pressures and problems John Calvin set up Geneva as a city of God. This was not accomplished without difficulties and great dangers, but Calvin carried through a marvelous venture for the glory of God in Geneva. Ezra faced similar difficulties, but he too persevered with the help of God, and Jerusalem became, for a time, a city of God.

How fully are our minds subject to God's promptings today? How long has it been since your spirit was "raised," with the result that you started "building" for the glory of God? Such work entails sacrifice and self-renunciation, and it is not exempt from frustration and pressure, but we may trust God for the results.

Ezra was an example to each man of God who followed. His reading and discerning of the law produced fruit as it strengthened those whom he taught. His prayer life was one to be studied and followed. Not only could the great men of faith throughout history benefit from Ezra. We today can also benefit from his life. Each of us must take time to thoughtfully and prayerfully read God's Word and earnestly seek Him in believing prayer. Then, as ministers of God's grace and with the Spirit's guidance we can "feed . . . [others] with knowledge and understanding."[2]

[1] Ezra 1:5-6.
[2] Jeremiah 3:15.

     ❧   ❧   ❧

EZRA 3–6
EZRA 6

> And that which they have need of, . . . let it be given
> them day by day without fail.[1]

WHAT A DECREE King Darius had made during this time of
Ezra's working with the people of God. What would they
need? Young bullocks, rams, lambs for burnt offerings;
wheat, salt, oil. All these they would be given. God never
fails an obedient and trusting people. How well this is illustrated in this chapter.

What is your need today? Are you asked to sacrifice
something for God's glory? Think of Abraham in obedience
taking his son of promise, Isaac, to be given to God. "Where
is the sacrifice?" questioned the child, and the answer came
back, "God will provide." Darius provided for the sacrifices of the people of God with young bullocks, rams, and
lambs. God has provided for you also. Possibly you need
a good look at the Lamb of God, our true Sacrifice for sin.
In looking at Him by faith, you will find forgiveness of sin
and new life.

Darius the king gave wheat to the people. It is possible
you stand in need of provision physically and spiritually.
"My God shall supply all your needs according to his riches
in glory by Christ Jesus."[2] How bountiful is His provision
for time and for eternity!

King Darius offered salt to the people of God. We consider salt a daily necessity. How flavorless food is without
salt. Remember in II Kings when the salt was cast into the
poor water and the waters were healed? God must so deal
in our lives by His Spirit. Possibly your soul is agitated by
sin or by an unjust action. Selfish reaction makes the waters
bitter. The Holy Spirit convicts by the Word, and that
irritates and causes discomfort. But there is healing in believing and obeying God's Word. As youngsters we used to

put salt on sores in our mouths. At first it would smart but soon it was better. God's Word is like salt in that it pricks and penetrates; but as we yield to it, how beneficial it is.

Oil! The people were provided with an abundance of oil. The oil of the Holy Spirit makes any Christian life run smoother. The cogs of our wheels sometimes stick. What a difference His oil makes in our lives and ministries.

"And that which they have need of." Whatever your need is today, the King has it available. "Let it be given . . . without fail."

[1]Ezra 6:9.
[2]Philippians 4:19.

❧ ❧ ❧

Ezra 7–8
Ezra 7

> For Ezra had prepared his heart to seek the law of the Lord, and to do it, and to teach in Israel statutes and judgments.[1]

A NEW CHRISTIAN asked her minister how she could become a good Sunday school teacher. She was willing to work hard and do whatever would be necessary. The minister gave her the example of Ezra. His example should be followed not only by those who would teach or preach but by all who would be useful in the kingdom of God.

The instructions are almost elementary. Christ in your life is the first certainty that must be established. Then a willing and loving heart must follow, with complete trust in His guidance and explicit obedience to His Word.

Ezra knew the God of Israel. His was a rich experience. He was "a ready scribe in the law of Moses, which the Lord God . . . had given."[2] He had shown his love and trust in God through the long and difficult journey he had taken.

There had been times of peril, but the hand of God was truly upon him. Today, a personal relationship with Jesus Christ is essential. To us who would teach, He must not just be known as the great Teacher, or Example, but also as our Saviour.

Ezra's heart was willing and prepared. He had long been in preparation for the very day when he would lead the people. He took the scrolls and studied them to find the messages of God contained therein. He resolutely determined to know the mind of God. He learned "to teach in Israel statutes and judgments" by precept and example. To teach, one must know what is to be taught.

Ezra trusted in God to illumine his mind. He sought the law, he meditated in it, he thought upon it, and he wrestled with things he did not understand. In searching the Scriptures we too will find truth. Ezra sought truth in a manner pleasing to God. He was not searching for contradictions or problems, as some today are apt to do. He sought to teach the whole undefiled law.

Ezra, a man of distinguished ancestry and attainments, could well have sought other sources of wisdom and truth. But no, he knew that God was truth and he followed the exhortation "Acquaint now thyself with him, and be at peace."[3] He was not just seeking for seeking's sake but "to do it." This is real obedience.

As a teacher, Ezra was a graphic example. Make the truth your own, practice it in your own life, and then impart it to others. The diligent search for and discovery of truth are essential to teaching, also being a good example by your own life. "Whosoever shall do and teach them, the same shall be called great in the kingdom of heaven."[4]

[1]Ezra 7:10.
[2]Ezra 7:6.
[3]Job 22:21.
[4]Matthew 5:19.

❧ ❧ ❧

EZRA 9–10
EZRA 9:1–10:2

> I fell upon my knees, and spread out my hands unto the
> Lord my God, and said, O my God, I am ashamed and
> blush to lift up my face to thee, my God: for our iniqui-
> ties are increased over our head, and our trespass is
> grown up unto the heavens.[1]

EZRA'S INTENSE CONCERN for the people was similar to Jeremiah's concern of some sixty years before. Both sought the
Lord in reverent apology for the iniquities of their nation.
Both were incensed. They felt a sacred hatred for sin.
Wrote Jeremiah, "Were they ashamed when they had committed abomination? nay, they were not at all ashamed,
neither could they blush: therefore they shall fall among
them that fall: at the time that I visit them they shall be
cast down, saith the Lord. Thus saith the Lord, Stand ye
in the ways, and see, and ask for the old paths, where is the
good way, and walk therein, and ye shall find rest for your
souls. But they said, We will not walk therein."[2]

How true but sad is the statement that too many wink at
sin when they should be weeping. Our sin separates us
from God. If we regard or cherish iniquity in our hearts
the Lord has said He will not hear. He is as one cut off,
until the sin is confessed and communication is reestab-
lished.

Most Christians often pray the Lord's Prayer. How meaningful are the words to us, "Deliver us from evil"?[3] Is there
an eagerness to be kept by the power of God, to be kept
from evil things, to be delivered from ourselves and our
own wicked inclinations? Deliverance is possible because
Jesus Christ "gave himself for our sins, that he might deliver us from this present evil world."[4] The present world
is an evil world, but He is strong to deliver.

How enamored are we with the ways of the world? Do

we esteem the pleasures and sins which are only for a season more than the riches of God which are eternal? We should thoroughly sift our motives as did David, and make our prayer his: "Search me, O God, and know my heart: try me, and know my thoughts: and see if there be any wicked way in me, and lead me in the way everlasting."[5]

Do we blush to speak our Lord's name? Do our hearts truly "seek good, and not evil"?[6] Let us remember that "he that overcometh shall inherit all things."[7]

[1]Ezra 9:5-6.
[2]Jeremiah 6:15-16.
[3]Matthew 6:13.
[4]Galatians 1:4.
[5]Psalm 139:23-24.
[6]Amos 5:14.
[7]Revelation 21:7.

❧ ❧ ❧

May 15

NEHEMIAH 1-4
NEHEMIAH 1

O Lord, I beseech thee, let now thine ear be attentive to the prayer of thy servant.[1]

NEHEMIAH WAS WELL EMPLOYED. As the king's cupbearer he was surrounded with luxury. He held a high position in the imperial court. He went about his job faithfully, even though his heart was heavy. He prayed to God, confessing his sins and those of his people. Then he presented his request to the king. Nehemiah interceded with God and with the king for God's people. Then he left the matter in God's hand.

God granted Nehemiah favor with the king, who gave him permission to return to Jerusalem, the city of his fathers, and to rebuild it. Nehemiah's attitude of faith has been described as first cautious and then courageous. He was cautious in approaching the walls of Jerusalem to view them, for very few were with him and he was not ready to share the details of his mission. He wrote, "Neither told I any man what my God had put in my heart to do at Jerusalem."[2] But much courage followed his caution. He started the work at once. The achievements of faith are great.

Nehemiah shared the work with the people and the response was ready, eager, and willing workers. They said, "Let us rise up and build. So they strengthened their hands for this good work."[3] There was no loitering among Nehemiah's men. They were builders. Scripture quotes his words: "So we laboured in the work . . . from the rising of the morning till the stars appeared."[4] They put in a full day. Those who did their jobs well were recorded in writing to this day. There were a few who are remembered only because they "put not their necks to the work of their Lord."[5]

The God of Nehemiah commissions us to build for Him today. We, too, have been given the warning to work, for the night approaches. What do we build? Lives that are pleasing to the Lord and effective for His service? Homes that are centered about Jesus Christ and His teachings? Churches which become the focal points of our cities and communities? These are big undertakings. But Nehemiah, an ordinary man with superordinary zeal and love for the Lord, proved that such work can be done.

Marcus Aurelius left us some provocative words: "In the morning when thou findest thyself unwilling to rise, consider thyself presently, if it is to go about a man's work, that I am stirred up; or was I made for this, to lay me down and make much of myself in a warm bed!"

May our prayers take action. "Rise up and build."

[1] Nehemiah 1:11.
[2] Nehemiah 2:12.
[3] Nehemiah 2:18.
[4] Nehemiah 4:21.
[5] Nehemiah 3:5.

Nehemiah 5–7
Nehemiah 6

> And I said, Should such a man as I flee? and who is
> there, that, being as I am, would go into the temple to
> save his life? I will not go in.[1]

RECENTLY A MOTHER was prosecuted for telling her child, in
a thoughtless and agitated moment, to "go play in traffic."
Unfortunately the child obeyed her sarcastic injunction and
was seriously injured. The judge explained that life was
so continually beset by danger that thoughtlessness was not
sufficient excuse to warrant pardon.

How true it is that dangers seen and unseen lie in our
path each day. We must pray for wisdom and discernment
to know what is right, and we must seek the protection of
the One who cares for us.

Nehemiah was a man surrounded by danger in his rebuilding Jerusalem. He had his share of obstacles and
heckling. There were those who tried to deceive him to
hinder his efforts, but the Lord helped him discern the right
from the wrong. Some were simply jealous of the prosperity
which the king's cupbearer had in the task God had given
him to do, and purposely placed danger in his way. To
those who sought to entice or deceive him he spoke firmly.
"There are no such things done as thou sayest, but thou
feignest them out of thine own heart." At once he turned
again to the Lord and prayed, "O God, strengthen my
hands."[2]

Christians are often faced with subtle situations. There
are those who would deceive us. The deceitful ones suggested to Nehemiah that they meet together in the Temple
for worship. How often the house of the Lord has been mis-
used! Yet when Nehemiah spoke, he spoke with the authority of the Lord, refusing protection from personal danger. He said in essence, "Should such a man as I flee? Why,

when I have Jehovah with me, and His power can cast an army aside? Why, when I have been given a specific job to do? Should I waste time with those who would undo or slow down the progress of God's work? My job is for the living God. I am His servant. I must give an account to Him of my time and labor."

Should we not count it a great privilege to stand fast for Christ when the enemy would seek to destroy? Paul had his enemies and his dangers. But he refused to flee from them. He wrote confidently, "And in nothing terrified by your adversaries: which is to them an evident token of perdition, but to you of salvation, and that of God. For unto you it is given in the behalf of Christ, not only to believe on him, but also to suffer for his sake."[3]

Dangers? Yes, but they must not prevent our progress in fulfilling the King's business.

[1]Nehemiah 6:11.
[2]Nehemiah 6:8-9.
[3]Philippians 1:28-29.

❧ ❧ ❧

May 17

NEHEMIAH 8–10
NEHEMIAH 8

> Then he said unto them, Go your way, eat the fat, and drink the sweet, and send portions unto them for whom nothing is prepared: for this day is holy unto our Lord: neither be ye sorry; for the joy of the Lord is your strength.[1]

AS A RESULT of continued disobedience, the children of Israel had been exiled from their own land for seventy years. Their bread had been the bread of bondage, their way was one of uncertainty, they had no homes and no place to worship. One can only neglect the law of God for so long and worship contrary to His instructions. Repentance must

228

come, and only then will He deliver. The remnant had been led back and, under Nehemiah, had rebuilt the city. What a day of rejoicing there was when, after all the years of exile, the Temple was once more open for worship and the Word of God was read! No doubt Ezra, the ready scribe, had made available copies of the law of Moses. This special day could be classed as a day of revival.

What a graphic picture is given of the feast those people had that day: "Eat the fat, drink the sweet, and send portions unto them for whom nothing is prepared." Nehemiah's message should sink into our hearts, for we never leave the presence of God without this threefold experience.

"Eat the fat." Truly we are to feed on the Word of God. We may start out with the "sincere milk of the word,"[2] but we must mature, grow, and be fed from Him. A solid diet of Scripture has a tremendously strengthening effect on any Christian.

"Drink the sweet." How sobering to hear a man of God explain that many may glory in their "strength" in the Lord, but they miss the "sweetness" which He has for them. There is little merit in being strong, if we are not sweet!

"Send portions to those for whom nothing is prepared." When the cup is filled, it runs over and over and cannot help but spill on that one next door to you. The person who sits at the next desk will share in the blessed experience when you recognize that portions are to go to those who need them.

Revival sends people out with a message to those who have never heard. Revival in individual hearts strengthens and sweetens, and it results in sharing! Then every day is holy unto the Lord, and the "joy of the Lord is your strength."

[1]Nehemiah 8:10.
[2]I Peter 2:2.

❧ ❧ ❧

229

NEHEMIAH 11–13
NEHEMIAH 13

Remember me, O my God, for good.[1]

NEHEMIAH HAD BEEN FAITHFUL. These few words are his last recorded prayer. What he says here is great, but its implications are greater when we realize that remembering God was his constant experience. He truly practiced the presence of God until God was as close as breath itself, not only in the solitude of his private devotion but during the rebuilding of the Temple. Walking down the streets, helping build the walls, seeking direction and instruction, and just visiting with God, were natural experiences. We know that he was in the habit of remembering God or the prayer would never have been uttered.

"We are what our thoughts are," is a common saying. In the Christian life this is very true. If our thoughts are continually on the Lord and His mercies and goodness, so that we are continually rejoicing in Him, it shows in our Christian character. It has been said that "Nehemiah's remembrance of God was spontaneous and free: it sprang up on all occasions, like water from a fountain, or music from a bird, or light from the sun. It was part of a life—the life of faith and devotion: a life hid with Christ in God."[2]

When we take communion, we hear the familiar words, "This do in remembrance of me." How often do we really have remembrance of Him? Was this special gift of remembering God imparted only to Nehemiah? No, no! It is for us if we will take the time and foster the determination to learn to remember Him. It must be cultivated. It must be daily developed. It does not come in a few minutes or weeks, but the rewards are eternal. "Yea, in the way of thy judgments, O Lord, have we waited for thee; the desire of our souls is to thy name, and to the remembrance of thee."[3]

230

Remembrance of God is not quick or easy to attain, but it is possible and exceedingly profitable.

I was slow to realize that all men of God through the centuries—patriarchs, prophets, reformers, martyrs, ministers, and laymen—have had hindrances to devotion in their lives. But they have overcome. They will inherit the kingdom. And we may too!

Scholars point out that there was no Pharisaism in Nehemiah. His first prayer and his last were made in humility. He made no claims to merit, but looked for mercy. He *was* remembered!

[1]Nehemiah 13:31.
[2]J. H. Goodman.
[3]Isaiah 26:8.

❧ ❧ ❧

ESTHER 1–4
ESTHER 4

> And who knoweth whether thou art come to the kingdom for such a time as this?[1]

AS WE STUDY the Bible we become increasingly aware that God plans to win men through men. Throughout the history of Israel we see those who were destined to assume leadership. In Esther's time there was also a deliverer for those who relied on God. In our time, there is One who directs our affairs, choosing whom He will to introduce those in bondage to freedom in Christ.

God guides the affairs of men. He is not surprised by world events. Before a conflict arises, He has His hand on a leader. One would be foolish to suspect that George Washington merely appeared on the scene when the tyranny of George the Third threatened liberty. He did not just rise to the occasion. He was well grounded and prepared for the task. So, day by day we are being trained in the forces of the almighty God, to be used when and where He desires. God's circle of influence is not limited. He may be forging you for "such a time as this."

Esther had great influence and power. An unusual privilege and opportunity had been granted to her. On the other hand, her people were doomed to death and in great peril. A thoughtful heart recognizes this situation of "opportunity versus extremity." However, "man's extremity is God's opportunity," and Esther had been prepared to be a leader. When opportunity and extremity are brought together, what is impossible for everyone else always proves possible for our God.

What utter tragedy it would have been if Esther had missed her oportunity! The price may have seemed high for redemption, but Esther was willing. What if Jesus Christ had missed His opportunity? Mankind would have been doomed to death and eternity without God.

You may feel that your scope of opportunity is small. Perhaps the extremity that comes into your life does not entail life or death. If you miss, maybe only one would pass into eternity without hope. Is that so tragic?

This *you* must answer. Discover your influence in the service of God and the opportunities He has given you, and in faith fulfill each. You will find yourself greatly used for "such a time as this."

¹Esther 4:14.

❧ ❧ ❧

> Then said the king unto her, What wilt thou, queen
> Esther? and what is thy request? it shall be even given
> thee to the half of the kingdom.[1]

A MOVING SKETCH of Queen Esther before the king, who is
holding out his golden scepter, is superimposed on a larger
sketch of the King of kings with His hand outstretched. The
caption speaks of the larger illustration and says, "Dost thou
want nothing, O poor soul?"

Esther had approached her king with great courage. The
scepter held out meant that she was accepted, and she gave
her request. Time passed, and she gave it again. Her peti-
tion was laid fully before the king, and it was granted.

Why are we, as children of God, so fearful to go before
Him with our petitions? We have a Mediator, the Man
Christ Jesus, who is ever ready to make intercession for us.
His arm is outstretched to receive us, and the result of asking is receiving. "Dost thou want nothing, O poor soul?"
Is there nothing you have to ask? Does the Father not know
that your heart is breaking with requests and your needs are
great? Do not wait. Present them all to Him. When you
pour out your request to Him it goes from your heart to the
heart of God. If you have seen His generosity before, you
will see it again, and He does not withhold that which you
should have. "Cast thy burden upon the Lord, and he shall
sustain thee."[2]

In doing this we must be willing for the Lord to ask us
this question: "What wilt thou that I shall do unto thee?"[3]
When we tell Him our needs, we must in return give Him
obedient hearts and wills. Trust and faith are required of
us. We must express our love to Him. If we want His answer, we must do what He requires.

What does He require of me? "Fear the Lord thy God,

. . . walk in all his ways, and . . . love him, and . . . serve the Lord thy God with all thy heart and with all thy soul."⁴

The scepter was outstretched. Esther drew near and touched the top of it. "What wilt thou, queen Esther? . . . it shall be given thee to the half of the kingdom." His hand, the almighty Hand of our God, is reached toward us. Come near, child of the heavenly Father. Your step of faith brings you to the hand of God. He grants not just a part but all to those who are His own.

¹Esther 5:3.
²Psalm 55:22.
³Luke 18:41.
⁴Deuteronomy 10:12.

❧ ❧ ❧

May 21

JOB 1–5
JOB 1

> There was a man in the land of Uz, whose name was Job; and that man was perfect and upright, and one that feared God, and eschewed evil.¹

JOB IS PICTURED as the real person that he was. He was not a fictitious man but real. His character, his family, and his position find parallels in people we may know. We catch a glimpse of his private life and see that he loved the Lord and hated evil. It is said that "earth is the theater where the godly man is tried." Job was about to be tried and his human experience is shared with us in the book called by his name.

"Now there was a day . . ."² We read about some of Job's grave trials, and then see the phrase repeated: "Again there was a day . . ."³ Job lost his wealth and within a short time was reduced to poverty. Then he lost his children. His good health left him. He lost the sympathy of his wife, who proclaimed, "Curse God and die."⁴ His friends became fewer and he lost his sense of relationship with God, but he had not lost God.

A mother once sat outside a hospital emergency room. Her face was haggard and she was exhausted. "This was a day," she mournfully acknowledged, "a day to remember no more." I was in the hospital about a month later and a nurse knew I had made acquaintance with this sorrowing mother. She told me that "again there was a day," and that within those few weeks three of her children had been critically ill, and one had died. Their father had left her. Her self-respect was gone. How well she could comprehend the words of Job's story, for she too had been reduced to nothing.

Those "days" are bound to find their way into our calendars. Unfortunately, they are never announced in advance. They come without warning. But they come! And the strain and pain of their presence seem unbearable. More than a century ago a writer explained, "It is only through the temporary exclusion of light that we come to know what light is. To finite comprehension there is no other way of knowing light except through contrast, and so we experience the conditions we call 'darkness' and 'light' alternately."[5] We need the darkness with the light. "All things work together for good to them that love God, to them who are the called according to his purpose."[6]

His grace is sufficient for disaster as well as for delight. There is no doubt that for the man in the land of Uz who feared God there were dark days. However, the darkness led to the light and to his greatest days of truly knowing God.

[1]Job 1:1.
[2]Job 1:6.
[3]Job 2:1.
[4]Job 2:9.
[5]Sutphen.
[6]Romans 8:28.

❧   ❧   ❧

JOB 6–9
JOB 6

> My days are swifter than a weaver's shuttle, and are
> spent without hope. They are passed away as the swift
> ships.[1]

"MAKE USE OF TIME if thou lovest eternity; yesterday cannot be recalled; tomorrow cannot be assured; only today
is thine, which if thou procrastinate, thou losest; and which
lost is lost forever. One today is worth many tomorrows."[2]

The Scriptures give us varied pictures of time and of life.
A flower, a vapor, a dream, a watch in the night, a weaver's
shuttle quickly moving, and swift ships. Something that
is here and then is gone.

In Job's distresses he recognized how quickly the time
was passing. This good man had anticipated a long life.
Now death seemed so imminent to him. "My breath is cor-
rupt, my days are extinct, the graves are ready for me."[3]
What a picture of suffering mankind! Job was learning
lessons from disease: the terrible power of Satan and the
effects of sin. Virtue and the fear of God do not exempt
man from testing and trial.

Job is not a book of solutions, but it portrays the experiences and humanness of one who suffered. He learned
the value of a moment when it looked as though there were
very few moments left to him.

Perhaps man needs to be broken to understand the value
and opportunity of time. The older he grows the faster it
goes, and he longs to recapture the fleeting commodity.

The Christian should ask God to impress on his soul the
value of time. May it not take distress and deep water to
make its value known. The Bible solemnly emphasizes,
"Now is the accepted time."[4]

> I woke one morning with time on my hands.
> What luxury this day would be!

Each moment I'd cherish, none would be lost,
They must count for eternity.

But the hours crept by as I basked in the time
I thought I was able to spare.
It was lost in the minutes that made the hours—
Lost! I was so unaware.

I woke the next dawn with a prayer on my lips:
"O Saviour, Giver of time.
Grant today's gain from yesterday's loss;
Make each moment truly Thine."

[1]Job 7:6; 9:26.
[2]Quarles.
[3]Job 17:1.
[4]II Corinthians 6:2.

❦ ❦ ❦

May 23

JOB 10–13
JOB 12

> But ask now the beasts, and they shall teach thee; and
> the fowls of the air, and they shall tell thee: or speak
> to the earth, and it shall teach thee: and the fishes of
> the sea shall declare unto thee. Who knoweth not in
> all these things that the hand of the Lord hath wrought
> this?[1]

WHAT? Creation without a Creator? Could a watch with its
intricate parts and minute springs and jewels suddenly just
happen and take shape? Impossible! It is even more impossible that there is not a God who made the heavens and
the earth and all that is in them.

Look to the "beasts" for a testimony. They will teach you.
See how they find their food, protect their young. The fowls
of the air—how they wing their way above the world and
sing their song of praise to the Creator. Think of the earth,
of that wonderful sunset painted across the western sky in

brilliant colors. Who can discern the sky? It is of God. "The heavens declare the glory of God; and the firmament sheweth his handywork."[2] The mountains, the streams, the deserts, all are part of His glorious creation.

Only God could have made and sustained the creatures that inhabit His earth. It is easy to become fascinated by the life cycles of fish. Salmon will lay their eggs upstream, and when the fish are hatched they swim down to the ocean. However, when the time comes to spawn, they fight their way over obstacles, up fish ladders and past rocks to return to their breeding place! Does this just happen? No, God has ordained all things to operate in their time and place.

Some little girls were out playing in the sand of the tide-flats close to our home. They were awed at some footprints in the sand. "Look," said Pegge, "someone else is out here!" We looked all around and could see no one in sight, but as we walked together, we knew of the existence of another being on the beach that day. Kathi, Pegge's sister, said, "It must be an awfully big person." And we agreed that the prints most likely belonged to a man because they were large and far apart. We picked up characteristics just from the impressions in the sand.

There is no doubt that our Creator has left His impressions on the whole world. If you ever doubt it, go up to the summit of a mountain at sunrise. Or watch the moon on the water and the stars sparkling over the waves. Or hear a newborn baby's first cry!

The little girls could not see a person the day we walked on the sand, but the prints were proof, even to young minds, that someone had been there. Let us not miss the evidences of His presence on earth, well knowing that each trace and touch speaks of God—our God, the Creator and Sustainer of the world.

[1]Job 12:7-9.
[2]Psalm 19:1.

❧ ❧ ❧

JOB 14–17
JOB 14

If a man die, shall he live again?[1]

THE QUESTION is centuries old and has been stated in many ways. Asked one grammarian, "Is death a period that brings the sentence of life to a full stop, or only a comma that punctuates it to a loftier significance?" Job was questioning, in simplicity, "If a man die, shall he live again?"

One need only to attend a funeral, and watch the facial expressions of those who mourn to recognize the impact of death and the importance of this question as it confronts those closest to sorrow. People are varied in their personal answers. Some will unequivocally say, "No, this man will not live again." Others will express hope that he will. History tells us that the Egyptians carefully preserved dead bodies to prepare them for what would follow.

When Adam sinned, death followed. In Adam all men sinned and were under sentence. The Bible is clear: "The wages of sin is death."[2] No one is exempt. "All have sinned, and come short of the glory of God."[3] The question about life after death has been asked ever since Adam, in fields and in temples, in wildernesses and in palaces. Each religion has its teaching on the world to come. Job, one of the earliest contributors to the Bible narrative, was confronted with the age-old question.

In Old Testament times, life and death were taught in a solemn way, but the question could not be fully answered until Jesus Christ came to earth, died, and was resurrected. He explained to His followers: "I go to prepare a place for you. And if I go . . . I will come again, and receive you unto myself; that where I am, there ye may be also."[4] He was speaking of heaven. He is preparing a home for those who are members of the family of God.

In Him we have the answer to Job's question. "If a man die, he shall live again!" He declared, "I am the resurrection, and the life: he that believeth in me, though he were dead, yet shall he live: and whosoever liveth and believeth in me shall never die."[5]

Is there hope within your heart that when you die, you will live in heaven with God? His peace and presence can give great certainty now. Job's question can only be answered affirmatively.

[1]Job 14:14.
[2]Romans 6:23.
[3]Romans 3:23.
[4]John 14:2-3.
[5]John 11:25-26.

❦ ❦ ❦

May 25

Job 18–19
Job 19

For I know that my redeemer liveth.[1]

A YOUNG MAN had recently been granted his master's degree, and soon would begin work for a doctorate. His times of coming back to see his family were increasingly few. Things were different now that his parents had come to know Christ. To him the teachings of Christ just did not seem to fit in with their social and cultural attainments, and they were "so ill-founded." On one visit home he had taken a great deal of time to explain to his mother and father the arguments he had learned in college and graduate school. When his mother said she was praying for him, he thought silently, *How naïve.* Belief in God was out of date, and the new group of "believers" in town must have been influenced by those who were quite narrow in their thinking. His arguments, well expounded and substantiated, were always brought to an end by his mother's words, "But,

240

John, I have met Jesus Christ, and I know that my Redeemer lives."

The years passed by and the young man continued his impressive professional career. The doctor's degree in a school of the sciences was granted. He settled down to translate his knowledge into use. Then a series of crises upset his life. One after another they came, like an unending earthquake of trouble and uncertainty. The young man asked, "Is there a God?" His friends denied such a possibility. He suffered alone. He recounted his afflictions and the severity of the past months to his mother, who for the first time sensed a response in his heart. Together they searched the Word of God, talked of Job, not just as a mythical character from some dreamer's pen but as a man who lived and worked and struggled as we do. Finally the son saw the light. In the simplicity of a child he fell to his knees and committed himself to God unreservedly.

From pain and desolation a clear testimony may emerge. Such a testimony came from the son with the same assurance in which Job had previously spoken. "I know!" Here is language of certainty. There is no hesitation. "I know!" What did the son know? "My redeemer liveth!" A redeemer in Old Testament days delivered a captive, an enslaved soul, from bondage. The name applies to the God who is Redeemer and Deliverer of His people.

The young doctor derived comfort from the personal pronoun "my." Faith and love had helped him to clearly see the God he had thought did not exist. And now he knew Him as his own. God was not *a* redeemer but *"my* Redeemer," his Redeemer, forever and ever!

¹Job 19:25.

❧ ❧ ❧

Job 21–23
Job 23

> But he knoweth the way that I take: when he hath tried me, I shall come forth as gold.[1]

THE APOSTLE PAUL wrote, "We are troubled on every side, yet not distressed; we are perplexed, but not in despair; persecuted, but not forsaken; cast down, but not destroyed; always bearing about in the body the dying of the Lord Jesus, that the life also of Jesus might be made manifest in our body. For we which live are alway delivered unto death for Jesus' sake, that the life also of Jesus might be made manifest in our mortal flesh."[2] Paul was saying that such afflictions should be lightly worn. "For I reckon that the sufferings of this present time are not worthy to be compared with the glory which shall be revealed in us."[3]

Glory in sufferings? "Christ also suffered for us, leaving us an example, that ye should follow his steps."[4] It is here evident that a Christian is perfected through suffering. When afflictions come and the pressure almost passes the bearing-point, remember that the "fiery trial" is for our refining.

Our Lord is the perfect Refiner. The trial may be to rid us of the "dross and sin," our self-life and carnality. "I will turn my hand upon thee, and purely purge away thy dross, and take away all thy tin."[5] Isaiah further wrote, "I will make thee a new sharp threshing instrument."[6] God will be with us throughout the process. He did not desert Job. Job's despondency and affliction could not separate him from God. Job still remembered that God was an ever-present help in trouble.

The purifying process is not a hurried one. It takes time to refine gold to its purest form. The rough state of diamonds must be improved upon. Grinding and polishing make the gems valuable. Yes, and it also takes time for us to be formed in the image of God.

The process has purpose. "And he shall sit as a refiner and purifier of silver: and he shall purify the sons of Levi, and purge them as gold and silver, that they may offer unto the Lord an offering in righteousness."[7]

A saint of yesterday wrote, "The present circumstance which presses so hard against you is, if surrendered to Christ, the best-shaped tool in the Father's hand to chisel you for eternity."

[1]Job 23:10.
[2]II Corinthians 4:8-11.
[3]Romans 8:18.
[4]I Peter 2:21.
[5]Isaiah 1:25.
[6]Isaiah 41:15.
[7]Malachi 3:3.

❧ ❧ ❧

May 27

JOB 24–27
JOB 27

> My righteousness I hold fast, and will not let it go: my heart shall not reproach me so long as I live.[1]

JOB HAS HERE GRASPED a truth which is essential for our everyday Christian living. Christ made our righteousness possible, but we must work to make it practical in our lives, as "faith without works is dead." It is a natural thing for a new Christian to rejoice that Jesus paid it all. This is true, but the responsibility does not end there. It just begins. He granted us new life, everlasting life, but He still has given us powers of choice and reasoning. We must will to "walk in newness of life."[2] God could have created us to do only as He pleases, but instead He redeemed us and made us free agents to accept or reject His gracious, eternal gift.

He grants the power, but we must appropriate it. The

Christian's walk has been described as a circle. The heavenly half is completed, the earthly half requires continual vigilance. It takes prayer for wisdom and guidance. It takes Bible study to learn more of the One who has made our redemption complete. Another essential is the time of worship and communion with the Lord. These fill in our part of the circle and keep the circumference of Christianity unbroken and related to its center, Christ.

How well Job knew of what he spoke: "My righteousness I hold fast, and will not let it go." Each believer needs to assume this responsibility. Out of ceaseless pain and the loss of family and friends and fortune, Job acquired a new understanding of suffering and saw his part in his relationship to God. "My heart shall not reproach me so long as I live."

It was a warm May day. Two youngsters were setting up their first lemonade stand of the season. The mother of the one boy had made the drink, his father built the stand, and his sister purchased the cups. The other little boy stood by and watched. He liked the idea of equal profits without any expenditure. However, he was reduced to tears when the first nickel was not shared. "You have done nothing," said the little worker, "but just stand there." The reply from the second partner was noted: "But I've stood here!"

Too often, dear friend, we stand and expect God, in the partnership He has prepared for us, to do it all. He has provided the policies, the fellowship, and the capital. He asks that we give Him our hearts and, instead of being idle, do our share, joining Him to "work the works of him that sent" us.[3] Is this too much to ask?

[1] Job 27:6.
[2] Romans 6:4.
[3] John 9:4.

❧   ❧   ❧

Job 28–30
Job 30

> I was eyes to the blind, and feet was I to the lame. I was a father to the poor: and the cause which I knew not I searched out.[1]

THIS IS A CHAPTER of retrospect on Job's part. He talked of his past happiness, comparing it with the present conditions of his life. We again glimpse his character and in so doing see our Christian responsibility. In him we see demonstrated a fear of God, as he refers back to the opening chapter. This fear of God produced his real love for mankind.

"I was eyes to the blind." The child of God has much responsibility, not only to the physically blind but to those without spiritual sight. Their eyes must be opened to see the goodness of God. Spiritual darkness means darkness forever, not temporarily. We who have the remedy must bring His sight to those without it. It is an awesome experience to visit an eye bank, where those who have willed their physical eyes leave hope of sight to many who wait for the dawn of a new life. There, sightless ones are tested and their needs determined. Darkness and light—blindness and sight—all in a day's work if your job is in the eye bank. We Christians have a tremendously challenging charge to help open the eyes of those who are blinded to the message of Jesus Christ.

"I was feet to the lame." Here again, the reference is not just to the handicapped but to those who need to get on their feet in the faith. "As ye have therefore received Christ Jesus the Lord, so walk ye in him."[2] But some are like little children; they do not know how to stand on their feet. We must take them and lift them up to His life of growth and strength. Some may be lame from sin or its consequences. Let our feet be swift to assist such in their need.

"I was father to the poor." Again in a spiritual sense, dear friend, we may provide for those who are poor. No poverty is greater than barrenness of soul, emptiness of heart, longing of spirit.

In the story of the Good Samaritan, the Levite and the priest passed along the highway. Possibly they could have been on their way to some special service, but they had no time to stop. There lay a poor wounded victim in his blood until a man came along who also may have been en route to a place of worship. He stopped because his heart held compassion. All of our worship and devotion is of little merit if we do not minister to others and meet the test of Job, of the Good Samaritan, and of Christ, who came not to be ministered unto but to minister.

[1]Job 29:15-16.
[2]Colossians 2:6.

❧ ❧ ❧

May 29

Job 31–33
Job 31

Doth not he see my ways, and count all my steps?[1]

I REMEMBER COUNSELING one summer a group of unusually active high school girls. Each was special in herself, and together they made up one of those never-to-be-forgotten tentfuls. What one did not think of, another did, and their minds were churning with ideas at night as well as during the day. My co-counselor and I were kept running from dawn until after dark, and then there would be new ideas. One night, when the girls just couldn't settle down, they pleaded for a moonlight walk up a neighboring mountainside. Because we loved them and longed that they expend their energy, we complied. Twenty happy, healthy girls sang at the top of the hillside, while two tired counselors sat

246

quietly on a rock. Said the other to me, " 'Doth not he see my ways, and count all my steps?' "

I will never forget the reaction this verse had on me, and has had so many times since, when seeking to do His work, especially when bone-tired. It helps lift the load and lighten the burden when I know that He actually sees my ways and counts my steps! He must be a God who cares deeply, to be interested in my ways and my steps. My heart delights at His personal interest in me, a most undeserving child.

"Habits, like paths, are the result of constant actions. It is the multitude of daily footsteps which go to and fro which shapes them. Let it light up your daily wanderings to know that there—in the quiet bracing of the soul to uncongenial duty, the patient bearing of unwelcome burdens, the loving acceptance of unlovely companionship—and not on the grand occasions, you are making your eternal future. It is the multitude of little actions which makes the great ones."[2]

As I recognize that He truly sees, and sheds light on my pathway, I find it more difficult to displease Him. Someone said, "The queen's command is never broken when she is looking on." In a much greater sense He is looking on at all times. "Whither shall I go from thy spirit? or whither shall I flee from thy presence? If I ascend up into heaven, thou art there. . . . If I take the wings of the morning, and dwell in the uttermost parts of the sea; even there shall thy hand lead me, and thy right hand shall hold me. . . . Yea, the darkness hideth not from thee; but the night shineth as the day: the darkness and the light are both alike to thee."[3]

God's omniscience is a fact which should delight the hearts of all who rejoice that He does see our ways, and counts all our steps.

[1] Job 31:4.
[2] J. B. Brown.
[3] Psalm 139:7-12.

   ❧   ❧   ❧

> Remember that thou magnify his work, which men behold.[1]

I'LL NEVER FORGET the teacher who came to Sunday school with a magnifying glass one Sunday morning. She laid it down in the middle of the round table, and every child was eager to pick it up and enlarge the scene about him. How carefully our teacher stressed the importance of keeping our eyes on Christ. By doing this, we would magnify Him, so that others around us could see Him too. She had two pictures, one of a human being, the other of Christ. She picked up the magnifying glass and when it was centered on Christ, the class clearly saw Him. When she turned around and held it in front of the other picture, the other person was more clearly seen.

Surely no child left that class without the profound impression that each Christian has in a sense the opportunity to be a magnifying glass for Christ. We can make Christ real and definite to others, or point away from Him and bring into focus something that is not eternal or helpful. However, only through pointing to Him, emphasizing Him, can we make Him real and bring Him near to others.

A young housewife was struck one day with the thought that she magnified the wrongs of her neighborhood by much unnecessary talk and little constructive suggestion. With a great feeling of guilt and concern she went for her Bible and concordance. To better use the concordance, she looked for her magnifying glass. And that gave her an idea. One by one she looked up the verses about magnifying the Lord.

First she read this from Job: "Remember that thou magnify his work . . ." She continued in the Psalms: "Let them shout for joy, and be glad, that favour my righteous cause: yea, let them say continually, Let the Lord be magnified, which hath pleasure in the prosperity of his servant. . . . I will praise the name of God with a song, and will magnify him with thanksgiving."[2] She read in II Samuel, "Let thy name be magnified."[3] On into the New Testament she read of Mary during the annunciation when she said, "My soul doth magnify the Lord, and my spirit hath rejoiced in God my Saviour."[4] The housewife thought of the Apostle Paul and knew he could not have been petty about neighborhood problems, for he had written, "According to my earnest expectation and my hope, that in nothing I shall be ashamed, but that with all boldness, as always, so now also Christ shall be magnified in my body, whether it be by life, or by death."[5]

Let us, by our lives and our actions, point others clearly to Jesus Christ. "O magnify the Lord with me, and let us exalt his name together."[6]

[1]Job 36:24.
[2]Psalm 35:27; 69:30.
[3]II Samuel 7:26.
[4]Luke 1:46-47.
[5]Philippians 1:20.
[6]Psalm 34:3.

🌿 🌿 🌿

May 31

JOB 38–42
JOB 42

> I have heard of thee by the hearing of the ear: but now mine eye seeth thee.[1]

IT IS ONE THING to hear, but quite another to actually see. Many people have heard about Jesus Christ, and some have believed in Him, but precious experiences come when an individual truly "sees"!

In reading the book of Job this month, we have come to know a man, a very human one, although he was a good man and feared God. Job was prosperous in the land of Uz, between Arabia and Syria. He had a large family and all was well until one day, out of an unclouded sky, the storm broke loose. One affliction followed another. His friends condemned him without cause. A series of personal, shattering crises encompassed his life. At first, he feared God, but even so he harbored some self-righteousness. Then he began to learn lessons. His righteousness became inconsequential. Sufferings and pain brought him to an understanding and appreciation of the gifts of God. Sorrow brought him closer to God. He had heard with his ears, but there was such a difference after he had seen with his eyes![1]

You say, "Why must I suffer? I have tried to please the Lord and walk with Him, and do His will. I have been first to offer my service when there is a job to be done. Many late hours and long days are spent at my church. Why? Why me? Is it that I am to be punished or chastened?" To a child of God there comes assurance: "Whom the Lord loveth he chasteneth."[2] Sorrow, pain, perplexity are sent our way to teach us valuable lessons. "And this," you ask, "comes from a God of love?" Yes. Of Christ we are told, "Though he were a Son, yet learned he obedience by the things which he suffered."[3]

George Macdonald wrote some stirring lines: "Two men looked out through prison bars. The one saw dirt, the other stars!" In looking up to Christ, we can behold His glory, even in affliction. He can heal every heartache, and in Him we may find the solutions to all the puzzlements of life.

As we end another month we pray, "Show me Thy glory." Sufferings may be the steps leading to that place where we can say with Job, "But now mine eye seeth thee" and Thy glory.

"The sufferings of this present time are not worthy to be compared with the glory which shall be revealed in us."[4]

[1] Job 42:5.
[2] Hebrews 12:6.
[3] Hebrews 5:8.
[4] Romans 8:18.

❦ ❦ ❦

June

PSALMS 1–8
PSALM 1

> And he shall be like a tree planted by the rivers of
> water, that bringeth forth his fruit in his season; his
> leaf also shall not wither; and whatsoever he doeth shall
> prosper . . . For the Lord knoweth the way of the
> righteous: but the way of the ungodly shall perish.[1]

"PSALMS FOR SUMMER" was the title of a series of messages
in a certain church. This book of doxology has provided
rich blessing and unfolded great treasures for readers in
every season. However, with plans for warm-weather activity, vacations, and the closing of school, it is a good thing
to take time to check up on our spiritual welfare, and make
sure our true delight is in the Word of the Lord. Then,
though surrounded by summer activity, we will not neglect
our time with Him. In His law we will "meditate day and
night."[2]

The righteous man has been likened to a tree which has
its roots by the river. Growth and foliage in such a location
are likely to be healthy, green, and sturdy. So the righteous man can be pictured as strong and straight. One who
grows day by day, sustained by a constant supply of the
"water of life," cannot help but bear rich fruit.

Let us consider ourselves today as living trees of God.
When we met Him, we were likewise planted at the source
of true life, rivers of living water. Attachment to Christ is
vital. As Jesus illustrated in another context, that of the
vine-branch relationship, "I am the true vine. . . . Abide in

me, and I in you. As the branch cannot bear fruit of itself, except it abide in the vine; no more can ye, except ye abide in me."[3]

A strong tree may some day be cut down to serve another purpose. It may be made into a telephone pole and, in its new place of service, transmit messages around the world.

The Christian must be ready to be transplanted by his Owner, for use in God's garden of glory. He has a message to transmit, an eternal, life-giving message for a world that needs desperately to receive it.

Our fruit-bearing this summer is essential. With a living, vital relationship to Him, we cannot help but yield a harvest.

As we prayerfully enter Psalms and summer, let us be steadfast, strong, and straight for Him who today reminds, "Ask of me, and I shall give thee the heathen for thine inheritance, and the uttermost parts of the earth for thy possession."[4]

[1]Psalm 1:3, 6.　　　　[3]John 15:1, 4.
[2]Psalm 1:2.　　　　　　[4]Psalm 2:8.

❧　❧　❧

June 2

PSALMS 9–16
PSALM 16

> I will praise thee, O Lord, with my whole heart; I will show forth all thy marvellous works. I will be glad and rejoice in thee: I will sing praise to thy name, O thou most High.[1]

IT IS SAID of a Wesleyan preacher of the eighteenth century that he died "full of faith . . . and while he had breath, he praised god." All of us know special times of enthusiasm when we are exhilarated, when answers to prayer abound, when spontaneous song bubbles in our hearts. Unfortunately these occasions are often limited to favorable circumstances. If we are truly sincere, we will find that there are many times when we do not say, "I will praise thee, O Lord, with my whole heart."

It is easy to give thanks for abundance, but in drought we find it more difficult. How can you give thanks when your new automobile has become disfigured by five dents, all incurred when it was standing still? For our family it was not easy!

Someone asks, "How can I sing praise to His name when my husband, only five years out of medical school, and an effective Christian, is taken suddenly from me, and from a new church that needed his help?" How? We can all look to David. There were many times when he was frankly in no mood to praise God. As you read the Psalms you will often come across these times of trial. Once David said, "I was dumb with silence, I held my peace, even from good; and my sorrow was stirred."[2]

But David learned that he must look back to lessons learned in the past, and forward to fulfillment of God-given promises, and make a firm resolution regarding both: "I will praise thee."

Like the Wesleyan preacher, true praise can become part of living, almost as natural as breathing. The true source of this spirit of praise is not in circumstance but in God.

Horatius Bonar prayed:

> Fill Thou my life, O Lord my God,
> In every part with praise,
> That my whole being may proclaim
> Thy being, and Thy ways.

God grant that we too may cultivate lives of praise—perpetual praise—to our God.

[1]Psalm 9:1-2.
[2]Psalm 39:2.

❧ ❧ ❧

Psalms 17–19
Psalm 17

> As for me, I will behold thy face in righteousness: I
> shall be satisfied, when I awake, with thy likeness.[1]

How few things really satisfy! Some may temporarily
quench a thirst or appease an appetite or fulfill a desire.
However, most prove to be only transitory. Have you ever
long anticipated a great event? For months there was careful preparation in hopes that all would go well and the
occasion would be the happiest yet! The trouble was that,
though the event came, it passed so quickly and was over,
and a disappointing letdown followed.

In Christ, the Christian has a true source of eternal satisfaction. He does not disappoint us. His promises and
blessings do not come and quickly go. They are steady and
constant. There is no uncertainty with Him. He is entirely
sufficient. He gives glorious confidence and assurance that
no one else, nothing else, can give.

These are uncertain days. Power structures shift and
problems mount. Hope sinks, but the Christian has an
anchor of faith for times such as these. We behold His face
in righteousness as we stand secure before God because of
Christ's finished work for us on Calvary. Our righteous-
nesses, as Isaiah declared, "are as filthy rags."[2] God gives us
no choice. He bares our lack of qualifications for righteousness. Our so-called morality is all to no avail, and we must
recognize that there is nothing to be done but to rely totally
on the mercy of God. When we come to this realization, we
look up in His face and, seeing His love, compassion, grace,
and mercy, become satisfied indeed.

Some day we shall awaken in His likeness. Imagine it!
We shall be in the likeness of God's Son!

We shall be satisfied when some day we share His glory.
On the morrow we shall be in His presence. Everything that

we thought would satisfy on earth will fade into insignificance when we behold Him. It would be impossible to begin to describe the glory that will be ours in being with Him, nor could our finite minds ever comprehend it.

Is this not sufficient to take us day by day on the pilgrim way until we join Him and are overwhelmingly satisfied?

[1]Psalm 17:15.
[2]Isaiah 64:6.

❧ ❧ ❧

June 4

PSALMS 20–25
PSALM 25

> Turn thee unto me, and have mercy upon me; for I am desolate and afflicted. The troubles of my heart are enlarged: O bring thou me out of my distresses.[1]

IN THE FOYER of a church stood a lovely Christian mother, one who was faithful in all the activities of the church and taught Sunday school. Many in the congregation had turned to her for help and counsel in times of need. This particular day her expression was troubled and her countenance pale. Her answer to my inquiry was scriptural and most descriptive: "The troubles of my heart are enlarged!"

Most of us have experienced at one time or another heavy hearts that literally felt overloaded with adversity. It seemed as if one more blow would shatter us, and we felt desolate and discouraged. It is this type of experience that causes some people to overindulge in sleeping pills or to seek to escape reality by jumping from a high bridge.

In this condition of utter helplessness, many Christians have become defeated. The mother at the church, gifted with many human resources and material advantages, when weighed down by a troubled heart, came to realize she had been too dependent on a backlog of knowledge rather than on the Lord. When laid low, with no means of eliminating the problem, she came to humbly cast her care on the Lord. At last she experienced the reality of the words of Christ in which He put His finger on the problem of those who try to take things into their own hands: "Without me ye can do nothing."[2]

God made me and He sustains me. I had no control over my coming into this world, and there is no way I could change the color of my skin or influence my ancestry. In this I am utterly helpless. My troubles, which I am powerless to change, are evident to God. In fact, they are ordained by Him for my good. In facing my condition, I can utter this prayer of helplessness: "The troubles of my heart are enlarged: O bring thou me out of my distresses."

The prayer must come in honesty, with all self-sufficiency renounced. It must come recognizing that "man can receive nothing, except it be given him from heaven."[3] As we pray, our helplessness is an invitation to Almightiness, and the hearts we thought were crowded with enlarged problems will find sufficient space for praise.

[1]Psalm 25:16-17.
[2]John 15:5.
[3]John 3:27.

   ❧   ❧   ❧

Psalms 26–32
Psalm 26

> Wait on the Lord: be of good courage, and he shall
> strengthen thine heart: wait, I say, on the Lord.[1]

GOD OFTEN SPEAKS of the heart, that interesting vital organ
which is so intricate and complex. The heart is a constant
reminder, as it beats day by day, that God Himself gave us
life. Even the most minute cell lives only because God made
it.

Of paramount importance, in considering our hearts, is
the solemn question, "Is your heart right with God?" Has
He put within your "heart" that life-restoring power and
Presence that spiritually speaking makes man pass from
death to life? If so, you are a candidate for His strength.

God strengthens the hearts of believers in different ways.
I have always been impressed by the story of the famous
New York preacher, Dr. A. B. Simpson. He was greatly
used of God in speaking, teaching, and writing. However,
he was limited by many physical complications. One was a
heart condition. At one time his physicians reported that
his days were definitely numbered. At this time he began
searching the Scriptures and waiting on the Lord. He was
convinced that the Lord had an interest in strengthening
him physically. One day he climbed a mountain and of the
experience he wrote, "The world of weakness and fear was
lying at my feet. From that time on I had literally a new
heart." He used his health and heart for the glory of God.

God strengthens other hearts in different ways. Some have
found that their strength of body was not renewed, but that
their souls flourished. Amid the great weakness a strength
was given which was "made perfect in weakness."[2]

Whether your need today is physical or spiritual, God
can work miracles in your heart. "Wait on the Lord: be of

good courage," and you will be able to testify, "God strengthened my heart!"

¹Psalm 27:14.
²II Corinthians 12:9.

❧ ❧ ❧

PSALMS 33–36
PSALM 34

> O taste and see that the Lord is good: blessed is the man that trusteth in him.¹

THE COUNTRY was Puerto Rico. It was a very warm afternoon and I was both hot and hungry. I knew it would be several hours before my friends met me for dinner. A little way from the hotel I had previously noticed a fruit stand, and now, as I approached it again, it was a vision of delight: melons, papayas, bananas, all larger and more beautiful than any I had ever seen. In line ahead of me was an elderly man. He fingered the fruit from the time I arrived and continued to do so for about ten minutes. His questions were abrupt and impatient. "Is this fresh?" "Is this ripe?" He would look some more, then ask, "Is this as good as this? When was the fruit picked?"

My watch ticked off the minutes as he picked up a beautiful juicy-looking orange. He held it up, encircled it with his hands, weighed it on the antique scale, and said to the attendant, "Are you sure it is good?" The frazzled Puerto Rican plucked the orange out of his hand, ripped off the skin in three quick movements, and blurted out, "Taste it, and see for yourself!"

The picture always comes back to my mind when I read this little verse, or hear someone who keeps asking questions about the Christian life. Many folks are well-meaning like the elderly man. They have heard the testimony of others and have even handled the Word of God. They may even compare Christianity with another religion. Yet when the moment of decision comes, they do not make their choice.

Would to God that we Christians could be with them at that time to unfold the living Word of God, carefully proclaiming that "we have seen and do testify that the Father sent the Son to be the Saviour of the world. Whosoever shall confess that Jesus is the Son of God, God dwelleth in him, and he in God."[2]

We can pray that the Holy Spirit will "peel back" the darkness that is keeping others from enjoying the delights of the Gospel.

> Until they taste, they cannot see
> God's goodness
> Which has come to me.
> But I can live and surely show
> The choicest fruit
> God can bestow.

[1]Psalm 34:8.
[2]I John 4:14-15.

🍀 🍀 🍀

259

PSALMS 37–41
PSALM 37

> Fret not thyself . . . trust . . . delight . . . commit . . .
> rest . . . wait patiently for him.[1]

LITTLE CHERI bounded in the back door. "Mother, mother," she cried, "God has a secret in the Psalms." The youngster could not remember much of the lesson but she did remember that God had a secret.

In this blessed Thirty-seventh Psalm, God has a secret, it is true, but it is a secret He has shared with us. It is the secret of a happy Christian life. Just as we have laws for physical health and happiness, so God has very explicit laws for our spiritual well-being. Some rules are laid down in the first seven verses.

"Fret not thyself." Said a wise man, "Most of my problems have been caused by worrying about burdens that were not mine to bear and by answering questions I was never asked!" It is easy for us to fret about those around us, about the way evil abounds, about what our neighbors do or don't do, but God says we should not fret. If we desire His peace, we must "fret not."

"Trust in the Lord." This is the opposite of fretting. Relinquish one and adopt the other. Trust Him for your every need. If you are committed to Him He will care for you.[2]

"Delight thyself also in the Lord." The heavenly Father desires that we delight in Him as a child delighteth in a well-loved parent. Someone has said, "Delight in the Lord and He will delight in you." It is an essential truth that to those who delight in Him, the desires of the heart are granted.

"Commit thy way unto the Lord." Literally, "shift the load onto" Him. God will handle your affairs. A God-planned and controlled life is prosperous.

"Rest in the Lord." We rest when our labor is finished.

So it is with our care. Until we give up control, we cannot rest. We are prone to be full of planning, scheming, rushing, and doing, and there is no time to learn the secrets of rest.

"Wait patiently." Physicians tell us that impatience drains our energy. Have you experienced spiritual dyspepsia by trying to hurry up an answer to prayer or even going ahead of God's plan? At such times, God has to wait for us!

I am glad God reveals His secrets to the children of men, and I pray that we will learn to fret not, to trust, delight, commit, and rest. Then we will learn to wait until He moves.

[1]Psalm 37:1-7.
[2]I Peter 5:7.

❧ ❧ ❧

June 8

PSALMS 42–48
PSALM 46

> Be still, and know that I am God: I will be exalted among the heathen, I will be exalted in the earth.[1]

IN EVERY CLASSROOM there usually is a would-be scholar who is constantly questioning the teacher, bothering a fellow pupil, or speaking out. This type of student often has difficulty in school. He cannot learn much, for he won't take time to listen.

There are children of God who resemble this student. Their scope of learning revolves about constant questioning, much talking, but very little listening.

If we are sincere about getting to know the Lord, this text gives us the sure clue: "Be still." Divine instruction comes in stillness and quietness before God. The distractions will diminish as we seek Him and become more eager for time alone with Him.

I read about a scholar and poet who was telling a pious

261

Quaker woman how each moment of his day was spent. He did not believe in wasting time. He explained that he studied Portuguese grammar while he shaved, read Spanish for an hour before breakfast, and each additional waking moment was assigned to a task or to beneficial indulgence. The Quakeress listened patiently and waited for a moment when he would stop for breath. Then she quietly asked, "Friend, when dost thou think?"

It is easy to be busy, even for the Lord. We are going, and doing, studying a lesson, and rushing to the next task. But, "friend, when dost thou think?"

In the stillness and quietness of being with God, our thoughts become established, our goals made clear, and there is peace so that we can hear His voice.

This is another of God's secrets: "He that dwelleth in the secret place of the most High shall abide under the shadow of the Almighty."[2] In His shadow we are secure, and in the stillness we will know God!

[1]Psalm 46:10.
[2]Psalm 91:1.

❧   ❧   ❧

PSALMS 49–55
PSALM 51

> Have mercy upon me, O God, according to thy loving-
> kindness: according unto the multitude of thy tender
> mercies blot out my transgressions.[1]

PSALM 51 is the great psalm of confession. It is intensely
and intimately searching, and should cause us to take careful spiritual inventory.

The Bible has told us that David was guilty of several
crimes. For a time they remained unconfessed until Nathan
was used to confront him with them and make him realize
that they were an open insult to God. We are sure that
David was conscious of his sin, but nevertheless it remained
unconfessed. He finally came to God with great penitence
and specifically laid his guilt before Him, without qualification.

Then David was ready for the cleansing and forgiveness
that God would give him. "Hide thy face from my sins,
and blot out all mine iniquities. Create in me a clean heart,
O God; and renew a right spirit within me."[2]

How often do we stop and realize what grief our sin
brings to God? We frequently go our willful way, unconcerned and unconfessed, because we have not stopped to
think of God's pain at our wrongdoing. The consequence is
grave. "If I regard [cherish] iniquity in my heart, the Lord
will not hear me."[3] God cannot tolerate our sin, and His
abhorrence for it should motivate us to seek forgiveness and
let His blood cleanse and cover it forever.

David had known the joy of salvation, but after sinning
he had missed God's gracious fellowship. He prayed, "Restore unto me the joy of thy salvation; and uphold me with
thy free spirit."[4] This needed restoration was granted and
brought him peace. Is it needed in your life?

St. Augustine, who was marvelously converted in A.D. 387,

and who left us many of his confessions, wrote: "Power of my soul! Enter into it, and fit it for Thyself, that Thou mayest have it and hold it without spot or wrinkle. This is my hope; therefore do I speak." When that Power was hindered by sin, Augustine quickly acknowledged, "What could be hidden in me, tho' I were unwilling to confess it? For I should hide Thee from myself, not myself from Thee!"

Oh, that we too might be spiritually sensitive to the strategies of the evil one, and quick to acknowledge, "Against thee, thee only, have I sinned."[5] May we each be "throughly" washed and emerge clean vessels for our Master's use.

[1]Psalm 51:1.
[2]Psalm 51:9-10.
[3]Psalm 66:18.
[4]Psalm 51:12.
[5]Psalm 51:4.

❧ ❧ ❧

June 10

Psalms 56–63
Psalm 57

> My heart is fixed, O God, my heart is fixed: I will sing and give praise.[1]

I HAVE HEARD Christians say that in reading about David's "fixed heart" they feel an almost sacred jealousy stirring within them. If such a thing could take place within their lives, they feel it would be joy unspeakable!

David had been through trials, sins, disappointments, but in all things he had learned that his God was merciful and gracious, forgiving and loving. David had determined that his was to be a "fixed heart" with a steadfast purpose and goal.

At a man-of-the-year banquet, the recipient of the award was introduced without the usual pomp and pageantry. The master of ceremonies quietly said, "Friends, meet a man with a fixed purpose in life." Those who knew the man receiving the trophy knew that his fixed purpose stemmed from a fixed heart.

This civic leader had had in his early years great hardships and problems, making barely enough to live in surroundings that were unbelievable. From the bitterness of his past came the resolution to better his future. He would let nothing deter him. From then on his steadfast thoughts and careful plans helped him reach the goal of unusual accomplishment.

If we could have looked into David's heart, we would have found these qualities in even greater proportion. He loved the Lord and longed that the Lord would be exalted. His affection for Him grew from a personal walk with Him.

David's thoughts were of God. Each morning when he woke he would think of his Lord and commune with Him, well knowing that "he slumbers not." Oh, that our waking thoughts would first be of the Lord. What a difference it would make in our day! How true the statement that we are what our thoughts are.

David's intentions were for the glory of God. "Be thou exalted, O God, above the heavens: let thy glory be above all the earth."[2]

God looks into the heart of man. What is the condition of your heart today? Could it be somewhat sluggish in its purpose, uncertain, divided? Or is it steadfastly "fixed"?

[1]Psalm 57:7.
[2]Psalm 57:11.

    ❧   ❧   ❧

> Thou visitest the earth, and waterest it: thou greatly
> enrichest it with the river of God, which is full of wa-
> ter: thou preparest them corn, when thou hast so pro-
> vided for it.[1]

IN HIGH SCHOOL I had a teacher in social studies who took
one period to describe the Nile River and its value to those
in the area surrounding it. Its presence and fullness provide life-giving water in a dry and barren desert. What a
tragedy it would be if it ceased to flow!

A Christian could be called a "river of God." Each one is
destined to be a channel of blessing. What a great tragedy
if we become dry and cut off the life-giving flow to those
about us who are faint with spiritual thirst.

"The river of God," writes the Psalmist, "is full of water."
To be filled with Himself must be our daily concern and desire. "Be filled with the Spirit,"[2] wrote Paul to the Ephesians. Perhaps he thought of the resultant fruit of "love,
joy, peace, longsuffering, gentleness, goodness, faith, meekness, temperance."[3] Only those who have drunk deeply of
the river of God's fullness can bring forth the fruit of the
Spirit of God. "Whosoever drinketh of the water that I shall
give him shall never thirst; but the water that I shall give
him shall be in him a well of water springing up into . . .
life."[4]

True, our degrees of fullness may vary, but that divine
reservoir is ours on which to draw. God is the Source of
the life-giving water, and we are to be the open channels to
receive it.

I have watched a river which has been clogged by silt or
debris carefully being dredged. The waste is piled to one
side as the passageway is opened. This is essential so that

activity on the river may continue without interruption, unhindered.

So it is in our lives. At times they may become clogged with those things which stop the flow of God's blessing and provision. The "river" may be reduced to a trickle until the waste is cleared away and we again become useful.

May we each be a life-giving conduit for God, a channel of blessing, so that His refreshing fullness may flow through our lives to others.

[1]Psalm 65:9.
[2]Ephesians 5:18.
[3]Galatians 5:22-23.
[4]John 4:14.

❧ ❧ ❧

June 12

PSALMS 69–72
PSALM 71

> For the zeal of thine house hath eaten me up.[1]

SOMETIMES when I read the Word, a phrase or sentence will strike a resonant note in my heart. Today's verse did just that.

Enthusiasm for the things of Christ often becomes less evident as a person grows older in the faith. This is cause for concern, for the church cannot increase if our zeal decreases.

Just recently at a Christian Women's Club meeting I met a woman who was wonderfully introduced to Jesus Christ. She described her past as "thirty years of gross sin." The one who was used to sow the seed was a neighbor, who herself had found Christ through reading her child's Bible and acting in faith on the divine promises she read. She was so thrilled with the change in her life, and with the transforming power of the Bible, that she just had to go next door and tell the good news. She knew the woman next door was cold and hard and unconcerned about such things, but this did not deter her. Over she went and instead of a closed mind, she found an open door and a friend who was ready to come to Christ.

The woman at the club was so impressed with her neighbor who cared, that she has followed the example and taken every opportunity to "go and tell."

In the same room that afternoon was another lady who listened to the story and later confessed to me that she too had had zeal when she met Christ. However, something had happened, and she had not witnessed since.

I have spent much time asking God to show me how and where we lose that first love. What cools the fervency, the fire that once was kindled in our hearts? Why do we now remain cold and indifferent?

The answer keeps coming to mind, "If any man will come after me, let him deny himself, and take up his cross daily, and follow me."[2] Crossbearing isn't popular. Our first holy zeal carries us for a time; then we become weary of the load and simply give up. We must first realize the lack in ourselves, then acknowledge the sufficiency of the Lord to take the burden and help us.

I pray for a new willingness to bear my share of the load, as God gives me opportunity, and as His love constrains, well knowing that He will pour out His grace, peace, and power. Then I will be "eaten up" with His zeal and will respond in quenchless devotion.

[1]Psalm 69:9.
[2]Luke 9:23.

❧ ❧ ❧

PSALMS 73–77
PSALM 73

> Nevertheless I am continually with thee: thou hast
> holden me by my right hand. Thou shalt guide me with
> thy counsel, and afterward receive me to glory.[1]

A LITTLE GIRL was learning to ride a bicycle. She was frightened and unsteady. She practiced and fell. She practiced
again. One day as her mother opened the kitchen window
to let in the warm sun, she saw her young daughter come
around the corner, grasping the handlebars gingerly, and
audibly praying, "Hold me, Jesus!"

All of us have had experiences when we prayed that
child's prayer. One of mine was in the mountains of South
America. I was in a small plane being carried to a mission
base. The weather was turbulent and so was my heart! The
treetops were too close. I must confess I did not feel it was
the time to be transported to glory. Hence my cry, "Hold
thou my hand!" Calm came with His gracious response,
"I am continually with thee."

The road we walk today holds many surprises. There
are twists and turns and detours. Crossroads confuse the
traveler. Ascents and descents make him weary. He stops
often for refreshment.

"I will instruct thee and teach thee in the way which
thou shalt go: I will guide thee with mine eye."[2] "The steps
of a good man are ordered by the Lord: and he delighteth
in his way."[3]

The journey may be continued in confidence. "This is
the way, walk ye in it."[4] The goal is straight ahead and our
future is assured. Some day we shall be received into God's
glory.

It is a wonderful experience to feel His arms of love
about us, our hands placed in faith and confidence in His,
knowing that He keeps His promises.

Hold Thou my hand, when the way is unsure,
In Thy hand of love I am safe and secure.
No crossroads confuse, nor detours cause fear.
"Behold, I am with thee . . . be of good cheer."

[1]Psalm 73:23-24.
[2]Psalm 32:8.
[3]Psalm 37:23.
[4]Isaiah 30:21.

❧ ❧ ❧

June 14

PSALMS 78–80
PSALM 78:1-11

> The children of Ephraim, being armed and carrying
> bows, turned back in the day of battle. . . . But he, being
> full of compassion, forgave their iniquity, and destroyed
> them not: yea, many a time turned he his anger away,
> and did not stir up all his wrath.[1]

"RECORD THE WHOS, whats, whens, and whys, and you will
have a complete account of the battle," a naval officer told
one of his mates. "Then you will have presented the complete picture."

The first of today's verses lends itself to such simple scrutiny, though I do not profess to understand all its implications.

Who? The children of Ephraim. The group stands for
all the children of Israel. They had seen the glory of God
in provision and guidance. They had been led by Joshua
into the Promised Land. Their parents were the true blue
bloods of the day. These children of Ephraim were well
armed.

What? They forsook their responsibility. In the time of
great crisis and need they turned their backs. They knew
well that the battle of Canaan was before them, but they
turned around. The consequences were grave and Canaan
was lost.

Why? The Word tells us, "They kept not the covenant of God, and refused to walk in his law; and forgat his works, and his wonders that he had shewed them."[2]

C. H. Spurgeon said, "They turned back, because they had poor memories!" The works and wonders of God had been dismissed from their minds and they had grown indifferent to all the wonderful things He had done for them.

What were the results? Their Father mourned deeply over what they had done. Here was heartbreak supreme.

We as Christians are placed on a battleground. We have before us the complete history of God's accomplishment in our lives and in the lives of our predecessors. Do we dare, being armed with the Spirit, to turn back? What grief it will be to our Father if we, as the children of Ephraim—yes, as the children of God—do not go forward in daily victory.

[1]Psalm 78:9, 38.
[2]Psalm 78:10-11.

❧   ❧   ❧

PSALMS 81–85
PSALM 85

> Wilt thou not revive us again: that thy people may
> rejoice in thee?[1]

MY HEART WAS WARMED during a missionary conference to
hear a veteran worker from Africa share her thoughts on the
subject of revival and its source.

Her field of service was small. There were but three
other laborers in her communications area. Their times together were limited, and their fellowship rare. Because of
these circumstances she became burdened that their hearts
and lives might be so revived that each meeting together
would result in great rejoicing.

From studying this verse, she recognized God as the Author of revival. Nothing that the four could do would generate revival. As the missionary said, "Spiritual awakening
is not worked up, it is brought down." So she began praying, first for the Lord to work her over. In studying she
deduced that if God was the Source, it was only natural for
her to be the subject. The subject could only be one who
was first reborn in Christ and then desired revival in Him.
She continued praying. Then the day came when all four
missionaries met to pray together. The result was revival.
And their labor flourished!

"Oh," you say, "when I pray for revival, I mean the kind
that causes sinners to be converted. I never think of Christians obtaining new joy in the Lord!" This dear woman in
Africa wanted a revival of joy, of unity, of goals and purposes, with the ultimate purpose of winning nationals to
Christ.

The Source of revival remains the same, but the subjects
need constant renewing. Evan Roberts of the Welsh Revival prayed, "O God, bend me!"

I wonder how willing we are to be "bent" in order to see revival in our times, first as individuals, and then as a nation?

¹Psalm 85:6.

❦ ❦ ❦

June 16

PSALMS 86–89
PSALM 86

> Bow down thine ear, O Lord, hear me: for I am poor and needy. Be merciful unto me, O Lord: for I cry unto thee daily. For thou, Lord, art good, and ready to forgive; and plenteous in mercy unto all them that call upon thee.¹

SEVERAL MOTHERS were debating which words meant most when they were honestly spoken by their children, "I love you" or "I'm sorry." In daily life the two cannot be separated, for to be truly sorry you must first love the one whose forgiveness you seek, and true love always seeks forgiveness for wrongdoing.

God is surely the God of forgiveness. He forgives because He is good. The Psalmist spoke again from experience. There was a time when he was harboring unconfessed sin, yet the moment he broke in confession to God, he knew he was forgiven. He said, "Lord, thou art good and ready to forgive."

God is always ready to forgive—seventy times seven times, and more. His forgiveness comes from His storehouse of "plenteous mercy."

A refugee came to the United States. He had been told it was a land of plenty. Before he arrived, he asked what "plenty" was, and someone told him it was "the opposite of poverty." Then he understood. He well knew poverty. "Plenty" would be a full glass of milk, possibly some meat once a week, maybe a blanket for the cold nights. He arrived in America. His first job was on a dairy farm. He had free access to all the milk he could drink and all the meat he could eat. Blankets were stacked in the bunkhouse. Plenty! He was just beginning to understand the meaning.

We have sinned. Our souls are in poverty. Then we read of "plenteous mercy." Possibly the meaning is not clear to us. It is difficult to understand how the Lord could forgive when our sins have been so many, so repeated, and sometimes so deliberate. Then we are brought face to face with Him. We pray, "Bow down thine ear, O Lord, hear me: for I am poor and needy." And He hears and helps us.

Our definition of "plenteous" was inadequate. We now experience its true meaning as individuals. It means "forgiveness which knows no barriers nor limitations." No matter how guilty we are, there is enough and more to cover our needs. If we are truly sorry for sin, it is because we do love Him whose forgiveness we seek. May the words come from our lips in devotion and sincerity, "I love You—I'm sorry." His "plenteous" mercy will be our portion.

¹Psalm 86:1, 3, 5.

❧ ❧ ❧

PSALMS 90–94
PSALM 90

> Lord, thou hast been our dwelling place in all genera-
> tions. Before the mountains were brought forth, or ever
> thou hadst formed the earth and the world, even from
> everlasting to everlasting, thou art God.[1]

A GIRL SCOUT LEADER was giving instructions to her new charges at summer camp. At twilight, some became frightened as shadows lurked about and swaying trees made their dark pictures on the ground. Her advice was good: "If you are afraid of the night, look up above the shadows into the stars."

How ordinary the perspective when we focus our sight at eye level. How delightful the picture when we focus our sight up, on the One who formed the earth, who "from everlasting to everlasting" is God.

This prayer of Moses is perhaps the oldest of the Psalms, and could well have been written as he saw the people of God dying because of their unbelief. Yet, even at such a time he could take his eyes from the human level and look up toward God. In looking up, he was sustained.

Do things in your range of sight look out of perspective? Does darkness loom over, casting shadows of doubt and fear? Look up, and find in God a refuge and dwelling place.

In Mexico, close to Christmas one year, I met a woman with the Salvation Army. Her testimony was gracious and sweet, and she greatly encouraged my faith. She shared some of the disappointments of her work along with the blessings. I noticed, however, there was still joy in her face as she mentioned the times of trial. Our conversation uncovered the reason.

In words something like this she summed it all up. We must keep God in focus. Knowing just where to look is essential. Looking back could discourage us. Looking ahead could frighten us. Looking around tends to confuse us. So we look up—up to the eternal One. We seek to live in heavenly places.

Knowing where to look is essential. "He that dwelleth in the secret place of the most High shall abide [take residence] under the shadow of the Almighty."[2]

[1]Psalm 90:1-2.
[2]Psalm 91:1.

❧ ❧ ❧

PSALMS 95–100
PSALM 100

> Serve the Lord with gladness: come before his presence
> with singing.[1]

"GOD REQUIRES NO SLAVES!" The statement could well be used as a reminder to many well-meaning so-called servants of Christ.

In a small city in Washington, a church was preparing for a banquet. The women of the church were working with all their might. Decorations, food preparation, programs—all were being readied for the final stages of work. Some were delighted at the opportunity to serve. Their faces were lit up in happy anticipation of another occasion which would be dedicated to the Lord. Some hummed as they worked, others broke out in triumphant song. Working toward the back were some new Christians who could not get over the fact that this labor, too, could be counted to the glory of God. How they rejoiced!

However, amid the joy there was one lady whose attitude was a contrast. She frowned, she scowled. Her fingers were quick in their work, but her heart seemed cold. It was so noticeable that one of the other women went back to cheer her up. "Say," she said, "what kind of a master do you serve? He must be a taskmaster!" The unhappy woman was silent. The statement carried much greater impact than originally intended.

Each of us, dear reader, is given an opportunity to serve the Lord. What kind of a master do we serve? The Psalmist reminds us, "The Lord is good."[2] We serve a good Master. One who calls on us to do service out of affection for Him. "We are his people, and the sheep of his pasture."[3] The Shepherd gave His life for the sheep. The angels serve Him with song, not sorrow. We are given the invitation: "Come before his presence with singing."

Too many people think that the Christian church is a negative one, one where don'ts overshadow dos, one where we are like slaves or robots to a master.

With joy and gladness springing from a heart of love to Him let us show forth that it is the very King of kings and Lord of lords whom we gratefully serve.

[1]Psalm 100:2.
[2]Psalm 100:5.
[3]Psalm 100:3.

❧   ❧   ❧

PSALMS 101–104
PSALM 103

> Bless the Lord, O my soul, and forget not all his bene-
> fits.[1]

THE MEANING of the word *benefit,* according to Mr. Webster, is "an act of kindness, a gift, a benefaction, whatever
promotes welfare."

Surely each Christian has experienced daily demonstrations of the glorious benefits which are made available to
us through Christ.

"Who forgiveth all thine iniquities."[2] Daily we are
cleansed by His blood and experience the forgiveness that
He makes possible.

"Who redeemeth thy life from destruction; who crowneth
thee with lovingkindness and tender mercies."[3] Notice the
present tense throughout the Psalms. These blessings were
not meant only for men of old; they are for today, every
day. God's benefits continue, and they surpass our continuing needs.

"Who satisfieth thy mouth with good things; so that thy
youth is renewed like the eagle's."[4] The Chinese have an
old saying that the eagle, instead of growing older, grows
younger. Isaiah referred to the eagle when he wrote, "But
they that wait upon the Lord shall renew their strength;
they shall mount up with wings as eagles; they shall run,
and not be weary; and they shall walk, and not faint."[5] In
Him we can renew our strength from the eternal source of
life.

"He made known his ways unto Moses, his acts unto the
children of Israel."[6] Even so today, He makes known His
ways to us through His Word. What a gift this is, a great
act of kindness. Does it not promote our welfare in the divine sense?

Blessing the Lord is something we do together, but it is also a personal, individual act. "Bless the Lord, O my soul." We want to join in the heavenly throngs that sing His praise, remembering that it takes individual voices to make up that host!

I don't want my heartful of joy to be crowded out in the chorus. I want to lift my soul, individually, in untiring gratitude for "all his benefits" to me.

¹Psalm 103:2.
²Psalm 103:3.
³Psalm 103:4.
⁴Psalm 103:5.
⁵Isaiah 40:31.
⁶Psalm 103:7.

❧ ❧ ❧

June 20

PSALMS 105–106
PSALM 105

> Glory ye in his holy name: let the heart of them rejoice that seek the Lord. Seek the Lord, and his strength: seek his face evermore.[1]

IT WAS D. L. MOODY who said, "If you have so much business to attend to that you have no time to pray, depend on it you have more business on hand than God ever intended you should have."

The statement serves as a good reminder to me that God wants my devotion more than my service. I honestly delight in serving the Lord. Nothing is more exhilarating than a calendar full of engagements for Him. There have been those days when the devotion was crowded out. For some time I could rationalize that this was all right. Was not I serving the Lord? Were not others hearing about Him? All the arguments were weak. He does not want my good works for Him. He wants me!

I must "seek the Lord, and his strength: seek his face evermore." It is His strength which I can impart to the discouraged one who finds life unbearable. My strength will not help. It is His strength I am called upon to share with that one who has lost a loved one and finds no consolation. Mine would not suffice. I must seek His face before another can be pointed to Him. Yesterday's vision could well be clouded if I don't see Him, in all the fullness of His glory, today!

It is rather difficult to describe someone whom you have not met or from whom you have long been separated. You may have heard a good recommendation of him, seen his picture, or read some of his writing. However, if you are called upon to introduce that one, your introduction will lack the strength of an introduction made from firsthand acquaintance.

You are daily called on to describe the Lord. By your life you are showing Him to your neighbor. How vivid will be the picture if you have not recently seen Him yourself? How well prepared can be the Sunday school lesson on personal devotion if yours does not equal what you require in others?

Let us conclude that we are too busy if time alone with Him is pushed aside, even in the name of Christian service. We must never cease to make time to "seek his face" and to do it "evermore."

[1]Psalm 105:3-4.

❧ ❧ ❧

> Then they cried unto the Lord in their trouble, and he
> delivered them out of their distresses. And he led them
> forth by the right way.[1]

The Psalms are all expressions of experiences in reality and
in life. Those who wrote the Psalms walked real roads,
faced specific situations, and were as human as we are.

The Psalmist was acquainted with the burden of cares in
this world. He knew the meaning of temptation. He knew
what it was to actually be in trouble, serious trouble. The
picture of him with his harp in shady green pastures, with
only peace and pleasantness around, is not the David I read
about. All was not music and happiness for him. I am
sure he knew comedy, but he also knew tragedy. We know
he had times of rest and delight, but they came after he rose
from the depths of despair.

Psalm 107 is a good example of this. David talks of the
solitary way, the hunger and thirst, the distress and trouble,
which he knew. Yet, out of his cry to God, out of the depths
of his human experience, comes the desire to turn to God
in salvation.

Such may be your experience. Inexpressible darkness.
Situations that are hard to bear. Every way but the right
way has been tried. Peace has been sought in many places
without success.

Seek the Lord. "Then they cried unto the Lord in their
trouble, and he saved them out of their distresses."[2]

Night may have swallowed up your hopes, but the light
of God will shine through simple faith and trust in Him,
and you will be delivered from your aimless search and wanderings.

This is God's offer to us. This psalm brings comfort to

our hearts. Out of the wilderness experience shines the wisdom of God, and He is able to deliver. Rejoice that

> The best is yet to be,
> The last of life, for which the first was made:
> Our times are in His hand
> Who saith, "A whole I planned. . . ."
> Trust God . . . nor be afraid.[3]

[1]Psalm 107:6-7.
[2]Psalm 107:13.
[3]"Rabbi ben Ezra," Robert Browning.

❧ ❧ ❧

PSALMS 110–115
PSALM 110

> He shall drink of the brook in the way: therefore shall
> he lift up the head.[1]

HOW OFTEN we have heard the expression, "I am dying of thirst!" Thirst is not a pleasant experience. Where there is an abundance of water, thirst is easily satisfied.

All too many of us are dying of thirst today, not in a physical sense but spiritually. The thirst-quenching brook is as close as the Bible, and we need only drink to be satisfied.

Summer particularly lends itself to slackening off from time to drink from God's brook. How many vacation preparations include everything for our pleasure, but little for our Lord's!

Christ drank of the brook of humiliation for us. He went farther and drank the cup of suffering and of death. He did this so that we in turn might "drink" from the river of life and live.

Spiritual refreshment is the secret of going on in the Christian life. Time in His presence renews us in every way. I must confess that one year I caught myself reading chapters ahead in my Bible to get ready for vacation. How foolish this was! Surely I would not spend extra time in the kitchen drinking extra amounts of water so that my thirst would be quenched for the next two weeks! It is humorous but also humiliating. Our reasoning goes out of control when self comes ahead of the things of the Lord.

God never intended His pilgrims to faint along the way. He knew all about the heat of the journey and so He prepared refreshing streams. "He restoreth my soul."[2]

Imagine the privilege that is ours to taste of God's "brook," even before the time comes for us to spend an eternity with Him in heaven. Today each of us can partake!

Bow down to drink. Lift up your head to face life refreshed.

[1]Psalm 110:7.
[2]Psalm 23:3.

❧　❧　❧

Psalms 116–118
Psalm 116

> For thou hast delivered my soul from death, mine eyes
> from tears, and my feet from falling. I will walk before
> the Lord in the land of the living. Precious in the sight
> of the Lord is the death of his saints.[1]

WHAT IS DEATH? No one seems to come up with a completely satisfactory answer. The physician can explain the physical phenomenon. The theologian can lead you beyond the
grave. But neither can lift the veil which hangs over the
thought of death to those outside of Christ.

To the Christian, death is a step to life eternal in the
Lord's presence. Because of this, our souls have been delivered from death. For this reason, we anticipate the day
when we will be with Him in the true land of the living.

The land of the living has special significance for our
family. When my father went to be with the Lord, an
acquaintance suggested that it was not for him we mourned
but for us who remain. We live today in the land of the dying. Daddy had been transported into God's land of the
living. Because of this thought, our eyes were delivered
from tears.

A mother had experienced the sorrow of losing three children at birth. The years went by and at last she and her
husband were overjoyed that she had delivered a live infant.
The child grew and with it their hopes and anticipations
for its future. They thanked God continually for the precious gift He had given them. They fully recognized that
children are from the Lord, and that God places them in
the parents' hands only to be nourished and trained for His
pleasure.

At thirteen months, the baby died. At first the sorrow
was unbearable, not only for the mother and father but for
other loved ones who were aware of what this child meant.

It not only left a vacancy in their home but heaviness in many hearts.

The mother one afternoon was reading in the Psalms, "Precious in the sight of the Lord is the death of his saints." God granted her, through His Spirit, new understanding. She had been called upon to give back the child that had been loaned to them for the brief period. In seeking further light, answer came more clearly through an old truth which had new significance. Even when the gift is an only child, "God loveth a cheerful giver!"[2]

May He grant us spiritual perspective in order to bring every area of our lives into His eternal perspective.

[1]Psalm 116:8-9, 15.
[2]II Corinthians 9:7.

❧ ❧ ❧

June 24

PSALM 119:1–88
PSALM 119:1–8

> Blessed are the undefiled in the way, who walk in the law of the Lord.[1]

OBEDIENCE for the Christian cannot be overemphasized. We know there is a wide divergence among us as to degree of personal obedience. Yet we know obedience is a distinguishing mark of the true, sincere child of God.

The character of an obedient child of God is found in Psalm 119. Some of the evidences are clearly outlined:

> They are undefiled in the way.
> They walk in the law of the Lord.
> They keep His testimonies.
> They seek Him with their whole heart.
> They do no iniquity.
> They keep God's precepts diligently.
> They learn His righteous judgments.[2]

Suppose someone chooses a path of partial obedience. He walks with divided loyalties, and still hopes his faith will grow. At times the Scriptures are searched and the Word of God heard. However, the faith is not sufficiently nurtured, and good works are neglected. There can be no progress, for faith without works is not alive.

The story is told of a man who was thrown down to the ground from a high tension pole he was working on. At the hospital he was pronounced dead. At the undertaker's, a man saw his eyelid barely flicker, and called an ambulance. The man is alive today. However, if he had not somehow evidenced his life, even by a little flutter of the eyelid, he would have been buried.

Faith, without works, indicates only partial obedience, not a wholehearted walk in the whole law of God. Is there at least a "flicker" of works in our lives? Or is our faith dead? In the home, the disobedient child is the unhappy child. In the family of God, the child disobedient to His commands cannot be truly happy. Our love and obedience to the Lord must be manifested in love and faith, in patience and kindness, to others. "They [God's children] are peaceful and pleasant," said a pilgrim of old, "in their blessed state with God." He added, "Any breach of His commands leads to the utmost of wretchedness."

Are you satisfied today with the state of your soul? If you love God, keep His commandments, and evidence such commitment in your daily walk.

[1]Psalm 119:1.
[2]Psalm 119:1-8.

❧   ❧   ❧

Psalm 119:89–176
Psalm 119:97–112

> O how love I thy law! it is my meditation all the day.
> Thy word is a lamp unto my feet, and a light unto my path.[1]

CHRIST, the living Word, offers Himself to us as the Light of the world. His brightness and glory penetrate a darkened world. In the light of God's Word we seek daily instruction for heart illumination that will ultimately light up the hearts of others. Thus God's Word lights the path for us and for others.

Christ said, "Man shall not live by bread alone."[2] He knew that the Word of God was essential for feeding His flock and for sustaining them. Light in the Word can not only show up imperfections but give specific direction as to the way we should walk and the work that we must do.

Christ lights the way to the exercise of prayer. By His example, He highlighted its importance. Mark described it thus: "Rising up a great while before day, he went out and departed into a solitary place, and there prayed."[3] In times spent alone with God in prayer, we gain true enlightenment for our life.

Yesterday we talked of obedience. Christ was obedient. He often made clear to those about Him that His very meat was doing the will and work of the One who sent Him. This was uppermost in His mind. The light of Scripture often shines on our reaction to God's commands. It shows clearly that there is only one way, His way.

As a lamp and light, God's Word can give illumination on any problem the Christian may face.

> There is a light which cannot fail.
> It shines from heaven above.

It has its center and its source
In Christ's redeeming love.
The light illuminates my path,
Makes clear God's holy Word,
And, through me, penetrates the dark
Of those who've never heard.

¹Psalm 119:97, 105.
²Matthew 4:4.
³Mark 1:35.

❧ ❧ ❧

PSALMS 120–127
PSALM 121

> I will lift up mine eyes unto the hills, from whence
> cometh my help. My help cometh from the Lord.¹

"MAMA," asked eight-year-old Susan, "what help comes from
the hills?" Mother was somewhat confused as to her daughter's query until Susan continued by quoting the chapter
she was memorizing for Sunday school.

How easy it is to quickly read over words and miss the
entire message. What the Psalmist is saying is, "I will lift
up mine eyes unto the hills." But it is not from the hills
that his help comes. His local surroundings cannot solve
his problems. His help is beyond personal circumstances,
beyond the hills and the mountains. The next words should
start a new sentence, and it should end with a question
mark. "From whence cometh my help?" The sure answer
follows: "My help cometh from the Lord, which made
heaven and earth." Psalm 123 expresses it another way.
"Unto thee lift I up mine eyes, O thou that dwellest in the
heavens."²

Several of the Psalms are called "songs of degrees." Others
are described as "ascents." We are told they stem from
pilgrim songs, sung by those going to Jerusalem for feasts

288

at various times of the year. The children of God, however, marching to Zion, are also led higher in their worship of Him, and in their approach to His presence through the Psalms.

How vividly this psalm also expresses the keeping power of God. We lift our hearts to Him, beyond the hills, and all our circumstances are entrusted to Him. Six times in eight short verses His keeping power is presented.

One writer points out the exquisite sequence of the phrases in reference to this wonderful keeping power. It is sustained by day and by night. God guards, as He slumbers not nor sleeps. He preserves our goings and our comings. He keeps us, body and soul. The promise is timeless. "The Lord shall preserve thy going out and thy coming in from this time forth, and even for evermore."[3]

Lift up your eyes beyond yourself and past your problems, into the limitless expanse of God's power and sure promise!

[1]Psalm 121:1-2.
[2]Psalm 123:1.
[3]Psalm 121:8.

❧ ❧ ❧

> Blessed is every one that feareth the Lord; that walketh
> in his ways. For thou shalt eat the labour of thine
> hands: happy shalt thou be, and it shall be well with
> thee.[1]

THESE ARE TRULY wonderful words. "It shall be well with
thee." That is something we all would like. Everything we
plan for stems from our desire for well-being. Physically,
mentally, and spiritually this is true.

This psalm has been called a "portrait of a godly man and
his family." The man of the house is described as one that
fears the Lord and walks in His ways. He is reverent and
devoted to the cause of the kingdom of God. His home has
been built on the Rock, Christ Jesus, for he knows that
"except the Lord build the house, they labour in vain that
build it."[2]

The woman of the house competently attends to the details of their homelife. Her housework is dedicated to the
Lord, no matter how menial the duties may be. She is a
source of strength to her husband. The vine is a symbol of
grace and fruitfulness, and she exemplifies both.

The children are likened to olive plants symbolic of those
who are raised in a godly atmosphere. They will be vigor-
ous and able to stand alone for the cause in which they have
been nurtured. They will also bring joy to their parents.

Such families are desperately needed today for "peace
upon Israel." They will not only be blessed but they will
be a blessing in all their pursuits. The church will be enriched by their membership and their example will challenge others.

> "Is it well with you?"
> Comes the question clear,

"And with your home
And children dear?

"Do you fear the Lord
And walk His ways,
And seek Him first
Throughout your days?"

[1]Psalm 128:1-2.
[2]Psalm 127:1.

❧   ❧   ❧

June 28

PSALMS 136–139
PSALM 139

> In omniscience, the all-knowing God
> Planned the past and future path I plod.
>
> He is omnipresent. He is everywhere!
> He surrounds my life and lifts my care.
>
> His omnipotence is power indeed
> For strength when I have none—and all I need!

THESE DIVINE ATTRIBUTES of God make us stand still in awe and wonder that such a God could be interested in us!

God knows all about us. He knows our "uprisings." To me this means not only our daily rising from sleep but also those moments when our spirits are lifted; the times when we have dared to speak for Him and the results were blessed; days when the future was all bright and our hearts were filled with praise. "Uprisings" can recall a special instance of His presence.

God knows our "downsittings." How well that word illustrates the days when the future looks dark, when we are weary and almost exhausted; times when we are completely discouraged with ourselves; times when we fall so short of His glory. "Downsittings" are not only times of physical weariness but also the shadow experiences of life.

God's omnipresence brings great joy. We are never alone. He is ever with us and in us. A Puritan of old wrote, "God's center is everywhere, and His circumference is nowhere." Literally feeling His presence is an untold comfort to one who feels he walks alone.

God's power is not an abstract thing. It too can be demonstrated in our lives. Throughout the Old and New Testaments men and women witnessed this power in their lives. It has continued to work through the centuries and is as real and vital today as it was when David wrote the Psalms.

These three attributes of God, His omniscience, His omnipresence, and His omnipotence, should lift our hearts, for "this God is our God for ever and ever."[1]

[1]Psalm 48:14.

❧ ❧ ❧

Psalms 140–145
Psalm 145

> The Lord is nigh unto all them that call upon him, to
> all that call upon him in truth.[1]

How OFTEN we have sung the words, "There is a place of
quiet rest, near to the heart of God." When we close the
hymnbook our thoughts may focus on the spiritual significance. Oh, to stay in that place of rest, near to the Lord.

We watch great Christians and wonder what is their secret of close relationship with Him. We devour books on
how to know Him better. But second-hand knowledge seldom uncovers the pattern for drawing near. It is not a
complicated pattern. It is simple and sure. *Prayer* brings
us closest to God. "He is nigh unto all them that call upon
him." How strange that we seek afar to find Him when He
is as close as prayer. Why do we make such a large "pro-
duction" of meeting One who already abides within?

Our conversation with Him can be carried on not just
early in the morning, or late at night, but throughout the
day—while going to work, while cleaning the kitchen, before
meeting a client, while going to class, continually. Let us
want to say with David, "I am continually with thee."[2]

Nearness brings dearness. We want to be with one whom
we dearly love—not just on brief occasions but continually.
Communication is unhindered only as we keep a constant,
unbroken, and growing relationship.

A little girl was learning to pray. It was very hard for
her to close her eyes and believe that God, whom she could
not see, was able to hear. Even though young, she had a
strong desire that her daddy know Christ too. So she prayed
on. One day she told her mother, "I have to pretend very
hard that God is right here with me, and yet the pretend
isn't pretending at all. I hope God knows that!"

God did know, and we too would do well to practice His presence, for He surely is with us.

[1]Psalm 145:18.
[2]Psalm 73:23.

❧ ❧ ❧

PSALMS 146–150
PSALM 147

> He healeth the broken in heart, and bindeth up their wounds. He telleth the number of the stars; he calleth them all by their names. Great is our Lord, and of great power: his understanding is infinite.[1]

WHEN WE THINK of the magnitude of the world in which we live, the complex explanation that science is giving for its origin, and man's philosophies in every realm of human knowledge and experience, we may become puzzled. Not too many years ago we looked at the stars and in all simplicity watched them twinkle and shine, without knowledge of some facts that now begin to unveil their mystery. We are aware that the universe is infinite, and our finite minds are wondering, "How can the Master Architect be interested in me individually?"

This psalm might further complicate the issue, especially when we think of the uncounted number of stars in the heavens. But the Psalmist dispels speculation: "He telleth the number of the stars; he calleth them all by their names." Marvelous? Yes, but lest we should still wonder at the tremendous implications of this statement, the Scripture becomes intensely personal. "He healeth the broken in heart, and bindeth up all their wounds." Here is a fantastic contrast. God's interest in the unlimited scope of space, and His compassion for one broken heart!

Here He becomes not just the Creator and Sustainer but

the Master Cardiologist. His heart was once broken for us. Out of this heart flow love and compassion and matchless understanding. He also gives spiritual treatment for sin-sick hearts. If your heart is full of sin, He has promised, "A new heart also will I give you, and a new spirit will I put within you: and I will take away the stony heart."[2] Such an exchange shows His personal interest in each of His children.

St. Augustine once wrote, "O Lord, Thou hast made us for Thyself. Our hearts are restless until they find their rest in Thee."

God's heart of love continually seeks us out. "Great is our Lord, and of great power: his understanding is infinite."

[1]Psalm 147:3-5.
[2]Ezekiel 36:26.

❧ ❧ ❧

July

PROVERBS 1–3
PROVERBS 2:1-6; 3:1-6

> My son, hear the instruction of thy father. The fear of
> the Lord is the beginning of knowledge.[1]

THE VOICE OF WISDOM, speaking to the heart of youth, or the
message of a father to a son. This is the setting of Proverbs,
sometimes called the "Hebrew wisdom literature."

Wisdom is here set forth in the true spiritual sense. It
stems not only from the head but also from the heart. This
is knowledge of God and His ways, and a holy fear and understanding of Him. Did you realize that wisdom is often
listed with other virtues like charity and honesty?

The writer tells us how such wisdom may be obtained:
"The Lord giveth wisdom."[2] The Psalmist wrote, "The
entrance of thy words giveth light."[3] Our growth is determined by our heart-reception of God's words. Following
reception there must be retention. Receiving must never be
a temporary thing when it comes to the Word.

"Incline thine ear unto wisdom, and apply thine heart to
understanding."[4] This is only accomplished with much diligence. We know the words of wisdom are received in only
one way, by His Word through the Spirit. As one would
pan for gold or mine silver until the treasure is uncovered,
so the believer must study and search the Word diligently,
looking to the Spirit to illuminate it.

"If thou liftest up thy voice for understanding . . ."[5]
Here is a phase of prayer which should not come last but

should be first. Without understanding, prayer cannot be definite or effective. God truly is the giver of all knowledge, and it is in asking that we receive.

All knowledge is in God. As we begin to read the book of Proverbs let us each ask God to open it to us. This is a book we need for knowledge of Christian conduct. It is packed with wise sayings of wise and holy men. Proverbs are short moral sentences, each with a profound meaning. Let us ask the Holy Spirit to enrich their significance as we drink from this fountain of wisdom.

[1]Proverbs 1:8, 7.
[2]Proverbs 2:6.
[3]Psalm 119:130.
[4]Proverbs 2:2.
[5]Proverbs 2:3.

❧ ❧ ❧

July 2

PROVERBS 4–7
PROVERBS 4

> Let thine eyes look right on, and let thine eyelids look straight before thee. Ponder the path of thy feet, and let all thy ways be established. Turn not to the right hand nor to the left: remove thy foot from evil.[1]

"PONDER THE PATH of thy feet." Remember how, as children, we took great delight in walking narrow paths, or gingerly conquering walls and fence tops? A father watching his son practice on a tightrope noted the distortions of his mouth and commented, "It's not just the way you hold your mouth; it's your feet too!"

As we ponder our path as Christians, we must realize it is important that we not only express our wisdom but that our feet also walk accordingly.

A teen-ager took delight in associating with a circle of friends who did things that did not befit a child of God.

297

Her continual excuse was found in the lines of a well-known hymn: "Anywhere with Jesus I can safely go." Her teacher was greatly concerned and called her in for a special talk. The teacher related a story she had heard of another young girl who visited a coal mine with some high school juniors. A determined girl, she set out to prove she could wear a white dress and still come out clean. She descended, clean and scrubbed, into the mine in all its blackness. She arrived home black and covered with dust and soot. The teacher went on to explain that as Christians we must ponder the path of our feet, lest the surroundings overpower us.

May we walk circumspectly. This very moment we are pondering a path. It may be one of blessing or of shame. It may be one of danger or of great delight. The farther we venture into the wrong path, the longer it takes us to find the right road again. Because of this, we must take time to "ponder" and consider our ways. A false step could prove eternally fatal.

Said a wise man, "Keep your feet and eyes joined, and your ways will be established." "In all thy ways acknowledge him, and he shall direct thy paths."[2]

[1]Proverbs 4:25-27.
[2]Proverbs 3:6.

❧ ❧ ❧

The blessing of the Lord, it maketh rich, and he addeth no sorrow with it.[1]

"I AM INDEED RICH," said an elderly woman who had lived in virtual poverty as a missionary for almost a half century. "I am rich because my Father is rich, and I live with true royalty." In beautiful assurance she spoke the words of a familiar hymn:

> My Father is rich in houses and lands,
> He holdeth the wealth of the world in His hands!
> Of rubies and diamonds, of silver and gold,
> His coffers are full, He has riches untold.[2]

Her mouth spoke the abundance of her heart. Her riches consisted not in the extent of her possessions but in the eternal treasure and inheritance which were hers in Christ.

Surely, His blessing in our lives does make for riches. Material blessings? No, it is not such that I have in mind, for the older one grows, the more one realizes that the good and perfect gifts are from above. Think today of the blessing of sins forgiven! Remember the great High Priest who is touched with the feeling of our infirmities! There is great blessing in anticipation. Think of the future we will have with Him forever! That is a glorious hope.

There are the blessings of friends and loved ones. And the still greater blessing of the sure knowledge that God loves me, and that nothing can separate me from that consistent and persistent love.

There is the blessing of our land, and the handiwork of God displayed profusely throughout it. Our admiration of the beauty that surrounds us should lift our hearts in praise and add to the rich inventory that is already ours.

Have you taken recent stock of all that is yours in Christ? Riches indeed! Some may be material riches, granted to you for your wise care. But the greatest riches are spiritual. These are not marked or marred by evil, and there is no sorrow with them. Let us seek the blessing of God upon every detail of our lives. For it truly "maketh rich"!

[1]Proverbs 10:22.
[2]Harriet E. Buell.

❧   ❧   ❧

July 4

PROVERBS 12–15
PROVERBS 14

> Righteousness exalteth a nation: but sin is a reproach
> to any people.[1]

INDEPENDENCE DAY is an appropriate time to look back and review our fight for freedom. Probably no other nation can make the claims that ours can in relation to this text. Our history books tell us of the struggles of those who braved unknown peril and danger in order to leave a place where there was all too much tolerance for evil, to come to a place where they could live righteously, free of former fears and frustrations.

Many of our dedicated founders were devout men of God who put Christ first, and wanted their children reared where righteousness prevailed. Our nation grew and flourished. It has been said, "Righteous founding fathers made us what we are. Sinful sons can cause our fall to be as great as that of the Roman Empire!" We know that no country has long prospered that has set aside the way of national righteousness.

"Sin is a reproach to any people." This was illustrated in the Old Testament in the nation of Israel. They remain a constant object lesson for us. As long as they were obedient, and esteemed God, they prospered. When sin overtook them, they became a reproach.

We love our United States and the liberty for which our country stands. But in order that our nation be righteous under God, we Christians must take a firm stand for Christ and country. Someone has truly said, "Until we uproot vice and implant virtue, secure peace and prosperity, and remove sin, there can be no exalting of a nation."

We know this is not easily accomplished. Until man's heart is cleansed and changed, righteousness will not endure. "How can I change the nation?" you ask doubtfully. "How am I going to remove national sin?" The answer comes not in changing the nation but in changing individuals. God alone can do this. When a person receives a new heart and a new life, and he allows righteousness to excel in his life, then prays for it to spread next door, the power of the gospel is released. And other lives are reached and transformed in ever-widening circles.

If we all do our part, as "laborers together with God,"[2] as a nation we will know righteousness and not reproach.

[1]Proverbs 14:34.
[2]I Corinthians 3:9.

❧   ❧   ❧

> Commit thy works unto the Lord, and thy thoughts
> shall be established.[1]

ESTABLISHED THOUGHTS. How often we long for them. Oh,
with Paul, to "have the mind of Christ"!

A saint of yesterday said that to commit one's works to
the Lord means literally to give one's soul a holiday! The
burden of the day has been rolled onto Him, and His Spirit
will develop those needful details.

There is no doubt that God uses various methods to lead
us, but what is vital and essential is that we recognize that
He does lead! Psalm 32 is not just a series of lovely sentences. These are living words that may be daily experienced: "I will instruct thee and teach thee in the way that
thou shalt go: I will guide thee with mine eye."[2] Guidance
may come from the Scriptures, from circumstances, or even
from a friend. But the real source, if we have committed
our lives to Him, is the Lord.

How wonderful to awake to a day that is filled to the
brim and overflowing with responsibility, and quietly and
confidently say, "Lord, I commit it entirely to You—the
major jobs and the minor ones, the big problems and the
little ones, the seen and the unseen." The Master Planner
is continually at work to do His will and pleasure in me.
The outcome can only be one of divine organization, bringing fresh realization that "this is the day which the Lord
hath made."[3] So, I will rejoice and be glad in it. I will
rejoice because my works are committed. I will be glad because my thoughts are established.

Then there are those who battle with their thoughts.
Often fear, or discouragement, or lack of victory in a specific area of life, is most difficult to overcome. "Too often,"
wrote an acquaintance, "my thoughts feed on fear and I

have little control." Christ can conquer these thoughts also, if He is given a chance. Paul challenged us about "bringing into captivity every thought to the obedience of Christ."[4]

Starve those thoughts that are not on Him by feeding on His words. The result will be Christ-established thoughts.

[1]Proverbs 16:3.
[2]Psalm 32:8.
[3]Psalm 118:24.
[4]II Corinthians 10:5.

❧   ❧   ❧

July 6

PROVERBS 19–22
PROVERBS 22

> Train up a child in the way he should go: and when he is old, he will not depart from it.[1]

AN ARCHERY TEACHER admonished her class, "If an arrow is to fly straight, it must be started right." This is good advice to parents, teachers, and all those who have responsibility in pointing youngsters in the right direction.

I remember a Sunday school teacher saying that since she was not a parent, she paid little attention to this proverb. Another teacher was shocked, as she had felt—and rightly so—that this is for all of us. The verse has been paraphrased, "Initiate a child concerning the way he should go." Starting a child right by spoken words is not enough. Example is essential. Teachers and friends as well as parents have the responsibility of that five-letter word, *train*.

To train takes patience and perseverance. It may be in Sunday school with difficult third graders, but we are training by our preparation, our devotion, and our sincerity. It is not enough to quickly pray the Lord's blessing on those we work with. Our work must be backed up with fervent, diligent prayer and preparation.

The question arises, "But what of those who found Christ late in life? Those who did not have the opportunity to be trained for Him by dedicated people." Almost always, somewhere in their background, someone has been faithful in prayer and concern. Few find Christ late in life, and this proves again the need and value of early regeneration.

David was trained from his youth. Samuel's mother determined, before he was born, to put his feet on the right path. The result of a godly heritage was shown in the life of Timothy. "When I call to remembrance the unfeigned faith that is in thee, which dwelt first in thy grandmother Lois, and thy mother Eunice; and I am persuaded that [it is] in thee also."[2]

Let us recognize today the benefits of early piety and seek in practice and precept to instill it in the children God brings under our influence.

[1]Proverbs 22:6.
[2]II Timothy 1:5.

❧   ❧   ❧

PROVERBS 23–27
PROVERBS 23

> Boast not thyself of tomorrow; for thou knowest not
> what a day may bring forth.[1]

"THE PRESENT is given man in order that he may act in view of the future." I first read that provocative sentence on the desk of a very busy statesman. To him, and often since to me, it has proved a vivid reminder to do today what today requires.

The future is always uncertain. We do not know what tomorrow will bring forth. Therefore, today has been given us to fulfill the sacred trust of God, another day for His glory.

Said the statesman, "If God tarries until tomorrow, tomorrow in itself will be enough. If today's cares are combined with tomorrow's, they will be more than I can handle." In his life he has often seen this illustrated. Often he promised to take his son who had polio on a proposed outing "tomorrow." Procrastination, that thief of time, finally robbed him of the opportunity forever. The boy had to be returned to an iron lung, and soon passed away.

The same man had a fellow colleague about whom he was burdened. Many times he tried to clear his calendar for lunch with him to tell him about Christ, and to give him a Bible. Meetings were planned and delayed, made and cancelled, until again it was too late. The colleague died of a heart attack.

No wonder we are told to boast not ourselves of tomorrow. Only the omniscient God knows what will come to pass. The uncertainty of the future compels us to act today. Planning without Him tends to "invade the providence of God."[2] Let us not be guilty of this.

Personal devotions are too often put off until tomorrow. We do this in the name of getting a fresh start. We propose beginning a new week or year with the Lord, and so we delay. But, putting it off again and again may mean we never will start, for delay often causes us to lose the desire. If you have been waiting for the perfect time, "Now is the accepted time."[3]

The Spanish have a proverb that too often proves true: "The road of by-and-by leads to the house of never." Let us not be guilty of procrastination in expressing our devotion to God.

[1]Proverbs 27:1.
[2]Harry Ironside.
[3]II Corinthians 6:2.

❧   ❧   ❧

July 8

PROVERBS 28–31
PROVERBS 31

> Where there is no vision, the people perish: but he that keepeth the law, happy is he.[1]

TODAY WE NEED VISION. The lack of it is causing our world to perish. It is an awesome and frightening thought. Most of us boast sight but lack vision.

Two men stood on top of a hill where a church was located. They were part of an experiment. Each was asked what he saw as he looked over the panoramic sight below. The first quickly said he saw lots of rooftops, some lawns that needed mowing, and buildings. The other, more thoughtful and more slow to answer, came up with a statement which showed true vision. He saw houses, yes, but thought of what lay beneath those rooftops. He was concerned about the little children who were not in the Sunday school. He saw scores of parents who regarded Sunday as no different from the other six days. His heart was challenged and moved by the experiment.

Vision often reveals a *division* in thoughts as this experi-

306

ment proved. Thus it is important to look through the eyes of God and see the world as He sees it, lost, without Christ, and without hope. He sees not only the exterior but also the interior, and knows the deepest needs of people.

The results of the test brought some *revision* to the Sunday school planning. Why were those homes still untouched by the evangelization program of a church that had stood for almost half a century? Visitation at once was started and a survey made. A concentrated program to "bring them in" is proving successful.

God has made every *provision* for our needs in reaching those outside of Christ. He has promised to supply the needs we have in reaching those who are receptive to the Story. And after each has been planted, watered, and cared for, God will give the increase. Under the *supervision* of the Holy Spirit we can only go forward.

Rooftop sight is one thing. Vision of what lies beneath is what we should seek, and then go forward to be faithful ambassadors for our Lord.

¹Proverbs 29:18.

❧   ❧   ❧

ECCLESIASTES 1–3
ECCLESIASTES 3:1-15

> To everything there is a season, and a time to every purpose under the heaven.[1]

A FEW DAYS AGO we talked about the importance of spending time with the Lord for personal devotions in His presence. Some may have resolved that very day to start, others may still be looking for a more convenient "tomorrow."

Again, let me urge those who have not set aside a specific time with God or who have not deliberately resolved to make time, to do so at once. How strange it is that we can find time for anything we really want to do! To postpone spending time in God's presence points to our lack of desire. Why do I emphasize this? My own soul has felt the barrenness of crowding Him out in the name of being busy—busy even with important things. Daily I learn there is no substitute for communion with Him. My longings are satisfied in Him. My yearnings are fulfilled. Why should I live in emptiness when His fullness is available?

If you would resolve to experience personally what it means to shut out all else and step into God's divine Presence, you would be satisfied.

"To everything there is a season and a time":

> A time to meet my Lord and seek His face.
> A time to feed on Him, present my case.
> A time to seek His plan, and then to trace
> The intimate instruction of His grace.
>
> A time to bring to Him my every care;
> Time to confess my sin and guilt He'll bare;
> A time for others when with them I share.
> A will to take more time with God in prayer.

Take time, today, to be holy! Take time to listen and wait.

God should have priority to that precious gift He has given you. Some day He will ask you to account for each moment of your time.

[1]Ecclesiastes 3:1.

❧ ❧ ❧

ECCLESIASTES 5–8
ECCLESIASTES 5

Better is the end of a thing than the beginning thereof.[1]

THE BOOK OF ECCLESIASTES is a sermon which shows that anything—worldly pleasure, profit, wisdom—proves worthless when it comes to satisfying our inner needs. Without the reign of God within, all is vanity.

Frequently we meet a living illustration of the truth in today's reference, someone who has sought pleasure and riches, and found each unrewarding. They may have turned to a form of religion which did not fulfill their needs. Their ultimate conclusion: there is no profit in life. Their problem is too great to confront, and they wait, most miserably, the inevitability of death.

When such an individual finds abundant life in Christ, he is prime proof that the end can be much better than the beginning. This can also be true of those who have known Christ for most of their lives. Many a Christian has had a bitter beginning, but then experienced much glory in his later years through the "altogether lovely" One.[2]

Even Jesus Christ had a lowly and humble beginning. "He is despised and rejected of men; a man of sorrows, and acquainted with grief: and we hid as it were our faces from him. But he was wounded for our transgressions, he was bruised for our iniquities: the chastisement of our peace was upon him; and with his stripes we are healed. Yet it pleased the Lord to bruise him; he hath put him to grief:

when thou shalt make his soul an offering for sin, he shall see his seed, he shall prolong his days, and the pleasure of the Lord shall prosper in his hand."[3] His beginning was one of rejection, but the "end" remains eternally glorious.

Have you experienced some of this rejection of the message of Christ? Have neighbors made you a laughing stock so that you shuddered at their scoffing? Possibly you bear battle scars for Christ! How triumphant an ending there will be for those who, in these days of beginning and continuing, bear His "brand" of suffering! Yes, Solomon was right. "Better is the end of a thing than the beginning thereof."

[1]Ecclesiastes 7:8.
[2]Song of Solomon 5:16.
[3]Isaiah 53:3, 5, 10.

        ❧   ❧   ❧

ECCLESIASTES 9–12
ECCLESIASTES 12

> Cast thy bread upon the waters: for thou shalt find it
> after many days.[1]

A CHRISTIAN soon learns that he cannot outgive God. "Give,
and it shall be given unto you."[2] "Cast thy bread"—the
bread of kindness and understanding, with no hope of return—and "thou shalt find it after many days." When we
give to God, the return is as He promised: "good measure,
pressed down, and shaken together, and running over."

> Only one life, 'twill soon be past.
> Only what's done for Christ will last.

Much of our work on earth will perish, yet that which has
sterling value will abide. "He that doeth the will of God
abideth for ever."[3] Good deeds and actions will spring up
from the everlasting fount of His goodness as it is shown
to others, and unselfishness will never be fruitless. The
blessing will be preserved by God.

The Good Samaritan gave expecting nothing in return.
He stopped and cared for the wounded man not because
he hoped he was a millionaire in disguise. His kind heart
led to his action. God's reward for these acts is eternal
treasure.

A story comes from a family who were vacationing years
ago on Lake Michigan. In their morning devotions they
read this verse. It gave the teen-age boy an idea: next time
he sailed out into the lake, he would put a little Bible he
had inside a bottle after writing his name and address in
it, and a brief, personal testimony. It was his secret, and the
bottle was carefully prepared after the family retired. Each
day of his life he fervently prayed for the Bread of Life
he had cast upon the waters. The years passed. In 1963,

eleven years after the little Bible had been tossed into the lake, a letter addressed to the teen-ager, now grown, came to the family home. The young man's prayers were answered. The bottle had been found, and a lost soul found the Saviour. Now he is teaching his own family this vital principle.

Line upon line, precept upon precept, to rich and to poor, we must in faith "cast our bread upon the waters," knowing we shall "find it after many days."

[1]Ecclesiastes 11:1.
[2]Luke 6:38.
[3]I John 2:17.

❧ ❧ ❧

July 12

Song of Solomon 1–4
Song of Solomon 2

I sought him, but I found him not.[1]

PASTED ABOVE the "lost and found" window in a downtown department store is a little saying: "First look for it where you dropped it; it is most likely there."

The Song of Solomon, or the "Song of Songs" as it is called, pictures the believer's beautiful relationship with God. It typifies the holy love God has for His church. When our fellowship with Him is lost, it is time that we look for it—where we lost it.

Sometimes a misunderstanding arises between friends, often because of lack of communication. When that is restored the friendship flourishes.

Could it be that lack of communication with Christ impairs your relationship to Him? Once you loved Him with all your heart. The words of this book were real to you. He was your beloved. You could say, "His right hand doth embrace me."[2] But that close, sweet communication has been severed for a time. He patiently waits and lovingly

312

deals with you. Return to where you lost vibrant, satisfying communion. You will again hear His voice and thrill at His love. The constant sense of His presence will return to you, and there will be great joy.

It is possible that the "cares of this world, and the deceitfulness of riches, and the lusts of other things entering in, choke the word, and it becometh unfruitful."[3] Return to the place of the problem, and meet Him there as you admit your wrongdoing. Let His fragrance again fill your life. He is "the rose of Sharon, and the lily of the valleys."[4] His beauty can reflect in your life and on your face so that others will desire Him too.

Many have agonized with Job, "Oh that I knew where I might find him!"[5] Seek His wisdom and presence, as you look back to the joys that were yours. Confess the hindrance that separated you from His great love, and return to that glorious, sacred reality: "My beloved is mine, and I am his."[6]

[1] Song of Solomon 3:1.
[2] Song of Solomon 2:6.
[3] Mark 4:19.
[4] Song of Solomon 2:1.
[5] Job 23:3.
[6] Song of Solomon 2:16.

❧ ❧ ❧

> He is altogether lovely. This is my beloved, and this is
> my friend.[1]

CHRIST TRULY is the altogether lovely One. In reference
to Him, the Psalmist wrote, "My heart is inditing [bubbling
over with] a good matter: I speak of the things which I
have made touching the king: my tongue is the pen of a
ready writer. Thou art fairer than the children of men:
grace is poured into thy lips: therefore God hath blessed
thee for ever."[2] How appropriate are the words! How utterly amazing that He condescends to become our friend.

The basis for friendship with God is mutual love. How
great was His love in giving His life for us. Can our love
match His? His friendship is precious and excellent, constant and never-changing. Are we worthy of such a Friend?
Worthiness is measured by obedience. "Ye are my friends
if ye do whatsoever I command you."[3]

Our profession of love ought not to be hidden. If we
truly cherish the Lord our admiration should be shared.
Said a Puritan of old, "What the heart intensely feels, the
lips will naught conceal. I am enjoined to God by Christ;
my actions and love must prove befitting."

"He is altogether lovely . . . my beloved . . . my friend."

> Have I an object, Lord, below,
> Which would divide my heart with Thee—
> Which would divert its even flow
> In answer to Thy constancy?
> O teach me quickly to return,
> And cause my heart afresh to burn.
>
> Have I a hope, however dear,
> Which would defer Thy coming, Lord—
> Which would detain my spirit here

(Where naught can lasting joy afford)?
From it, my Saviour, set me free
To look and long and wait for Thee.

Be Thou the object bright and fair
To fill and satisfy the heart.
My hope to meet Thee in the air,
And nevermore from Thee to part;
That I may undistracted be
To follow, serve, and wait for Thee.[4]

[1]Song of Solomon 5:16.
[2]Psalm 45:1-2.
[3]John 15:14.
[4]G. W. Frazer, in the *Little Flock Hymnbook*.

❧ ❧ ❧

July 14

Isaiah 1–4
Isaiah 1

> To what purpose is the multitude of your sacrifices
> unto me? saith the Lord: I am full of the burnt-offerings
> of rams, and the fat of fed beasts; and I delight not in
> the blood of bullocks, or of lambs, or of he goats. And
> when ye spread forth your hands, I will hide mine eyes
> from you: yea, when ye make many prayers, I will not
> hear.[1]

THE BOOK OF ISAIAH is often called the heart of the Old
Testament. The prophet vividly presents the suffering and
sovereignty of Christ. How the rebellion of God's chosen
people grieved His heart! Their sins were many, and they
were ungrateful. Yet, many continued to bring offerings
and sacrifices to the Lord. Little wonder that He could
not accept their gifts. The spirit behind them was false.
  If we could hear a playback of our own lives, we would
see how closely we resemble the children of Israel. Though
God's faithfulness has been demonstrated daily, we are still
rebellious. However, we continue to offer our sacrifices to

315

Him, perhaps in the form of an offering for our church program. Or a missionary passing through may have needs, and out of a feeling of necessity, or even duty, we contribute. To us too comes this stinging indictment: "To what purpose is the multitude of your sacrifices unto me?"

Why do we give our money, or our time? Are we "men-pleasers," or, as Isaiah wrote, are "our hands . . .full of blood"? If this is the case, our service and savings are in vain. They are fruitless and insignificant.

We may tremble to face these things, but they must be faced in the presence of our God. We are rejected for our wrong attitudes, and we are called to repentance and reformation: "Wash you, make you clean; . . . cease to do evil; Learn to do well. . . . Come now, and let us reason together, saith the Lord: though your sins be as scarlet, they shall be as white as snow; . . . If ye be willing and obedient, ye shall eat the good of the land."[2]

How can we resist such gracious reasoning? May our sacrifices come from clean hearts and be offered up to Him in adoration and praise.

[1]Isaiah 1:11, 15.
[2]Isaiah 1:16-19.

❧ ❧ ❧

Isaiah 5–8
Isaiah 6

> Also I heard the voice of the Lord, saying, Whom shall
> I send, and who will go for us? Then said I, Here am I;
> send me. For the Lord spake thus to me with a strong
> hand.[1]

MANY AND VARIED are the experiences which people have
related in regard to the call of Christ for service. Some are
given the divine call to care for the home, while others are
called to minister on a foreign mission field. Some are confident God has placed them in an office as a faithful witness,
while others feel called to work in hospitals or to train and
encourage the handicapped. Whatever our calling, God
deals with us as individuals, according to our needs, our
capabilities, and our desire to be led.

Isaiah heard the call of God to be a prophet and, being
obedient, he quickly responded. From a yielded heart came
the willing answer, "Here am I; send me."

The Apostle Paul, then known as Saul, was journeying to
Damascus. Truly God spoke to him with a "strong hand,"
and though his background had been one of bias and persecution against the cause of Christ, his life was spectacular-
ly changed, and was subsequently characterized by devotion
to the One who stopped him so suddenly that day on the
dusty road.

Reading the life of John Bunyan, we may be moved by
the account of the divine hand that gripped Bunyan as he
played on Elstow Green. His startling work and ministry
followed, and his writings today are an inspiration to all
Christendom.

You may be thinking, *I am classified only as Mr. (or
Miss, or Mrs.), so insignificant! No matter how firm the
hand that takes hold of me, I have so little to offer.* Remember that little is much when God is in it. His almightiness

makes all the difference, when linked with our nothingness. All we must proffer is willingness to do what He commands. When we so surrender He draws near and calls and commissions.

John Jowett wrote, "My Father God, I pray that Thy strong hand may lead me when I am in spiritual danger. Grip me even with violence if I am going astray. Speak to me with a hand that cannot be resisted, and keep my feet in the way of life."

May our prayers reflect submission that will result in renewed service for the Lord.

[1]Isaiah 6:8; 8:11.

※ ※ ※

July 16

ISAIAH 9–12
ISAIAH 12

> For unto us a child is born, unto us a son is given: and the government shall be upon his shoulder: and his name shall be called Wonderful, Counsellor, The mighty God, The everlasting Father, The Prince of Peace.[1]

MANY YEARS BEFORE Christ's birth, Isaiah prophesied the advent of the Son of God. Of the names attributed to Him, one stands out in my mind, not just during the Christmas season, when we hear this familiar verse so often, but during the entire year. It is "The everlasting Father." As the Father of the ages, He plans and puts together those things which accomplish the will of God. But it is even more personal—He is my Father. I am a member of the family of God.

God deals with us as sons. Those who do not know Him are told, "But as many as received him, to them gave he power to become the sons of God, even to them that believe on his name."[2] By simply coming to Him in faith, and

318

acknowledging Him as Saviour, we can begin to understand what it means to be born into the family of God. Here the fatherhood of God is seen. Theology may confuse us, but not the simple relationship of father and son. In this relationship we begin to see and know His love and goodness. "If ye then, being evil, know how to give good gifts unto your children, how much more shall your Father which is in heaven give good things to them that ask Him?"[3]

In this relationship we are dealt with as sons, not strangers. God has a special, personal interest in every area and activity of our lives. It may bring discipline or denial, but it ultimately brings delight.

The story is told of a young boy who visited a blind man's home. On arrival, the blind man carefully fingered each feature of the boy's face. The boy was confused until the sightless one explained, "I'm examining your features for evidences of your father's likeness!"

As members of God's family, can others trace in us the features of our Father? Are His graces evident in us? Paul admonished, "Be God's children, blameless, sincere and wholesome, living in a warped and diseased world, and shining there like lights in a dark place."[4]

May we walk pleasing to our Father.

[1]Isaiah 9:6.
[2]John 1:12.
[3]Matthew 7:11.
[4]Philippians 2:15, J. B. Phillips translation.

❦　❦　❦

Isaiah 13–16
Isaiah 14

IN SEEKING FOR CLARITY of these verses, Dr. James Moffatt presented the following translation:

> The Lord of hosts has sworn: "As I have planned, so shall it stand, as I have purposed, so shall it be; the Assyrians I crush within my land, and on my hills I trample them, till from my people's shoulders shall their load be shifted, and from their neck the Assyrian yoke be lifted. So is it in my purpose for the world, so I stretched out my arm against all nations. The Eternal's purpose who can disannul? His outstretched arm, who turns it back?"[1]

It is thrilling to note that in the Old Testament when God was foretelling a future event, at the same time He brought to pass another event which the people could see at once. Isaiah in these chapters told of the coming destruction of Babylon. When he wrote about it, this event was many years away. However, to confirm the immutability of God's Word, Isaiah foretold an incident that would shortly come to pass, namely, the destruction of the Assyrian army.

These object lessons are granted to us today also. We know that Christ has promised to return again for us, to take us to be with Him forever. However, He continually shows us current signs and wonders to remind us that He does what He says. "As I have planned, so shall it stand. As I have purposed, so shall it be."

It is exciting to be a Christian. We do not worship a God who is far away or unconcerned about His people. He has not concealed Himself from us, but daily reveals Himself so His continuing presence is a reminder of the future events coming to pass.

Recognizing that "the powers that be are ordained of God,"[2] the same God who is at work in me, a mere individual in the kingdom, I can only lift my head up in praise, and rejoice with Isaiah. "The Eternal's purpose who can disannul? His outstretched arm, who turns it back?"

Yes, the Lord has done and will do what He has promised.

[1]Isaiah 14:24-27, Moffatt.
[2]Romans 13:1.

   ❧ ❧ ❧

July 18

Isaiah 17–21
Isaiah 17

> Thou hast forgotten the God of thy salvation, and hast not been mindful of the rock of thy strength.[1]

A LITTLE SPEEDBOAT pushed its way through the calm water, leaving a rooster tail of foam behind. All was going well. The mountain's reflection sparkled on the water as the sun shone on the setting. The two pleasure riders in the boat talked happily. In their complacency they failed to remember the rock. For generations the rock had been there, almost submerged at high tide. But those who knew the shoreline were aware of its presence. *Crash!* Forgetfulness had led to disaster.

When all is well on the sea of life, how often we too tend to become complacent. We sit back and enjoy our surroundings: a good home, ample provision, and a church packed with friends and fellowship. We subconsciously reflect, *It is well with my soul.* At these times we are in danger of forgetting God and not being mindful of the Rock of our strength. Too often the result is a crash. Our lives suddenly are turbulent because we are thrown out of the calm boat and into the dangerous waters. All the while it could have been avoided. Our course is divinely charted. Disaster comes only in forgetting the God of our salvation. That Rock is immovable.

Comforts have a way of lulling one to sleep. How easy it is to forget. Dr. John Jowett profoundly illustrated this verse:

> Here is a forgetfulness that is born when we have recovered from some weakness. Our weakness helps our remembrance of God: our strength is the friend of forgetfulness. And so our strength is in danger of becoming our drug. It is an opiate which ministers to spiritual forgetfulness.

We are given to discouragement over physical illness, yet this may be the very means God must use to remind us that our strength lies in weakness. Being unmindful of Him has its disastrous consequences. Let the strength and energy derived from Him be used for His honor and glory.

¹Isaiah 17:10.

❧ ❧ ❧

Isaiah 22–25
Isaiah 25

> And in this mountain shall the Lord of hosts make unto
> all people a feast.[1]

OLD TESTAMENT SCHOLARS tell us these verses definitely refer to the end times. Observe the place to which the Lord
will take us, up to the mountain, and think of the blessings
that go with mountaintop experiences.

The mountain refers to Zion, which typifies the church
of Christ. As members of that church, do we enjoy our
place on the mountain with Him?

The mountain is a place of elevation and exaltation. The
spirit soars and the soul lifts heavenward as we see Him
"high and lifted up." We are in the world, but not of the
world. A Christian is above the strife and sin that make up
so much of earthly life. The elevation is obtained by daily
scaling the mountain heights, step by step, over the cliffs,
past the valleys, but always pressing upward. Sometimes
our feet sink or slip, but the sin is not a permanent obstacle if we, with His strength, start up again and progress.

The mountain is a place of stability. "Upon this rock I
will build my church."[2] Doubtful influences will try to
deter the climb, but such efforts need not succeed. The
mountain is immovable. So the Christian should be "sted-
fast, unmoveable, always abounding in the work of the
Lord."[3]

A high mountain is known for its visibility throughout
the countryside. On a clear day in the western part of the
state of Washington, many millions see Mount Rainier in
its elevation of over 14,000 feet. To us it is a symbol of
elevation, of stability, of permanence. From a distance it
makes an impression, even as it does to one standing in its
foothills. It is especially beautiful on those days when the
sun shines upon it and it cannot be hid.

The Sun of Righteousness shines on His church. It must not be hid in clouds or shadows, but must be a constant reminder of the visible church. Invite others to "come," to know the mountaintop experience of life in Christ.

[1]Isaiah 25:6.
[2]Matthew 16:18.
[3]I Corinthians 15:58.

❧   ❧   ❧

Isaiah 26–29
Isaiah 26

He that believeth shall not make haste.[1]

ONLY A PHRASE, but what depth of meaning! How often we prove in varied ways that haste makes waste.

Guests are coming for dinner and in the hustle of getting prepared, the hostess hurries. More often than not, the results are disastrous. The gardener is in the orchard pruning the fruit trees. It looks as if the rains are about to descend and he quickens his pace. By mistake, vital limbs may be severed, with a resulting dearth of fruit.

A Christian approaches the presence of God. The day has been discouraging and he knows he needs a lift. Fumbling through the pages of the Bible he looks for a thought for meditation. Too often the mind is filled with other thoughts crowding in, and the message is missed.

In the rush of the morning hours, we hastily ask God's blessing upon the day. There is not time for communion or fellowship, and then we wonder why the answer is not quick to come. A teacher once pointed out that if God answered our prayers in the haste with which we pray them, and with the same negligent attitude, it would be a good lesson for His children. God does not teach us this kind of lesson for revenge, but He has given us some object lessons that are for our profit.

324

"Enter into his gates with thanksgiving, and into his courts with praise."[2] God reminds us that we are to take time to be holy and to speak often with Him. To His disciples Jesus said, "Tarry ye here, and watch."[3] Time spent in prayer can be time saved. This can be proved only as we are willing to spend time and spend it freely on our knees.

We also sin in impatiently insisting that God bring to pass our desire, or in anticipating a given time for our answer to come. In running to and fro, we resemble those who are at their wits' end. This is not a commendable condition for a child of God who has already experienced that "all things work together for good."[4]

"He that believeth shall not make haste."

[1]Isaiah 28:16.
[2]Psalm 100:4.
[3]Mark 14:34.
[4]Romans 8:28.

❧ ❧ ❧

Isaiah 30–33
Isaiah 31

> Woe to the rebellious children, saith the Lord, that take
> counsel, but not of me; and that cover with a covering,
> but not of my spirit, that they may add sin to sin.
> Therefore shall the strength of Pharaoh be your shame,
> and the trust in the shadow of Egypt your confusion.[1]

THESE TWO CHAPTERS, Isaiah 30 and 31, could be entitled
"Instructions for Times of Trouble." God's message to
Israel can teach us plain truths and deliver us from wrong
paths. The inspired history tells us that Israel was planning an alliance with Egypt although this had been forbidden by God. These rebellious ones did not seem to realize
that temporary deliverance would cause permanent problems.

Egypt is often pictured as the world apart from Christ.
It is no wonder that God's first word was negative: *woe*.
If a time of testing comes your way, stay away from Egypt.
The consolation or comfort you may receive in the world is
only temporary.

God says it is wrong to take counsel outside of Himself.
In Him are the answers! "Call upon me in the day of
trouble: I will deliver thee."[2]

God's instructions include waiting on Him. "Wait on the
Lord: be of good courage, and he shall strengthen thine
heart: wait, I say, on the Lord."[3] This is not always an easy
thing to do, but it is essential, and the promised result will
come. "They that wait upon the Lord shall renew their
strength; they shall mount up with wings as eagles; they
shall run, and not be weary; and they shall walk, and not
faint."[4] Our afflictions may be many and varied, but the
prophet speaks of God's goodness to those who will take
time to wait upon Him: "And therefore will the Lord wait,

that he may be gracious unto you . . . for the Lord is a God of judgment: blessed are all they that wait for him."[5]

There is a glorious ending to God's instructions for our times of trouble. They can be used for His glory and our good. "And though the Lord give you the bread of adversity, and the water of affliction, yet shall not thy teachers be removed into a corner any more, but thine eyes shall see thy teachers."[6] Out of these trials come patience and wisdom.

> Resurrection mornings only follow crucifixions.
> Pentecost is dated from the Passover.
> The land of milk and honey is ever beyond Jordan.
> It is the rain that filled the pools where we drink in the
>   sunshine.[7]

[1]Isaiah 30:1, 3.
[2]Psalm 50:15.
[3]Psalm 27:14.
[4]Isaiah 40:31.
[5]Isaiah 30:18.
[6]Isaiah 30:20.
[7]T. M. Morsey.

❧   ❧   ❧

July 22

ISAIAH 34–37
ISAIAH 35

> And an highway shall be there, and a way, and it shall be called The way of holiness; the unclean shall not pass over it.[1]

NOTHING CAN HURT the true Christian who walks the way of holiness with God. His beauty, reflected on a human being, produces a picture that has caused many to stop and wonder, *What makes that one different?* Christ said, "I, if I be lifted up, will draw all men unto me."[2] The Spirit of God seeks to draw men to Christ through yielded believers.

Holiness has been defined as beauty of thought and action. Through holiness God's peace is graciously portrayed. Yet another expression of holiness, which we do not commonly recognize, is the beauty of holiness in the spoken Word. How much of that Word is used in our daily conversation?

I was somewhat astonished to learn that some day I will be judged for my words. How easy it is to drift into the sea of conversation with little thought and much talk. Recognizing that God is listening and evaluating, should put a guard on my tongue. Remember how Peter betrayed the Lord with his lips? He was greatly grieved afterward and asked for the Lord's forgiveness, but I am sure he wept sorely many times for the words that could not be taken back. The writer of the book of Isaiah made the confession that he was of "unclean lips." Both Peter and Isaiah were desirous to use their words for the glory of God, and because of their dedication and determination, we have their living words with us.

Do our words cause God joy or grief as He listens? Are they true words, pure words, thankful words, gracious words?

In Proverbs is the saying, "A word fitly spoken is like apples of gold in pictures of silver."[3] What beauty! Our words can also be significant in causing a sinner to turn to God in repentance, or a discouraged one to look up in faith and hope. It is most important that we have His divine approval on all that proceeds from our mouths.

"Give unto the Lord the glory due unto his name; worship the Lord in the beauty of holiness."[4]

[1]Isaiah 35:8.
[2]John 12:32.
[3]Proverbs 25:11.
[4]Psalm 29:2.

❧ ❧ ❧

Isaiah 38–40
Isaiah 40:28-31

> Hast thou not known? hast thou not heard, that the
> everlasting God, the Lord, the Creator of the ends of
> the earth, fainteth not, neither is weary? there is no
> searching of his understanding. He giveth power to the
> faint; and to them that have no might he increaseth
> strength.[1]

A TRUCKLOAD of youngsters was ascending a very steep hill.
In the front seat with the driver was a woman who was
frightened that the truck would not make it to the top.
"It's lagging," she said. "Stop, or do something!" The
driver grinned and shifted into a special gear. The surge of
strength pulled the truck right to the top without any further hesitation. The lady had wanted the driver to unload
the vehicle for the power necessary. All he had to do was
increase its strength for the extra steepness.

Is this not a simple illustration of what God does for His
children? We are on an uphill journey. Along the ascent a
burden is added here, another care there. We start chug-
ging spiritually! Instead of upsetting the load or casting
the responsibility aside, we can turn to One who increases
our strength. In Him we are more than conquerors.

There are times when we would like to level the load to
make it a bit more easy to bear. At these times God often
increases our strength, enabling us to carry its weight lightly. In fact, He invites us to cast our burdens on Him.

In India, where men and women often carry their burdens on their heads and backs, it is not uncommon to see
resting places provided along the road. Missionaries tell us
that stones just the height of the burdens are set up along
these hot trails and roads. There a man can lay his heavy
possessions and pause until he is refreshed and able to con-

tinue. A national who had recently been converted said to the missionary, "Ah, friend, Christ is my Rest Stone!"

Is Christ your Rest Stone? For us in our weariness He is such a rock. He says, "Come unto me, all ye that labour and are heavy laden, and I will give you rest."[2] Rest, so that your strength may be renewed. God can equip you with the needful power for His work.

[1]Isaiah 40:28-29.
[2]Matthew 11:28.

❧   ❧   ❧

July 24

Isaiah 41–43
Isaiah 41

> I, even I, am he that blotteth out thy transgressions for mine own sake, and will not remember thy sins.[1]

A MOTHER was trying to help her son forget his acts of wrongdoing. Over and over she said, "Try to forget it, dear. Erase it from your mind." She was well meaning, and sincerely thought she was lessening the child's feelings of guilt.

Psychologists are quick to explain this is not good. Their theories advocate confession instead of repression of the guilt feelings, for mental health, and exposing wrongdoings rather than covering them.

The Psalmist had keen insight into divine psychology when he wrote, "Blessed is he whose transgression is forgiven."[2] Sins against God cannot be hidden or tucked under a rug in the corner of your heart-house. They must come into the light of God's truth. "If we confess our sins, he is faithful and just to forgive us our sins, and to cleanse us from all unrighteousness."[3] Basically every sin is against God, so confession must first be made to Him—confession that we are sinners and in need of His cleansing. Then, as

330

His children, we need daily purging and searching of our hearts to keep them pure and forgiven.

The son spoken of in the opening paragraph was visited by a minister who led him to Christ. The young man acknowledged his sins one at a time as an individual matter between himself and his heavenly Father. He then made right things which had caused grief to many around him. His mother saw the tremendous difference and inquired of him. His answer was simple: "Mother, I got myself off my own hands and into the hands of God!"

Another young man went to a college professor to admit cheating on a term paper. He told the professor it had bothered him and he had asked God to forgive him and now wanted the professor to do so also. The wise professor said, "Yes, I will forgive you, but now you must do the work over. Rewrite the paper, and the grade will be your own!"

It is one thing to ask forgiveness, but we must be willing to make everything right. God is forgiving and loving and keeps His promise to blot out the confessed transgressions and remember them no more.

[1]Isaiah 43:25.
[2]Psalm 32:1.
[3]I John 1:9.

❦ ❦ ❦

Isaiah 44–47
Isaiah 46

> Remember this, and shew yourselves men.[1]

THROUGHOUT HISTORY outstanding Christians have been willing to show themselves men! Exploits like theirs require devotion to Christ that cannot be gained in the few minutes we reserve out of our day for meeting with God. Such devotion gives Him more than a portion of our time and money. Such devotion gives the title deed to ourselves to Him!

The fear of the Lord must far surpass the fear of men. In Ephesians Paul wrote, "Not with eyeservice, as menpleasers; but as the servants of Christ, doing the will of God from the heart."[2] We must not merely exemplify good; we must represent God. He is seeking men and women who will selflessly minister to others in His name, witness to sinners of His saving power, and thus hasten His coming again.

Though you may feel insignificant, when you give yourself to God, even your smallest and most humble act can contribute to His glory and the furtherance of His kingdom. Most movements that have advanced the Christian church have had minute beginnings.

It was at a tiny prayer meeting beneath a haystack at Williamstown, Massachusetts, that Adoniram Judson and some other students became concerned about the world around them. The result was a missionary movement which has been felt around the world. Martin Luther was a man alone, but he had the compulsion to extend a single inspired truth, justification by faith, and he altered European history. D. L. Moody, Charles Finney, John Wesley, and Billy Graham, all dominated by the love of Christ and burdened for the extension of His message, have been the means through whom untold millions have heard the gospel story.

Said a teen-age boy, when we were discussing great men of faith, "I just realized that they were all young nobodies, just like me. We have one common denominator, God. Why can't He use me too, if I am willing?"

Why can't He? He will, if we will show ourselves men. And He gives this promise: "I will go before thee, and make the crooked places straight: I will break in pieces the gates of brass, and cut in sunder the bars of iron: and I will give thee the treasures of darkness, and hidden riches of secret places, that thou mayest know that I, the Lord, which call thee by thy name, am the God of Israel."[3]

[1]Isaiah 46:8.
[2]Ephesians 6:6.
[3]Isaiah 45:2-3.

❧   ❧   ❧

July 26

Isaiah 48–52
Isaiah 49

> But thus saith the Lord, Even the captives of the mighty shall be taken away, and the prey of the terrible shall be delivered: for I will contend with him that contendeth with thee, and I will save thy children . . . and all flesh shall know that I the Lord am thy Saviour and thy Redeemer, the mighty One of Jacob.[1]

OUT AND OUT COMBAT, when it comes to winning people to Christ? Surely the One who was called "meek and mild" did not intend His followers to conquer the enemy in battle? Taking captives from the mighty is no mean task. Is this what Jesus Christ requires of those who have professed to accept Him?

Such was the discussion among some businessmen at their men's fellowship dinner. Disagreement, desires, disappointments, and victories in soul-winning were shared from man to man. The text was these verses and the topic, "Taking Men for God."

The men of the church were grounded in the faith, and knew the preparations that were needed for being good ambassadors. However, they varied greatly in the armor they felt they needed. One, a banker, said he could never be aggressive in his dealings with unsaved friends because he felt the best approach was by example and life. When people saw he was different they would come to him about the Lord. Another felt that what God had told Moses in ages past was a commission for him today: "Now therefore go, and I will be with thy mouth, and teach thee what thou shalt say."[2] Confident in the Lord's promise, he would go and tell.

A third man, known for his diplomacy, and a member of the local city council, recommended a combination of both tactics. Then the minister stepped in. Example by life was important, holy boldness directed by the Holy Spirit essential, but why discuss so much the human aspects when God had laid down the divine procedures. He could have sent angels to earth to "sing" the message to all people. He could have painted the message across the sky in a sunset, calling sinners to repentance. However, God had chosen each in that room to bring others in. If it meant spiritual battle as Isaiah had described, God had provided adequate armor and a powerful weapon, His Word. God had chosen to work through men.

The men left the dinner, their differences of approach forgotten, but the message of Paul on their lips: "I continue . . . witnessing both to small and great."[3] Their prayer was to win others by every means.

[1]Isaiah 49:25-26.
[2]Exodus 4:12.
[3]Acts 26:22.

❧   ❧   ❧

334

Isaiah 53–56
Isaiah 53

> Enlarge the place of thy tent, and let them stretch forth
> the curtains of thine habitations: spare not, lengthen
> thy cords, and strengthen thy stakes.[1]

ONE NEEDS only to listen to the news analysts or read the morning paper, to be compelled anew to face the shortness of time left on God's eternal clock. His voice must be heard louder and clearer today. It must resound around the globe. Dare we slacken our efforts? Can we merely hold our own in the battle of Christ against sin?

We need to enlarge our scope of service. You may complain that it is straining now, but He has commanded, "Lengthen thy cords."

As never before we need to work in the strength of the Lord. We must be well fortified for the task ahead. We must spend more time in prayer, more time in His Word, more time with Him, alone. In this we are strengthening the stakes. It is not an easy process. This reminder may help impress the worthwhile result in our hearts:

> Trees are strengthened by storms.
> Fruit is borne by pruning.
> Wheat is gathered by threshing.
> Steel is tempered with heat.
> Gold is purified by fire.
> Hardships and difficulties are among our greatest blessings.
> These are God's tools for perfecting, maturing, and strengthening us.[2]

Our outreach must extend into the world. So often we hear, "Why *foreign* missions when America is in such need?" We are reminded that this text was given to God's people. As we lengthen the cords by going into all the world and preaching the gospel, we are literally strengthening our own position. This task is not easy to accomplish, but it is essential.

Attending missionary conferences one becomes aware of the problems missionaries face: new customs, climate, prejudices, and barriers. Yet, when the needs for prayer are made known, those in the church at home become more concerned and can pray more intelligently. They have a part in the harvest of the seed they helped to plant. A difficult job is always more stimulating than a simple task. Seeing victories accomplished abroad, the Christians at home are encouraged to trust God for their personal victories.

Today's verse and this thought were on the back of a missions leaflet:

> Church of the living God, awake!
> They slumber. Oh, how guilty, how cruel!
> Thy husband, thy Redeemer, bids thee wake
> And what He says to all, He says to each—awake!

Let us awake! May our service be enlarged as we "spare not" for Him.

[1]Isaiah 54:2.
[2]T. M. Morsey.

$$\text{✤} \quad \text{✤} \quad \text{✤}$$

July 28

ISAIAH 57–59
ISAIAH 58

> And the Lord shall guide thee continually, and satisfy thy soul in drought, and make fat thy bones: and thou shalt be like a watered garden, and like a spring of water, whose waters fail not.[1]

> To those who have chosen to walk by His side
> He lovingly says, "I'll continually guide."

336

His daily direction gives light on my way,
It enters my heart as sincerely I pray.

"Father in heaven, as I come apart
I give You my will, my love, and my heart.

Take them, indwell them, may Your Spirit lead
And the answers You grant I accept indeed.

As we walk together, You and I,
May my thoughts submit to Yours on high.

May my life reflect in all that I do
That in starting this day, I have been with You."

I come from the "closet," from casting each care;
Assurance o'erwhelms me that He has been there.

He'll surely continue, each day He has made,
To lead and to guide me. I walk unafraid.

GOD'S PROGRAM for guidance is continuous. What blessed
assurance! He is with you, wherever you go. A pioneer
preacher of yesterday used to say, " 'Whithersoever thou
goest' covers a lot of territory!" There is no place where
God is not with us. He will not leave us nor forsake us.
This continual guidance will surely make the bones fat
and satisfy the soul in drought. Guidance is available to
each believer and its Source is never quenched, nor the
receiver satiated. It continues, as does His compassion.
His blessings are new every morning.

To a young person contemplating the future, there is
instruction; to the mother who wonders how she can finish
her household tasks, a plan; for father, whose job is demanding, a way in the wilderness of work; to those ready
and anxious to follow their Guide, a way "through the
valley of the shadow of death." In each case there is no
fear, for we can confidently affirm, "Thou art with me."[2]

[1]Isaiah 58:11.   [2]Psalm 23:4.

> Thy people also shall be all righteous: they shall inherit
> the land for ever, the branch of my planting, the work
> of my hands, that I may be glorified. A little one shall
> become a thousand, and a small one a strong nation:
> I the Lord will hasten it in his time.[1]

THE MORNING PAPER made a statement that caused me to
reflect on the verses from Isaiah which I had read earlier. It
stated that one thousand dollars invested five years ago
in the common stock of a particular item would today
yield about two hundred fifty thousand dollars. "A little
one shall become a thousand." Imagine the increase that
Isaiah was talking about!

How is it with your investment in God today? How many
years ago did you commit your life to Jesus Christ? Have
you invested all in Him? If not, can you claim high returns? In the days of the early church, a few made a spectacular impact on the world. That small band of believers
became a large and strong worldwide fellowship. They
invested their lives in the Lord and had vast returns. Their
commitment was not divided between God and their personal interests. They knew, as James wrote, that to be
double-minded is to be unstable. All had to be forsaken
for Christ. As a result of their all-out investment, scores
believed.

The newspaper columnist stated in the article, however,
that over one thousand companies went broke in a given
ten-year period with a loss of one hundred million dollars
in capital funds. How discouraging!

This information was a warning and an admonition to
me. Could it be that over the past decade we have gone
broke spiritually? I do not say it lightly. If our lives are
not bringing in returns for God, they are definitely liabili-

ties rather than assets to Him and to ourselves. We can ill afford such lack of progress when we think of standing before Him on the judgment day.

God has given us territory to possess for His glory, with the promise that "one shall become a thousand." He will bless each effort and strengthen us in each endeavor for Him. And some day He will say, if we are diligent, "Well done, thou good and faithful investor!"

¹Isaiah 60:21-22.

❧ ❧ ❧

July 30

ISAIAH 63–64
ISAIAH 64

> Oh that thou wouldest rend the heavens, that thou wouldest come down.[1]

HAVE YOU NOT HAD DAYS when you wished with all your heart that the Lord would rend the heavens and come down, right down into your room, into your situation? I have. The circumstances seemed too involved or the problems too deep to warrant anything but an actual visit from my Lord! Possibly there have been days when you sought His help and, instead of waiting patiently for the answer, said, "Oh, if He were here right now I would know." Childish? Perhaps, but even the most mature feel as needy as a child at times, especially in hours of great need.

As our cries for help increase, we long for Christ's coming again. To be with Him forever is a joyous anticipation! Reading on in this chapter of Isaiah even increases our appetites. "For since the beginning of the world men have not heard, nor perceived by the ear, neither hath the eye seen, O God, beside thee, what he hath prepared for him that waiteth for him."[2] Expectation unlimited!

Remember the experience of Elisha when the crops

339

failed. God provided food for him and sustained him during the drought. Could Elisha ever doubt again? Has not God provided for you too? Should you ever doubt Him again? At times of desperate crisis it is good to look back and review His goodness to us in the past, for in doing so, we are assured that He will not fail us now.

Wait upon God in prayer and meditation. Feed upon the wonderful inspired Word He has given us. As you draw near to Him, His presence will be real and precious not only at these times of special need but every day.

The prophet continues: "Thou meetest him that rejoiceth and worketh righteousness."[3]

In times of stress let us encourage our hearts with the fact that He will come again. In days of trouble we wish for that day of days to be hastened. However, while we wait and anticipate, let us also work and witness as we have never done before, to bring others to Christ, that they too may have the sweetness of His Spirit's indwelling, and the knowledge of hope everlasting.

[1]Isaiah 64:1.
[2]Isaiah 64:4.
[3]Isaiah 64:5.

❧ ❧ ❧

> Thus saith the Lord, As the new wine is found in the cluster, and one saith, Destroy it not; for a blessing is in it: so will I do for my servants' sakes, that I may not destroy them all.[1]

In sections of western Washington there are many who grow grapes. One such family had a crop that was in serious danger of widespread blight. In going through the arbors, the owner would test and retest. Where a good cluster was found surrounded by ruined and blighted fruit, the owner would not have the complete vine destroyed. His comment was that there might be enough strength in the good fruit to compensate for the destructive disease.

Isaiah had been representing the terrible sins of men. The result of their idolatry, hypocrisy, and blasphemy was a curse. Because of their rebellion God had allowed them to be afflicted and His blessing had been withheld. Yet, even in this period, the Lord said He would be a shield to those who remained faithful. They were called a "remnant."

The "cluster" of Christians are surrounded by a world of corruption, but God desires that they bear fruit and flourish for Him. He can use them on His vine as an example of good. They also are to be the means of saving the blighted about them.

We have a friend who constantly prays that she will be a part of God's remnant. Her life is totally dedicated to the Lord. She faithfully serves Him in her job and her place of worship. Her witness is gracious, and her face exemplifies the beauty of holiness. She may be on a bus, in a little fruit market, or in an elevator, but she is a cluster with blessing in it. Sinful people surround her, but she diligently prays for these rebellious ones. The burden of their guilt is heavy upon her because she believes that, if she is faithful in life and prayer, they will be saved.

A day is coming when all will be judged. "For I know their works and their thoughts: it shall come, that I will gather all nations and tongues; and they shall come, and see my glory."[2]

God grant that we will each be a good cluster. May your and my prayer be "Show me Thy glory so I may impart it to others."

[1]Isaiah 65:8.
[2]Isaiah 66:18.

❧ ❧ ❧

August

JEREMIAH 1–3
JEREMIAH 1

> But the Lord said unto me, Say not, I am a child: for
> thou shalt go to all that I shall send thee, and whatso-
> ever I command thee thou shalt speak. Be not afraid of
> their faces: for I am with thee to deliver thee, saith the
> Lord. Then the Lord put forth his hand, and touched
> my mouth. And the Lord said unto me, Behold, I have
> put my words in thy mouth. See, I have this day set
> thee over the nations and over the kingdoms, to root
> out, and to pull down, and to destroy, and to throw
> down, to build, and to plant.[1]

SEVERAL PERIODICALS have carried the following provocative
item in recent days:

> The average age of the world's great civilizations has
> been 200 years. These nations progressed through the
> following sequence:
>
> > From bondage to spiritual faith
> > From spiritual faith to great courage
> > From courage to liberty
> > From liberty to abundance
> > From abundance to selfishness
> > From selfishness to complacency
> > From complacency to apathy
> > From apathy to dependency
> > From dependency back into bondage.
>
> In 1976 the United States will be 200 years old. This
> cycle is not inevitable—it depends on you![2]

We read such statements with great concern. However, we see a picture of what faced Jeremiah in the days preceding the final fall of Jerusalem and the destruction of Judah.

What kind of man was Jeremiah? We might think he was powerful and strong, courageous and brave. Yet these were not his chief attributes. At heart he was timid and sensitive. Facing the task to which God had called him, he said, "I cannot speak: for I am a child." He trembled at the sight of the faces of those about him. Yet his meekness was not weakness. God had chosen him before his birth to speak for Him in an age of failure. Those whom God calls He equips for service. He never gives us a job without sufficient guidance and strength.

We ask God for a Jeremiah today, one who would call men back to the realization that all ruin and national decay are due to forgetting God. "Righteousness exalteth a nation: but sin is a reproach to any people."[3]

God may be calling you. If He is, do not fear; He will equip you for the task ahead. "Behold, I have put my words in thy mouth!" As we study Jeremiah, may our hearts be impressed with what God can accomplish through a man in whom His Spirit resides.

[1]Jeremiah 1:7-10.
[2]*International Rotary.*
[3]Proverbs 14:34.

🍀 🍀 🍀

JEREMIAH 4–6
JEREMIAH 5

> Your iniquities have turned away these things, and
> your sins have withholden good things from you.[1]

THE MESSAGE OF JEREMIAH is a message for us today. In
the depravity of the people and the resulting destruction he
saw God's attitude toward sin. "Thine own wickedness
shall correct thee, and thy backslidings shall reprove thee:
know therefore and see that it is an evil thing and bitter,
that thou hast forsaken the Lord thy God, and that my
fear is not in thee, saith the Lord God of hosts."[2] Ruin is
the result of sin, and God most surely punishes sin. He cannot and He will not condone it. Neither would Jeremiah
shrink from his responsibility to tell his nation that sin
had caused their destruction. The cost to him was great:
stripes, brutality, and the dungeon. His own personal life
was filled with grief over the sin of the people. "Mine eye
runneth down with rivers of water for the destruction of the
daughter of my people."[3]

Those who heard the message of "the weeping prophet"
responded as does a bad patient in a hospital. Instead of accepting the true diagnosis and cooperating with the "doctor," they rebelled. How well we know that those who do
not follow their doctor's orders do not get well. If he pre-
scribes a strict diet, it must be adhered to. If after an accident he says, "Exercise," you must exercise even if you
feel another step is impossible!

When the great Physician says, "Your iniquities have
turned away these things, and your sins have withholden
good things from you," take note. Only by obeying His
orders can our lives and land be healed. He does not leave
us in the grip of sin. Repentance stems from obedience and
brings victory.

How beautifully and clearly the sovereignty of God is

illustrated in the simple message of the clay and the potter. "O house of Israel, cannot I do with you as this potter? saith the Lord. Behold, as the clay is in the potter's hand, so are ye in mine hand, O house of Israel. And the vessel that he made of clay was marred in the hand of the potter: he made it again another vessel, as seemed good to the potter to make it."[4] This was the message of Jeremiah, and it lifts our hearts in praise to God.

We have displeased Him. We are marred in the sight of the Master Potter. Our utter helplessness results. If we repent, we shall rejoice! "He made it again . . . as seemed good."

[1] Jeremiah 5:25.
[2] Jeremiah 2:19.
[3] Lamentations 3:48.
[4] Jeremiah 18:6, 4.

❧ ❧ ❧

August 3

JEREMIAH 7–10
JEREMIAH 10

> O Lord, I know that the way of man is not in himself:
> it is not in man that walketh to direct his steps.[1]

WHO EVER HEARD of taking a trip without first making provision for one's needs along the way? How carefully plans must be made for supplies and emergency supplies. In stories of our American pioneers who traveled west it is interesting to note how thoroughly they made preparation for the long journey ahead. Except for rare occasions, there were no stores nor stations dotting the route. Everything needed for sustaining life was carried on the wagons. Even food and water supplies had to be carried rather than depending on infrequent water holes and game along the route.

Christians travel a pioneer path on the journey of life.

It is essential that their steps be guided and kept on the right road. Constantly there are choices between two ways, only one of which can be right. A false step might cause a fall. The wrong road is beset with dangers. Each step must be carefully considered. Our provision for every day cannot come from within ourselves. It must come from a higher source. How well this is pointed out in Jeremiah. "It is not in man that walketh to direct his steps." Solomon said that he recognized he was but a child when it came to directing his life. This is true of men throughout the human history. Think of the wanderings of the children of Israel; their kings and leaders tried, but failed. Consider the blunders and errors of the centuries. "The world by wisdom knew not God."[2] Too often we seek to follow the way of conscience, but the eye of reason has become dimmed so that the right path is not always discerned.

In bewilderment there is concern. Where shall I turn? If I cannot guide myself, who can? If one can, where may I find him? I can turn to the Word of God. "Thy word is a lamp unto my feet, and a light unto my path."[3] The Bible speaks of One who has said, "I will instruct thee and teach thee in the way which thou shalt go: I will guide thee with mine eye."[4]

Christ is the only sure guide. "Follow me," He invites. He will order our steps and lead safely, surely through the intricacies of life, through the valleys and over the mountains.

St. Augustine made a statement which is most appropriate for each Christian: "I am a little child, but my Father is my sufficient Guardian."

[1] Jeremiah 10:23.
[2] I Corinthians 1:21.
[3] Psalm 119:105.
[4] Psalm 32:8.

❧ ❧ ❧

JEREMIAH 11–14
JEREMIAH 12

> But thou, O Lord, knowest me: thou hast seen me, and
> tried mine heart toward thee.[1]

JEREMIAH APPEALS to us as a fully dedicated and spiritually
minded prophet. He was a true forerunner of the Lord.
He was a sensitive man. He was not to take a wife or know
the blessing of children. Thus his whole life was wrapped
up in God. From experience he could say that the Lord
knew him, had seen him and tried him. Jeremiah learned
a great deal about God's character as well as some of the
principles by which He works.

It is not uncommon to hear even a Christian lament,
"No one really understands me." Possibly that feeling has
grown through unfortunate circumstances or misunderstandings. A well-known counselor often asks such individuals, "Do you really understand yourself?" That is
something to think about! Few may comprehend your position or your problem, but Jeremiah learned what we can
all learn, that God understands! At such times portions of
Psalm 139 are illuminating: "O Lord, thou hast searched
me, and known me. Thou knowest my downsitting and
mine uprising, thou understandest my thought afar off.
Thou compassest my path and my lying down, and art
acquainted with all my ways. For there is not a word in my
tongue, but, lo, O Lord, thou knowest it altogether. Thou
has beset me behind and before, and laid thine hand upon
me. Such knowledge is too wonderful for me; it is high,
I cannot attain unto it."[2]

> Search me, O God! My actions try
>   And let my life appear
> As seen by Thine all-searching eye—
>   To mine my ways make clear.

Search all my thoughts, the secret springs,
  The motives that control;
The chambers where polluted things
  Hold empire o'er the soul.

Search, till Thy fiery glance has cast
  Its holy light through all,
And I by grace am brought at last
  Before Thy face to fall.[3]

[1]Jeremiah 12:3.
[2]Psalm 139:1-6.
[3]F. Bottome.

❧   ❧   ❧

August 5

JEREMIAH 15–18
JEREMIAH 18

> Thy words were found, and I did eat them; and thy
> word was unto me the joy and rejoicing of mine heart:
> for I am called by thy name, O Lord God of hosts.[1]

A MISSIONARY MOTHER was having great difficulty teaching
her children to read. They lived on an outpost station and
few luxuries were theirs. However, she knew the youngsters would derive great joy from books, so she early began
their instruction. Neither her five-year-old son nor her
six-year-old daughter showed any interest. Then one day
some friends kindly sent a case of Hershey chocolate bars.
The mother had an idea! A candy bar would be the reward for each page well read. At once there was new enthusiasm. An incentive spurred their reading and before
long each child had acquired a love for books and a joy in
their contents.

There is much wisdom in what Jeremiah says. "Thy
words were found, and I did eat them." Eat the Scriptures?
You raise an eyebrow in wonder. Then it becomes clear.
You eat candy piece by piece. It is chewed, swallowed, di-

gested, and assimilated. It becomes part of you. There is a simple parallel in reading the Word. "Break off" a verse. Read it, meditate on it, digest it, and before long it will become part of yourself. Then you will taste the sweetness in it, for in each verse, on every page, the goodness of God is manifest.

In Jeremiah 18, God said to the prophet, "Arise, and go down to the potter's house, and there I will cause thee to hear my words."[2] Jeremiah went and saw the potter take a piece of clay and put it on the wheel. It was molded and fashioned according to the mind of the potter. But suddenly the plan was thwarted. Did the potter discard the vessel with the blemish? No, he took it again—the same piece—and remolded it to make another vessel that was good.

Jeremiah saw this not just as an incident but as an object lesson. He thought on it until it became part of him. God made it clear. "Cannot I do with you as this potter? So are ye in mine hand!"[3]

The Potter has a pattern. "Thou art . . . thou shalt be."[4] And the plan is found in His Word. Find those words and eat them, and they will be the joy and rejoicing of your heart.

[1]Jeremiah 15:16.
[2]Jeremiah 18:2.
[3]Jeremiah 18:6.
[4]John 1:42.

❧ ❧ ❧

JEREMIAH 19–22
JEREMIAH 20

> Then I said, I will not make mention of him, nor
> speak any more in his name. But his word was in mine
> heart as a burning fire shut up in my bones, and I was
> weary with forbearing, and I could not stay.[1]

SOME OF Jeremiah's experiences were similar to our Lord's.
He despised sin and suffered because of it. He was faithful, but he was also human, and one day his soul was discouraged. Although he is distinguished as a great prophet
in our eyes, he received little recognition from his people,
and he was discouraged. He loved his nation and had a
burning desire that they would turn back to God; but they
gave him a difficult time. The pressures mounted and
he suffered greatly. Undoubtedly he had cause to complain.
The chief governor in the house of the Lord had treated
him cruelly by putting him in stocks. Jeremiah was in-
dignant. He complained against God, saying that He had
deceived him. Yet God had warned him that princes and
people would rise against him. Possibly, he felt, as some
do today, that a Christian should be exempt from suffering.

What precedes discouragement? Jeremiah was beaten
by orders of the son of the priest and put in stocks as a
criminal. He wrote, "I am in derision daily, every one
mocketh me."[2] This was the background of his hurt, and
he was ready to blame God. There may be an attempt to
forget Him and His ways, but the true child of God is
brought back, sometimes with quite a jolt! Jeremiah confessed, "His word was in mine heart as a burning fire shut
up in my bones."

The Word purifies as it enlightens. As a fire, it burned
out the rebellion and rekindled the flame of love and zeal

in Jeremiah's heart for the work of the Lord. What a relief when the chaff is driven away and consumed.

We must expect discouraging days. God tries our faith and in so doing multiplies His grace and builds our character. Even discouragement can be used for the glory of God and for our good. Be encouraged. "It is God which worketh in you both to will and to do of his good pleasure."[3]

[1]Jeremiah 20:9.
[2]Jeremiah 20:7.
[3]Philippians 2:13.

❧   ❧   ❧

August 7

JEREMIAH 23–25
JEREMIAH 24, 25:1-14

> Behold, I will send and take all the families of the north, saith the Lord, and Nebuchadnezzar the king of Babylon, my servant, and will bring them against this land . . . and will utterly destroy them.[1]

As WE READ the Scriptures we cannot doubt that truly "the powers that be are ordained of God."[2] One may rise and another may fall. Some may serve the Lord while others disobey Him, but to fulfill His will, God uses even the wrath of man to praise Him.[3]

Nebuchadnezzar was being used unconsciously by God for His purposes. God's plan was to bring together the northern nations, under Nebuchadnezzar, and then to bring them against Judah. Nebuchadnezzar thought he was serving only his own purposes, and considered himself a conqueror. However, the plans of our omnipotent God are always fulfilled. He would use this captivity to mold His people into instruments for His divine service. No matter how powerful a person or a nation, all are weak in relation to almighty God.

"God does not will the present evil, but we must believe

352

Him able to turn it to a redemptive use. He used the Caesars to unify the ancient world and so prepare it for the Christian mission. And He is still God."[4]

We take heart in such knowledge. A Christian is one in whom Christ lives. A Christian is one in whom the purposes of God are to be completed. A Christian does not fear the future, for it is in God's hands and He has His unique ways of effecting His plans.

Thomas Jefferson wrote, "When great evils happen, I am in the habit of looking out for what good may arise from them as consolation to us, and Providence has so established the order of things that most evils are the means of producing some good." To one on God's side, is it too elementary to believe that "all things work together for good"?[5]

God directs the powers and the projects of man. "Thus saith the Lord, the God of Israel . . . I will set mine eyes upon them for good . . . and I will build them, and not pull them down . . . And I will give them an heart to know me, that I am the Lord."[6]

[1]Jeremiah 25:9.
[2]Romans 13:1.
[3]Psalm 76:10.
[4]Source unknown.
[5]Romans 8:28.
[6]Jeremiah 24:5-7.

❧ ❧ ❧

Jeremiah 26–30
Jeremiah 30

> For I know the thoughts that I think toward you, saith
> the Lord, thoughts of peace, and not of evil, to give you
> an expected end. Then shall ye call upon me, and ye
> shall go and pray unto me, and I will hearken unto you.
> And ye shall seek me, and find me, when ye shall search
> for me with all your heart.[1]

ONE THOUGHT can enrich and transform your Christian life:
God is thinking about you. To our finite minds this is incredible. Our reasoning power says, "Impossible!" Yet
God speaks specifically: "I know the thoughts that I think
toward you . . . to give you an expected end."

On the days when discouragement comes and the clouds
crowd into your joy, accept this with certainty: God *is*
thinking about you. He has thoughts of your day and your
future. He well knows each tomorrow, and you must learn
to trust.

If we truly believed this we would be different. We
would seek after God in a way hitherto unknown. We seek
guidance, although seldom with our whole heart, because
we lack the faith to go forward.

A minister used a simple illustration, but I have never
forgotten the truth behind it. His church had sponsored
an old-fashioned "treasure hunt" for a dozen underprivileged children. Objects were hidden in various places and
the instructions given. At the time to begin, each child set
off, some with fervor, but most of them only halfheartedly.
The sponsors were concerned and called time. The group
reassembled and the idea of the hunt was reiterated. One
sentence changed the whole tenor of the activity. An adult
emphasized, "Remember, everything you find is your very
own to keep!" It was like an electric charge. Off they went,
scampering, running, dashing, climbing, and uncovering.

Their search had a purpose. What they found they would keep.

Oh, the revolution that would take place in our innermost hearts if we really understood that God is thinking of us and has a plan for us! The success of our search for His plan and His purpose, and for our riches in Christ is somewhat commensurate with the zeal and fervor put into the search. The truth revealed to the underprivileged children is equally true for the impoverished soul. "What you find is yours to keep."

[1]Jeremiah 29:11-13.

   ❧ ❧ ❧

August 9

JEREMIAH 31–32
JEREMIAH 32

> Ah Lord God! behold, thou hast made the heaven and the earth by thy great power and stretched out arm, and there is nothing too hard for thee.[1]

IS IT NOT EASY to put ourselves in the place of Jeremiah when he uttered this prayer? How many times we approach the hallowed ground of prayer with hearts full of requests and needs, yet in the stillness of the sacred surroundings we find utterance difficult. We cannot find words to express what has made our hearts full, but we realize that God is there. "Groanings which cannot be uttered are prayers which cannot be refused." Our hearts cry out of fullness or heaviness, "Ah Lord God!"

These three words can stem from belief or disbelief. The latter may have been the feeling of Jeremiah as he came to God. He doubted that there was any merit in the purchase of the land God had commanded him to obtain. He had misgivings, his soul was bewildered. "Ah Lord God!" The experience has undoubtedly been yours. In coming to God in prayer you may have the feeling that He simply does not understand. The spirit of reproach may be taking root within. Here the heart that staggers in unbelief must stop and ponder as Jeremiah did.

"Thou hast made the heaven and the earth by thy great power and stretched out arm and there is nothing too hard for thee." Think of the story of creation, how God created the world by the Word of His mouth. In my circumstances I doubt that He can make something from nothing. How wrong I am! We are not dealing with a man but with the almighty God. He can take a destitute sinner and re-create him. David prayed, "Create in me a clean heart . . . and renew a right spirit within me."[2] The same God who created the world made me, and the same power is available for my need.

I cry, "Ah Lord God," but I do not stop there. I remember His goodness and righteousness and, most of all, His almightiness. Here I come to the place of Jeremiah's confidence: "There is nothing too hard for thee."

When you are prone to doubt that there is a solution for your situation, know that these words are for your comfort and encouragement. If God made the world out of nothing, then nothing is too hard for Him.

[1]Jeremiah 32:17.
[2]Psalm 51:10.

JEREMIAH 33–37
JEREMIAH 33

> Call unto me, and I will answer thee, and shew thee
> great and mighty things, which thou knowest not.[1]

SOMEONE HAS SAID, "We are inclined to pray as though
this world were in the grip of cold, fixed laws, with only
the remote possibility that God might occasionally break
through."[2] What a rebuke this is to the King of kings and
Lord of lords. Faithless, unbelieving prayer grieves His
heart and deprives His children of what He waits to give.

The president of a corporation was holding a sales meeting. He had made promises to the salesmen on various occasions and always backed them up. One day he decided to
make an offer such as he never had made before. At stake
was a good percentage of the company stock. It would be
given for those willing to "call and discuss it with him."
When the meeting was over, the men broke into little
groups. They casually dismissed his offer as something unbelievable or as a joke. Why would he be offering stock
when there were many established stockholders? No one
wanted to be laughed at, so the offer went unacknowledged.
The men did not know what was in the heart of their president. He was looking for someone who was willing to "call
and discuss" something that seemed to be beyond their
reach or grasp. As a result the reward was left unclaimed
and the offer was never repeated.

Why are we Christians so reluctant to call on the name
of the Lord? Why are we so timid in approaching God?
The offer He has made for us to call and let Him show us
great and mighty things which we know not all too often
stands unclaimed. Such an offer is unbelievable. Since we
cannot really understand it, we ignore it or shy away from
it. The reward is thus not granted.

Some say that the Lord does not answer just the way they pray. Others fail to see what is hindering their calling on the Lord. The fact that God's answer may not always be what we hoped, does not alter the fact that He does answer. Amy Carmichael wrote, "God answers us in the deeps, never in the shallows of our soul." This could account for frustration which comes when we rely on sight rather than faith.

Call, and He will answer.

[1]Jeremiah 33:3.
[2]Vance Havner.

❧ ❧ ❧

August 11

JEREMIAH 38–41
JEREMIAH 39

> Now the word of the Lord came unto Jeremiah, while he was shut up in the court of the prison, saying, Go and speak to Ebed-melech the Ethiopian, saying, Thus saith the Lord of hosts, the God of Israel; Behold, I will bring my words upon this city for evil . . . But I will deliver thee in that day . . . because thou hast put thy trust in me, saith the Lord.[1]

A WELL-KNOWN CHRISTIAN in the eastern United States tells a story that encourages my heart. He was brought up in a godly home by parents who feared the Lord above everything. The way of salvation was clearly shown to him at an early age, but the instruction fell on disinterested ears. Open rebellion and resentment brewed within him as his brothers and sisters followed Christ. He determined to know nothing of salvation or the Christian way. This was a source of heartbreak to his family but they knew God was still over all, and they fervently prayed.

His father, who knew many mighty men of God and Christian leaders, asked them one by one to speak to his son. These men made little impression on him. At last he left home and for years had no contact with his family.

Then, one summer, the son was in a minor accident. He was temporarily hospitalized, not because of known injury but because of a lack of response. The doctors felt that there must be some internal injury which had not yet shown up. One day a nurse stood by the patient's bedside. He looked perplexed, troubled, and in pain. Her question was simple. "Where does it hurt?" He did not answer in the way she had anticipated. Instead, he started telling her his life story. The nurse, a child of God, quickly realized the Spirit had granted her an opportunity. When her shift was over, she returned to the room and answered her own earlier question. "I know where it hurts," she said. "The hurt is in your heart." Thus a nurse, unknown to this day, brought the son of a Christian family to Christ.

As we read the Bible, we become increasingly aware that God uses those we may class as "unknowns" to accomplish His purpose. When we secretly wish we could be someone special, it is good to remember that unknowns have been given a great task too.

In reading of Jeremiah we see his life saved by an unknown man. Only the man's name is given—"Ebed-melech" —but because of his service, God faithfully remembered him.

At times it is good to carefully consider if, in this life, we are anxious to be known by God or known by men. There is a great difference, when eternity's values are viewed.

¹Jeremiah 39:15-18.

❧ ❧ ❧

JEREMIAH 42–47
JEREMIAH 42

> Whether it be good, or whether it be evil, we will obey
> the voice of the Lord our God, to whom we send thee;
> that it may be well with us, when we obey the voice of
> the Lord our God.[1]

As WE READ Jeremiah's history, we find God's recorded provision for guidance. The chapter simply unfolds a pattern that may answer your need today. The decision to "obey the voice of the Lord" is extremely important.

Picture this "remnant," as the Scriptures call them, coming to Jeremiah and saying, "Let, we beseech thee, our supplication be accepted before thee, and pray for us unto the Lord thy God . . . that the Lord thy God may shew us the way wherein we may walk, and the thing that we may do."[2] They were willing and eager to know and do the will of God. Willingness to ask God for guidance is indicative of a sincere heart. That heart must also accept the word *whether*: "whether it be good, or whether it be evil." The Psalmist wrote, "The meek will he guide in judgment: and the meek will he teach his way."[3]

First there must be willingness to ask, and then willingness to wait for the answer. It is significant that the answer came to this remnant "after ten days." Sometimes the answer does not come that soon, and the days stretch into weeks and months, even years. Little wonder we are told, "For ye have need of patience, that, after ye have done the will of God, ye might receive the promise."[4] Isaiah wrote, "Blessed are all they that wait for him."[5]

Then comes the real test. We ask, the answer comes, but will there be obedience to God's will? To the remnant Jeremiah gave God's answer: "If ye will still abide in this land, then will I build you, and not pull you down, and I will plant you, and not pluck you up."[6] They would rather have heard that they could leave the land for a more peaceful place. Would they obey or disobey? To obey would be to see the mercy of God. Disobedience would bring grave consequences: "Then shall it come to pass, that the sword, which ye feared, shall overtake you."[7]

When a decision must be made, look to God in prayer, then wait and obey.

[1]Jeremiah 42:6.
[2]Jeremiah 42:2-3.
[3]Psalm 25:9.
[4]Hebrews 10:36.
[5]Isaiah 30:18.
[6]Jeremiah 42:10.
[7]Jeremiah 42:16.

❧ ❧ ❧

August 13

Jeremiah 48–50
Jeremiah 49

Dwell deep.[1]

ONLY TWO WORDS but they speak volumes. Their message to Christians is profound, as the Scriptures clearly illustrate.

In Jeremiah the words were spoken to the residents of Edom. The enemy was pursuing and God spoke: "Flee ye, turn back, dwell deep."

God speaks thus to us in the twentieth century. There is no doubt that the enemy approaches. His attacks are varied and subtle, and we can meet them only by dwelling deep. Some Christians, after they meet Jesus Christ, temporarily glory in His presence. However, through neglect of the Word and prayer, their profession becomes shallow and unsatisfying. The Christian "dwells deep" only as he is nourished by the Word and instructed in and matured by the deep things of God. As he is refreshed with those rivers

361

of living waters, he remains a healthy Christian who is dwelling deep.

Prayer protects from the enemy and makes one sensitive to the attacks of Satan. Knowledge of the Scripture straightens and strengthens the soul.

The Apostle Paul wrote, "Eye hath not seen, nor ear heard, neither have entered into the heart of man, the things which God hath prepared for them that love him. But God hath revealed them unto us by his Spirit: for the Spirit searcheth all things, yea, the deep things of God."[2] His Spirit waits to reveal these things, but they come only after digging and dwelling deeper and deeper in the Word of God.

> Care and trial, stripes and pain,
> Are the ropes that let us down;
> But our Father holds them well,
> And His peace our lives will crown.
> Worldlings take the surface show,
> Then but dust and ashes reap.
> Would you win life's purest joys?
> You must then dwell deep![3]

[1]Jeremiah 49:8.
[2]I Corinthians 2:9-10.
[3]May Stephens.

✄ ✄ ✄

JEREMIAH 51–52
JEREMIAH 52

> And it came to pass . . . that Evil-merodach king of
> Babylon in the first year of his reign lifted up the head
> of Jehoiachin king of Judah, and brought him forth out
> of prison, and spake kindly unto him, and set his throne
> above the throne of the kings that were with him in
> Babylon, and changed his prison garments: and he did
> continually eat bread before him all the days of his life.
> And for his diet, there was a continual diet given him
> of the king of Babylon, every day a portion until the
> day of his death.[1]

FRANK NOVAK was a very special friend of our family. His
story was much like the story of Jehoiachin. He came to
the United States from Lithuania. He read stories of "bad
men with guns," emulated those men and found himself in
prison with a death sentence. There he found Jesus Christ
and was pardoned first from his sin, then from the crime
of which he had been convicted. How vividly he likened
putting off the prison garments and taking on the garments
of a free citizen to casting off the chains of sin and being
clothed in the garments of Christ's righteousness. Mr. Novak had "put on the new man, which is renewed in knowledge after the image of him that created him."[2]

Mr. Novak like Jehoiachin was a prisoner set free. The
King of kings had invited him to sit at His table all the days
of his life. How he fed on the Word of God. It was his
continual spiritual diet and his daily portion until the day
God called him home to heaven.

Our friend never forgot that he could not keep what he
had obtained for himself alone. As a plumber he faithfully
served the Lord, offering his skills to assist Christian camps
and individuals. During off hours he was a witness in jails
and penitentiaries. He carried with him the official pardon
releasing him from death row. He also always carried the

Bible with its record of his pardon from sin through faith in Jesus Christ. "If we confess our sins, he is faithful and just to forgive us our sins, and to cleanse us from all unrighteousness."[3] How often Mr. Novak would point to the verses in I John for the "official record." "And this is the *record,* that God hath given to us eternal life, and this life is in his Son. He that hath the Son hath life; and he that hath not the Son of God hath not life."[4]

Let us never forget that one day Jesus Christ exchanged our garments, spotted with sin, for the robe of His righteousness, and allowed us to sit at the King's table. For us He has provided a continual feast of His pardon, peace, and presence. Let us well represent the One who has given us this undeserved position in the royal family of God.

[1]Jeremiah 52:31-34.
[2]Colossians 3:10.
[3]I John 1:9.
[4]I John 5:11-12.

❧   ❧   ❧

August 15

LAMENTATIONS 1–2
LAMENTATIONS 1

> Is it nothing to you, all ye that pass by? Behold, and see if there be any sorrow like unto my sorrow, which is done unto me.[1]

LAMENTATIONS is like an echo and re-echo as Jeremiah pours out his broken heart after the destruction of Jerusalem. He truly wept for the people and for their sin as he looked out over the ruins after the captivity of the nation.

Here we see a picture of our Lord Jesus Christ looking over a people crushed beneath the load of sin and captive to the power of Satan. The Lord could ask the same question that Jeremiah addressed to the passerby: "Is it nothing to you?"

It meant a great deal to Jesus Christ. He could not bear to see a world passing into eternity without God and without hope, and He did something about it. He went to the cross and died bearing your sin and mine. Are His sufferings for our sake of no interest or concern to us? Are you not moved by the fact that He who was perfect died for His enemies? "Is it nothing to you?"

A motorist was involved in a three-car accident. Although he was not the cause of the accident, he later confessed that possibly he could have helped to avoid it, but instead chose to teach the young driver a lesson in driving courtesy. He did not realize that his intended lesson to the boy in the wrong would cause the death of another person. The anguish on the motorist's face will never be forgotten. He said to the judge in court, who had declared him free of guilt, that he still must confess his guilt, for possibly the accident might have been avoided.

Some day we will be facing the Judge of all the earth. My heart stirs within me as I realize that passing before me are scores who I might lightly say are not my concern. Yet Jesus Christ died for all, and thus I have some guilt if their death is without hope, for I am responsible to tell others of Him.

"Is it nothing to you?" Christ prayed in Gethsemane, and some of his disciples slept. He is interceding above, on the right hand of the Father. Are we spiritually asleep? When contemplating the picture of the suffering Saviour on the cross to save mankind, only the most hardened, uncompassionate soul would say, "It is nothing to me." God grant that by our actions we will daily prove ourselves concerned and dedicated to reaching those that "pass by" our lives.

[1]Lamentations 1:12.

❧ ❧ ❧

LAMENTATIONS 3–5
LAMENTATIONS 5

> It is of the Lord's mercies that we are not consumed,,
> because his compassions fail not. They are new every
> morning: great is thy faithfulness.[1]

AMONG THE FIVE ELEGIES which make up the Lamentations of Jeremiah we find these two verses which have lighted the darkness for many believers and have replaced the silence of despair with a song. This middle elegy, different from the other four, is very personal and human. At times Jeremiah lamented things that appeared too great to bear, but God's mercy and compassion emerged there. "Great is thy faithfulness."

Whatever the difficulty or trial of yesterday, each today brings another opportunity. Though I failed my Lord yesterday, I know that today brings a new gift of twenty-four hours. And my faithfulness must first be shown in my own heart and in my devotion to Him rather than in what others can see.

Days in which I fail the test are days to really consider His compassion. Though I am weak and helpless, and fail to do what my heart cries to do, His compassions fail not. They are always the same and always in abundant supply.

Here we see Jeremiah looking above himself to a God who waits to be gracious. In looking up we see our trials in different perspective as we gain confidence that God does care and that His grace is sufficient. Why be underneath the circumstances when it is so simple to rise above them? Why live in the depths of despair when the mount of mercy is set before us? Instead of looking at afflictions and trials as evidences of His wrath let us consider that afflictions are for our edification. Strengthened by His compassion, we can look up and sing with praise and gratitude.

Each experience we are allowed to pass through is another

step in the process of molding and refining our lives for His better service. Some are grave and some gracious, but it takes both to mature.

A children's dentist had this little motto above two sets of teeth in his office:

> "Too many sweets cause decay
> Eat what's right for you today."

A diet of "all goes well" with no reversals can be detrimental to your experience as a child of God. Your health will be enriched as you too "eat what is right," the bread of adversity, or the sweetness of success. It takes both, but in both, Jeremiah's promise can be ours: mercies—new every morning—and great faithfulness.

[1]Lamentations 3:22-23.

❧ ❧ ❧

August 17

Ezekiel 1–4
Ezekiel 2

> And he said unto me, Son of man, stand upon thy feet,
> and I will speak unto thee.[1]

Ezekiel was greatly influenced by Jeremiah. He too was called to be a voice of God. He too was to remind Israel of the awfulness of sin and call them to repentance.

As we read Ezekiel, it is good to remember that the book deals largely with the prophetic history of the Jewish nation. The author's visions took him beyond the days of their scattering to the time when they would be brought together with the Messiah in Palestine.

Ezekiel's call to the prophetic ministry is most interesting for us to note. "Son of man, stand upon thy feet, and I will speak unto thee." This was his commission to his life's work for God, and his responsibilities followed.

How easy it is for us to stand when the surroundings are familiar and the situation favorable. However, when the pressures come what do we do? Quit? Fold up and retreat? Ezekiel stood when the siege of Jerusalem began and everything went against him. He would not retreat but continued to proclaim the message. In difficulties he claimed the promises of God. He drew strength and courage by communing with God. Divine reinforcements saw him through to victory. In standing with God we look up and can face the world on our feet!

Ezekiel did not wait for others about him to rise and do the job. He himself worked and prayed and faithfully proclaimed God's message. He had been given a solemn charge from God, words that are written for us too: "When I say unto the wicked, Thou shalt surely die; and thou givest him not warning, nor speakest to warn the wicked from his wicked way, to save his life; the same wicked man shall die in his iniquity; but his blood will I require at thine hand. Yet if thou warn the wicked, and he turn not from his wickedness, nor from his wicked way, he shall die in his iniquity; but thou hast delivered thy soul."[2]

No doubt we all believe that the Great Commission must be obeyed, yet all too many of us pass the responsibility to our ministers and missionaries. Christ has commissioned each believer to be a missionary. The term means "one on a mission." It particularly relates to religion and does not involve location.

Each Christian is called to be God's witness, here and now, to those next door and around the corner. "Stand upon thy feet, and I will speak unto thee."

[1]Ezekiel 2:1.
[2]Ezekiel 3:18-19.

❧ ❧ ❧

368

Ezekiel 5–9
Ezekiel 8

And when I looked, behold a hole in the wall.[1]

William Edward Biederwolf used to tell the story of two brothers, architects, who were celebrated in Greek mythology. They were Trophonius and Agamedes. They were in the employ of King Hyrieus. While they were building him a treasury they became increasingly impressed with the great wealth of the king and made a plan. They placed a certain stone so that it could later be removed, giving them access to the treasure. The work was so planned and precisioned that they could purloin the treasury without detection.

The king became concerned. His treasury was well built and it had guards and seals. Yet the place was being entered frequently and his wealth was diminishing. Trophonius and Agamedes had a perfect plan. They were never discovered.

How well this illustrates the life of some Christians. The armor of God is put on, and supposedly the life is one of victory. However, there is one place where spiritual vitality is tapped, and the Christian becomes drained. His plight has one basic difference from that of King Hyrieus. The king could not find the vulnerable spot. The Christian knows it, as does his God.

Ezekiel saw the hole in the wall of the house of Israel. In his vision the Lord said, "Go in, and behold the wicked abominations that they do here."[2] How foolish were those within. They said, "The Lord seeth us not."[3] Are we so blinded that we go on cherishing some idol or wrong in our lives and think that the Lord does not see us?

We cannot hide from God. The Psalmist confessed, "Whither shall I flee from thy presence?"[4] He knew there was no place where God would not see him and know him.

God knows that "hole" in our spiritual foundation. It may seem peripheral or insignificant, but it is causing the depletion of our spiritual resources.

David found his weakness and stopped it up by praying, "Search me, O God, and know my heart . . . Create in me a clean heart . . . Cleanse thou me from secret faults."[5]

May we guard well the treasure in the temples of our hearts.

[1]Ezekiel 8:7.
[2]Ezekiel 8:9.
[3]Ezekiel 8:12.
[4]Psalm 139:7.
[5]Psalm 139:23; 51:10; 19:12.

❧ ❧ ❧

August 19

EZEKIEL 10–13
EZEKIEL 10

> And every one had four faces: the first face was the face of a cherub, and the second face was the face of a man, and the third the face of a lion, and the fourth the face of an eagle. For there shall be no more any vain vision nor flattering divination within the house of Israel.[1]

TODAY'S READING is an illustration of the way Ezekiel wrote. Some refer to his style as "Ezekiel's hieroglyphics." The visions of this man were symbolic. These symbols are significant to the thoughtful reader.

In the cherub, we see one of God's special messengers who lives near the throne of Deity, the place of devotion. The second face was in the vision of a man. Here are pictured humility and communication. The next was the face of a lion. Here is an illustration of strength. Last, there was the symbol of a soaring eagle, which speaks of fervency and zeal.

The four are described thus by G. Campbell Morgan: "The cherub was a symbol of service, man the symbol of manifestation, the lion the symbol of supremacy, and the eagle a symbol of mystery. Supremacy suggested kingship. Service suggested sacrifice. Manifestation suggested the unveiling of life at its best, and mystery, the unfathomable."

Is such symbolism too complex for us? Do we shy away from such teaching and truth? Think of a telescope. There are two ends, the small one which brings things otherwise not discernible into clear focus, and the large end, which makes distant the things at hand. Too often we look into the large end of our spiritual telescope when it comes to understanding these words of the prophets. It is much easier to push them away into the distance than to bring them into view by careful and patient focus to learn the things God intends us to know.

It is said that an eagle has telescopic vision to view the earth below and the heavens above. Our God sees all, but He also sees me, not far away and in the distance but close to His heart of love.

[1]Ezekiel 10:14; 12:24.

🍀 🍀 🍀

Ezekiel 14–16
Ezekiel 16

> When I passed by thee . . . I said . . . Live.[1]

NIGHTS WERE LONG for a lonely man who lived in a solitary way. His schedule was unrelieved day after day: eat, walk, rest, eat, then retire as the shadows darkened. Life held little meaning and no zest. One afternoon he sat on a bench in a nearby park. Off in the distance he heard some children's voices. They were singing and he moved closer to listen.

> The whole world was lost in the darkness of sin;
> The Light of the world is Jesus;
> Like sunshine at noonday His glory shone in,
> The Light of the world is Jesus.[2]

Light? In his dark world? It wasn't long before a little boy brought over a booklet and handed it to the intent listener. "It's for you," he said, and passed on.

As he read the words in the booklet, the desolate, weary man responded to the echo of the children's voices:

> Come to the Light, 'tis shining for thee;
> Sweetly the Light has dawned upon me;
> Once I was blind, but now I can see;
> The Light of the world is Jesus.

At eighty-six years this man became a recipient of God's mandate of mercy. "When I passed by thee . . . I said . . . Live." In just a moment life everlasting had become his.

Though elderly, this man began studying the Word of God. There was a spring in his step and joy in his heart as he became better acquainted with the One who had said, "Live." He mentioned to a friend that there was a verse in Ezekiel which he really understood: "Son of man, What is the vine tree more than any tree, or than a branch which is among the trees of the forest?"[3] The friend looked puzzled until the old man explained, "I am a new vine in God's vineyard. By his love and goodness and mercy, even in old age I have been put in rich, rewarding soil. I have no place for pride as the only thing I can rest upon is the merit of Jesus Christ. If I bear fruit it is because of my relationship to Him, and the increase will be His. God took an old man and made him a new man. I cannot say I am better or greater than those that live in my area. Except for Jesus Christ I am nothing. With Him, I can do all things."

Our experience with Jesus Christ is the same. One day as He passed by He said to us, "Live." We also are true debtors to Him. The hymn writer expressed the thought aptly: "Boasting excluded, pride I abase; I'm only a sinner saved by grace."[4]

[1]Ezekiel 16:6.
[2]"The Light of the World Is Jesus," Philip P. Bliss.
[3]Ezekiel 15:2.
[4]"Only a Sinner," *James M. Gray.*

❧ ❧ ❧

August 21

EZEKIEL 17–19
EZEKIEL 18

> And all the trees of the field shall know that I the Lord have brought down the high tree, have exalted the low tree, have dried up the green tree, and have made the dry tree to flourish: I the Lord have spoken and have done it.[1]

TODAY'S VERSE is a portion of a paragraph which refers to the ultimate setting up of Christ's kingdom. In His kingdom things will be set up in a manner quite unfamiliar to our worldly wisdom. How often in the Word He speaks of the last being first, and exhorts those who would exalt themselves to be humble. We are continually reminded that "man looketh on the outward appearance, but the Lord looketh on the heart."[2]

An illustration comes from the story of Queen Esther. Haman and Mordecai were at opposite ends of the political register. The first was greatest and exalted and could be called "the high tree." Mordecai had no authority and represents the "low tree." In the final struggle we might expect Haman to win. He had the power and the position. This is where the plan of God enters in. Instead of the "low tree" being destroyed, it was exalted, and the "high tree" executed.

In such living pictures, Ezekiel tells us a story in which we may see pictures of Jesus Christ. He was born in lowly circumstances. Isaiah pictured him as "despised and rejected . . . oppressed and afflicted . . . he is brought as a lamb to the slaughter, and as a sheep before her shearers is dumb, so he openeth not his mouth. Yet it pleased the Lord to bruise him; he hath put him to grief: when thou shalt make his soul an offering for sin, he shall see his seed, he shall prolong his days, and the pleasure of the Lord shall prosper in his hand."[3] Yet Jesus Christ, the "low tree," will overcome. His name will be "from everlasting to everlasting."

There are deep doctrines and great philosophies, but profound as they are, they seem insignificant beside the reality and meaning of the Cross. Here the "low tree" becomes supreme. The righteous man has been likened to a "tree planted by the rivers of water, that bringeth forth his fruit in his season; his leaf also shall not wither; and whatsoever he doeth shall prosper. For the Lord knoweth the way of the righteous: but the way of the ungodly shall perish."[4]

[1]Ezekiel 17:24.
[2]I Samuel 16:7.
[3]Isaiah 53:3-7, 10.
[4]Psalm 1:3, 6.

❧　❧　❧

Ezekiel 20–22
Ezekiel 22

> And I sought for a man among them, that should make
> up the hedge, and stand in the gap before me for the
> land, that I should not destroy it: but I found none.[1]

AN ADVERTISING EXECUTIVE has said that God is constantly
running a sacred "want ad." He is looking for men and
women who will step up and apply for the position of
"stand[ing] in the gap" to "make up the hedge." The qualifications are high, requiring the applicant to bear the standard of the Cross. It takes conviction and courage, with consecration to Jesus Christ alone.

As we study the history of Israel in Ezekiel, we find a sum-
mary which allows us to draw a parallel to the times in
which we live. There were breakdowns in the civil life of
the people. They refused to look to God as their leader and
tried to get what they wanted without restriction. The
social life of Israel went through a serious breakdown also.
Impurity and degeneration took their grave toll. What
naturally followed was the rejection of the religious side of
life. The Scriptures tell us that the priests, the princes, and
even the prophets were guilty of self-seeking and indifference. The spiritual emphasis was forgotten with chaotic
results.

It has been said, in reference to Israel and to our own
nation, that "fundamentally we are alike; superficially we
differ." God searched then and searches still for one who
would meet the challenge. His Son was the supreme example of standing in the gap and taking another's place.
He was willing to die that we who were already dead in
sin could live.

What of our conviction today? Are we concerned with
the needs of those about us, or will we remain indifferent

and inactive toward others? Do we have courage within to face up to the sin and general breakdown that surround us?

A little girl was urging her mother to come into the water. The mother was fearful and barely dampened her toes. In impatience, the child shouted, "Mamma, just jump in!" That was all it took and Mamma learned to swim! We need to do just that, "jump in," into our responsibility in the kingdom of God.

Our consecration stems from our devotion. In giving up our own interests we receive God's bounty in abundance. Patiently but urgently He speaks: "And I sought for a man . . ."

[1]Ezekiel 22:30.

❧ ❧ ❧

August 23

Ezekiel 23–25
Ezekiel 24

A YOUNG LUTHERAN MINISTER stood in his pulpit one Sunday morning with a look of determination which his parish had not seen before. In the second row were his four sons, but his wife was missing.

He read the Old Testament lesson as follows:

> Son of man, behold, I take away from thee the desire of thine eyes with a stroke: yet neither shalt thou mourn nor weep, neither shall thy tears run down. Forbear to cry, take no mourning for the dead, bind the tire of thine head upon thee, and put on thy shoes upon thy feet, and cover not thy lips, and eat not the bread of men. So I spake unto the people in the morning: and at even my wife died; and I did in the morning as I was commanded.[1]

The young pastor had been through a shattering experience, but through it he was steadfastly determined, that first morning after his wife's death, that it would not interfere with his ministry. In his heart he grieved, but he would continue in the work of the Lord.

The death of Ezekiel's wife was an object lesson to the children of Israel. It was to be symbolic of their attitude when Jerusalem would fall. In having Ezekiel "forbear to cry" God was reminding him that He had intervened. This was an illustration to the children of Israel of how God might interpose in their behalf. Ezekiel's wife had been taken quickly by a stroke—with no warning. God would so deal with the sin of a guilty nation. Through this the prophet himself had become a sign. In seeing his personal grief, the people might understand the grief that would come with Jerusalem's destruction.

The story also typifies the greater Prophet. The will of God in His life a severe test to His followers. How devoted the disciples were to Jesus Christ. His words to "follow" brought out their unreserved response and they gloried in His presence. Then the day came when God said He must die. It was incredible that suddenly He was to be taken from their midst. Oh, the grief and sorrow, the emptiness, the darkness in the hearts of those who called him Lord. For the minister as well as for these disciples the bottom had dropped out. Life becomes a void unless the higher purposes of God are realized. Jesus Christ overcame death to give us new life, new purpose, and new hope.

The young minister learned that when one's world collapses, the master Builder is right there to rebuild for those whose trust is in Him. He can erect a new structure that can never be destroyed. Because of his keen spiritual understanding, the minister could stand in the pulpit the morning after the tragedy and do as he felt God wanted. We serve a living Christ. His purposes are without question the only ones we must seek.

¹Ezekiel 24:16-18.

❧ ❧ ❧

> We have also a more sure word of prophecy: where-
> unto ye do well that ye take heed, as unto a light that
> shineth in a dark place, until the day dawn, and the day
> star arise in your hearts.[1]

A CLASS OF TEEN-AGERS were discussing what might happen
in our world in future generations. They tried hard to
imagine the year 2000. They were full of ideas but no
one was about to publish them for they were mostly speculation. Finally one commented that no one really knows
what the future will be, and here their true discussion began. They took the Bible and, with the help of a teacher,
sought to find out what God has said about the future.
Such revelations are called "prophecy." The young men
and women were extremely attentive as they heard about
Bible prophecy, much of which has already been fulfilled.

Ezekiel foretold some remarkable prophecy about a place
called Tyre. Chapter 26 outlines the judgment that was to
come upon this place: "Therefore thus saith the Lord God;
Behold, I am against thee, O Tyrus, and will cause many
nations to come up against thee, as the sea causeth his
waves to come up. And they shall destroy the walls of
Tyrus, and break down her towers: I will also scrape her
dust from her, and make her like the top of a rock."[2]
Ezekiel's words even included the name of Nebuchadnezzar,
king of Babylon, one of those who would conquer Tyre.

Was that prophecy fulfilled? To the very letter. History
gives the story of how King Nebuchadnezzar came in to
surround Tyre, to break its walls and destroy the city. The
city was rebuilt in a different location when the king left,
thus the prophecy of Ezekiel was only partially fulfilled.
However, more than two hundred years later, Alexander
the Great, the conqueror from Greece, came in. Ultimate-

ly he used up the old ruins of the city to build a causeway, finally scraping up the dirt to get to the rock beneath!

We are most fortunate to live in a time when we may daily see the confirmation and fulfillment of God's Word. There are increasing proofs of the infallibility of the Scriptures. Read on with new assurance that these are inspired words and that the Word of our God will endure forever.

[1]II Peter 1:19.
[2]Ezekiel 26:3-4.

❦ ❦ ❦

August 25

Ezekiel 29–32
Ezekiel 29

> I will give thee the opening of the mouth in the midst
> of them; and they shall know that I am the Lord.[1]

AT CERTAIN TIMES Ezekiel had been silent. Now the Lord gave him the opportunity and liberty to proclaim His message. Thus God opened the mouth of His servant to comfort the people and to give praise to God and make Him known.

We cannot appreciate the freedom we have to speak for our Lord until we visit a country where such speech is limited or even forbidden. As one Christian refugee woman exclaimed, "In America I can open my mouth without fear of it being forever closed." Until we understand the power and malevolence of Satan, her statement cannot be completely understood. She lost her husband, who was preaching the gospel, by martyrdom. He was falsely accused of subversive activity and would not renounce the Lord. Her children were put in schools to be brought up without mention of God. She knew of what she spoke.

With our wonderful opportunities to share the riches available in Christ, some of us still keep our mouths closed.

What a tragedy that we remain silent while the doors are wide open! A word in season could bring eternal life to the one who hears. Ours is the glorious opportunity to shed light in darkness.

For those frightened to speak, the Lord has promised to guide the thoughts and supply the words that will bear fruit. Thus we do not share the good news alone but in the Presence and with the Power of the Spirit of God. He brings to mind the words to be used and graciously assists us. We will be enriched as we experience the reality.

When, by faith, we speak the words of Christ to those who have been on our hearts, it is a glorious experience. We may draw assurance from a background of prayer and Christian concern and the knowledge that His Word does not return void. "Hear, O my people, and I will testify unto thee: O Israel, if thou wilt hearken unto me; I am the Lord thy God, which brought thee out of the land of Egypt: open thy mouth wide, and I will fill it."[2]

[1]Ezekiel 29:21.
[2]Psalm 81:8, 10.

❧ ❧ ❧

For thus saith the Lord God; Behold, I, even I, will both search my sheep, and seek them out. As a shepherd seeketh out his flock in the day that he is among his sheep that are scattered; so will I seek out my sheep, and will deliver them out of all places where they have been scattered in the cloudy and dark day.[1]

"HERE THEN is the beauty and glory of Christ, as a Redeemer and Saviour of lost man, that He goes before, always before, and never behind His flock. The works of love that He requires from us, in words, are preceded and illustrated by real deeds of love, to which He gave up all His mighty powers from day to day. He bore the cross Himself that He commanded us to take up and bear after Him. In all which He is our Shepherd, calling, but never driving; bearing all the losses He calls us to bear; meeting all the dangers, suffering all the cruelties and pains which it is given us to suffer, and drawing us to follow where He leads."[2]

See the tenderness and care of the Good Shepherd. He not only leads but He feeds. "And I will feed them in good pasture, and upon the high mountains of Israel shall their fold be: there shall they lie in a good fold, and in a fat pasture shall they feed upon the mountains of Israel."[3] As the Psalmist says, so may the Christian, "I shall not want."[4]

Our Lord knows the pastures that are best for His sheep. Each individual must not question nor doubt where he is led. The greenest of pastures may be in the hot climate of adversity. The troubled waters are made calm when the Shepherd causes them to "be still." The path may be far from home and friends but, if it is His choice, it is a place of safety and growth and great joy, for He, the Good Shepherd, is there.

A new Christian came into the fullest understanding of

the term "my Shepherd" when one day she realized that if God knew her by name, had the hairs of her head numbered, and her path prepared, He had certainly made a study of her and surely would reveal this path to her. He had long sought for her before she searched for Him. Most certainly her times were in His hands.

"The Lord is *my* shepherd."

[1]Ezekiel 34:11-12.
[2]Horace Bushnell.
[3]Ezekiel 34:14.
[4]Psalm 23:1.

❧ ❧ ❧

August 27

EZEKIEL 36–37
EZEKIEL 37

> Then said he unto me, Prophesy unto the wind, prophesy, son of man, and say to the wind, Thus saith the Lord God; Come from the four winds, O breath, and breathe upon these slain, that they may live. So I prophesied as he commanded me, and the breath came into them, and they lived, and stood up upon their feet, an exceeding great army.[1]

WE MUST USE our imaginations to recapture the vision of Ezekiel as he stood in the midst of "the valley which was full of bones."[2] The scattered bones were symbolic of the house of Israel dispersed throughout the world. The purpose of the vision was to unfold the future plan of the Lord to gather His people together and reign forever with them.

As Ezekiel pondered the scene of hopelessness and death, the Lord put a question to him: "Can these bones live?" The prophet's answer came back, "O Lord God, thou knowest." Then God spoke to him again. "Prophesy upon these bones, and say unto them, O ye dry bones, hear the word of the Lord."[3]

Ezekiel was obedient to the heavenly vision, and suddenly the bones took human form but were without breath. "Breathe upon these slain, that they may live." The breath of heaven brought life, and power, for "they stood up upon their feet" and were brought together, "an exceeding great army."

We know that in reading the Scriptures it is important to keep the setting in mind and know for whom the message was intended. Here God was speaking about Israel, but we can apply this to ourselves in the twentieth century without fear of going astray. A lesson comes to life.

Man is spiritually dead until the breath of God comes upon him and he is quickened. All too many walk around with flesh and bones but are spiritually dead until the Spirit of life makes them alive. On being made alive, they must come to the place of receiving power. "But ye shall receive power, after that the Holy Ghost is come upon you."[4] The power of God's breath caused the men in the vision to stand up. The power of God in our lives gives us what is necessary to truly be counted for God. The hymn writer expressed it well:

> Breath of Calvary! Breath of Calvary!
> Let us feel Thy quickening power
> Cleansing, energizing, filling,
> Every moment, every hour.[5]

It is wonderful to realize that the breath of the Spirit not only quickened and gave power but brought them together. The scattered were united. How we need to be brought together today, to bury our differences, and in unity carry forth the plan He has for us.

[1]Ezekiel 37:9-10.
[2]Ezekiel 37:1.
[3]Ezekiel 37:3-4.
[4]Acts 1:8.
[5]*George Hall;* Herbert Tovey, copyright owner.

❧ ❧ ❧

THESE TWO CHAPTERS are the subject of much discussion and varied interpretation. Gog seems to be a king and Magog the kingdom. Since this is a devotional book and not a book of prophecy, we will not attempt to do what expositors are equipped to do. However, we can conclude with certainty that God is on the throne, and that there will be a fierce onslaught against all enemies of truth.

Ezekiel was told to prophesy againt Gog. He did not mince words: "And the word of the Lord came unto me, saying, Son of man, set thy face against Gog, the land of Magog, the chief prince . . . and prophesy against him, and say, Thus saith the Lord God; Behold, I am against thee."[1]

God not only sees His past enemies and the present ones but He also looks into the future. Though there will always be those who will be rebellious against Him, we know that even the wrath of man will praise Him.[2]

It has been pointed out how careful God was in these chapters to warn of coming troubles and dangers. He explained that in the end all will work out well for those who place their trust in Him. The conclusion is, "Then shall they know that I am the Lord their God, which caused them to be led into captivity among the heathen: but I have gathered them unto their own land, and have left none of them any more there. Neither will I hide my face any more from them: for I have poured out my spirit upon the house of Israel, saith the Lord God."[3]

We may rest assured, during the uncertainty of the future, that the providence of God concerning His own is for their good. God is with His children in their times of calamity and captivity as well as in times of comfort and security.

Who is the true Israel? Dr. A. Lange has said, "The true Israel, the people of the Spirit. The outpouring of the

Spirit of Jehovah is the end of all the ways which He has gone with Israel in the Christian Church."

The Psalmist prayed, "Take not thy holy spirit from me."[4] "The indwelling of the Spirit is an infallible pledge of the continuance of God's favor."[5] May His Spirit permeate our lives and cause us to keep looking up, knowing that our redemption is on the horizon.

[1]Ezekiel 38:1-3.
[2]Psalm 76:10.
[3]Ezekiel 39:28-29.
[4]Psalm 51:11.
[5]Matthew Henry.

❦ ❦ ❦

August 29

Ezekiel 40–42
Ezekiel 40

THE STORY IS TOLD of an old harp that for years stood unused in the music room of a palace. Once it had produced beautiful melody and harmony. Now it only gave out discordant sounds and its notes were harsh and shrill. The palace officials had invited many musicians into their music room to tune the harp, but none had been successful.

One day an elderly guest asked the prince if he still had the old harp. The prince was interested that the gentleman remembered it and took him to where it was covered. At once the guest sat down and began to tune it. His precision with the pegs was most remarkable. At last he sat forward, tipped the instrument back to his shoulder, and filled the room with sweet music. The prince was amazed at what the man had accomplished until he learned that the guest was the one who had made the harp. Discord becomes harmony only when the discordant strings are tuned.

The vision of Ezekiel recorded in these closing chapters has been considered one of the most difficult to understand.

For many it is out of tune and without harmony. The Jewish people recommend that it be read only by those over thirty years of age. However, the Christian knows One who can bring harmony out of the confusion that may come to souls through lack of understanding. Christ can remove the painful discord of not knowing what comprises the future. Believing "that the sufferings of this present time are not worthy to be compared with the glory which shall be revealed"[1] will bring glad harmony into one's life.

This vision of Ezekiel came in his twenty-fifth year of captivity. God was cognizant of the length of time the yoke had been worn and the burdens borne. The vision was of the restored Temple and the reinhabited land. Such vision is reserved for those who are spiritual and perceptive. These visions of God bring revelations of His character and His plans.

Surely He who made us can take the world, no matter how out of tune with Him, and bring it back into harmony with His purpose. In the interim, let us be instruments pitched to His glory and praise.

[1]Romans 8:18.

     ✄   ✄   ✄

Ezekiel 43–45
Ezekiel 44

> And it shall be unto them for an inheritance: I am
> their inheritance: and ye shall give them no possession
> in Israel: I am their possession.[1]

THE MORNING PAPER carried the story of a man who had
been living in complete poverty and now had become heir
to a quarter of a million dollars. It was titled "Missing
Heir Discovered."

One cannot help but wonder how many missing heirs
there are to the kingdom and riches of God. All too many
are content to continue in spiritual poverty, tasting only
fragments of the Word and experiencing insufficient peace
when a limitless inheritance awaits! Too many are "pre-
tenders" to the throne of grace. It is no wonder that they
come away unfilled.

Our Father is King and the wealth of the world is His.
He is willing to give in abundance, but He requires first
that we give ourselves to Him. We do not become heirs by
merely pronouncing ourselves as such. We must first be
born into the family. "The Spirit itself beareth witness with
our spirit, that we are the children of God: and if children,
then heirs; heirs of God, and joint-heirs with Christ."[2] This
is a relationship of responsibility, but it also yields each believer a rich heritage.

What God gives us we are to use in His service. The spiritual and material blessings can be used for stepping-stones
or stumbling blocks. In the royal family there should be
no question as to which are produced. The challenge is
given in these lines by an unknown author:

> To each is given a bag of tools,
> An hourglass, and a book of rules;
> And each must build e'er his work be done
> A stumbling block or a stepping-stone.

387

Our Father has not left us without a Guidebook, in which we are reminded that time is of the essence. As His possession we must work the works of Him that sent us. There is much to be accomplished.

If only we could realize the possession we have in Christ. If only we could comprehend how much we need Him. He is more than a friend, closer than a family. Today claim your inheritance in Him. If you have lived like a missing heir, discover your riches in Christ.

¹Ezekiel 44:28.
²Romans 8:16-17.

❧ ❧ ❧

August 31

Ezekiel 46–48
Ezekiel 47

> Afterward he brought me again unto the door of the house; and behold, waters issued out from under the threshold of the house.¹

THE BOOK OF EZEKIEL ends with the vision of the river of water of life. Its source was not from the Temple but from the One whose glory filled it. Ezekiel had looked around the Temple many times. He had surveyed and admired it and rejoiced in all that it represented. But it took a special revelation to show him the waters that were proceeding from under the threshold and to bring him to an awareness of their source.

How easy it is in our accelerated way of life to be engrossed with the things close to us to such a degree that we miss much that is more important. We must come to the threshold of the house of God and stop to pray and meditate until, with David, we can say, "All my springs are in thee."²

The river is pictured as having a small beginning, but

it widens and deepens as it flows from the Temple out into the distance. If we could trace its course we would learn of barren land refreshed, of soul-thirst quenched, and of desert lands becoming fruitful.

Does this not bear resemblance to the Christian life? The Christian is a temple of God, and rivers of living water should be flowing from him. At first they may be narrow and shallow, but as they go forth they will deepen and broaden and grow in their life-giving pursuit. They will expand in fullness of grace and peace and untold joy to many. The Christian's life will be a channel of God's blessing, and fertility will result—all for His glory.

Let us never be so involved that we forget the Source of the soul-refreshing life stream. Let us saturate ourselves in His Word. "Blessed are they which do hunger and thirst after righteousness: for they shall be filled."[3]

When we are filled, the wells within will overflow to others in a new and vital way, and the words of Ezekiel will become a reality. "Everything shall live whither the river cometh."[4] And God's glory will thus be seen.

[1]Ezekiel 47:1.
[2]Psalm 87:7.
[3]Matthew 5:6.
[4]Ezekiel 47:9.

❧ ❧ ❧

September

DANIEL 1–3
DANIEL 1

> But Daniel purposed in his heart that he would not de-
> file himself with the portion of the king's meat, nor
> with the wine which he drank: therefore he requested
> of the prince of the eunuchs that he might not defile
> himself. Now God had brought Daniel into favour and
> tender love with the prince of the eunuchs.[1]

DANIEL was a remarkable young man whose life of faith
and obedience to God has been influential to countless
souls through the centuries. Historically, the text was recorded at a time of tragedy and drama in the life of an entire nation. All of Israel was in captivity. The king had
requested that some exceptional youths of Israel be brought
to him to be trained in the language and learning of the
Chaldeans. They were captive slaves whose lives were regu-
lated by the court. Each was apportioned certain food and
drink. However, the diet of Babylon was one to which
Daniel and his young companions from Israel objected because it contained foods forbidden by the laws of God.
Daniel, making himself spokesman for the few who were
willing to abstain, "purposed in his heart" to ask for something different. His request was granted for a ten-day period.
"At the end of ten days their countenances appeared fairer
and fatter in flesh than all the children which did eat the
portion of the king's meat."[2]

In considering this story, we know that God's special protection was with Daniel and his friends, for speaking against

the king and his table might have brought the death penalty. However, Daniel, described as "well favoured, and skilful in all wisdom, and cunning in knowledge, and understanding science,"[3] had seen the results of defilement in his people and was determined to stand strongly for what was right.

It has been said that "a noble heart-purpose is the strongest watchman over external conduct. It is the purposeless life that has no defenses." The one who has purposed in his heart to serve God is the happy, useful Christian. At times there may be offense to the world but, as in Daniel's case, it is better to offend a king than the King of kings.

How much easier it would be for the child of God to serve Him staunch in purpose rather than to play at his profession. There are some things that decidedly do not characterize a Christian. For true victory, my smallest sin must be crushed rather than cherished. I must let God's divine purpose fill my life. Then there will be no doubt that "to me to live is Christ."[4]

[1]Daniel 1:8-9. [3]Daniel 1:4.
[2]Daniel 1:15. [4]Philippians 1:21.

❧ ❧ ❧

September 2

Daniel 3–4
Daniel 3

> If it be so, our God whom we serve is able to deliver us from the burning fiery furnace, and he will deliver us out of thine hand, O king. But if not, be it known unto thee, O king, that we will not serve thy gods, nor worship the golden image which thou hast set up.[1]

Picking up the morning paper or reading a news magazine makes one aware of the dark condition of the world. I heard a mother, terrified for the future of her children, frantically ask, "Is there any hope?" When nations are in a cold war and threats become increasingly grave, how can peace come about, as God has promised?

At such discouraging times it is well to read the story of Shadrach, Meshach, and Abednego. Here were three Hebrew children facing the furnace because they would not obey the king. They were confident that God could deliver them, but if not they still would be faithful to Him. Such trust is little known to those who have not faced the furnace of world disfavor. We pray to be kept from trials and persecution and misunderstanding that might come our way. We ask that sickness be removed from us. We plead that one we love greatly might be spared from death. These young men asked to be delivered but "if not" they would still be faithful to God, trusting for strength to go through the experience.

Remember the afflictions of Joseph. He longed to be spared his "furnace," but God was faithful to him and took him through, using him for a greater purpose. Moses' fate was decreed when he was a baby, but the king's daughter interceded in the providence of God. Think of Job, stripped of everything and afflicted, yet able to say, "Though he slay me, yet will I trust in him."[2]

A Christian must be willing to face up to the revealed purpose of God in his life. He must determine that no matter what comes, he will be true to Jesus Christ. This decision has meant death for some. However, with God in command of our lives, we can enjoy the cool assurance that was in the hearts of Shadrach, Meshach, and Abednego.

It sometimes takes the fire to give us a true sense of values, to make us realize that there is more to life than homes and books and flower gardens! The disciplines of God are purposeful. Let us go forward accepting what He gives and, in turn, giving thanks.

[1]Daniel 3:17-18.   [2]Job 13:15.

DANIEL 5–7
DANIEL 6

> And when he came to the den, he cried with a lamentable voice unto Daniel: and the king spake and said to Daniel, O Daniel, servant of the living God, is thy God, whom thou servest continually, able to deliver thee from the lions? Then Daniel said unto the king, O king, live for ever. My God hath sent his angel, and hath shut the lions' mouths, that they have not hurt me.[1]

WHY HAD DANIEL been cast into the den of lions? He would rather risk death than lose his privilege of prayer. He was there for breaking a royal decree prohibiting prayer to any but the king himself. Prayer to God was a matter of life and death to Daniel. He could not afford to continue without it and lose the favor and power of God. Here we have another evidence of God's providence in guiding the affairs of men. In simply closing the mouths of those lions, Daniel was protected. How can we doubt that God's wonders are daily performed, seen and unseen, though at times we may not understand nor comprehend His ways.

> Let my prayers ascend
> Unceasingly to Thee, my Lord.
> My devotion grow
> Increasingly, in will and word.
>
> With my window open
> I will pray unashamed,
> Waiting Thy fulfillment
> Of every promise I have claimed.
>
> So my every moment
> I leave surely in Thy hand,
> Every joy or trial
> By Thee perfected and planned.

Oh, that I might understand the life that God has planned, and let Him "perfect that which concerneth me."[2] Seeing Daniel's life-and-death purpose in prayer should make me resolve that nothing will prevent that vital time apart.

Too often we resemble those in the Far East who spin a wheel of prayer, or fasten prayer cloths to trees and bushes. Prayer should be true communication, spontaneous and unceasing. Our silence grieves God.

Let us reevaluate our prayer habits and, bowing low, reach up to Him whose outstretched arms are eager to receive and revive the soul who earnestly seeks His purpose.

[1] Daniel 6:20-21.
[2] Psalm 138:8.

❧ ❧ ❧

September 4

DANIEL 8–10
DANIEL 10

> O man greatly beloved, fear not: peace be unto thee, be strong, yea, be strong. And when he had spoken unto me, I was strengthened, and said, Let my Lord speak; for thou hast strengthened me.[1]

DANIEL WAS APPROACHING his ninetieth year. Much had transpired and by now he had seen his people restored to their own land according to the promise of God and by means of the edict of Cyrus. Then he saw a vision of the glory of God.

Daniel had expressed what he had experienced. He endured because God had strengthened and upheld him. With God's arm to hold and to gird, and His strength for our weakness, we too can endure and triumph. Daniel's experience can be ours in reality. "Jesus Christ the same yesterday, and to day, and for ever."[2] This is an eternal certainty. We falter but God does not. Our minds waver, but not the heart and mind of God. He who made Daniel strong when he prayed to Him, makes us strong when we communicate with Him. No matter how weak we are, His strength can energize our lives.

When Jesus Christ walked on the earth He showed His power in countless ways. There was the man crippled from birth. To him God the Son spoke and imparted His strength, and the man was made whole. There was one who was lame. His weakness would have followed him to the grave, but Christ spoke, telling him to rise and walk. Think of the man with the withered arm who was told to stretch it forth. What an experience it must have been to feel life coming into his hand and fingers! Picture him reaching out and grasping an object for the first time. No doubt he felt fresh strength and life in his entire being.

Christ showed His power on behalf of sinners also. Their lives were snared and broken by sin. When they met the Saviour their weakness was converted by His saving and strengthening power. They could then walk in the ways of the Lord.

God can speak to you today as He spoke to Daniel. Through prayer and meditation and reading His Word, you can be changed. And the more you listen as He speaks, the more you will cry, "Let my Lord speak."

[1]Daniel 10:19.
[2]Hebrews 13:8.

❧　❧　❧

Daniel 11–12
Daniel 12

> And they that be wise shall shine as the brightness of
> the firmament; and they that turn many to righteous-
> ness as the stars for ever and ever.[1]

As WE CLOSE the book of Daniel we find a verse which describes Daniel's last vision. A life of faith and trust in God
will not be without reward.

Who are the wise? They have been defined as "those
with wisdom," and wisdom as "that which chooses the best
ends and pursues them by the best means." To a Christian
there is no doubt as to the best end. "Man's chief end is to
glorify God and to enjoy Him forever."[2] Wisdom begins
with the true fear of the Lord. Wisdom comes from above
and its author is our God who is wise. "They that be wise
shall shine as the brightness of the firmament," said Daniel
by inspiration. His vision was also a promise of God.

"They that turn many to righteousness" is a description
of those who are soul winners. The literal translation says,
"They that make men righteous." There is no righteousness in us. "For therein is the righteousness of God revealed
from faith to faith: as it is written, The just shall live by
faith."[3] God justifies man by faith alone. His is the faith
way and not the works way. Faith is believing what God
says and acting in obedience to Him. Turning men to
righteousness has its real reward. However, all are not partakers in this divine privilege. What is the reason? Does
not the Lord know who wants to please Him and turn people toward the Way?

Turning men to righteousness has a prerequisite: "they
that be wise." It takes skill and courage to win men to
Christ and both must be tempered by God's wisdom. It
takes wisdom not in the ways of men but in the ways of
God. The outcome brings lasting reward.

The sun and stars in Scripture are often used as symbols. They denote dignity, exaltation, light, and joy. "Light is sown for the righteous, and gladness for the upright in heart."[4] "For ever and ever" speaks of everlasting life, of permanence.

Let us seek our place among the wise in God's family, well knowing that we will reign with Him forever and ever.

[1]Daniel 12:3.
[2]Westminster Catechism.
[3]Romans 1:17.
[4]Psalm 97:11.

※ ※ ※

September 6

HOSEA 1–3
HOSEA 1

> And I will betroth thee unto me for ever; yea, I will betroth thee unto me in righteousness, and in judgment, and in lovingkindness, and in mercies. I will even betroth thee unto me in faithfulness: and thou shalt know the Lord.[1]

HOW CAN GOD open a heart that has not been broken? Often the deep things of God gain entrance only through a broken heart. Hosea was a man with a broken heart. It was evidenced both in his domestic life and in his prophetic ministry. "He who has much to teach must suffer much; and he alone can speak of the deepest things in the economy of God who has sooner or later entered into fellowship with the suffering of God. Hosea passed into fellowship with that suffering through his own suffering."[2]

God had called Hosea to do a most unusual thing. He was to take a wife who was an idol-worshiper. She would be unfaithful and would fail to appreciate her blessings. Through their symbolic relationship and Hosea's broken heart God would speak to the heart of Israel.

Hosea loved Gomer his wife, even though she was not chaste and sought after others. His love in spite of her wanderings gave him a clear picture of God's love for unfaithful, wandering Israel.

Christ's love for His children is tenderly expressed as an everlasting betrothal. These words from Hosea are some of the most exquisite in the Scripture. The day is coming when we are to be married—a wedding of the soul with its Saviour! In the interim may each of us be faithful to the One who truly loves us. In tenderness and compassion He sought us even before we were aware of Him. Paul wrote, "I have you in my heart"[3] to those he loved in the Christian church. The position of the believer is near to God's heart also.

Dr. John Jowett wrote a prayer which is applicable to those who are the Lord's betrothed:

> Heavenly Father, I would be the friend of the Bridegroom. I would help Him to win His bride. Every day let me think how people can be wooed into a marriage contract with the Lord of glory. Let me be alert in the cause of the Bridegroom. Fill my life with holy gentleness that I may win and not repel those for whom He died. For His sake. Amen.

[1]Hosea 2:19-20.
[2]G. Campbell Morgan.
[3]Philippians 1:7.

❧ ❧ ❧

Hosea 4–7
Hosea 6

> Then shall we know, if we follow on to know the Lord:
> his going forth is prepared as the morning; and he shall
> come unto us as the rain, as the latter and former rain
> unto the earth.[1]

THE SUN does not move around us, but we are moving around the sun. The Christian in his "orbit" revolves around the Sun of righteousness.

The Scripture is marked with many invitations such as this: "Come, and let us return unto the Lord: for he hath torn, and he will heal us; he hath smitten, and he will bind us up."[2] As we move toward God, He moves toward us, for He eagerly awaits our coming. We are told that a portion of today's verse is translated thus in Arabic: "His coming is as certain as the dawn." Nothing hinders the breaking of the day. As long as men have lived, the dawn has never failed to rise in the east. Christ's return has the same certainty.

In preparation for this, we must "follow on" to know the Lord better and to make ready for His return. We do not know when it will be but we know that we must be ready. If we are willing to follow on to know the Lord better, our walk will be deeper and fuller in Him.

God's coming is likened to the morning. Light brings security, whereas darkness brings uncertainty. God's coming is likened to the rain also. Rain is symbolic of refreshing. It is of divine origin. God rains spiritual blessings on those who are His children, and through His graces there is an abundant yield in His harvest.

If we lived in preparation for Christ's coming, our values would alter and our goals change. Imagine you have been given a priceless treasure in a faraway country. However, for your journey you will be allowed but one suitcase. What will you take? Think over all your precious and needful possessions. Consider how little can be packed in one bag and how much exclusion would have to be done to arrive at that which is most valued and most useful.

We are stewards of all that God has given us. We journey toward the Promised Land. Let us not be bogged down with "things," but daily keep eternity's values in view as we watch for His coming.

[1]Hosea 6:3.
[2]Hosea 6:1.

❧   ❧   ❧

September 8

HOSEA 8–10
HOSEA .8

> For they have sown the wind, and they shall reap the whirlwind: it hath no stalk: the bud shall yield no meal: if so be it yield, the strangers shall swallow it up.[1]

WE ARE FAMILIAR with the parable of Christ which begins: "Behold, a sower went forth to sow."[2] The various soils and their effect on the seed give us clear illustrations. Today we have another picture. "For they have sown the wind, and they shall reap the whirlwind."

In the Old Testament the question keeps recurring: Why does Israel not learn her lesson? Why the consistent pattern of turning her back on God, of seeking and making alliances with nations who will only cause more oppression? Can she not learn? "For Israel hath forgotten his Maker, and buildeth temples; and Judah hath multiplied fenced cities: but I will send a fire upon his cities, and it shall devour the palaces thereof."[3] Here is the sobering result of "sowing to the wind."

"Sowing to the wind" is an expression used for laboring in vain or exerting futile effort. Lovers of this world, those who profess but do not possess true Christianity, may expect

400

the inevitable harvest, the whirlwind. In Proverbs it is written, "When your fear cometh as desolation, and your destruction cometh as a whirlwind; when distress and anguish cometh upon you. Then shall they call upon me, but I will not answer; they shall seek me early, but they shall not find me: for that they hated knowledge, and did not choose the fear of the Lord: they would none of my counsel: they despised all my reproof."[4] The picture of the whirlwind is awesome. It should at once turn us about face if we are not sowing in the ways the master Husbandman intended.

It is humbling to realize that what we sow we reap. Every thought, action, and deed is a seed that will become a plant. All will be harvested when the day of judgment comes. What we sowed yesterday we reap today, and all we sow during a lifetime is garnered for eternity. God is no respecter of persons. "For he that soweth to his flesh shall of the flesh reap corruption; but he that soweth to the Spirit shall of the Spirit reap life everlasting."[5]

[1]Hosea 8:7.
[2]Matthew 13:3.
[3]Hosea 8:14.
[4]Proverbs 1:27-30.
[5]Galatians 6:8.

❧ ❧ ❧

Hosea 11–14
Hosea 14

> They that dwell under his shadow shall return; they shall revive as the corn, and grow as the vine. . . . I am like a green fir tree. From me is thy fruit found. Who is wise, and he shall understand these things? prudent, and he shall know them? For the ways of the Lord are right, and the just shall walk in them: but the transgressor shall fall therein.[1]

Hosea experienced the art and heart of Jehovah's message. Tenderness, compassion, long-suffering must be extended to the sinner. In seeing Israel's sin in the light of the sin of one he loved, Hosea understood how God could love in spite of sin. So we see illustrated clearly what sin is and how necessary is its punishment. However, through it all we see the unerring love of God.

Today we need the message of God through Hosea. We scarcely understand the true love of God because we have not hated sin as He does, nor truly understood its consequences. We hesitate to admit we are guilty of spiritual adultery, for in the light of Hosea's writings, it would be better for us not to have known the truth than to fail to obey and honor it. However, along with the lesson on the awfulness of sin and judgment comes the message of God's love. In Hosea's time He said, "I will heal their backsliding, I will love them freely."[2] In our times, Jesus Christ has made this possible. "For God so loved the world, that he gave his only begotten Son, that whosoever believeth in him should not perish, but have everlasting life."[3]

Is your heart broken today by the things that break the heart of God? Does the unfaithfulness in your heart and in the hearts of His people cause you to seek, as never before, to walk in the ways of the Lord?

Each of us has known some form of unfaithfulness.

Through it God is speaking to us. We can let it become an instrument to show us how essential is complete faithfulness to Him.

Ephraim said boastfully, "I am like a green fir tree." But God said, "From me is thy fruit found." He may have to do some drastic pruning. Enemies of the fruit will seek to devour the source of fruitfulness. Just as a diligent gardener protects his trees, may we protect and cultivate our hearts. In so doing we will bend low with fruitful branches, ready for God's harvesting.

[1]Hosea 14:7-9.
[2]Hosea 14:4.
[3]John 3:16.

❦   ❦   ❦

September 10

JOEL 1–3
JOEL 2

> Fear not, O land; be glad and rejoice: for the Lord will
> do great things.[1]

JOEL IS INTRODUCED to us with little information as to his background. But we know for certain that he was a special servant of the Lord for a given time. It is significant that God sent several prophets at one time that they might strengthen one another. A single voice, or one standing alone, can be greatly encouraged and helped as others take their places at his side. How often we see the truth of this in our places of employment or in our neighborhoods. More than one voice for the Lord extends the opportunity for the message to be heard.

Joel was used, as were the other prophets, to help bring the people to repentance. Surely they had begun to see God's grace and mercy. Surely they would not turn their backs on God again. But this was not the case. God would have to judge them, this time by means of a small insect, the locust, which would intensively destroy their fruit and grain and vines. Repentance must precede God's deliverance.

Repentance would restore their rejoicing, and they would again see that the Lord does great things. In this story we see the fact vividly depicted by this distinctive writer that God delights in showing mercy. God clearly showed Joel that many outward blessings would follow if the people would repent. He would also pour out His Spirit upon them again.

How weak we are when it comes to obedience and faith in our great God who has repeatedly shown us His glory. When an "insect" eats away at our hearts, bringing disappointment, pain, or intense discouragement, we are quick to turn to other means for relief. But there is divine provision for our needs, there is strength for our weakness. The Lord is waiting to show us great things. Consider the promise to Joel: "Ye shall eat in plenty, and be satisfied, and praise the name of the Lord your God, that hath dealt wondrously with you."[2]

A friend takes pride in her roses and has won many prizes. But she relates the wealth and beauty of her flowers to the times she has had to deprive the bushes of light and water. Possibly our darkness and drought are being used to create something special in God's plan.

[1]Joel 2:21.
[2]Joel 2:26.

❧ ❧ ❧

Amos 1–3
Amos 3

> Surely the Lord God will do nothing, but he revealeth
> his secret unto his servants the prophets. The lion hath
> roared, who will not fear? the Lord God hath spoken,
> who can but prophesy?[1]

Amos was called the champion of social justice, but he was
much more than that. He was another in the long line of
prophets who faithfully proclaimed the drastic contrast between God's righteousness and holiness, and man's sin and
degradation. It is surprising how much of this book can be
applied to us today. Careful study will show you what
should be cultivated by God's Spirit in your heart, and what
can be imparted to others.

A middle-aged man who had not had the opportunity of
education said he was greatly encouraged by the book of
Amos. Amos was not a product of the schools for prophets.
He was trained in the wilderness. His call was simple but
certain. "Then answered Amos, and said to Amaziah, I
was no prophet, neither was I a prophet's son; but I was an
herdman, and a gatherer of sycomore fruit: and the Lord
took me as I followed the flock, and the Lord said unto me,
Go, prophesy unto my people Israel."[2] Amos' approach was
somewhat indirect. First he denounced the wrongs and
crimes of the surrounding nations and the disloyalty of
Judah. Finally he applied the message to Israel. Said one
Christian, "Amos' way of witness is the only way I can tell
people about Jesus Christ. I start out by telling them of the
things in our world that trouble me. Then I talk about
the disloyalty to God in my own heart for many years, and
then make it applicable to the one the Spirit has directed
me to speak to as a faithful witness." This Christian told of
borrowing one of Amos' phrases, "in that day," explaining

the coming judgment of God to his contacts, but also telling of His promised deliverance.

Christians sincerely seeking to serve the Lord and be messengers for Him may be reproved by the book of Amos when they confront the issue of "being at ease in Zion." One can talk a lot but do little, say much but not pray for those lost in sin, unless the heart has been warmed in devotion to Jesus Christ.

Another question may come into the mind. "Can two walk together, except they be agreed?"[3] It is a most logical question, and by it Amos was showing Israel that God's dealings with Israel were right and logical. The Lord has spoken—may we hear and obey.

[1]Amos 3:7-8.
[2]Amos 7:14-15.
[3]Amos 3:3.

❧   ❧   ❧

September 12

AMOS 4–6
AMOS 5

Seek ye me, and ye shall live.[1]

"SEEK NOT BETH-EL, . . . Seek the Lord . . . Seek him . . . Seek good, and not evil, that ye may live."[2] "Seek" is the continuous message of Amos.

Why seek the Lord? The question of sin must be answered. "By one man sin entered into the world, and death by sin; and so death passed upon all men, for that all have sinned."[3] Only Jesus Christ can grant redemption, and to each the message is presented: "Seek ye the Lord while he may be found, call ye upon him while he is near: let the wicked forsake his way, and the unrighteous man his thoughts: and let him return unto the Lord, and he will have mercy upon him; and to our God, for he will abundantly pardon."[4]

Our search for God must be diligent and earnest, with regret for our past sins and grievous ways. "And ye shall seek me, and find me, when ye shall search for me with all your heart."[5]

The outcome of seeking the Lord is peace that passeth understanding, joy that is unspeakable, and true assurance that we have been found by the Lord and that our future is secure in Him.

The believer must "seek good" as he walks with the Lord every day, knowing that his steps are ordered by the Lord. Amos exhorted men to prepare to meet God. This preparation may be applied to our daily walk as well as to eternity. We must accomplish those things we have been called upon to do, in preparing to give account to Him.

Amos, with his background of tending flocks, no doubt had sought God in many ways. How descriptive was his writing when he said, "Seek him that maketh the seven stars and Orion, and turneth the shadow of death into the morning, and maketh the day dark with night: that calleth for the waters of the sea, and poureth them out upon the face of the earth: The Lord is his name."[6] Many nights Amos must have watched the sun set and the stars come out. He would not be lonely in his shepherd's job, even though it meant being outside in the darkest of hours when dangers were greatest. The echo of "seek and live" was his comfort. And as the stars would fade in the dawn light, he would again seek for the day what he had claimed for the night. In everything he was sustained.

Seek and live.

[1]Amos 5:4.
[2]Amos 5:5, 6, 8, 14.
[3]Romans 5:12.
[4]Isaiah 55:6-7.
[5]Jeremiah 29:13.
[6]Amos 5:8.

❧ ❧ ❧

Amos 7–9
Amos 9

A basket of summer fruit.[1]

GOD HAD SPOKEN to Amos and showed him a basket of summer fruit, symbolic of the condition of Israel, ripe for its final judgment. This picture was recently illustrated for me by a letter from a dear missionary friend:

> It is harvesttime again, and the thing that strikes me this time as I watch the bustling workers is their joy. On my way back from the station, after my last visit there, having walked two and one half miles in the hot sun, I was very tired by the time I reached the bus stop. Feeling at the end of my rope, I flopped onto a rickety bench to wait for the bus. Close by there was a crowd. I could see that they were bringing in the yield from the day's harvesting, so I watched. Each one deposited his load and dropped onto the road with fatigue. But the moment the overseer came to measure the rice, the tiredness seemed to drop off like an unnecessary garment. They sat up and with a satisfied expression of joy watched as he measured the golden grain into each one's sack according to the work they had done. Then they had to carry it some distance to their villages. But their conversation was not about the difficulty of that, or of their weariness, but only of the good yield and the ample supply they were able to take home. I felt refreshed by watching them and was reminded that if only there is a good yield in the heavenly harvest in which we are engaged, the heat and toil are not worth thinking about.[2]

Israel faced its judgment just as God predicted through Amos. The day will come when we will meet our Lord in final judgment of our works. We are given to fatigue and some murmuring along the way. But what will be the outcome when we present Him with our harvest yield? Will

His expression be one of disappointment or delight? Will it be "Well done, thou good and faithful servant"? Or will He have to say, "Thou wicked and slothful servant"?[3]

The natives left rejoicing because their yields had been more than acceptable. The burdens along the way were forgotten in their present joy. Our goal must be more than mere "acceptable service" as we work in God's vineyard. Then He and we will be pleased that the labor was not in vain.[4]

[1]Amos 8:1.
[2]Olive Fuller.
[3]Matthew 25:21, 26.
[4]I Corinthians 15:58.

❧ ❧ ❧

September 14

OBADIAH
OBADIAH

> But upon mount Zion shall be deliverance, and there shall be holiness; and the house of Jacob shall possess their possessions.[1]

OBADIAH is a short prophetic book with the doom of Edom as its theme. It is significant that all of its prophecy and predictions have been completely fulfilled. The book is evidence that God speaks in manifold ways, through visions, reports, and judgments, that His revelation to man may become known and confirmed.

Of the book of Obadiah, Isidore wrote: "Among all the prophets, he is the briefest in number of words; in the grace of mysteries he is their equal." It is clear, then, that the brevity has nothing to do with the lasting message. Study of the twenty-one verses grants us assurance that "the word of the Lord endureth for ever."[2] His purposes are fulfilled. Along with His plan for Israel and other nations, He

has a plan for our lives. One day we shall indeed "possess
. . . [our] possessions" in Him.

> In Christ we are justified by faith alone;
> We are His possession, His very own.
>
> Reconciled to God by the death of His Son,
> Glorified with the eternal One.
>
> Possessions multiply. Sons of the King
> Victory in all things He daily will bring.
>
> Peace and joy amid trouble and strife,
> Guidance for our spiritual life.
>
> Inheritance assured from the Father above
> Brought as a gift to show wonderful love.
>
> Hope for the future! What a glad day
> When He will return! And so I pray
>
> That while on the earth I will take what He gives,
> Proving to others that surely He lives;
>
> That the tasks, large or small, that He has shared,
> Will be stored for me in the place prepared.
>
> I deserve not one blessing—this I know—
> But He gives them because He loves me so.
>
> I seek every day to learn His lessons
> And in doing so, I possess my possessions.

[1]Obadiah 17.
[2]I Peter 1:25.

❧ ❧ ❧

JONAH 1–4
JONAH 3

> And the word of the Lord came unto Jonah the second time, saying, Arise, go unto Nineveh, that great city, and preach unto it the preaching that I bid thee.[1]

JONAH, a runaway prophet, paid his fare and boarded a ship bound for Tarshish—a ship that would take him away from the responsibility God had given him. He must have been more than eager for the anchor to be hoisted and the vessel to sail in the opposite direction from the capital city where he had been called to minister. He knew God was a God of mercy, and he used that fact to justify his own sin. "Therefore I fled before unto Tarshish: for I knew that thou art a gracious God, and merciful, slow to anger, and of great kindness, and repentest thee of the evil."[2] How it must grieve the heart of God when one of His children wilfully sins in confidence that he may be forgiven! What a presumption on God's mercy! It must have been a rude awakening when he later realized how deliberate was his sin and how it displeased God. Oh, the grace that led him to repentance! Oh, the grace that granted him a second chance!

It has been pointed out that after Jonah's disobedience he was less competent to fulfill God's assignment. His powers had been impaired by his disobedience. Disobedience brings "moth and rust" to the soul. When we recognize this it should bring us to our knees to plead with God to make us faithful and adequate for the job we are given to do, and to be alert for every opportunity to serve, not missing that first call.

In my own life I have experienced the words of Jonah: "When my soul fainted within me I remembered the Lord: and my prayer came in unto thee, into thine holy temple."[3] Christ told His disciples to remember Him. We also are told to remember Him. My heart is heavy when I think of how often I forget, and it becomes heavier when I realize that He always remembers. At any time I may call on Him, and He is there. He does not forget to listen and show me the way.

Dear ones, we do forget, He forgives our forgetting. May the knowledge not make us complacent but compel us to be faithful and obedient, never harboring the thought that we could "catch the first ship to Tarshish," but knowing that "obedience is the Christian's crown."

[1] Jonah 3:1-2.
[2] Jonah 4:2.
[3] Jonah 2:7.

❧   ❧   ❧

September 16

MICAH 1–3
MICAH 2

> Do not my words do good to him that walketh uprightly?[1]

ALTHOUGH MICAH was a denunciatory voice for the God of Israel, he also spoke words of comfort and hope. His insight into the future was unusual. Micah was gifted in literary skills, and used them to glorify God in an uncompromising way. The Word of God was essential to him, and he expounded its benefits in his life. He consistently urged the people to "hear" the words of the Lord. He used God's words as though they were swords intended to cut into the core of man's being. He slashed at idolatry and oppression and contrasted them with the blessings of obeying God's Word. Micah had experienced that God's "words do good to him that walketh uprightly."

It is a dangerous offense when men oppose God's Word. His Word has been proved in human experience. His Word has condemning power, and men fear its light, for it will show up what they really are: men who love "darkness rather than light, because their deeds . . . [are] evil."[2] To those who will renounce their sin, the words of God are pure and precious, full of hope, joy, and consolation.

God is speaking in this verse. The people had said to the prophet, "Prophesy not." They would rather hear nothing than hear of their sin and guilt. But Micah shows the purpose of God which will be fulfilled by the Word, and the consequences of opposing it.

How vital it is that we hear the Word, read it, memorize it, and meditate upon it, asking the Holy Spirit to enlighten our hearts. The Word itself will not do what the Spirit does by the Word. He brings the knowledge of Christ to us through the Word, and Christ is made known, not speculatively but experimentally.

The Word has a way of rebuking. It will not flatter. "Thy word is true from the beginning."[3] There is no mistake about the way it deals with man. The Word quickens the mind to greater things. The Author shows Himself in its pages and endears Himself to us. "I will never forget thy precepts: for with them thou hast quickened me."[4] The Word encourages us in times like these. Nations may fail and empires cease, but God's Word endures, and in its endurance we have encouragement. "It shall not return . . . void,"[5] but shall accomplish its purpose. The Word does good to those who will walk uprightly.

[1]Micah 2:7.
[2]John 3:19.
[3]Psalm 119:160.
[4]Psalm 119:93.
[5]Isaiah 55:11.

❧ ❧ ❧

> Therefore I will look unto the Lord; I will wait for the
> God of my salvation: my God will hear me. Rejoice
> not against me, O mine enemy: when I fall, I shall
> arise; when I sit in darkness, the Lord shall be a light
> unto me.[1]

HOW DISCERNING was the man who said, "We must get into
us more of that which is above us or we shall give way
to that which is around us." Micah, during the conflicts
and evil that were the order of his day, learned that he
could not look around him and receive any consolation or
help. His only recourse was to look up. Life for him had
been a dark and dismal picture. After hearing him tell of
the grave situation about him, we would expect this verse to
conclude, "Therefore, I might as well give up!" Not
Micah, for his hope was in God. He feared no enemy. If
he fell, he would rise again; and if darkness covered him,
God would provide the light of His presence.

"We go to God by prayers, not by steps," said Bishop
Lancelot Andrewes. "God commandeth thee to ask, and
teacheth thee how to ask, and promiseth that which thou
askest, and is angry if thou asketh not; and yet, askest thou
not?" Until we realize this principle personally, we will
continue to seek the answers about us rather than above
us.

The period during which Micah predicted bore a strong
resemblance to the early Christian Era. He did his work
with strong resolutions which are set forth in these verses
and are worthy of our consideration. First, Micah had a
resolution of faith. The promises of God encouraged him
as he said, "I will look unto the Lord." To look to the
Lord is an act of faith. The will and affection and intellect
must be in accord to take this action of faith. Next, Micah

resolved to be patient. "I will wait for the God of my salvation." Patience, in times like these! It is difficult, but "they that wait upon the Lord shall renew their strength."[2] Resolving to "wait" for God's answers will spare us untold delay. Third, Micah said with true hope and confidence in his heart, "God will hear me." My cry may be weak, or the request great, but I know He will hear me. This gives me the encouragement to keep looking up because I too know that "when I fall, I shall arise," and God will triumph over all.

Keep looking up!

[1]Micah 7:7-8.
[2]Isaiah 40:31.

❧ ❧ ❧

September 18

NAHUM 1–3
NAHUM 1

> The Lord is good, a strong hold in the day of trouble;
> and he knoweth them that trust in him.[1]

IF YOU WERE TRAVELING today in the land about which Nahum wrote, you would be unaware of the one-time existence of the city which was then flourishing, but which was later destroyed according to Nahum's prophecy. It is significant that what he foretold long ago has become an actual page in history! Among the ruins, tablets, and inscriptions, many things have been found which prove that God is confirming His Word in our times.

Nahum represents a God of wrath: "God is jealous, and the Lord revengeth; the Lord revengeth, and is furious; the Lord will take vengeance on his adversaries, and he reserveth wrath for his enemies."[2] Today we prefer to shy away from the picture of an angry God, but if we could comprehend His heart, we would see how He hates sin and disobedience. His anger is real, not just invented, and we must not forget that "the Lord revengeth." Nahum's teaching does not end here. He shows how God's wrath is interpreted by His divine love. His wrath actually stems from His love.

Contrast God's anger and His goodness. "For a small moment have I forsaken thee; but with great mercies will I gather thee. In a little wrath I hid my face from thee for a moment; but with everlasting kindness will I have mercy on thee, saith the Lord thy Redeemer."[3] His goodness does endure forever and ever, and He is able to keep those whom He loves, no matter how unworthy they have been, safe in His care.

"The Lord is good." In the day of trouble and anxiety He builds a fortress about those who are His. His protection is better than that of armies, navies, or air forces. "He shall give his angels charge over thee, to keep thee in all thy ways."[4] "God is our refuge and strength, a very present help in trouble."[5] Through Him we can be more than conquerors of ourselves. "O wretched man that I am! Who shall deliver me. . .? I thank God through Jesus Christ our Lord."[6] God has made provision for our daily work and our daily needs. Our sufficiency must be entirely from Him. He is a stronghold from all who would afflict, and He has promised sufficient grace and strength for each day.

"For this God is our God for ever and ever."[7]

[1] Nahum 1:7.
[2] Nahum 1:2.
[3] Isaiah 54:7-8.
[4] Psalm 91:11.
[5] Psalm 46:1.
[6] Romans 7:24-25.
[7] Psalm 48:14.

❧ ❧ ❧

HABAKKUK 1–3
HABAKKUK 3

> Yet I will rejoice in the Lord, I will joy in the God of
> my salvation.[1]

HABAKKUK proclaims his message from personal experience. He shows believers the conflict and the triumph of faith. His wrestling with his beliefs and God's answers makes up the book. "Behold, his soul which is lifted up is not upright in him: but the just shall live by his faith."[2] Habakkuk faced difficulties even as we do, and at times circumstances made him question and doubt, but his ultimate conclusions were affirmative.

The prophet said, "I will stand upon my watch, and set me upon the tower, and will watch to see what he will say unto me, and what I shall answer when I am reproved."[3] What an important lesson to learn. "I will" in all things see what He has to say to me, and if I have been displeasing Him, I will take note. Timothy wrote, "All scripture is given by inspiration of God, and is profitable for doctrine, for reproof, for correction, for instruction in righteousness: that the man of God may be perfect, throughly furnished unto all good works."[4] Habakkuk sought to find what God would say to him, whether it was doctrine or reproof. As we approach the Word we too must affirmatively declare, "I will" and let God speak.

Habakkuk resolved that circumstances would not get him down. He had enumerated a long list of failures and dreary affairs but, though these existed, he declared, "I will rejoice." This is living above, not below, the circumstances. A strong "I will" ensures a triumphant heart. The resolution may be tested in sickness, or even in death, in uncertainty or disaster, but determination to persist in faith strengthens the heart. Habakkuk and the Apostle Paul had much in common. Paul declared what they both determined: "I know both how to be abased, and I know how to abound: every where and in all things I am instructed both to be full and to be hungry, both to abound and to suffer need. I can do all things through Christ which strengtheneth me."[5]

There is unspeakable joy in the "I wills" that are for God's glory. Let us make these resolves: "I will praise Thee. I will bless Thee. I will sing of the mercies of the Lord. I will joy in the God of my salvation." These "I wills" are in accord with His will for us.

[1]Habakkuk 3:18.
[2]Habakkuk 2:4.
[3]Habakkuk 2:1.
[4]II Timothy 3:16-17.
[5]Philippians 4:12-13.

❧ ❧ ❧

September 20

ZEPHANIAH 1–3
ZEPHANIAH 3:8-20

> In that day it shall be said to Jerusalem, Fear thou not: and to Zion, Let not thine hands be slack. The Lord thy God in the midst of thee is mighty; he will save, he will rejoice over thee with joy; he will rest in his love, he will joy over thee with singing.[1]

ZEPHANIAH was another of the prophets who announced "the day of the Lord." He had a burden and was not hesitant in sharing it. In the closing verses of the last chapter we see the results of God's dealing with the people. His work is designed to result in a pure and holy life, a life of service. He tells us that we must not hang down our hands in despair of judgment for past sins but we must work: "Let not thine hands be slack."

The Scripture tells us, in the words of Jesus Christ, "Occupy till I come."[2] Opportunity follows anointing, and God's call implies divine service. Special opportunities for

Him come during the course of our lives, just as they came to David and others, right where they worked. We will not be slack if we catch the vision of God's great delight in saving sinners, and of His power to do so.

Zephaniah's inspired expressions about our God are surely filled with encouragement. God is mighty to save us today. Even as He led the children of Israel through the wilderness, as He performed miracles by day and by night, so His power is unlimited today. Through providence He can accomplish anything He desires. Going a step further, we realize He not only saves but He delights in doing so. In the Parable of the Prodigal Son we see God's feelings when one of His own comes back to Him. He will punish the transgressor, but His compassion lasts long after punishment is past. "Having loved his own which were in the world, he loved them unto the end."[3]

The day of the Lord may be closer at hand than we recognize. Let us take up His banner zealously, each Christian vowing to be a worker, a warrior, and a witness.

[1]Zephaniah 3:16-17.
[2]Luke 19:13.
[3]John 13:1.

❧ ❧ ❧

HAGGAI 1–2
HAGGAI 1

Consider your ways.[1]

THE FOUR MESSAGES of Haggai were addressed to the people after their long captivity, and he commanded them to consider their ways. They were reminded that God could not bless them while their Temple lay in ruins. The people argued that the time was not right for reconstruction, and in their appeals they proved their selfishness. When they stopped to consider and change their ways, God visited them and said, "From this day will I bless you."[2] Even their fruit and grain increased manifold because of His hand upon them for good.

The message to "consider your ways" should impress our hearts during our quiet times of devotion with the Lord. How much time is spent for ourselves in relation to the time we give to the Lord? Is the ratio sadly out of balance? "Consider your ways." Does complaining come from our lips more than praise? Is it possible that meditation gives way to murmuring? "Consider your ways." Do petty irritations have their way of rubbing into our lives, in turn inflicting scars on others? "Consider your ways." The writer of Proverbs said, "In all thy ways acknowledge him, and he shall direct thy paths."[3] And He will!

In considering our ways, as in the time of Haggai, true repentance will bring the ultimate blessing of God. He will pour out His abundance in the riches of His grace and peace. His power and presence will be overwhelming. We will grasp a new urgency to be strong and work, and strength for the task will be available. How long has it been since we set a goal for God? Possibly a long-neglected friend needs encouragement, or a neighbor needs to know the Lord. Have we in faith accepted the challenge as an opportunity for His glory? It is said that people who are going places have to be willing to take risks to get there. Going with God is not a risk, for He will "keep thee in all places whither thou goest."[4]

The president of a corporation said, "Part of the talent or genius of the goal-setter is the ability to distinguish between the possible and the impossible—plus the willingness to get very close to the latter." Our God said, "The things which are impossible with men are possible with God."[5] "Consider your ways."

[1]Haggai 1:7.
[2]Haggai 2:19.
[3]Proverbs 3:6.
[4]Genesis 28:15.
[5]Luke 18:27.

❧ ❧ ❧

September 22

ZECHARIAH 1–2
ZECHARIAH 2

Be silent, O all flesh, before the Lord.[1]

THE HISTORY OF GOD'S DEALINGS with man is full of compassion and glory, but the history of man's response to God is utter shame. However, there is still hope, for His compassion does not fail. Thus the message of Zechariah is one of inspiration for the hearts of discouraged people. In seeing God's goodness and graciousness, His children can only worship in adoration and humiliation. With a holy hush of reverence for His mercy, they are silent.

Reverence is born from respect and a sense of mystery. Reverence toward God comes from a heart that has seen and felt the impact of His presence, and is aware of His holiness and majesty. He manifests Himself to us in countless ways, in creation and re-creation. And He is far more concerned than we can comprehend, unless we experience

His divine tenderness. "Reverence is more than a duty; it is the innate courtesy of the soul. Its garments are humility; its language is silence; its crown devotion."[2] If we say we are reverent toward God the posture of our lives will testify to our reverence. If we revere God we most surely cannot be proud or arrogant. In ourselves there is nothing worthy of exaltation, but He is high and lifted up. Our pride vanishes in the reality of what we truly are before God. If we revere Him, truth will come from our lips, for we cannot willfully speak in error knowing that where He stands we stand. We cannot commit sins of the tongue on that holy ground. We cannot ignore Him, or relegate Him to a lesser place in our lives. A Christian should strive to live always in Christ's presence.

The sanctuary of the church, the house of worship, is another place where our reverence may be noted. Our minds cannot be divided in worship, or irreverence takes precedence. It is a solemn occasion when we step into the house of God. Let us study to be silent and reverent before the Lord our God.

> Mine be the reverent, listening love
> That waits all day on Thee,
> The service of a watchful heart
> Which no one else can see.[3]

[1] Zechariah 2:13.
[2] A. G. Walton.
[3] A. L. Waring.

❦ ❦ ❦

422

ZECHARIAH 3–5
ZECHARIAH 4

For who hath despised the day of small things?[1]

WE ARE PRONE to measure success in terms of size and
quantity. Zechariah's question helps us to rediscover the
value of small things in the believer's life.

"A cup of cold water" does not go without reward in the
kingdom of heaven, and should not be undervalued nor
ignored. The greatness of our Lord was not manifest as
much on the Mount of Transfiguration as in His deeds to
His fellowmen. A blind man received sight; a sick woman
touched the hem of His garment, and He paused to meet
her need. Today our God shows His love and concern in
everyday life.

A small service to a friend, a little self-denial that makes
possible something for another, a passing word of sympathy
or understanding: these are the things which God ap-
proves. He does not ask that we seek great and mighty
attainments. He wants us faithful where we are. Too many
people long for that one big opportunity, that one break
that may come. Meanwhile they pass over the seemingly
insignificant ministries which may be most significant to
God.

I shall not forget a Sunday school teacher who gave her
students a bookmark. On one side was a picture of bricks,
sand, and a pair of hands, with a few drops of water in the
corner. On the other side there were rivers, mountains, and
a magnificent cathedral. The inscription was meaningful
in the light of today's verse. It read, "A big rushing river
is but the teamwork of numberless little drops of water. A
gigantic mountain is only the bulk of innumerable grains
of sand and particles of dust piled up. The worthiness of
the church is not expressed in terms of brick and mortar—

great cathedrals with massive domes—but in the gentle life and faithful service of its individual members."

"Who hath despised the day of small things?" May we daily be faithful in what we are given, ordinary or extraordinary, great or small, so that when we meet our Lord each of us can say, "I have completed the work You gave me to do."

¹Zechariah 4:10.

       ❧   ❧   ❧

September 24

ZECHARIAH 6–8
ZECHARIAH 6

> These are the things that ye shall do; Speak ye every man the truth to his neighbor; execute the judgment of truth and peace in your gates. . . . therefore love the truth and peace.¹

ZECHARIAH encouraged in the people the same qualities which the other prophets had been exhorted by God to proclaim: true judgment, mercy, and compassion.² They must learn to contend with anything that was not truth and to love mercy. Zechariah has been called "a great unveiler." Through his message people could see previously concealed truths. We are often prone, during adversity, to see only what affects us, or to listen only to what will be relevant to our personal needs. Zechariah's prophecy took the people up and beyond themselves, by means of his visions, to see out into the purposes of God.

In thinking about truth and peace we must elevate ourselves from what our eyes can see and our ears hear, and look into the total picture of God.

Truth—"A truthful character is of value beyond computation. Its transparency is beautiful. No darkening stains discolor the medium through which the soul goes forth in words, in looks, in actions. It is the only medium through which we can know God."[3] He is "the way, the truth, and the life,"[4] and to know Him we must "worship him in spirit and in truth."[5] Of the Word it is stated, "And ye shall know the truth, and the truth shall make you free."[6] Truth before God is a prerequisite to a genuine and sincere Christian life. Let us order our lives before God, and let Him mold and shape us according to His plans. We cannot hide from His searching. Said a Puritan of yesterday, "Before God I am what I pretend to be. About me there is no make-believe." Oh, that all Christians' lives were so transparent and real; that such truthfulness were evidenced in our every-day experience!

Peace—Peace is the opposite of strife. Our peace with God is first experienced as we become reconciled to Him. Then the believer can be filled with "the peace of God, which passeth understanding [which] shall keep your hearts and minds through Christ Jesus."[7]

"Truth is one of the brightest jewels in the crown of Deity, and peace is the very element of enjoyment." The two go together to characterize the gospel. "Therefore love the truth and peace."

[1]Zechariah 8:16, 19.
[2]Zechariah 7:9.
[3]E. Nichols.
[4]John 14:6.
[5]John 4:24.
[6]John 8:32.
[7]Philippians 4:7.

❧ ❧ ❧

ZECHARIAH 9–11
ZECHARIAH 10

> Ask ye of the Lord rain in the time of the latter rain;
> so the Lord shall make bright clouds, and give them
> showers of rain, to every one grass in the field.[1]

THERE IS BEAUTY in the promises of God. This promise is
special as we picture the "bright clouds" or lightning, the
harbinger of rain. God declares Himself in these before
He sends the shower.

"Ask ye of the Lord rain." Zechariah had promised that
blessings would rain on the people who had been spiritually parched—blessings both spiritual and temporal. The
blessings were prepared, but the people must ask for them.
Theirs was the promise that God had also extended to the
children of Israel: "And it shall come to pass, if ye shall
hearken diligently unto my commandments which I command you this day, to love the Lord your God, and to serve
him with all your heart and with all your soul, that I will
give you the rain . . . that thou mayest gather in thy corn,
and thy wine, and thine oil. And I will send grass in thy
fields for thy cattle, that thou mayest eat and be full."[2] But
they must "ask" to receive.

"The latter rain" alone is mentioned, but it is a continuation of what God had started by the first rain. Both are
used as symbols of the spiritual gifts of God. Osorius wrote,
"God exhorts all to frequently ask for the dew of the divine grace, that what had sprung up in the heart from the
seed of the Word of God might attain to full ripeness."

"So the Lord shall make bright clouds, and give them
showers of rain." While we ask He answers. At times He
does not immediately answer our prayers, but He makes the
bright clouds to give us encouragement while we wait. No
matter how dark the clouds may have been, God's power
enlightens them with the promise of showers of blessing.

"To every one grass in the field." Oh, the goodness of God to be interested in our individual needs. Wrote the Psalmist, "He causeth the grass to grow for the cattle, and herb for the service of man."[3] Each with his particular need has the personalized promise of provision.

"He is faithful that promised."[4]

[1]Zechariah 10:1.
[2]Deuteronomy 11:13-15.
[3]Psalm 104:14.
[4]Hebrews 10:23.

❧ ❧ ❧

September 26

ZECHARIAH 12–14
ZECHARIAH 14

> And one shall say unto him, What are these wounds in thine hands? Then he shall answer, Those with which I was wounded in the house of my friends.[1]

LET US TODAY grasp a truth which needs to be apprehended by every Christian. If we are not obedient and faithful to our Lord Jesus Christ we are inflicting wounds upon Him. "Do they hurt?" asked a little child when told how the Lord was wounded for us, and how deeply He feels about our disobediences. And the teacher answered, "Yes, they hurt!"

Judas and Peter are not the only ones who have denied Christ Jesus. Daily we are guilty if we call Him "Lord," but fail to do what He has commanded of us. Maybe I pass up an opportunity for witness as I rationalize, "I don't want to offend my neighbor. Tomorrow I'll speak, if the time is right." I may fail to give that cup of cold water—a simple deed but one of eternal import. Christ's deepest hurts must come from those who call themselves Christians. "Do they hurt?" "Yes, they hurt." They hurt beyond our comprehension.

The prophecy of Zechariah points to the Cross of Christ, and beyond, when He will come again. We have seen Zechariah's writings on the Messiah come to pass. They will be further fulfilled when our Lord returns in glory. When He came the first time, He was wounded and crucified among His own people. He was denied by those whom He had helped. What will be the situation when He comes again? Will he find us faithful?

The Son of God was wounded for us, in taking our sins, on the Cross, and bearing the scars in His hands, His feet, and His side. Have we not caused Him grief enough without continuing to inflict anguish and hurt by our disobedience?

> But drops of grief can ne'er repay
> The debt of love I owe;
> Here, Lord, I give myself to Thee,
> 'Tis all that I can do.[2]

[1]Zechariah 13:6.
[2]Isaac Watts.

❧ ❧ ❧

MALACHI 1–2
MALACHI 1

> The priest's lips should keep knowledge, and they
> should seek the law at his mouth: for he is the mes-
> senger of the Lord of hosts.[1]

JUST BEFORE the prophetic silence between the Old and
New Testaments fell on the world, God sent Malachi, "my
messenger," as a voice to Israel. We know nothing of the
man behind this voice other than that he was faithful with
his message. Malachi is the last of the minor prophets. As
did the other prophets, he denounced wrong and announced
mercy. He was also emphatic in his reproof of priests who
did not give to God what He deserved. "And if ye offer
the blind for sacrifice, is it not evil? And if ye offer the
lame and sick, is it not evil? Offer it now unto thy governor;
will he be pleased with thee, or accept thy person?"[2]

Malachi was saying that the people should take inventory
of the gifts they were laying on the Lord's altar. To make
the priests think seriously he asked, "Would you treat the
governor as you treat God?" A businessman said this indictment caused him to wonder what would happen if he
treated his taxes as he treated his tithes. When it comes to
God we often become negligent. How often we pacify our
consciences by a dollar or two in a Sunday offering. But
what does it really cost us? Nothing? We withhold from
ourselves the blessing of sacrificial giving, in both service
and substance.

Malachi's wrath could well make us sit up and take
notice. He said he would rather the doors of the Temple
were shut than to have people continue to bring in their
worthless sacrifices. Why kindle fire on God's altar for
nought? How many useless fires do we kindle in the name
of Christ and the church? How can we hold back when all
we have is already His?

The privilege of being a priest is great, but it brings responsibility. There must be a discerning mind and continuing communication with the Lord. There must be constant study of the Word of God impressing each page of inspiration on the heart and working with the compelling authority of "Thus saith the Lord."

A Christian is a member of a chosen generation and a royal priesthood. It is impossible to overestimate the privilege. Let us never be guilty of a blind sacrifice or a lame offering for expediency's sake. Let us daily fulfill our holy task with divine precision, living in the power of the Spirit of Him who made possible our priestly nearness to God.

[1]Malachi 2:7.
[2]Malachi 1:8.

❧ ❧ ❧

MALACHI 3–4
MALACHI 3–4

For I am the Lord, I change not.[1]

THE TWENTIETH CENTURY is known as the century of change. Science, medicine, cultures, and nations have undergone significant changes, and more are in store for us, if the Lord tarries as the dawn of the twenty-first century approaches. However, throughout all time the words of Malachi are certain to remain. "For I am the Lord, I change not."

When we become disheartened by the storms on the horizon, it is well to recognize that God is in charge. He is in command of this universe. He does not change in His holiness or judgment. His love and His mercy, His grace and His sufficiency remain the same. He is the same God whose creation of the heavens and the earth we read about in Genesis. And now in the last book of the Old Testament, He reminds us that He changes not.

The Psalmist reminds us of another great certainty. In a time when textbooks are rewritten and soon become obsolete, when some theories are disproved and others approved, we have God's Word which changes not. "For ever, O Lord, thy word is settled in heaven."[2] Daily the Scriptures are being confirmed to us in the field of archaeology, and even more dramatically in men's lives. "The grass withereth, the flower fadeth: but the word of our God shall stand for ever."[3]

We see man in Malachi as we saw man in Genesis—sinful and disobedient. In between we have read the history of God's patience and perseverance, along with His judgment. The record proves that until the heart of man is changed, man's ways cannot be changed. From Adam on, every man has needed forgiveness from sin and God's life and power to quicken and change his life and ways.

God's purpose for the world always will be under His control. His plan will culminate in the time when we will reign with Him forever. May this knowledge of our unchangeable God and His immutable ways draw us closer to Him. An old hymn writer expressed it like this:

> Change and decay in all around I see:
> O Thou who changest not, abide with me.[4]

[1]Malachi 3:6.
[2]Psalm 119:89.
[3]Isaiah 40:8.
[4]Henry F. Lyte.

❧   ❧   ❧

THE OLD TESTAMENT

A YOUNG LIBRARIAN was handed a copy of the Bible. She knew little about the Book, and was puzzled as to how it should be catalogued. On the index-reference card was a place for author's name and date. The young lady learned that there was no single answer. In her search for more knowledge on the unusual volume, she found that its contents were inspired by God but collected little by little over thousands of years. She learned that many men and women had given their lives for the cause of the Book, and that even nowadays there are those who will sacrifice self, circumstance, and convenience to uphold and extend its teachings and truths.

The librarian's desire for a way to display the Bible became more intense as she read the Book. As she read the story of creation in Genesis, she made a new beginning with Christ. The stories of the Exodus and the wanderings of the Israelites impressed her heart with the value of obedience. She studied precepts and teachings through the Books of the Law, then turned toward the Books of History. The promises of Joshua rejoiced her heart as she determined, "The Lord our God will we serve, and his voice will we obey."[1] She read and studied the Psalms, the "hymnbook" of the Bible, which lifted her heart in praise to the Lord. She discovered the good advice in the wise sayings of Proverbs.

The Major Prophets, Isaiah, Jeremiah, Lamentations, Ezekiel, and Daniel, made her aware of the preaching and teaching of the prophets, and their message of repentance and deliverance. The twelve Minor Prophets, beginning with Hosea, made her increasingly aware that the Bible is not a single book at all. There are many books, short and long, thirty-nine in all, in the Old Testament. But each book has a story, a continuing story of God and His dealing with people, and of people in their relationship with God.

Another librarian explained that there is no possible way to show the treasures of the Bible except in an individual life. Kings have bound the Book in rich leather and set it with stones. Artists are constantly attempting to illustrate it. Scribes dip pens in gold to copy its words. Yet none of these accouterments can show the riches within, which can be manifested only as they enter individual lives and are then daily passed on to others who have yet to discover the wonderful words of life. Make the treasure of both Testaments your own.

[1]Joshua 24:24.

❧ ❧ ❧

September 30

THE NEW TESTAMENT

Too few recognize the inseparability of the Old and New Testaments. Some sadly disregard the Old as they glory in the New. They fail to recognize that the truths of the New Testament grow out of the Old Testament and, for true understanding, each needs the other.

If the Old Testament is discredited, the foundations of the New are destroyed; yet the New cannot stand alone. It draws examples and principles from the stories that make up the thirty-nine books of the Old Testament, and fulfills some of its inspired prophecy. If we can envision the Garden of Eden and the stable at Bethlehem close together in God's mind, it will help us to comprehend both Testaments. Together they unfold the plan of God for our redemption. One deals with the preparatory stages, and the other with "the fullness of time."

The Old Testament starts with "In the beginning God. . . ."[1] In the New Testament, John takes the phrase "in the beginning" and writes, "In the beginning was the Word,

433

and the Word was with God, and the Word was God. The same was in the beginning with God. All things were made by him; and without him was not any thing made that was made."[2] In Hebrews creation was reaffirmed when the writer penned, "And, Thou, Lord, in the beginning didst lay the foundation of the earth; and the heavens are the works of thine hands."[3]

Paul pled with men to renounce vain things and "turn from these vanities unto the living God, which made heaven, and earth, and the sea, and all things that are therein."[4]

Hebrews continues to give recognition to men of faith who lived in Old Testament days: Enoch, Noah, Abraham, Moses, and many more whom we have met and followed through the Old Testament.

The story from Eden to Bethlehem is complete. Now we joyfully anticipate fulfillment of the prophecy of Christ's second coming given in the Old Testament, which was confirmed again in the New Testament, when He said, "Surely I come quickly."[5]

May the observations of one and the confirmations of the other erase the division between the Old and the New and merge the two into a vision of His glory, evidenced in both. "Whatsoever things were written aforetime were written for our learning."[6] "The holy scriptures . . . are able to make thee wise unto salvation."[7]

[1]Genesis 1:1.
[2]John 1:1-3.
[3]Hebrews 1:10.
[4]Acts 14:15.
[5]Revelation 22:20.
[6]Romans 15:4.
[7]II Timothy 3:15.

    ❧   ❧   ❧

October

MATTHEW 1–3
MATTHEW 1

> Now the birth of Jesus Christ was on this wise: When
> as his mother Mary was espoused of Joseph, before they
> came together, she was found with child of the Holy
> Ghost. And she shall bring forth a son, and thou shalt
> call his name JESUS: for he shall save his people from
> their sins. Now all this was done, that it might be ful-
> filled which was spoken of the Lord by the prophet, say-
> ing, Behold, a virgin shall be with child, and shall bring
> forth a son, and they shall call his name Emmanuel, . . .
> God with us.[1]

HERE IS THE GLORIOUS MIRACLE of God identifying Himself
with man! Jesus Christ was unusual not only in life but
also in birth. He was born without an earthly father. This
is expressed in our Apostles' Creed, which dates back to the
third century: "I believe in God, the Father Almighty,
Maker of heaven and earth, and in Jesus Christ, His only
Son, our Lord, who was conceived by the Holy Ghost, born
of the Virgin Mary."[2]

Today's scripture tells us something of Joseph. This passage refers to his "espoused wife." It is well to remember
that Oriental culture placed tremendous significance on
engagements. Each betrothal was sacred. Joseph must have
been perplexed and disappointed. His future wife was
expecting a baby. He was hurt. How prone he might have
been in his bitterness to "make a public example" of Mary.
Not Joseph. He was "a just man . . . he thought on these

things."[3] Matthew Henry writes, "It is the thoughtful, not the unthinking, that God will guide." While Joseph was pondering, the angel appeared to him saying, "Fear not." Joseph's mind was put at ease. God had given him his answer.

What a lesson for us in accepting the guidance of God. How wonderful to see the perfect plan of God unfold.

The birth of Jesus Christ is a historical fact and a vivid reminder that in each of us the Lord must be born through the work of the Holy Spirit. As Mary brought forth the Child and called His name "Emmanuel," may we experience the reality of its meaning in our individual lives—"God with us."

[1] Matthew 1:18, 21-23.
[2] Apostles' Creed.
[3] Matthew 1:19-20.

❧ ❧ ❧

October 2

MATTHEW 4–5
MATTHEW 5

> Then was Jesus led up of the spirit into the wilderness to be tempted of the devil. And when he had fasted forty days and forty nights, he was afterward an hungered. And when the tempter came to him, he said, If thou be the Son of God, command that these stones be made bread. But he answered and said, It is written, Man shall not live by bread alone, but by every word that proceedeth out of the mouth of God. . . . Then saith Jesus unto him, Get thee hence, Satan: for it is written, Thou shalt worship the Lord thy God, and him only shalt thou serve. Then the devil leaveth him, and, behold, angels came and ministered unto him.[1]

A YOUNG CHRISTIAN, realizing that the Lord was tempted in all points even as we are, expressed the fact that Christ's temptation left him with a mixed feeling of relief and un-

436

easiness. Relief, yes, because he knew Christ was tempted, so he did not stand alone in temptation; but uneasy because of His being tempted as we are, yet without sin. The young man listed some of our twentieth century temptations: selfishness, tension, immorality, power, materialism, and others. Surely Christ was not tempted in these areas of living? Yet the Bible is clear in stating He knows temptation and is familiar with our feeling of weakness.

The temptation of Christ makes us see anew the real enemy the Christian faces in Satan. He dared to assault even the Lord Himself. The same defense that our Lord used is readily available to us. It is the Bible. When Christ said, "It is written," Satan was forced to retreat. The knowledge that our Lord used this method should certainly make us more determined readers of the Word. Knowledge does not come from intuition; it takes hard, regular, attentive reading and meditation.

There is consolation in Christ's temptation. We have a sympathizing Saviour. "In that he himself hath suffered being tempted, he is able to succour them that are tempted."[2]

We are tempted; so was He! His ear is open to hear and His heart to understand. Times of temptation offer sweet experiences with the sympathizing Saviour.

Christians are photographs of Christ. In the darkroom of trial and temptation, God develops his loveliest reproductions.

[1]Matthew 4:1-11.
[2]Hebrews 2:18.

❧ ❧ ❧

MATTHEW 6
MATTHEW 6:1-13

> After this manner therefore pray ye: Our Father which
> art in heaven, Hallowed be thy name. Thy kingdom
> come. Thy will be done in earth, as it is in heaven.
> Give us this day our daily bread. And forgive us our
> debts, as we forgive our debtors. And lead us not into
> temptation, but deliver us from evil: for thine is the
> kingdom, and the power, and the glory, for ever.
> Amen.[1]

AFTER THIS MANNER . . ." But notice, it does not say, "In
these words." Prayer is the key to the morning and the
bolt to the night. "Evening, and morning, and at noon,
will I pray, and cry aloud: and he shall hear my voice."[2]
The pattern of prayer given to the disciples is simple, direct, and earnest. The prayer is reverent and unselfish.
Yet, how guilty we are of saying rather than praying, of
speaking rather than acting upon the sacred words. So our
prayers remain unanswered.

A man expressed concern to a Quaker teacher that his
long-continued prayers were not answered. During their
conversation the teacher made a poignant suggestion. Emphasizing the truth that "faith without works is dead,"[3]
she exhorted, "When you pray, move your feet!"

We know prayer as confession, gratitude, meditation, pe-
tition, communion in God's presence. But it is more. Unless it results in action, we have never experienced its power.

We pray, "Forgive us our sins, as we forgive those who
have sinned against us." We hope God will not be too hard
on us as we recall those things that have displeased Him, but
sin does not just dissolve. Something must be done about
it. Sin must be blotted out and forgiven through our confession before our prayers can again ascend unhindered.

We pray, "Deliver us from evil" but continue doing things which we know hurt God and cause Him grief.

We pray, "Thy kingdom come" but do so little toward the furtherance of kingdom business.

There is little doubt that the reason we fail to see God's power is that it works only through those who pray, believing. It is said that to be little with God is to be little for God.

Today, as we spend time in His presence, may the reality of Himself and His pattern for prayer stimulate our devotion so that it will result in service.

"As you pray, move your feet!"

[1]Matthew 6:9-13.
[2]Psalm 55:17.
[3]James 2:26.

❧ ❧ ❧

October 4

MATTHEW 7–8
MATTHEW 7

> Therefore whosoever heareth these sayings of mine, and doeth them, I will liken him unto a wise man, which built his house upon a rock: and the rain descended, and the floods came, and the winds blew, and beat upon that house; and it fell not: for it was founded upon a rock. And every one that heareth these sayings of mine, and doeth them not, shall be likened unto a foolish man, which built his house upon the sand: and the rain descended, and the floods came, and the winds blew, and beat upon that house; and it fell: and great was the fall of it.[1]

IN TEACHING THIS LESSON, as always, Christ spoke with authority and His listeners were astonished at His doctrine. People with authority demand our attention. One with authority is likening men to houses in the above verses. The people listening to Christ were amazed at His teachings. He stressed the temporary nature of earthly life. To get the most out of it we must build securely and for eternity.

Christ asked the group who were surrounding Him what kind of lives they were building. A good house must have a good foundation. During the intense heat of the Syrian summer, the soil bakes hard, and the most carelessly built shacks will stand. However, when the winter rains fall, only those places built to solidly grip the rock will stand. Inhabitants of that area understood from experience the meaning of the lesson.

Only you as an individual can know how you are building your life. Possibly no one, save the Lord, really knows of the sand of selfishness and worldliness which lies under the superstructure of your life. However, there may be a secret longing for that stability which comes from the Rock Christ Jesus. "Other foundation can no man lay than that is laid, which is Jesus Christ."[2] This is the starting point. Here is the security man cries out for when the rains of fear and storms of difficulty and winds of the unknown "beat upon that house."

Once the foundation is laid, a good house needs good materials. Christ gave this lesson to impress the importance of building in Him. May we accept its message and daily seek to erect structures to His glory and praise.

[1]Matthew 7:24-27.
[2]I Corinthians 3:11.

❧   ❧   ❧

MATTHEW 9–10
MATTHEW 9:35-38; 10:1-6

> And Jesus went about all the cities and villages, teaching in their synagogues, and preaching the gospel of the kingdom, and healing every sickness and every disease among the people. But when he saw the multitudes, he was moved with compassion on them, because they fainted, and were scattered abroad, as sheep having no shepherd. Then saith he unto his disciples, The harvest truly is plenteous, but the labourers are few; pray ye therefore the Lord of the harvest, that he will send forth labourers into his harvest.[1]

THESE CHAPTERS introduce a new phase of Christ's ministry. As He walked among the villagers and by the sea, His heart was moved with compassion. So much need, and so few to carry the message. He had chosen, prepared, and instructed twelve disciples. Now that they had studied His life they would represent Him. In Matthew 10, the disciples are referred to as apostles, "ones sent forth." We too have a responsibility, as His disciples, to heed His words. "Learn of me."[2] "As my Father hath sent me, even so send I you."[3]

"Pray for laborers and you will become a laborer. Begin as a disciple and you will become an apostle."[4] Little did Christ's disciples dream that their names would be engraved on the foundations of the New Jerusalem. "And the wall of the city had twelve foundations, and in them the names of the twelve apostles of the Lamb."[5]

Let Christ's compassion compel you to act as one sent from God. Strive to be a foundation for future generations, to His glory.

> How little we know of compassion today,
> Of love that shows others the Christian way,
> Of the Saviour's heart as He knelt to pray
> For a flock that had scattered and gone astray.

441

He preached and He healed, He gave and He went.
We must love as He loved; 'tis for this we are sent.

[1]Matthew 9:35-38.
[2]Matthew 11:29.
[3]John 20:21.
[4] F. B. Meyer.
[5]Revelation 21:14.

🍀 🍀 🍀

MATTHEW 11–12
MATTHEW 11

> Come unto me, all ye that labour and are heavy laden,
> and I will give you rest. Take my yoke upon you, and
> learn of me; for I am meek and lowly in heart: and ye
> shall find rest unto your souls. For my yoke is easy, and
> my burden is light.[1]

How FAMILIAR are these words to the Christian. Scores of
times I have read them, heard them expounded and illustrated, but it took a personal experience to make them live
to me.

It happened on the island of Jamaica. I never learned
the woman's name, but the circumstances and history of her
eighty years were clear. She spoke in a patois in which
words were omitted and final consonants clipped. The in-
tonation was totally different from ours, but she could be
understood. Her home was a one-room shack in such di-
lapidated condition that a breeze endangered its struggle
to stand. Food was scarce other than breadfruit, and that
came by begging. Life had been filled with hardship, struggle for survival, and much disease.

One day the missionaries came to her village and took
time for some "shack to shack" visitation. In the words of
today's verse, she had labored, she was heavy laden, she
knew little of rest, and nothing of God. In the days that
followed the missionaries' visit, this woman learned more

of God from a fellow native, and then accepted the invitation "Come unto me." Oh, the joy she found in the rest that Christ gives! Though totally ignorant, she learned of Him through the teachers and workers. She found His yoke no burden and her formerly heavy heart became much lighter.

The immediate change in the life of this poverty-stricken woman illustrated the complete simplicity of Christ's offer in His invitation "Come unto me." There are no prerequisites, no works, nothing to be accomplished. That day, in her helpless condition, her eligibility lay in her willingness to come.

God is no respecter of persons. To the rich and the poor, to the unlearned or the educated, He says, "Come unto me." "And him that cometh to me I will in no wise cast out."[2]

[1]Matthew 11:28-30.
[2]John 6:37.

❧   ❧   ❧

443

Matthew 13–14
Matthew 13

> Again, the kingdom of heaven is like unto treasure hid
> in a field; the which when a man hath found, he hideth,
> and for joy thereof goeth and selleth all that he hath,
> and buyeth that field. Again, the kingdom of heaven is
> like unto a merchant man, seeking goodly pearls: who,
> when he had found one pearl of great price, went and
> sold all that he had, and bought it.[1]

HERE WE HAVE our glorious gospel likened to a hidden
treasure. People who live in lands which fear invasion are
often forced to take their riches and conceal them. From
Japan comes a story of a family that did just that.

For generations their ancestors had been pearl divers.
There was always a thrill in opening the oyster and examining its contents. To an untrained eye, many of the pearls
they found would appear to be "of great price." But experts would point out the imperfections: a speck here, a
dent there, too oblong; and so it was as day after day the
pearls were brought to the surface and examined. Then
one day the eldest son of the family had found an unusually
rich oyster bed. He stayed down too long and soon afterward died. But he had brought up with him an oyster
containing the most perfect pearl the family had ever seen.
At last they had obtained their pearl of great price, but it
had cost them a son. The family came to the United States
and then World War II broke out. During their intern-
ment the pearl was hidden. When they were released, they
knew the time had come to sell the treasure. It was ap-
praised, but on the day the buyer came to pick up the pearl,
the father of the house explained that they had made a new
decision. The pearl was beyond price, no amount of money
could console them for the costly death of their son!

The gospel too is a treasure, much of which was hidden

in the Old Testament, and then revealed when God gave His Son. The Son He sacrificed was beyond price, so salvation cannot be purchased. Nothing will buy it and no one can earn it. It is only granted as a free gift.

This short, stirring parable likens Christ to the precious pearl, and we through faith may possess Him. It is time to reflect on the treasure that becomes ours when we receive the gift of God, the treasure of life and truth, and know for a certainty it is beyond price. Let us not be guilty of burying the treasure. May we recognize that its value becomes greater as it is shared with another.

[1]Matthew 13:44-46.

✤ ✤ ✤

October 8

MATTHEW 15–16
MATTHEW 16

> Then said Jesus unto his disciples, If any man will come after me, let him deny himself, and take up his cross, and follow me. For whosoever will save his life shall lose it: and whosoever will lose his life for my sake shall find it. For what is a man profited, if he shall gain the whole world, and lose his own soul? or what shall a man give in exchange for his soul?[1]

A GROUP of college young people were discussing the cost of following Jesus Christ. As they read His demands, their expressions were solemn and thoughtful. "Christ really puts things on the line," said a young prelaw student, eager to serve the Lord but pondering what the cost would be. "Those are hard words to apply," said another who had volunteered for foreign mission service several months before, and who was aware that the field he had chosen might be one where sacrifice was required. Another told of reading the statement of a young martyr who had said, "He is no fool who gives what he cannot keep to gain what he cannot lose."[2]

If it had been possible for the disciples of Christ to be present that day, they would have added to the discussion. When the disciples first met the Lord they anticipated that He would set up an earthly kingdom, never realizing that to fulfill His purpose He must die. Possibly some even hoped for acclaim because of their association with Him, for after all, He was the great Teacher, the Good Shepherd, and had many times confounded the wise of His day. For them, and for us, the Lord corrected any misapprehensions. He spoke of cross-bearing, loss of life, self-denial. He stressed the value of man's soul, for which there can be no exchange, for the world is temporal, but the soul eternal.

Allegiance to Christ is costly. As the group talked it over, the one who was the missionary volunteer posed a new question: "What is the cost of not following Christ?" The group recognized the loss to Christendom of those they would never reach if they did not follow Christ. They thought of the sorrow to Christ, who gave His all, in seeing one of His own turn his back. They considered the personal loss of the rich young ruler who felt he could not sell all to follow the Master.

But the Lord does not leave us with only the thought of the cross to bear for Him. He reminds us, "The Son of man shall come in . . . glory."[3] Those who are faithful will exchange the cross for a crown.

[1]Matthew 16:24-26.
[2]Jim Elliot.
[3]Matthew 16:27.

❧   ❧   ❧

446

Matthew 17–19
Matthew 19

> Then answered Peter and said unto him, Behold, we
> have forsaken all, and followed thee; what shall we have
> therefore? And Jesus said unto them, Verily I say un-
> to you, that ye which have followed me, in the regenera-
> tion when the Son of man shall sit in the throne of his
> glory, ye shall also sit upon twelve thrones, judging the
> twelve tribes of Israel. And every one that hath forsaken
> houses, or brethren, or sisters, or father, or mother, or
> wife, or children, or lands, for my name's sake, shall
> receive an hundredfold, and shall inherit everlasting
> life.[1]

IN OUR ENGLISH BIBLE the word *regeneration* appears only
twice. To many it is unfamiliar, yet it may become a key
to unlock the door to richer and fuller service for God on
earth.

The best-known reference is found in Titus: "Not by
works of righteousness which we have done, but according
to his mercy he saved us, by the washing of regeneration,
and renewing of the Holy Ghost."[2] This reference illustrates what takes place when a person initially comes to
know Christ. There is a rebirth, a making over, a complete
change of nature.

The word as used in today's reading refers to the time
when Christ will come again and establish or "generate" a
new heaven and a new earth. This is the time when He
will reward His faithful followers "an hundredfold" for
sacrifice in this life.

A young woman who experienced the first regeneration in
a changed life was barred from her home. Her family and
friends forsook her and her material inheritance was cut
off. Although young in the faith, she knew she must follow
Christ. She settled down in a small midwestern town, un-

known and much alone. In time she began to meet Christians. Friendships and fellowship grew, and she started to witness. Her witnessing bore fruit. After many months she felt called to Bible school. The community gave her a farewell party. In attendance were exactly one hundred people, her friends, closer than those she had known before.

Her eyes were filled with happy tears as she boarded the train for school. She had been washed by regeneration, and had experienced part of the hundredfold reward in seeing many friends accept Christ as their Saviour. We may have a like experience.

[1]Matthew 19:27-29.
[2]Titus 3:5.

❧ ❧ ❧

October 10

MATTHEW 20–21
MATTHEW 21

> Now in the morning as he returned into the city, he hungered. And when he saw a fig tree in the way, he came to it, and found nothing thereon, but leaves only, and said unto it, Let no fruit grow on thee henceforward for ever. And presently the fig tree withered away. And when the disciples saw it, they marvelled, saying, How soon is the fig tree withered away! Jesus answered and said unto them, Verily I say unto you, If ye have faith, and doubt not, ye shall not only do this which is done to the fig tree, but also if ye shall say unto this mountain, Be thou removed, and be thou cast into the sea; it shall be done. And all things, whatsoever ye shall ask in prayer, believing, ye shall receive.[1]

IT WAS IN THE MORNING, and Jesus was on His way to Jerusalem with the disciples. He was looking for fruit. The barren fig tree provided an illustration for the disciples. Christ has been criticized for causing the tree to wither away. However, I remember in high school botany a teach-

448

er more than once uprooted plants and trees to provide the students with a learning situation.

Might this not be a picture of our Christian lives, full of leaves, but barren of fruit? Possibly we may have a lovely outward appearance, but no love, no joy, no inward peace, no message of Christ to give to friends?

Biblical scholars tell us that the incident also pictures the Jewish church of the time when the Lord was on earth. It had everything for an exterior show, with daily services, lavish feasts, and elaborate rituals. But the Jewish church lacked fruit. In the future, it too would be deprived of its outward ornaments, and its members would be scattered as Jerusalem would be destroyed.

What of the church today? Is it not in danger of becoming a withered tree? Many of its members have brilliant professions but lack holiness. Church-going has become a ritual but not a necessity to self-sufficient man. How clearly the Lord spoke on another occasion when He said, "By their fruits ye shall know them."[2]

Dear reader, do not be satisfied with leaves. Ask God for fruit.

[1]Matthew 21:18-22.
[2]Matthew 7:20.

❦ ❦ ❦

MATTHEW 22–23
MATTHEW 22

> But when the Pharisees had heard that he had put the
> Sadducees to silence, they were gathered together. Then
> one of them, which was a lawyer, asked him a question,
> tempting him, and saying, Master, which is the great
> commandment in the law? Jesus said unto them, Thou
> shalt love the Lord thy God with all thy heart, and with
> all thy soul, and with all thy mind. This is the first and
> great commandment. And the second is like unto it,
> Thou shalt love thy neighbour as thyself. On these two
> commandments hang all the law and the prophets.[1]

ENVISION A GROUP of Pharisees gathered around Jesus. They
were undoubtedly a learned group: attorneys, teachers, and
some grammarians. The lawyers in particular were scholars
in the law of Moses and had anticipated questioning the
Master. On the surface their question seemed superficial.
Were not all the aspects of the law equal in importance?
One writer suggests that it was not Christ's knowledge but
His judgment they were weighing that day.

His answer summarized the law. It has been called the
gospel in a nutshell. His brief answer spoke volumes. Love:
what a magnificent answer! After all, love fulfills the law,
and obedience stems from love.

"Thou shalt have no other gods before me,"[2] states the
first commandment. If we love God, He will be supreme.
To love Him with heart, soul, and mind brings each area
into control. From our hearts comes affection, from our
minds, comprehension, and from our souls, volition.

"And thy neighbour as thyself." This has been classed as
a prescription. Putting it to use—esteeming others, honoring our fellowmen—is true Christianity. Cain asked, "Am I
my brother's keeper?"[3] There are those who prefer to think
that the best philosophy is for each to do as he pleases.

Selfishness and negligence are covered by the rationalization "Live and let live."

Christ foresaw this kind of attitude; thus He clearly exhorted, "Love thy neighbour as thyself." This eliminates doubt. I am my brother's keeper. A wise man of Old Testament days admonishes us today to "hear the conclusion of the whole matter: Fear God, and keep his commandments: for this is the whole duty of man."[4]

[1]Matthew 22:34-40.
[2]Exodus 20:3.
[3]Genesis 4:9.
[4]Ecclesiastes 12:13.

❧ ❧ ❧

October 12

MATTHEW 24–25
MATTHEW 25

> Then shall the King say unto them on his right hand, Come, ye blessed of my Father, inherit the kingdom prepared for you from the foundation of the world: for I was an hungered, and ye gave me meat: I was thirsty, and ye gave me drink: I was a stranger, and ye took me in: naked, and ye clothed me: I was sick, and ye visited me: I was in prison, and ye came unto me. Then shall the righteous answer him, saying, Lord, . . . When saw we thee a stranger, and took thee in? or naked, and clothed thee? . . . And the King shall answer and say unto them, Verily I say unto you, Inasmuch as ye have done it unto one of the least of these my brethren, ye have done it unto me.[1]

TODAY'S PASSAGE, which refers to the judgment of nations, provides us a lesson in true Christian concern. Those who know and love the Lord are confident of His return, and should recognize the job to be done in a world that is hungry not only physically but spiritually. For those who are thirsty, to whom natural water cannot give permanent satisfaction, comes the promise, "But whosoever drinketh of the water that I shall give him shall never thirst; but the water that I shall give him shall be in him a well of water springing up into everlasting life."[2]

It has been said that the subject of judgment does not make good devotional reading. However, we Christians will be judged on our concern for those around us, and it is well for us to remember the principles on which we shall be judged.

Judgment separates men into two companies; there is no neutral ground. The solemnity of recognizing that men are born again or forever lost should work in our hearts. Then works play a definite part as illustrated in the reading. Christ identifies Himself with His people, showing that what is done for them is done as unto Him, and later explains that what is withheld, is withheld from Him.

These truths must be applied. There is an unlovely person that should be visited, but she lives across town. It is inconvenient and I am so busy. Such thoughts often prevail. If I ask the Lord what should be done, the message comes: "Sick, and ye visited me." A day is coming when I will be judged for what I didn't do as well as for what I did. Day after day in the little things I must be faithful, though I may be obscure. My loving deeds may be unseen by men but His all-seeing eye does not miss them.

Our Christian concern needs to be encouraged and will only be effective as we bear one another's burdens and "so fulfil the law of Christ."[3]

[1]Matthew 25:34-40.
[2]John 4:14.
[3]Galatians 6:2.

❧   ❧   ❧

MATTHEW 26
MATTHEW 26:1-13

> There came unto him a woman having an alabaster box
> of very precious ointment, and poured it on his head,
> as he sat at meat. But when his disciples saw it, they
> had indignation, saying, To what purpose is this waste?[1]

OFTEN in our daily reading of the Scripture we come upon
something that startles us. Such, for me, is the story of the
alabaster box. It might be called an unexpected interruption in a chapter that tells of Christ's betrayal by Judas, the
agony of Gethsemane, and the denial of Peter. I wonder
about this woman, knowing that Christ did something very
special for her. Her background is completely unknown,
but we know that she had a great affection for the Lord.
Possibly He had healed her, or she had witnessed one of
His miracles. At any rate, her life had been drastically
changed through the power of this God-Man and her gratitude was overwhelming.

Mark tells us the worth of the perfume. It cost about a
year's wages. However, was this really sacrifice on her part?
Who would not sacrifice the wages of a year for eternal
gain? But the disciples, in their smug indignation, demanded, "To what purpose is this waste?" Should not the
poor be fed?

Christ accepted the gift and vindicated the giver. He
said, "Wheresoever this gospel shall be preached in the
whole world, there shall also this, that this woman hath
done, be told for a memorial of her."[2] And this prophecy
has been fulfilled, just in our reading the story today. Kings
and emperors and great people have been forgotten, but
not this humble and loving woman.

A brilliant young doctor with a fine practice decided to
sell all and go to the mission field. Those closest to him in
utter disgust demanded, "To what purpose is this waste?"

Could not he do more in his own community, helping the poor, healing the sick? The doctor had given God the gift of his life. He, with scores of others who are faithful to Christ, and the woman in our story, whether giving medical help, a cup of cold water, or ointment from an alabaster box, will not be forgotten. The fragrance of such lives will linger long, and one day each will be rewarded by the One who said, "Them that honour me I will honour."[3]

[1]Matthew 26:7-8.
[2]Matthew 26:13.
[3]I Samuel 2:30.

❧ ❧ ❧

October 14

MATTHEW 27–28
MATTHEW 28

> And Jesus came and spake unto them, saying, All power is given unto me in heaven and in earth. Go ye therefore, and teach all nations, baptizing them in the name of the Father, and of the Son, and of the Holy Ghost: teaching them to observe all things whatsoever I have commanded you: and, lo, I am with you alway, even unto the end of the world. Amen.[1]

WE HAVE A FRIEND who was all alone. She had no close relatives, and her mother, with whom she had lived her entire life, went to be with the Lord. She expressed the dark loneliness that encompassed her when she entered the house for the first time after her mother's death. It was too much! It was unbearable. In desperation she cried to the Lord, who graciously answered, "Lo, I am with you alway." From that moment, and through the years that have passed, she has yet to feel alone. Christ's presence has filled her life and home. Centuries have passed since the words were spoken by Christ—His last in Matthew—but today, in a little home in Portland, Oregon, they are being experienced.

454

Loneliness is a major social concern today. Yet God never intended man to feel lonely. God loves to fill the longing heart with His joy, peace, and satisfaction. We have accounts of His own desire for fellowship such as the times He called His disciples to be with Him. And we have recorded throughout the Bible God's desire that man should not be lonely but that he should have fellowship with Him.

Enoch walked with God.

Moses met with God on Mount Sinai.

Abraham was God's friend.

God gave Joshua the promise "I will be with thee."

The writer of the Psalms could face the "valley of the shadow of death" as he exulted, "Thou art with me."

Christ said to the disciples, "Lo, I am with you alway." Because of Jesus' concern about our loneliness, when He left earth He did not leave us alone but promised and gave us "another Comforter, that he may abide with you for ever."[2]

There is a difference between solitude and loneliness. We each desire and need those special times when we can go apart and be alone. But loneliness should be unknown to the Christian. No wonder our friend in Portland can answer friends who ask if she minds being alone by saying, "I am not alone. Christ is with me." Her heart sings:

> How can I be lonely when I've Jesus only
> To be my companion and unfailing guide:
> How can I be weary, or my path seem dreary,
> When He's walking by my side![3]

[1]Matthew 28:18-20.
[2]John 14:16.
[3]Haldor Lillenas.

❧ ❧ ❧

> Now as he walked by the sea of Galilee, he saw Simon
> and Andrew his brother casting a net into the sea: for
> they were fishers. And Jesus said unto them, Come ye
> after me, and I will make you to become fishers of men.
> And straightway they forsook their nets, and followed
> him.[1]

CHRIST was in eastern Galilee when He called a quartet of
fishermen, Simon, Andrew, James, and John. "Come . . . and
I will make you . . .," He said to the fishermen who had
spent much of their lives casting their nets into that sea.
They were laboring men and common in the eyes of their
neighbors, but Christ had a plan for each.

Simon, who was later called Peter, was impetuous. He had
been brought to Christ by his brother Andrew, who was
convinced that this was the Messiah. Andrew later brought
the boy with the loaves and fishes to Jesus. Andrew sensed
that Jesus always welcomed strangers. James and John had
been with their father that day and were busy mending nets.
But when Christ called, "Come," they left the ship and followed Him.

There is a clarion call to us today, real though not for
physical ears, to come. It is the first step that must be taken
before Christ can "make" us useful for Him. We must personally encounter Him. Intellectual assent is not enough.

Christ spent time with the disciples. "And they went into
Capernaum; and . . . he entered into the synagogue, and
taught."[2] They had so much to learn, and the best way
was by walking moment by moment with Him. "I am the
vine, ye are the branches: He that abideth in me, and I in
him, the same bringeth forth much fruit."[3] Daily fellowship
with the Lord is our source of instruction. We read, "And
they were astonished at his doctrine."[4] They needed to

master the doctrine if as disciples they were to represent Christ. It is one thing to be able to tell another person what the Lord has done for you, but it must be backed up by a knowledge of the "doctrine" which is in the Bible. The importance of a working knowledge of Scripture cannot be overemphasized.

The more the disciples were with Christ, the more they learned about Him and loved Him. They walked with Him, listened to Him, and with their eyes saw the miracles He performed. Together they agreed, "We cannot but speak the things which we have seen and heard."[5]

[1]Mark 1:16-18.
[2]Mark 1:21.
[3]John 15:5.
[4]Mark 1:22.
[5]Acts 4:20.

❧   ❧   ❧

October 16

MARK 4–6
MARK 4

And the same day, when the even was come, he saith unto them, Let us pass over unto the other side. And when they had sent away the multitude, they took him even as he was in the ship. And there were also with him other little ships. And there arose a great storm of wind, and the waves beat into the ship, so that it was now full. And he was in the hinder part of the ship, asleep on a pillow: and they awake him, and say unto him, Master, carest thou not that we perish? And he arose, and rebuked the wind, and said unto the sea, Peace, be still. And the wind ceased, and there was a great calm. And he said unto them, Why are ye so fearful? how is it that ye have no faith? And they feared exceedingly, and said one to another, What manner of man is this, that even the wind and the sea obey him?[1]

A MINISTER told of his experience in crossing the Sea of Galilee. Knowing its landlocked geographical position, he wondered why sudden storms often plagued the water. As he crossed, he noted that the oarsmen were very silent. Only the rhythmic sound of the oars filled the air. He questioned a fellow traveler who explained that these fishermen always row silently, seldom speaking a word. They carefully listen for the sound of wind that may be causing a storm in the mountains. It was one of these unexpected storms that struck the disciples in the boat that day, and they had become fearful.

Our Lord was asleep. He had spoken to the multitudes words of comfort and peace that day, and now was resting. His message had been heard by the disciples many times, but they were still unprepared for the storm. When it came they were frightened. "Master, carest thou not that we perish?" Quietly He rebuked the wind, and the calm returned. But His question challenged their faith in Him: "How is it that ye have no faith?"

Storms without warning are always a test of the Christian's trust. An unexpected change in events, new surroundings, or crises may cause sudden chaos. Our faith is shaken and we rush to the Master, crying, "Carest thou not that we perish?" So often we see His guidance and provision and overwhelming kindness, but then we become overconfident and start steering on our own. We too, like the disciples, are "piloting" the Lord! We chart our own course, until the storm! Then we rush back in fear and frantically seize on prayer like a life jacket, until the tempest passes over.

God help us to have faith that remains constant not only in the sunshine but during the storm.

[1]Mark 4:35-41.

❧   ❧   ❧

Mark 7–9
Mark 8

> And when he had called the people unto him with his disciples also, he said unto them, Whosoever will come after me, let him deny himself, and take up his cross, and follow me. For whosoever will save his life shall lose it; but whosoever shall lose his life for my sake and the gospel's, the same shall save it.[1]

WHAT A VAST CONTRAST between God and human nature! A similar contrast exists between the world and the Word. The world says, "Take care of yourself, and do not throw away your life for any cause." The Word says, "Whosoever shall save his life shall lose it; but whosoever shall lose his life for my sake and the gospel's, the same shall save it."

The natural man cries out, "Put yourself ahead." He will advise you to "get even" with the neighbor who has done you wrong. How easy it is to rationalize thus: *Fight back! Teach him a lesson!* And there may be some satisfaction in an upset, especially if there has been a real wrong.

The spiritual man disagrees. "Turn the other cheek. Bless them who despitefully use you. Bless and do not curse." If another crushes you along the way, pray for him, for as a Christian, there is no doubt that you are your brother's keeper. The world would say, "Feelings are not important, just get on top." The Word would contrast, "He that humbleth himself shall be exalted."[2]

Many are familiar with the story of John Williams who labored long in Tahiti. He had been concerned for the spiritual welfare of the long-neglected island. His ministry was fruitful, and the people were responsive. It was a tremendous shock to the natives when, after more than twenty years of service, he announced that he was leaving. "You may never come back," sobbed one woman as his ship was about to leave the port, and she was right. His new field was unfriendly, and savages beat him to death. The end? Oh, no, it was just the beginning. As the news of his martyrdom reached England, scores were stirred. The story came to the United States, where a small boy's heart was reached. His life was never the same and, as he grew up, A.B. Simpson became a true stalwart of Christian missions and the founder of one of our great missionary societies.

Jesus said, "Except a corn of wheat fall into the ground and die, it abideth alone: but if it die, it bringeth forth much fruit."[3]

[1]Mark 8:34-35.
[2]Luke 14:11.
[3]John 12:24.

❧ ❧ ❧

MARK 10–12
MARK 10

> And they brought young children to him, that he should touch them: and his disciples rebuked those that brought them. But when Jesus saw it, he was much displeased, and said unto them, Suffer the little children to come unto me, and forbid them not: for of such is the kingdom of God. Verily I say unto you, Whosoever shall not receive the kingdom of God as a little child, he shall not enter therein. And he took them up in his arms, put his hands upon them, and blessed them.[1]

"IF I COULD TOUCH JESUS," said nine-year-old Mickey, "I would know He was really real." The Sunday school class had been discussing Christ's interest in children just their age, how much He loved and cared for the little children, and how even in His very busy schedule He took time to bless and be with them. Mickey left Sunday school still unsure about the reality of Jesus. The Sunday following she pranced into class with a happy expression. "Mother said if Jesus comes to earth again, she will take me to see

Him." Recognizing the confusion that was still in the child's mind, the teacher prayed for wisdom. Enlightenment came through a fellow student. Chris was nine years old too, and well versed in primary teachings. "Jesus has already been here," he said, a bit upset with Mickey's lack of knowledge. "He did what He was supposed to do a long time ago. Besides, if He was in Jerusalem today, you are in Seattle, and I doubt if you could go that far to see Him, so you had just better believe that He was there, and now He is everywhere."

The nine-year-old boy had more to say, but the teacher came in. She asked if Mickey knew about Abraham Lincoln. Yes, she had heard about him and read about him in school. The teacher asked how she could know that Mr. Lincoln was "really real" if she had never touched him? Mickey thought and thought as her teacher told more about Jesus on earth and how He had gone to heaven. The teacher said that it is easier to talk with Him today than it was a long time ago; that we can be introduced to Him through prayer, and then talk to Him as often as we wish. Mickey began to grasp the reality of Jesus.

The teachableness of children, their simple trust, and their dependence and submission make them so easy to reach. Is it any wonder that Christ said to adults, "Except ye become as a child . . ." We too need to be teachable, to be obedient, to want to grasp as the children do, and to really believe. Parents must sometimes learn from their children. Happy are those who grasp, as a child, that God is real, and that we can touch Him through prayer and trust.

Entrance into the kingdom of God is through Christ Jesus the "door." In that kingdom there is no place for worldly wisdom or human power.

¹Mark 10:13-16.

❧   ❧   ❧

MARK 13–14
MARK 14

> And they came to a place which was named Gethsemane: and he saith to his disciples, Sit ye here, while I shall pray. And he taketh with him Peter and James and John, and began to be sore amazed, and to be very heavy; and saith unto them, My soul is exceeding sorrowful unto death: tarry ye here, and watch. And he cometh, and findeth them sleeping, and said unto Peter, Simon, sleepest thou? couldest not thou watch one hour? Watch ye and pray, lest ye enter into temptation. The spirit truly is ready, but the flesh is weak.[1]

WE CANNOT READ Mark's account of the agony in Gethsemane without a desire to love Christ with increased devotion. He was about to be betrayed, and had taken His dear ones about a half mile from Jerusalem, up the Mount of Olives, to a garden called Gethsemane. Peter, James, and John were asked to go beyond the place where some of the other disciples would wait. Christ then sought solitude a few steps from them.

Gethsemane must have been a lovely location for prayer. It was surrounded by olive trees, quiet because it was almost midnight, and the very presence of the Lord should have warmed the hearts of the waiting trio. As Christ prayed, He suffered and agonized, and asked His Father to "take away this cup. Nevertheless not what I will, but what thou wilt."[2] He rose from His knees, walked toward the disciples, and found them asleep. His heart was already broken. Three times the same thing happened, and three times his friends failed. The words must have gone deep when He said to Peter, "Couldest not thou watch one hour?" There was no answer.

How often my heart is overwhelmed within me, and those words, "Couldest not thou watch one hour?" penetrate

462

deep. The day is ended, and I pause to talk with Him. The mind begins to drift and the eyes become heavy. How many unfinished prayers, half-spoken, half-whispered requests, ascend meaninglessly. How it must grieve His heart —the heart that was broken for me.

How little Christians know of agonizing prayer. Small wonder that our lives are ineffective for Him. It is well to look beyond ourselves, out into the distances of God, where we see a suffering Saviour, and view multitudes for whom He died, but who still have never heard of His great love. Let me climb a personal Mount of Olives and tarry there.

[1]Mark 14:32-34, 37-38.
[2]Mark 14:36.

♣   ♣   ♣

October 20

MARK 15–16
MARK 16

> And it was the third hour, and they crucified him . . . and laid him in a sepulchre which was hewn out of a rock, and rolled a stone unto the door of the sepulchre. And very early in the morning the first day of the week, they came unto the sepulchre at the rising of the sun. And entering into the sepulchre, they saw a young man sitting on the right side . . . And he saith unto them, Be not affrighted: Ye seek Jesus of Nazareth, which was crucified: he is risen; he is not here: behold the place where they laid him. But go your way, tell his disciples and Peter that he goeth before you into Galilee: there shall ye see him, as he said unto you.[1]

THERE WAS inexpressible joy that early resurrection morning—Christ was alive! Could their finite minds comprehend the miracle? The followers of Christ had suffered much in the past hours. Their leader was gone. The guilt of Peter's denial left a hurt in his heart which could not be assuaged. But there was good news. Christ had risen indeed! "Go your way, tell his disciples and Peter." (This is a tender touch. The Lord knew of Peter's grief, of his downcast condition. He felt for Peter in his weakness, and He had left special word for him.) The disciples had become eyewitnesses to a glorious truth that had been hinted at in Old Testament days, and now had been fulfilled.

A missionary statesman described the event by saying, "All conditions were GO that day," and though the term is borrowed from missile-launching procedure, how descriptive it is. "Go ye into all the world, and preach the gospel to every creature."[2] Go work, go seek, go tell. We are told that the word appears two hundred and fifty-two times in the New Testament. "Go." And they went, for they had much to tell.

Mary Magdalene, the first to whom Jesus made Himself known, after she realized who it was, answered, "Rabboni!" The word means "my master." The risen Christ surely became the core of her conversation for the rest of her life. Of course, there were those who doubted, but even Thomas experienced the "feel" of His hands and the depths of those scars, and sincerely believed.

One by one they went forth, in ecstasy and wonder, in awe and relief. They "preached every where, the Lord working with them, and confirming the word with signs following."[3] How well they came to appreciate Christ's statement: "Because I live, ye shall live also."[4]

[1]Mark 15:25, 46; 16:2, 5-7.
[2]Mark 16:15.
[3]Mark 16:20.
[4]John 14:19.

❧ ❧ ❧

Luke 1–2
Luke 2

> And lo, the angel of the Lord came upon them, and the
> glory of the Lord shone round about them: and they
> were sore afraid. And the angel said unto them, Fear
> not: for, behold, I bring you good tidings of great joy,
> which shall be to all people.[1]

READING THE STORY of Christmas in October ought to be a
stimulating experience! There is no tinsel, no rushing to
town, not any of the happy confusion that surrounds the
holidays. One can carefully examine the story and gain an
enriching experience.

Mary's visit with her cousin Elisabeth was a sacred occasion. The two had much to talk about, and so much to
plan for. I can hear Elisabeth telling Mary of the angel's
appearance to her husband, Zacharias, and recounting the
message: "Thy prayer is heard; and thy wife Elisabeth
shall bear thee a son, and thou shalt call his name John."[2]
It had been many years since Zacharias and Elisabeth had
prayed for a child. Elisabeth was old, and well past child-
bearing age, but their prayers of years ago had been heard,
and were now being answered.

There is much to think about in that small statement
"Thy prayer is heard." Perhaps you have a loved one for
whom you have prayed for years. Possibly a prayer offered
a decade ago may be answered tomorrow. It was so for
Elisabeth.

As for the angels, the Bible has much to say about these
"ministering spirits."[3] Both Old and New Testaments tell
of their appearance and service. The Psalmist said, "He
shall give his angels charge over thee, to keep thee in all
thy ways."[4] Angels gave the good news to these two women,
and today, along life's way, we too may realize the presence
of angels.

A **missionary** friend felt an angel's protection in the heart of Africa. It could only have been an angel, she said, that made her aware of a poisonous snake hidden in her room.

Angels unaware are more common than we think, and I cannot help but believe that their visitation as in today's story is reenacted in our daily lives. Though unseen, they are real helpers of God. We will do well to heed their message given that first Christmas: "Fear not."

¹Luke 2:9-10.
²Luke 1:13.
³Hebrews 1:14.
⁴Psalm 91:11.

🍀 🍀 🍀

LUKE 3–5
LUKE 5

> Now when he had left speaking, he said unto Simon, Launch out into the deep, and let down your nets for a draught. And Simon answering said unto him, Master, we have toiled all the night, and have taken nothing: nevertheless at thy word I will let down the net. And when they had this done, they inclosed a great multitude of fishes: and their net brake.¹

IT WAS THE HABIT of the fishermen to fish at night. Now morning had dawned and there had been no catch. The nets were pulled up and the toilers were ready to give up. Simon was still new in the Christian faith, and undoubtedly his spiritual legs were unsteady. When the Master commanded, "Launch out into the deep, and let your nets down for a draught," he must have wondered just what the Lord knew about fishing! "Master, we have toiled all the night, and have taken nothing." There was a question in Peter's mind and he did not try to hide it, but he did yield to higher authority. How significant is the word that follows: *nevertheless.*

Life for the Christian is often one great "nevertheless." There is almost perpetual conflict. Our obedience is tested. One way seems tempting and easy, and the other challenging, demanding. Simon could have pondered the situation for a few minutes, analyzed it, as we say today; but no, swiftness is part of obedience. "Nevertheless at thy word I will let down the net." It was an act of faith, and faith is always rewarded. The catch was so great that the fishermen could scarcely believe it. Everyone got together and helped, even some from the shore.

Here is a true-to-life parable. The fishermen represent Christian workers, the ship the church, the net the gospel, the sea the world, and the shore eternity. As the disciples talked these things over, they better understood their work on earth, and Christ further clarified it in the next verses. "Henceforth thou shalt catch men"—a catch for eternity.

"Launch out into the deep" is a command for us today as well. It demands a prompt, personal response. Simon later learned still more of obedience. I wonder if he recalled this incident on the Day of Pentecost, when he cast forth the net which brought in three thousand souls. On that day he preached long and earnestly. And again his obedience was rewarded, this time with the catch of men! "Nevertheless at thy word I will let down the net."

[1]Luke 5:4-6.

❧   ❧   ❧

And why call ye me, Lord, Lord, and do not the things
which I say?[1]

THERE ARE MANY NAMES given to Jesus: Emmanuel, Saviour,
Son of the living God, the unspeakable Gift, and others.
There are names of reverence and respect, names of worship and adoration. However, the name "Lord" demands
much more than just address. It demands allegiance and
submission, loyalty and devotion. How really meaningful
is the term. It is not enough to hear His words or to lightly
profess a relationship to Him. Think back over Christ's
earthly career. People lauded and honored Him as He rode
triumphantly into Jerusalem. They called him "King" and
"Master," and some even called Him "Lord." There were
those who paid Him homage. Where were their endearing
terms several days later, when He went to Calvary? Judas
called Him "Lord," and all the time Christ knew of the betrayal that would come from him.

Those who heard Jesus' teachings inquired, "Lord, what
of this, and that?" He would answer, and they would hear
His parables, listen to the interpretations, witness His miracles, and yet remain indifferent to Him. No wonder He
asked one day, clearly and bluntly, "Why call ye me, Lord,
Lord, and do not the things which I say?" Words must be
confirmed with deeds. If we call Him Lord, we must bow to
His will and to His right to rule our lives.

There are three kinds of people who could here be described: those who do not call Him Lord, and do not the
things which He has spoken; those who call Him Lord,
possibly on Sunday morning, but heed not the responsibility
of obeying Him the other six days; and those who call Him
Lord and are obedient.

Categorize yourself. Are you completely indifferent to Him, or are you echoing the crowd and calling Him Lord on occasion because it is the thing to do? Or is there complete dedication without compromise in your heart? Is it lifted prayerfully, gratefully, and obediently to Him? Can you truly say, "My Lord and my God"?

[1]Luke 6:46.

LUKE 8–9
LUKE 8:43-48

> And a woman having an issue of blood twelve years, which had spent all her living upon physicians, neither could be healed of any, came behind him, and touched the border of his garment. And he said unto her, Daughter, be of good comfort: thy faith hath made thee whole; go in peace.[1]

F. B. MEYER calls this instance a story of "nobody, somebody, and everybody." Here was a woman who truly was a nobody. She had been excluded from worship because of a technicality in the Rabbinical law. She was no doubt divorced from her husband, and most likely separated from society. Her living was all gone, spent on physicians who could not heal her. The account in Mark tells us she was getting worse.

However, because of the love and compassion of Christ, this woman became a somebody. Christ noticed her. He "felt" her touch the hem of His garment. No doubt as she drew water in the village square she had heard of the Great Physician. Or possibly her curiosity was aroused by the multitude and, having nothing else to do, she joined the throng. When she listened to Him, she was amazed at the authority which He demonstrated, coupled with His gracious manner. She had no doubt. She believed. So many

469

were around Him that she dared not bother Him, outcast that she was. So she quietly slipped through the crowd, just within reach. She grasped His hem—and she was healed.

Christ took the opportunity to strengthen the timid faith which had just been displayed. He asked who had touched Him. He looked over the crowd. It must not have been difficult to pick her out. Ill people can easily be distinguished, and after years of ostracism and pain she was noticeable for the deep lines that sickness carves. She came forward trembling, and made confession "before all the people." Strength was coming into her body as she bore witness. Christ could have healed her with just a word and let her go on her way but, as with the man with the withered arm, an indication of her faith was required. By stepping out she acknowledged her faith and the cure was confirmed.

The story represents everybody because within the next few minutes Jairus evidenced a strengthened faith by remaining with Jesus in spite of the word that his daughter had died. Undoubtedly others were encouraged to believe when they heard what Christ had done. Through the centuries it has strengthened countless others who, like the woman, have been at the end of the rope, and have dared to touch the "hem of his garment." Through faith they also have been made whole!

[1]Luke 8:43-44, 48.

❧ ❧ ❧

470

LUKE 10–11
LUKE 10:21-42

> And Jesus answered and said unto her, Martha, Martha,
> thou art careful and troubled about many things: but
> one thing is needful: and Mary hath chosen that good
> part, which shall not be taken away from her.[1]

HOW GLAD WE ARE that Scripture records this heartwarming
story about Mary, Martha, and Lazarus. Their home was a
refuge for Christ amid His busy schedule. Our attention is
focused primarily on two sisters who were true individual-
ists. Mary was quiet, and loved to listen to the Lord, literally sitting at His feet. Martha was busy keeping house,
cooking, cleaning, and took the responsibility of seeing that
each guest had everything he needed. When Christ came
to Bethany to visit with them they ministered to His different needs. Martha provided the food and physical attention
which He needed. She was right in serving. He also needed
a listener and one who could minister to His heart's need.
Mary was right for listening.

A blend of both service and devotion is needed in the
well-rounded Christian. I know a woman who spends the
best part of five days a week in the church, working, cleaning, visiting; yet how little she knows of true prayer and
worship. Only God can give the true balance that is needed.
The trouble with the Marthas is that they tend to be so
busy that they deprive themselves of a satisfying visit with
Christ.

We need a good measure of tolerance when viewing the
varied ways in which people serve the Lord, and a reminder
that loving Him is the first and great commandment. Christ
loved both Mary and Martha, and appreciated Martha's
untiring service. But He also pointed out that "Mary hath
chosen that good part, which shall not be taken away from
her."

If there were a choice between service and devotion, devotion would win, for it is the source of true service. As we live for the Lord, He will direct the ministries to which each of us has been appointed in His kingdom.

[1]Luke 10:41-42.

❧   ❧   ❧

LUKE 12–13
LUKE 12

> Let your loins be girded about and your lights burning; and ye yourselves like unto men that wait for their lord, when he will return from the wedding; that when he cometh and knocketh, they may open unto him immediately. Blessed are those servants, whom the lord when he cometh shall find watching: verily I say unto you, that he shall gird himself, and make them to sit down to meat, and will come forth and serve them.[1]

GIRD YOURSELVES, and keep the lights burning. The Bible, which is not just a book of poetry and preaching, clearly forecasts that the Lord will come again. We have the first coming of Christ foretold in minute detail. Long before His birth, we were told how He would be born and where. We were told of His ministry to men and of His betrayal by men. Those prophecies were all fulfilled. Just as real—and just as positive—is the prophecy that He will come to earth again.

In preparing for His return, we are told to let our "loins be girded about." The people in Christ's day dressed differently than we do today. They wore long, loose outer garments. If they were going on a journey, the garments would get in their way, so they were in the habit of fastening them up for easier walking. If the trip was at night, they would take along lamps to help them see the way.

Christians today often have many entanglements, like the

472

loose garments, which could easily hinder the preparation for that great journey. Some things must be given up. Paul described it like this: "Let us lay aside every weight, and the sin which doth so easily beset us."[2] Then we will be prepared.

I have a friend whose husband constantly travels. Due to the nature of his employment he is never sure when he will be home. Because she loves him dearly, she has gotten used to being constantly prepared. Every morning that he is gone, she arises with the thought that he might come home that day. The house and the children are in readiness. At night, she makes sure again that things are ready, and the light remains on constantly. One day she explained that she "lived prepared," and when she read these verses, they helped her to seriously start making ready for the Lord's return as well as for her husband's.

The Lord came the first time as the Author of salvation. He will come the second time as the Finisher of our faith. Be alert. Be vigilant. "Be ye therefore ready also: for the Son of man cometh at an hour when ye think not."[3]

[1]Luke 12:35-37.
[2]Hebrews 12:1.
[3]Luke 12:40.

   ❧   ❧   ❧

> And whosoever doth not bear his cross, and come after
> me, cannot be my disciple. So likewise whosoever he be
> of you that forsaketh not all that he hath, he cannot be
> my disciple.[1]

WE HAVE TALKED a lot about discipleship these past days.
Too much cannot be said on this vital subject. How little
we truly know of the disciplined life which is required of a
real disciple. All too few could offer up their "reasonable
service" without adding many resolutions to do better soon.

Bill and Betty were a young couple from strong Christian backgrounds. Before going to work, Bill quickly read
a few thoughts from the Bible. When Betty had time, she
would do likewise. Because they were well known in the
church, the college department asked them to give a series
of talks on discipleship as it related to everyday living.
Both were pleased with the invitation.

Betty borrowed her dad's concordance and looked up
everything on what is required of a disciple. Bill was to or-
ganize their talks. It did not take much research or soul-
searching for them to realize that they were unqualified.
Instead of withdrawing from the assignment they set out to
enrich their barren Christian experience. First, they established a regular quiet time. Both had given talks on its
importance in the past, but neither had ever set aside a
specific time apart. Betty read a quote from Samuel Chad-
wick that spoke to her: "Hurry is the death of prayer." So
they took fewer requests and presented them slowly before
the Lord. From references Betty had read, Bill decided to
reorganize their budget. They increased their giving and,
instead of just sending a check hit and miss for the cause
of Christ, made a study of the true need for money in God's
service. This opened a new door, for as they met mission-

aries and surveyed fields via circulars, they better understood the needs and increased their support. Jesus knew what He was saying when He said, "Where your treasure is, there will your heart be also."[2]

Next they became witnesses and shared their Christian experiences with others. They invited not only Christians but those outside of the church, and oh, how their outreach grew.

The Sunday arrived for their ministry to the college group. The series of talks was prepared as a spiritual diary. Their downfalls and uprisings, their joys and mistakes were all recorded from the day Betty truly defined in her heart what a disciple was. Bill's closing thought was solemn: "Suddenly we realized there were two groups of Christians: producers and consumers. We had been the latter. But not any more." Their values had changed and so had their lives. Betty was bursting to interrupt, and finally couldn't wait. She wanted the group to know that Bill's boss had accepted Christ in their home the previous night!

How grateful they were to have been called upon to talk about discipleship. Their spiritual accounting and individual inventory might never have been made. What of your life? Can you be counted as a disciple?

[1]Luke 14:27, 33.
[2]Matthew 6:21.

❧ ❧ ❧

LUKE 17–18
LUKE 17

The kingdom of God is within you.[1]

THERE ARE MANY interpretations of the kingdom of God: what and where it is, and how it affects us. Some theories are remote and involved. I prefer the uncomplicated, and find joyous satisfaction in believing the kingdom can also be in my own heart.

In a world that is distressed and perplexed, there is peace. In seeking the kingdom folks often turn toward the world, looking hopefully, searching diligently for an intangible. Or they scan prophecy and become so involved with things to come that they miss the goal. It is almost too easy to understand that by opening one's heart the King can come in, take rightful place on His throne, and establish His kingdom within.

Here in the soul He takes residence. The outer confusion of everyday living, the fears of tomorrow, the petty irritations and doubts, cannot help but subside as we commune with Him—within. But we must listen also. "Be still, and know that I am God."[2] Stillness in the rush of the day? Yes, stillness, even silence, before Him. It is then that His reign brings forth the realities of His promises:

> Casting all your care upon him; for he careth for you.[3]
> Peace I leave with you, my peace I give unto you.[4]
> Commit thy works unto the Lord, and thy thoughts shall be established.[5]
> Rest in the Lord.[6]

Should I not be able to face every situation that comes, in quietness and confidence because the King of kings reigns? Not just beyond my reach but constantly around me, before me, beside me, and yes—the most glorious, transforming reality—the kingdom of God is *within* me. How can I help but have a tranquil heart?

The tranquil heart is one that lives
In tune with heaven above,
Well grounded in the ancient faith
And rooted in God's love.
The tranquil heart is unperturbed
When fortune brings great gain;
It is a chance to share the cup
With those in grief and pain.
When doubts arise and cares oppress,
And faith grows cold and dim,
The tranquil heart turns not aside:
For it is filled within.
Amid the burdens of the day
And cares that never cease,
The tranquil heart goes bravely on
In God's abiding peace.[7]

[1]Luke 17:21.
[2]Psalm 46:10.
[3]I Peter 5:7.
[4]John 14:27.
[5]Proverbs 16:3.
[6]Psalm 37:7.
[7]"The Tranquil Heart," T. B. Gleave.

❧   ❧   ❧

October 29

LUKE 19–20
LUKE 19

And he said unto him, Well, thou good servant: because thou hast been faithful in a very little, have thou authority over ten cities.[1]

ONE OF MY EARLIEST recollections is that of my mother reading to me a small booklet entitled *Little Is Much When God Is in It*. Through the years I have begun to recognize the significance of the words. The little things do count. The gift of gifts, salvation, comes through the simplicity of believing. God has promised great rewards for giving just a cup of cold water in His name. Planting a seed, no matter how small it may be, can be the beginning of tremendous growth.

It was only five dollars—a small amount when you think of the great sums we are spending today. But five dollars went into little gospel tracts, two hundred and fifty of them. Carefully distributed and prayerfully remembered, they too sowed the little seeds of the gospel. Within weeks the seed fell on fruitful ground, and seven children had found Jesus Christ. A small investment, true, but another proof that "little is much when God is in it."

He was a small man with no arms or legs. Corregidor had been his place of duty for the United States. He returned broken in body but not in spirit. Home would be a veterans' hospital. During the months of rehabilitation he asked God to help him. So little he now had to offer— so little that he would hum a hymn and change its words: "Of my life there's nothing to bring, Yet to Your cross I strongly cling." He was little in his own eyes, and his handicap was great, but he influenced not just his ward but the entire hospital.

What do you have to give? It may be small, it may be a frail effort, but the promise of God does not designate the degree of ability or the amount of money. It is a challenge to us to be faithful with what we have. As Christians we have business to do with God in the world today.

God never asks for more than we can give, but He says, "Give." Give of yourself, your time, your resources, your talents. "Give, and it shall be given unto you." Being faithful in the little brings big results. "Pressed down . . . running over." "Little is much when God is in it!"

¹Luke 19:17.
²Luke 6:38.

☙ ☙ ☙

> And the Lord said, Simon, Simon, behold, Satan hath
> desired to have you, that he may sift you as wheat: but
> I have prayed for thee, that thy faith fail not: and when
> thou art converted, strengthen thy brethren.[1]

How LITTLE we really know ourselves. And here is a good
illustration. Christ knew that Simon Peter, though he had
just pledged, "Lord, I am ready to go with thee, both into
prison, and to death,"[2] was about to deny Him.

God looks on the heart. He knows the nature of our
loyalties. How easy it was to be faithful to Him when His
popularity was at an all-time high, when the crowd chorused,
"Hosanna." Then in the space of just a few days the glorious hosannas changed to enraged shouts of "Crucify him."

"Satan desires to have you, that he may sift you as wheat."
Perhaps God allows Satan to sift us for the purpose of removing the chaff. Oh, the malice of Satan. Some choose
to neglect the fact of his existence among us. But God
warns us over and over to build a strong garrison against
him.

Christ is our defense against ourselves. "My father, which
gave them me, is greater than all; and no man is able to
pluck them out of my Father's hand."[3] As King of our
lives He has power to protect us. So much so that the
Psalmist rejoiced audibly: "God is our refuge and strength,
a very present help in trouble."[4] If the battle becomes too
strong, we are reminded, "Do you think that I cannot appeal to my Father, and he will at once send me more than
twelve legions of angels?"[5]

Oh, that our faith would keep firm so that we could
strengthen our brethren. We stumble and fall in the path
of faith. But it is important that we do not turn back. The
failures, the weaknesses, even the betrayals, teach us humili-

ty and give us insight into our own inadequacies as well as those of others. Thus, through Him, we become more capable of understanding our neighbors.

Do not trust yourself, but "trust in the Lord with all thine heart; and lean not unto thine own understanding. In all thy ways acknowledge him, and he shall direct thy paths."[6]

[1]Luke 22:31-32.
[2]Luke 22:33.
[3]John 10:29.
[4]Psalm 46:1.
[5]Matthew 26:53, RSV.
[6]Proverbs 3:5-6.

❧ ❧ ❧

October 31

LUKE 23–24
LUKE 24

> Their eyes were opened, and they knew him . . . And they said one to another, Did not our heart burn within us, while he talked with us by the way, and while he opened to us the scriptures? Then opened he their understanding, that they might understand the scriptures.[1]

WHAT A GLORIOUS EXPERIENCE it is when the Lord reveals Himself to a believer in a new way! This was the case that special day on the Emmaus road. Since His resurrection Christ had appeared to several disciples and had given unquestionable evidence that He was alive. As He walked along the road with the two sad ones, He expounded to them the significance of the past events. They did not know that it was the Lord. Later in the journey they asked Him to stop with them for supper. As he took bread and blessed it, they recognized their guest to be the Son of God. Their conversation was recorded: "Did not our hearts burn within us, while he talked with us . . . while he opened to us the scriptures?"

They rose quickly from the table and went back to Jerusalem. They must tell the disciples and others of their time with the Lord. Here He reappeared, and it is small wonder that, after He ascended into heaven, "they worshipped him, and returned to Jerusalem with great joy: and were continually in the temple, praising and blessing God."[2] They had seen and beheld His glory!

Three openings were here significant: First, He "opened" their eyes that they might know Him. It was a very personal experience when firsthand they recognized their Lord. Second, He "opened" the Scriptures. David had prayed for the same experience back in the book of Psalms: "Open thou mine eyes, that I may behold wondrous things out of thy law."[3] Third, He "opened" their understanding. It is one thing to read the Bible, but it is another to truly understand. Philip, in talking with the Ethiopian eunuch, asked a searching question: "Understandest thou what thou readest?" Too often we lack understanding, and must confess with the eunuch, "How can I, except some man should guide me?"[4] The Holy Spirit can open our understanding and shed light upon the Word.

The resurrection of Christ is the great hope of Christians. Without it our faith would be dead and buried. We have the positive witness of friends, soldiers, people like Cleopas, angels, that He did rise again! God grant that each of us will also bear individual witness, that our lips will be open to say triumphantly with Paul, "It is Christ that died, yea rather, that is risen again."[5] Have you seen His glory? Have you told others?

[1] Luke 24:31-32, 45.
[2] Luke 24:52-53.
[3] Psalm 119:18.
[4] Acts 8:30-31.
[5] Romans 8:34.

    ❦   ❦   ❦

November

JOHN 1–3
JOHN 3

> There was a man of the Pharisees, named Nicodemus, a
> ruler of the Jews: the same came to Jesus by night, and
> said unto him, Rabbi, we know that thou art a teacher
> come from God: for no man can do these miracles that
> thou doest, except God be with him. Jesus answered and
> said unto him, Verily, verily, I say unto thee, Except a
> man be born again, he cannot see the kingdom of God.[1]

THE MEETING of our Lord and Nicodemus brings to mind
a true story of two men of the twentieth century. One was
a true man of God, the other a brilliant and religious millionaire. Their meeting might be termed a "summit meeting," for they met at a mountain resort. The religious man
had heard about God and Christ throughout his life. He
was a true intellectual and an ardent reader. He had studied philosophies and ideologies. He was acquainted with
the major faiths of the world.

The daily paper had told of the religious leader's visit to
this resort city. It told of people finding Jesus Christ, and
of others just coming to inquire and see what was happen-
ing. In the circle of this businessman's friends, one had
come to Christ. He had been completely changed. This
made the millionaire puzzled and curious, so a late evening
meeting was arranged for him and the minister.

The inquirer found himself surprised at many things
which he heard during the hour he talked with the man of

God, who was young, yet had a tremendous knowledge of the Word of God. The Word was like a sharp sword. As it was deftly quoted with power it pierced the seeker's heart. Sometimes during the visit, the millionaire would change the conversation. As Nicodemus did with Christ, he started to give his personal credentials. He told of the good he did: his civic accomplishments and his great contributions to charity. The minister kept going back to the Scripture, and at last ended with John 3:16: "For God so loved the world, that he gave his only begotten Son, that whosoever believeth in him should not perish, but have everlasting life." The Scripture found its mark. The inquirer believed.

In such simplicity Jesus talked with Nicodemus. Being a judge, Nicodemus weighed the facts of the case. He proved Jesus' testimony to be true, and his own actions guilty. He was religious and learned, but he became as a child and was born into the kingdom. His final verdict was that Christ was the Messiah. Nicodemus did not keep the knowledge to himself. As a believer he later showed courage.

Each of us must encounter Christ in a personal summit experience, weigh the evidence, and decide his eternal destiny. May the right choice be made. Its results will tell for both time and eternity.

[1]John 3:1-3.

❧   ❧   ❧

John 4–5
John 5

> Search the scriptures; for in them ye think ye have eternal life: and they are they which testify of me.[1]

ON MY DESK are two books. One is a dictionary, which is a great asset to me, and the other is my Bible. To know their contents I must read them. To be understood, both must be studied. The Bible differs from the dictionary, however, in that one must know the Bible's Author to fully glean its secrets and apply their meanings. This must be done by searching. Searching implies thorough investigation and examination.

In the precise instruction to "search the scriptures," we uncover an important fact. All too many Christians delight in searching books about the Bible, or in using devotional aids such as this book. However, these are only helps, and should never become substitutes for God's Word. It is said that too often "people prefer to drink at any source other than the original."

Great treasures will be uncovered by searching God's Word. Do it daily as the writer of Proverbs admonishes: "Blessed is the man that heareth me, watching daily at my gates."[2] Do it diligently. Peter reminds us, "Of which salvation the prophets have inquired and searched diligently." Do it with delight as the Psalmist says: "But his delight is in the law of the Lord, and in his law doth he meditate day and night."[4] Do it lovingly rather than with a sense of duty. David wrote, "O how love I thy law!"[5]

In Sunday school I heard the story of a man who died and willed a great treasure to his sons. He made it known that this treasure was hid in his vineyard. How diligently the young men searched, carefully overturning all the dirt, and spading every inch of the ground! They raked and scraped and labored, as they never had before. How disappointed they were to find no treasure. However, the next year the yield in the vineyard was so great from their toil in churning the soil that they found themselves rich. It was then they discovered what their father had done. He had left them a wealth in the soil, and he knew what must be done to bring it to fruition.

God left us great wealth in His Word. But it is only by work and serious search that we too may discover our riches in Him.

[1]John 5:39.
[2]Proverbs 8:34.
[3]I Peter 1:10.
[4]Psalm 1:2.
[5]Psalm 119:97.

❧ ❧ ❧

John 6–7
John 6

> Then Jesus said unto them, Verily, verily, I say unto you, Moses gave you not that bread from heaven; but my Father giveth you the true bread from heaven. For the bread of God is he which cometh down from heaven, and giveth life unto the world. Then said they unto him, Lord, evermore give us this bread. And Jesus said unto them, I am the bread of life: he that cometh to me shall never hunger; and he that believeth on me shall never thirst.[1]

HOW DISCERNING our Lord was. He spoke in a way that all could understand. In using His well-known "I am's," in each case He was speaking of something familiar. When He said, "I am the bread of life," everyone could envision what He illustrated. Bread is universal to man, as it has been the common denominator of all civilizations.

Simple, ordinary bread was the object of Christ's message that day. First he had broken bread and fed the five thou-

485

sand. Impressed? They certainly were, for they had been hungry. It was not surprising that immediately they wanted to make Him their king. It has been said that in His saying, "I am the bread of life," Jesus had had no intention of setting up a bread line but was referring to a lifeline. His primary intention was to offer not physical bread to the masses but rather spiritual bread. As bread feeds man and gives him strength and energy, so Christ meets man's basic needs. He gives the Christian an ever-abundant supply of faith, love, joy, peace, patience, goodness, and truth. These things, like ordinary bread, are essential to health and happiness.

In the Lord's Prayer He said, "Give us this day our daily bread."[2] Daily we must eat and be filled; also daily we must partake of His Word. It is sad but true that people spend a good part of Sunday "storing up" enough of the Bible to last the week. I have yet to hear of anyone eating enough in a single day to be physically sustained for a prolonged period!

Deep in our hearts we all long for the bread that does not perish. How blessed is the Christian who knows the source, and how barren the man who eats from other sources but remains starved. May we recognize our responsibility to share the Bread of life. "This is that bread which came down from heaven: not as your fathers did eat manna, and are dead: he that eateth of this bread shall live for ever."[3]

[1]John 6:32-35.
[2]Matthew 6:11.
[3]John 6:58.

❧ ❧ ❧

> I must work the works of him that sent me, while it is
> day: the night cometh, when no man can work.[1]

BENJAMIN FRANKLIN advised his friends to inquire of themselves each morning and each evening, "What good shall I do today?" and "What good have I done today?"

So often the Lord made the statement, "I must be about my Father's business." Throughout the Gospels we have accounts of His busy days, of His time spent with believers and unbelievers. What an example to follow! Time is given to all men in equality. How it is spent remains our individual accountability.

"What good shall I do today?" It may be that you are reading this in the early hours and there is a day before you with its richness of opportunity. A telephone call which should be made, a letter or check sent to a missionary who has been on your mind, or a witness to a friend or loved one. What of today? It is daylight, but we know that darkness is coming, when the opportunity will be lost.

In the Body of Christ, each of us has been given a great work to do. It is wonderful to come to the close of a day feeling genuinely tired, but having the assurance that someone's load has been lightened, a burden has been borne, and Christ has been honored in some measure.

There is urgency in the words "night cometh, when no man can work." Each of us has a vocation. You may work in a dairy or preside over a court of law. You may be a housewife or a nurse. However, no matter what your temporal work, you are also granted a Christian calling. How your time is spent will be of paramount significance in God's Book of Remembrance. We all have the solemn reminder, "It is appointed unto men once to die, but after this the judgment."[2]

We are impressed with the shortness of time, yet there is sufficiency of time. No matter your age or your limitations, Christ has work for you to do today. Ask Him to guide you, then thank Him, and tonight you will be able to reflect on the good you have done today for His glory and honor.

[1]John 9:4.
[2]Hebrews 9:27.

❧ ❧ ❧

November 5

JOHN 11–13
JOHN 11

> And when she had so said, she went her way, and called Mary her sister secretly, saying, The Master is come, and calleth for thee. As soon as she heard that, she arose quickly, and came unto him.[1]

THOSE WHO MAKE frequent trips to the United States Post Office may remember a large poster which for a year was displayed inside. It was bright and colorful with a picture of Uncle Sam in his red, white, and blue uniform, looking very serious and pointing his index finger. The caption read, "I need you!" A local recruiting office tells us that the message was so stirring that many responded to the call of their country, and truly took personally the statement "I need you!"

In this chapter of John, the words were spoken directly to Mary, but they still have universal application, for this single incident applies to all. There is cause for rejoicing today. The Master has come and He calls us—each day, wherever we are. Just as Jesus sent Martha to her house to get her sister, so He comes to our homes, right where we live. The circumstances of His calling vary. In one home He calls a sinner. "I came not to call the righteous, but sinners to repentance."[2] In another home, He finds a depressed, purposeless youth to whom He says, "I am come that they might have life, and that they might have it more abundantly."[3] He even called one man who was up a tree! Recall the story of Zacchaeus. The Lord needed him, sinner though he was.

Paul, then known as Saul, was on the road to Damascus. His past was enviable by worldly standards. However, he had persecuted Christians. Then came Christ's word, as a pointed finger: "I need you!" Saul accepted the challenge, and his life was spent in the service of his Lord and Saviour.

Just as many people in the post office passed by the message of our country, some refusing to give it a second thought, so many men and women today pay little heed to the Master's beckoning call.

Think back today on the call He gave you: a call specifically for you, a call which if answered could change other lives as well as your own. Christ calls us as He called Mary, who quickly responded: "As soon as she heard that, she rose quickly, and came unto him."

[1]John 11:28-29.
[2]Luke 5:32.
[3]John 10:10.

❧   ❧   ❧

Job 14–17
John 14

> Let not your heart be troubled: ye believe in God, be-
> lieve also in me. In my Father's house are many man-
> sions: if it were not so, I would have told you. I go to
> prepare a place for you. And if I go and prepare a place
> for you, I will come again, and receive you unto my-
> self; that where I am, there ye may be also. And whither
> I go ye know, and the way ye know. Thomas saith unto
> him, Lord, we know not whither thou goest; and how
> can we know the way? Jesus saith unto him, I am the
> way, the truth, and the life; no man cometh unto the
> Father, but by me.[1]

HERE WE FIND the disciples and Christ in serious conversation. Christ knew they were troubled about many things,
especially about the fact that He would leave them. How
true it is that when we love our security, we often lose our
bearings. Our world is made up of family and friends, of
hopes, dreams, and aspirations. If something happens to
shatter that world, it seems to us that the end has come.

The world of the disciples was breaking up, but Christ
spoke words of comfort: "Let not your heart be troubled."
He knew "the world passeth away . . . but he that doeth the
will of God abideth for ever."[2] Christ wanted to get their
eyes off the present and on the future. In going away, He
was preparing a place for them in the world without end.

When Christ asked if they knew the way to where He
was going, Thomas said no, but Jesus was not angry with
his answer. He took time to explain carefully: "I am the
way," the key that unlocks the door to eternal life. "I am
the truth," the key to all knowledge. "I am the life," the
key to abundant, eternal living. "I will not leave you com-
fortless: I will come to you."[3] This is Christ manifesting
Himself physically while on earth, but telling His disciples
He will dwell by His Spirit in the hearts of believers.

The indwelling Christ is a glorious reality. No matter what happens, our hearts should rejoice and our happy faces should reflect the peace and contentment of untroubled souls.

Some day soon Christ is coming again for His own. What a blessed hope and tremendous challenge! We need to live each day as though it were that glorious one.

¹John 14:1-6.
²I John 2:17.
³John 14:18.

❧ ❧ ❧

JOHN 18–21
JOHN 20

> Then saith he to Thomas, Reach hither thy finger, and behold my hands; and reach hither thy hand, and thrust it into my side: and be not faithless, but believing."¹

WE CONCLUDE our readings in the Gospels today, having touched on the story of Christ from the different viewpoints of four inspired writers. Matthew gave us a narrative of Christ's life from the standpoint of a pious tax collector. He quoted many times from the Old Testament to prove prophecy fulfilled. He proclaimed Christ as King. Mark prepared the next Gospel (which was the first to be written), and proclaimed Christ as Servant. Luke, though not an eyewitness to what he wrote, made a careful survey and did much research to tell the unequivocal truth of the story he had experienced in his heart. He presented Christ as Son of Man. Our last Gospel, written by the Apostle John, pictured Christ as God's Son. John, more than the others, developed the contrast of faith and doubt.

Different and varied? Definitely, yet their inspired words tell the same wonderful story of Christ's life on earth, His work, His death, and His resurrection. They all confirm, beyond doubt, that Christ showed Himself alive after death. That fact was the basis of their enthusiasm in proclaiming His message.

After four such books, our faith should be so strengthened that we cannot doubt. But we go back to Matthew: "And when they saw him, they worshipped him: but some doubted."[2] A communicants' class was talking over the resurrection story. After we had considered all those who had seen Christ with their eyes, one young lad said, "I can see why there was doubt." Positive proof had been set before the young people, and this person in particular had a strong Christian background, but still he doubted. A young lady in the class said, "But I can see why they worshiped!" Her heart had been stirred, and for her the message confirmed that He is risen indeed! The two reminded me of the conflict that will surely continue between faith and doubt. It is the same when two Christians experience an answer to prayer. One will thank God and his faith will grow, while the other will observe, "Well, it might have happened anyway!" Someone has said, "True faith learns to look away from the human factors and difficulties, away from the human opinions and impossibilities, and rests securely in the promises and faithfulness of the living God."

That is what we need—strong, growing faith, carefully nurtured so that it will triumph over doubt. We have heard, now may our spiritual eyes behold Him as our Lord and God.

[1] John 20:27.
[2] Matthew 28:17.

❧   ❧   ❧

ACTS 1–3
ACTS 1

> But ye shall receive power, after that the Holy Ghost is
> come upon you: and ye shall be witnesses unto me both
> in Jerusalem, and in all Judaea, and in Samaria, and un-
> to the uttermost part of the earth.[1]

ACTS IS THE STORY of men infused by Christ and enthused
about Him. They became evangelists, tellers of the good
news. Their backgrounds were varied, but each had a similar message on the transforming power of Christ in a life.
They spoke with confidence and determination so that others might know of the Lord's gracious invitation for salvation. They told of forgiveness and hope which He had
made available to those who would trust in Him.

Christ, before He ascended into heaven, bequeathed to
the disciples the power of the Holy Spirit. "The power,
though natural in operation, is supernatural in character."
The Spirit is simply defined as "God in action." The Spirit
is our source of power—power in a person for a purpose.
And the purpose? To enable men and women to truly witness for Christ, to tell about something that really happened.

A prerequisite to having this power is dedication rising
from an earnest desire to share the good news. The Spirit's
power grants new insight into the Word, as the Holy Spirit's
office is to illuminate the Word. This power incites new
desire for prayer. It generates courage, all to the end of
knowing Him better and sharing Him with others.

Mr. F. B. Berry, writing in an article from England, says,
"Are the resources of the Holy Spirit limited? Is He not
infinite? Are not all things possible with God? We have
waited six thousand years for steam and electricity; but
these forces existed even in the Garden of Eden, and might
have been used if we had only known how. We have waited

two thousand years since Christ for the promised conversion of the world. The power to bring it about exists. It is possessed by the Holy Spirit. Shall we have it? Have it now? Or wait another two thousand years, while the world goes on in iniquity and generation after generation pass into Christless eternity?"

This transforming, vibrant power may be ours. It is easy to become more concerned with the eternal destiny of the men eight thousand miles away than the ones working next to us at business. It is easy to plan our outreach for Sunday, and neglect Monday-through-Friday contacts. True, we must express concern for the lost on foreign shores, but let us not neglect those next door. We are all evangelists, called to tell what we have individually experienced, with His power to make the message acceptable and effective.

¹Acts 1:8.

❧   ❧   ❧

November 9

ACTS 4–6
ACTS 4

> Be it known unto you all, and to all the people of Israel, that by the name of Jesus Christ of Nazareth, whom ye crucified, whom God raised from the dead, even by him doth this man stand here before you whole. This is the stone which was set at nought of you builders, which is become the head of the corner. Neither is there salvation in any other: for there is none other name under heaven given among men, whereby we must be saved.¹

How disconcerting the preaching of Peter, John, and the other early Christians must have been to the masses! They were proclaiming that the Messiah, for whom the Jews had been looking for years, had indeed arrived. There must have been discussions on the street corners and raised eyebrows among the priests and rulers. *Surely,* they thought,

*when Messiah comes He will be a leader. He will not suc-
cumb to death, as did this Man of whom the disciples
spoke.* Even when the early Christians were imprisoned,
their message did not change nor become less urgent. Peter's
defense, in today's reading, made the high priest take note.
Peter's boldness was astounding. The priests shook their
heads and, though the apostles were unlearned and ignorant
men, they marveled; and they took knowledge of them, that
they had been with Jesus.[2]

Their message was a resurrection message that firmly
avowed, "Christ lives." They revealed the source of their
faith, and zeal and power flowed as they would say, "We
have not only heard this story; we have seen it and experienced its significance." They would conclude their message
by teaching the listeners how to apply the principles they
had preached. They had personally experienced the pattern: repent, believe, start over, make restitution for wrongs,
don't conform but be transformed by the power of God.

This had happened to Peter himself. At one time he had
publicly repudiated Christ. Since then Peter had himself
become an apologetic for the Christian life through the zeal
and heart change he manifested. A changed life is an unan-
swerable argument for our faith.

We may be as uneducated as the disciples of Christ. Our
backgrounds and experiences vary, but the outside world
will see the difference if we have "been with Jesus." The
radiance and joy that come from being with Him cannot
help but reflect His goodness and plant a seed in the mind
of a nonbeliever which, when watered and cared for, will
reap a harvest. May the reality of knowing Him and experiencing the power of His Word grip our hearts so that
"we cannot but speak the things which we have seen and
heard."[3]

[1]Acts 4:10-12.   [3]Acts 4:20.
[2]Acts 4:13.

❧ ❧ ❧

ACTS 7–8
ACTS 8

> And the angel of the Lord spake unto Philip, saying,
> Arise, and go toward the south unto the way that goeth
> down from Jerusalem unto Gaza, which is desert. And
> he arose and went: and, behold, a man of Ethiopia, an
> eunuch of great authority . . . was returning, and sitting
> in his chariot read Esaias the prophet. Then the Spirit
> said unto Philip, Go near, and join thyself to this chari-
> ot. And Philip ran thither to him . . . and said, Under-
> standest thou what thou readest? And he said, How can
> I, except some man should guide me? And he desired
> Philip that he would come up and sit with him.[1]

PHILIP HAD FINISHED a successful meeting in Samaria, and
now he was suddenly sent to the desert without explanation. Philip did not question God. He was obedient and
went, and on arrival he knew why the mission was planned.

His encounter with the Ethiopian eunuch is well described. Here was a truly hungering soul. In the account,
we find him returning from Jerusalem where he had "worshipped." His deep interest was evidenced in the way he
was absorbed in the Bible. The writings of the Prophet
Isaiah were being devoured.

It is sad to realize that this man was returning from a
literal feast, but had come away starved. Philip came forward and introduced himself with a question. "Understandest thou what thou readest?" The eunuch's reply
made Philip's job clear. "How can I, except some man
should guide me?"

There is no doubt that God could have revealed His
truth to the eunuch, but here, as in many other instances,
He chose a man as His instrument. How wonderful that
God uses men, and how good it was that Philip was prepared to instruct. One must have understanding to believe,
but much more to teach. Philip's subject was Jesus Christ,

the central figure of Isaiah 53, which the man of authority had been reading. And the eunuch understood, saying, "I believe that Jesus Christ is the Son of God."[2] We are told that after the eunuch was baptized, as a confession of his belief in Christ, Philip was caught away. God had another job for him to do.

The following words in the story describe the one who had now found the way: "He went on his way rejoicing."[3] Philip, through the Holy Spirit, had accomplished more than all the religious leaders in Jerusalem. He served the all-powerful God. And this same power is available to us for God's purpose and is to be used so that the simplicity of faith will confound the wisdom of the world. May we be prepared to teach God's Word and to guide in His way because we truly understand, having been taught and led by His Spirit.

[1]Acts 8:26-31.
[2]Acts 8:37.
[3]Acts 8:39.

❧ ❧ ❧

November 11

ACTS 9–11
ACTS 11

> Now they which were scattered abroad upon the persecution that arose about Stephen travelled as far as Phenice, and Cyprus, and Antioch, preaching the word to none but unto the Jews only. And some of them were men of Cyprus and Cyrene, which, when they were come to Antioch, spake unto the Grecians, preaching the Lord Jesus. And the hand of the Lord was with them: and a great number believed, and turned unto the Lord.[1]

FOR MORE THAN TWO YEARS I worked for a wonderful company in their personnel office. When people came to be interviewed, it was not uncommon for me to have to remind them, "This job entails great responsibility." Some were willing to assume it; others would turn away, as the very thought of real concentration was against their way of life.

The book of Acts reemphasizes the tremendous responsibility every Christian is given. It cannot be put on one day and taken off another. It is not something that is for Sunday only. Being a Christian is a twenty-four-hours-a-day, seven-days-a-week job. Paul had a way of expressing it: "But as we were allowed of God to be put in trust with the gospel, even so we speak; not as pleasing men, but God, which trieth our hearts."[2] We have been put in trust—sacred trust —with the gospel. This thought is frightening if we fail to do with it what we are intended by God to do: extend it to others. We are God's means of communicating His message to others—from the heart of God to the heart of man. God has left people like you and me to express His message. It is with fear that I ask myself, "Am I responsible?"

The early Christians bore this responsibility courageously. They were persecuted, but it did not matter. They just spread out. They "scattered abroad . . . preaching the word,"[3] and because of these people the first Gentile church at Antioch came to birth. It was here that Christ's followers were first called Christians, "Christ's ones."

For those of us who may be prone to rely heavily on local pastors to do the job of witnessing, it is well to remember that among the great servants of God mentioned in Hebrews 11, only one pastor is named. The rest were people like us: a farmer, a shipbuilder, a military man—the kind we meet and live with, everyday laymen.

It is a great responsibility to be in the service of the King. It is imperative that we work in His strength, and are open channels, readily available and faithful so as not to break our sacred trust in His employ.

[1] Acts 11:19-21.   [3] Acts 8:4.
[2] I Thessalonians 2:4.

Acts 12–14
Acts 12

But the word of God grew and multiplied.[1]

IN A LITTLE COMMUNITY in northern California, a teen-ager
found Christ. He was not popular in school. His parents
were separated, and life had been quite meaningless until
he picked up a booklet on the street one Sunday afternoon.
Its cover was marked with heel prints, but the question was
still discernible on it: "Where are you going?" The youth
picked it up. He smiled a rather cynical smile and answered
the question audibly. "Nowhere!" The closest place to scan
it was a bus station a few yards away, so he went in and sat
down on a bench. The booklet told the simple, beautiful
story of salvation, and the sixteen-year-old responded to the
closing paragraph which explained the choice available to
man: to accept or reject, to travel the broad way or choose
the narrow path which leads to the celestial city.

The young man's first Bible was borrowed from the library. The first book he read was Acts, though it is not the
usual thing for a brand-new Christian to read. He quickly
became alert to his responsibility as a child of God.

One verse that compelled his attention in the borrowed
Bible was this: "And he said, The God of our fathers hath
chosen thee, that thou shouldest know his will, and see that
Just One, and shouldest hear the voice of his mouth. For
thou shalt be his witness unto all men of what thou hast
seen and heard."[2] He felt this verse was for him, and he
obeyed it.

He returned to school and first told the janitor, a man
who had been his friend in the past. Another day, he told
a sophomore, and then a boy in the band. Another verse
in Acts caused him to think: "I continue unto this day,
witnessing both to small and great."[3] To him "the great"
was the high school principal. He lingered restlessly after

school, but finally obtained the courage to witness to the principal. Much to his surprise he found he was already a Christian. However, the boy's literal interpretation of the Scripture was a challenge to the principal, and he began sharing the Word in a new way.

When this teen-ager did not know what to say for a witness, he would just start out, "Know what happened to me the other day? It was quite tremendous. I picked up a book which asked me a question I could not answer, and I'm wondering if you have thought about it: 'Where are you going?'"

I know there is nothing earthshaking, no headline material, in the above story, unless a changed life and a reason to hope can be counted as such. Yet the fruit of this lad's witness is most encouraging. In time the janitor, the band friend, and several others found Christ through this young man who simply learned in a natural way to tell what had supernaturally taken place within himself. "And the word of God grew and multiplied!"

[1]Acts 12:24.
[2]Acts 22:14-15.
[3]Acts 26:22.

❧ ❧ ❧

ACTS 15–17
ACTS 16

> Now when they had gone throughout Phrygia and the region of Galatia, and were forbidden by the Holy Ghost to preach the word in Asia, after they were come to Mysia, they assayed to go into Bithynia: but the Spirit suffered them not. And they passing by Mysia came down to Troas. And a vision appeared to Paul in the night; There stood a man of Macedonia, and prayed him, saying, Come over into Macedonia, and help us.[1]

TO THE CASUAL READER, our scripture may seem like a Biblical geography lesson, but there is much more in it than that. Here we have the Holy Spirit's guidance in a man's life, showing him where to go and where not to go. Did you ever stop to think that if they had been disobedient and had gone east rather than west, the story of the church today might be radically different? Possibly we might be in darkness, steeped in paganism and idolatry, while China, India, and Japan might be the so-called Christian nations.

The Apostle Paul had made plans. He was eager to visit some of the churches he had helped establish. Oh, how easy it is for us to do just that. To plan our lives, to chart our goings and comings, and set forth in determination to fulfill them. Sometimes we can mistake our own determination for the purpose of God. Paul wanted to preach in Asia, but he was detoured, then prevented from entering Bithynia and Mysia. Then he found himself in Troas, almost backed in a corner! Yet it was in Troas, not the previous places, that he had a vision. God speaks when we are where we ought to be. Everything came into focus, and Paul saw the unfolding plan of God. From Troas he had a clear view out into the world that was lost. His perspective changed and his outreach was astounding.

I recall visiting with a shut-in who had real plans for her

life. She was a Christian and loved the Lord. Her plans were well established but determined as they were, they were never fulfilled. She fought for what she wanted, and longed to serve the Lord in the big city from her wheelchair. Then she was forced into a personal Troas. It was a little country town without even a stoplight! Everything in her nature rebelled. She thought of Jacob in days of old, and uttered his cry, "Everything is against me." However, God had better plans than hers. The unfamiliar small town and difficult circumstances became for her, at last, a tower of observation. She accepted the call "Come over and help us" from the farms and unincorporated villages.

How well these verses illustrate that when the man of God accepts the plan of God, the call of God is real. Then the cry of Jacob is erased from the mind, and one rejoices with Paul that "all things work together for good to them that love God, to them who are the called according to his purpose."[2]

[1]Acts 16:6-9.
[2]Romans 8:28.

❧ ❧ ❧

ACTS 18–21
ACTS 20

> I kept back nothing that was profitable unto you, but
> have shewed you, and have taught you publickly, and
> from house to house, testifying both to the Jews, and
> also to the Greeks, repentance toward God, and faith
> toward our Lord Jesus Christ.[1]

IF IN YOUR BIBLE STUDY you find a few spare minutes, you
will find it interesting to think of the various degrees of
faith. In Scripture there are many, with varied descriptions. We read about those with "great faith," and those
with "small faith." We have accounts of "strong faith" and
"weak faith." Two young men, Stephen and Barnabas,
were described as being "full of faith."

In a man-on-the-street interview, I believe we would find
the majority of people saying that they possess faith, though
their descriptions of their faith and its degree would greatly vary. Just the other day I chatted with a sales representative who said, "I have lots of faith in lots of things."
It was a provocative though bland statement.

I have faith too, in a lot of things. Faith that when I sit
down to breakfast the fruit juice will be wholesome and
not poisonous, that the chair on which I sit is stable, that
the air I am breathing is fairly pure. This is faith, but not
the kind that has eternal value. Many say they have faith
but it is important to consider the object of their faith.
Faith may be in yourself, or in an employer or friend. However, human beings cannot always be trusted. We are
plainly told "it is better to trust in the Lord than to put
confidence in man."[2]

Real faith, a Christian's faith, takes God at His word.
Paul reveals the object of his faith: "faith toward our Lord
Jesus Christ." This is what counts. He is the One who re-
mains trustworthy when all else fails.

In establishing the real Object of spiritual faith, the degrees of faith may be analyzed.

Is your faith small? It can enlarge as will your heart, if you grant it opportunity.

Is it weak? It will gain strength as you use it in battle and experience it.

Is it strong? Thank God, but remember, if it is not properly exercised, it will not remain strong.

"Without faith it is impossible to please him."[3] God honors faith, the faith that we steadfastly place in Him, both for salvation and sustenance.

May He remain at the center of our lives, the true Object of faith for each believer, "our Lord Jesus Christ."

[1]Acts 20:20-21.
[2]Psalm 118:8.
[3]Hebrews 11:6.

🍀　🍀　🍀

November 15

ACTS 22–25
ACTS 22

> Then the chief captain came, and said unto him, Tell me, art thou a Roman? He said, Yea. And the chief captain answered, With a great sum obtained I this freedom. And Paul said, But I was free born.[1]

TO UNDERSTAND the conversation of Paul and the chief captain, it is well to recall a bit of history. During the time of Claudius' reign, Roman citizenship was often bought, the price being exceeedingly high. It is evident the captain had given much for the privilege of citizenship. Paul had been born a Roman citizen. He had not purchased nor worked for it.

This brings to mind the story of some refugees who came to America from Iron Curtain countries. On the day their long-awaited ambition to be United States citizens was confirmed, they made a statement to friends that anyone freeborn could not appreciate what they had gone through. The friends took the time to recount the cost of United States citizenship. They reviewed for the refugees the story of those who forced the Magna Charta on King John. They talked of the Huguenots, the Quakers, the signers of the Declaration of Independence, and those who survived Valley Forge. Both families saw anew the great price of freedom and liberty, and recognized what was needed to be free.

The captain and Paul were discussing Roman citizenship, but think for a moment of our Christian citizenship. We would profit from quoting these words as a spiritual challenge: "With a great sum obtained I this freedom." The cost to God of making freedom in Christ available was great. It cost Him His Son. Because He could never put a price on such a freedom He made it obtainable as a free gift. "If the Son therefore shall make you free, ye shall be free indeed."[2]

After the refugees had obtained their United States citizenship, they had to maintain it. The same is true for a Christian. Obtaining is the start, maintaining must follow. The price of liberty cannot be assured by the payment of an occasional premium, nor can ours, in Christ, by a few dollars here and there. The Bible says, "Study—learn—work," to keep the freedom.

The oldest of the refugees wrote back to her homeland, "Oh, if you but knew this freedom—if only it could be extended across the ocean!" She was sharing with others her joy. Our freedom in Christ can be "extended" across the street, throughout the city, and into the world. It takes sacrifice, but it is only as we maintain and extend that we appreciate what we have obtained through Jesus Christ: liberty which sets us free indeed.

[1]Acts 22:27-28.   [2]John 8:36.

❧ ❧ ❧

ACTS 26–28
ACTS 26

> To open their eyes, and to turn them from darkness to
> light, and from the power of Satan unto God, that they
> may receive forgiveness of sins, and inheritance among
> them which are sanctified by faith that is in me.[1]

I WAS GIVEN a little booklet outlining five ways to make a
sure sale. These instructions were so simple I pondered
their worth. The first was "Make a good introduction," the
second, "Tell the good points," next, "Eliminate doubt by
sharing misconceptions you may have had," fourth, "Tell
the results," and last, "Make your appeal."

The same evening I was reading the last chapters of Acts,
and I began to think about Paul's defense before King
Agrippa. It was very much a sales talk as he made his appeal—an appeal for acceptance of the most important gift.
There is much a Christian can learn from it.

Paul made a gracious introduction. He sincerely compli-
mented Agrippa on his background, recalling his great
grandfather, Herod the Great, and his knowledge of the
Jewish religion, and saying how glad he was to see him and
to know he was in charge of the case. It was a point of common interest. Many Christians fail in their witness for
Christ because they never find a point of mutual discussion.
It is important that we consider many introductions by
which we can bring people to the place of wanting to discuss the Lord.

Second, Paul told about his background and good qualifications, and established himself as worthy to be listened
to. A Christian may often relate how he has searched to find
truth, and thus identify himself with the seeking one. This
helps to eliminate doubt by sharing misconceptions you
have had. Paul did this in verses nine through eleven,

much as a salesman eliminates doubts by honestly mentioning specific drawbacks which he himself has found.

I like the fourth point: "Tell the results." Paul told of a changed life, and those who listened could not dispute the fact. The effects of being born again are immeasurable and no one can discount a changed life.

The last point is where Christians often lose out, or decide to wait for a more convenient time. "Make the appeal." It is as simple as a salesman saying, "Will you buy my product?" or as Paul asking, "Believest thou the prophets?"

May we study to show ourselves not just approved to men but to our God!

[1]Acts 26:18.

❧ ❧ ❧

ROMANS 1–3
ROMANS 1

> I am not ashamed of the gospel of Christ: for it is the
> power of God unto salvation to every one that be-
> lieveth.[1]

A SMALL MIDWESTERN TOWN's newspaper carried the story of
a well-respected judge who had faithfully interpreted the
law for over a decade. One day in court he faced a convicted criminal while the town awaited the sentence. What
an uproar resulted when he pronounced the man free! "An
outrage of justice," the newspaper headlined. "The judge
committed to upholding the law has broken it."

Romans is the story of what man is, compared with what
he ought to be. Every man is convicted in God's sight, but
we can be thankful that He is a true judge who can set
guilty men free without breaking His own law. He then
teaches man the way he should live.

I read of a convicted murderer who found Christ and
one day, through a series of unforeseen circumstances, he
was pardoned and set completely free. A magazine carried
a picture of the act of mercy by the President of the United
States. Do you think that man was ever ashamed of that
president, or of the proclamation which set him free? Never!

We were born in sin and under its power and condemnation. "As it is written, There is none righteous, no, not
one."[2] But God, through His redemptive power, made forgiveness possible. He paid for our sins by giving His Son.
A Christian is one who has accepted Christ's pardon. Dare
we be ashamed of the One who has set us free, or of His
proclamation, the Bible?

What is there about the gospel that could make us
ashamed? It tells of the Creator of the world and of His
way of justifying a man who has been condemned. It be-
queaths us eternal life with "an inheritance incorruptible,

and undefiled, and that fadeth not away, reserved in heaven for you."[3] The gospel is God's instrument of salvation.

When you feel hesitant to speak the name of Christ, think of Paul, and of his pondering to go to Rome. If I had been in his place, I fear I would have said, "Lord, any place but Rome!" The atmosphere of Rome reeked with wealth and prejudice. The leaders definitely frowned on this group of believers as offensive to Rome, but Paul's sin had been pardoned, and this pardon was his passport, in his thinking, to tell the world, rich or poor, bond or free, of his Redeemer. He agreed with the Psalmist: "I will speak of thy testimonies also before kings, and will not be ashamed."[4] Let not the rich be ashamed with "the unsearchable riches of Christ,"[5] nor the poor: "Let the brother of low degree rejoice in that he is exalted."[6] Let not the educated be ashamed of the gospel, for it unfolds the "manifold wisdom of God,"[7] nor the unlearned, for the gospel is "able to make thee wise unto salvation."[8]

As heirs of God and joint-heirs with Christ, we have no right to be ashamed of the gospel; nor can we afford to let the God of the gospel be ashamed of us.

[1]Romans 1:16.
[2]Romans 3:10.
[3]I Peter 1:4.
[4]Psalm 119:46.
[5]Ephesians 3:8.
[6]James 1:9.
[7]Ephesians 3:10.
[8]II Timothy 3:15.

❧   ❧   ❧

ROMANS 4–6
ROMANS 5

> Therefore being justified by faith, we have peace with
> God through our Lord Jesus Christ: by whom also we
> have access by faith into this grace wherein we stand,
> and rejoice in hope of the glory of God.[1]

As WE READ of the believer's benefits through justifying
faith, we join the Psalmist in grateful praise: "Bless the
Lord, O my soul, and forget not all his benefits."[2] We start
with our justification by faith alone. It is sometimes explained by the illustration of the man who goes broke. He
must not only have all his obligations paid for him, but he
needs something with which he can start again. Justification does just that. It gives us the needed resources to begin again.

Peace! This is not just peace of mind, but real peace
between God and ourselves. Sin within us causes lack of
peace. I remember visiting a hospital in Washington where
a great amount of construction was taking place. There
were derricks, earthmoving equipment, cement mixers, and
all sorts of noise and confusion. The administrator took
me out back for a picture of peace I shall never forget.
There, within just a few feet of the blasting and building,
was a mother duck, sitting on her eggs, looking quite unconcerned! The giant mixer was pouring no more than
three feet from the nest. However, through the years, the
lovely garden of the hospital had been her calm nesting
place. No one had harmed her, so why should the sudden
confusion cause her to fear? That is peace.

Hope! We can rejoice in hope. Think of those who are
without God and without hope. To have something for
which to hope is a blessing. "Hope maketh not ashamed;
because the love of God is shed abroad in our hearts by the
Holy Ghost which is given unto us."[3]

Love! Knowing the Lord is the richest experience in true love. He loved us enough to die for us. Herein is love.

Reconciliation! There was a gap between God and man until Christ provided a way to bring us into right standing with the Father. Reconciliation is part of salvation and makes possible life and joy in God.

Start with faith, and climb the staircase of the glorious benefits which are ours in Christ, and your heart will be responsive to Him who made it all possible.

[1]Romans 5:1-2.
[2]Psalm 103:2.
[3]Romans 5:5.

❧ ❧ ❧

November 19

ROMANS 7–9
ROMANS 8

> And we know that all things work together for good to them that love God, to them who are the called according to his purpose. He that spared not his own Son, but delivered him up for us all, how shall he not with him also freely give us all things?[1]

THE PROMISE "All things work together for good" is contingent on one simple suitable fact, that we love God. How well the Father provided for us! He knew the reassurance we would need that all things *do* work together for our good. To provide the "all things" it is well for us to remember that "he spared not his own Son."

How often, even in my lifetime, I have experienced the "all things." Some are hard to understand, and some are difficult to share, yet time has proved that God's Father-heart was working on my behalf, though at the time I was not certain.

Two couples were in a funeral home. The first couple were faithful church members, the other couple were completely cold toward any faith. The Christians were making funeral arrangements for their three-year-old daughter. Sudden death is a blow, yet together they radiated the peace which passeth understanding, knowing that death to the believer is not final and that their little one was in heaven. In the days that followed, the incident transformed their lives, and they both admitted, husband and wife, that "all things work together for good." The second couple, who had just lost a son, were unable to cope with death. They could not rise above its sting. So noticeable was the peaceful attitude of the Christian couple compared with the despair of the non-Christians, that the director of the mortuary called the Christians, and in time made a profession for Christ.

The "all things" can be little things or big things. There is no difference, for if we love God, if we are called according to His purpose, "all things work together for good." Read it, practice it, let it grip your soul, so that you never doubt its certainty. This is one of the believer's greatest encouragements. We have supernatural assistance along our natural path of life.

Like the children of Israel, we are so prone to murmur. We become impatient, so willful and disobedient. We want that visible pillar of fire or cloud to show us He is present, when day by day we experience His presence but will not acknowledge it. In eternity, we will thank Him for the "all things," when His purpose has been fulfilled. Child of God, why wait until then? Today you may accept His promise in advance, that truly "all things"—past, present, and future —will "work together for good."

[1]Romans 8:28, 32.

❧ ❧ ❧

ROMANS 10–12
ROMANS 12

> I beseech you therefore, brethren, by the mercies of God,
> that ye present your bodies a living sacrifice, holy, ac-
> ceptable unto God, which is your reasonable service.
> And be not conformed to this world: but be ye trans-
> formed by the renewing of your mind, that ye may
> prove what is that good, and acceptable, and perfect,
> will of God.[1]

IT IS INTERESTING TO NOTE Paul's use of the word *therefore*.
It often reoccurs with the same meaning throughout the
New Testament. In the first eleven chapters of Romans
Paul was describing just what Christianity is, what effect it
should have on men, and what God has done for men.
Someone has referred to this section as "eleven chapters of
straight theology." Then in chapter 12 Paul gives us some
Christian characteristics such as genuine love and brotherly
affection, which result in blessing those who persecute us,
living in harmony, and repaying good for evil. "In other
words," Paul says, "the doctrine I have given you must result in holy living. You have heard what God has done;
therefore be transformed."

Again in Ephesians we find the word *therefore*. The first
three chapters tell of Christ's work on the cross. Chapter 4
begins, "I therefore, the prisoner of the Lord, beseech you
that ye walk worthy." Again he is saying, "Because of
what Christ has done, *therefore* you should do as the Scriptures teach."

If you are ever in doubt as to what the Lord's will is for
you, think back over what He has done for you. Recall the
story of the Cross. Think through His many promises and
His goodness, and I believe you will be faced with a "therefore." So often our own selfish will is so superimposed on
our lives that we crowd out God's claim to us. In remem-

bering that He made us and purchased us, we begin to forget self and ambition, and humbly say, "Therefore, 'not my will, but thine be done.' "[2]

Paul is descriptive in explaining the will of God. First, it is "good." We may not always see it to be such, but by doing it we will prove the truth of David's admonition: "O taste and see that the Lord is good."[3] Then God's will is described as "acceptable." Let us be honest. Some things are so much more acceptable than others! We must learn to accept the pleasant and unpleasant, for then only His will becomes acceptable, not just by assent but by consent. God's will is "perfect." We can accept His will to be such because we realize His perfection. He never makes a wrong decision. Because of what He has done, and will do, therefore will I take His will to be good, acceptable, and perfect. I will steadfastly say, "I delight to do thy will, oh my God: yea, thy law is within my heart."[4]

[1]Romans 12:1-2.　　　[3]Psalm 34:8.
[2]Luke 22:42.　　　　 [4]Psalm 40:8.

❧　❧　❧

November 21

ROMANS 13–16
ROMANS 16

> For your obedience is come abroad unto all men. I am glad therefore on your behalf: but yet I would have you wise unto that which is good, and simple concerning evil.[1]

THE WORD *simple* in our common usage may be misunderstood. We must realize what the term "simple" meant when the Bible was translated in 1611. Then the term meant many things, all of them pleasant. In those days a "simple" person was straightforward, innocent, harmless, and honest. It was an honor to be called a simple person.

In today's verse Paul is saying to us, as he was to the Romans of his day, "Be wise unto that which is good, and simple concerning evil." He prayed that those to whom he was writing would be discerning as to what was good, and able to distinguish between good and bad doctrine. This meant that they must avoid even the appearance of evil, and not be gullible where evil was concerned. Because times have changed and words take on different meanings, it may help us to look at a more modern translation to understand Paul's concern for good and evil. In the Phillips paraphrase we read, "I want to see you experts in good, and not even beginners in evil." Could anything be more clear? What an honor to be called an "expert" in good. The Psalmist prayed, "Teach me good judgment and knowledge."[2] In Proverbs we are reminded that "a good word maketh it [the heart] glad," and "a good name is rather to be chosen than great riches."[3] We have much to learn to become expert in good.

Paul said, "I don't want you to become 'even beginners in evil.' " The consequences of evil are well defined, yet even Christians can stumble onto its ways. The Bible boldly pictures the heart thus: "For out of the heart proceed evil thoughts."[4] "Men loved darkness rather than light, because their deeds were evil."[5] Back in Genesis, in the beginning, we have awesome words: "And God saw that the wickedness of man was great in the earth . . . and it grieved him at his heart."[6]

Paul knew that sin grieved the Lord, thus he yearned that the Christians would be "wise unto that which is good, and simple concerning evil." Translate it as you wish, but let us seek discerning hearts regarding right and wrong, and work to do good, as we pray, "Deliver us from evil."[7]

[1]Romans 16:19.
[2]Psalm 119:66.
[3]Proverbs 12:35; 22:1.
[4]Matthew 15:19.
[5]John 3:19.
[6]Genesis 6:5-6.
[7]Matthew 6:13.

🍀 🍀 🍀

I Corinthians 1–4
I Corinthians 1

> For Christ sent me not to baptize, but to preach the
> gospel: not with wisdom of words, lest the cross of
> Christ should be made of none effect. For the preach-
> ing of the cross is to them that perish foolishness; but
> unto us which are saved it is the power of God.[1]

THE CROSS and its power are very meaningful to us Christians. We sing, "In the Cross of Christ I Glory" and other
beloved hymns. Yet there is a query as to just how the Cross
affects us in our daily walk with Him.

As I listened to the radio one day, a phrase from a sermon lingered with me: "power in a person for a purpose."
In recalling these verses, I wondered just what effect the
power of the Cross was having on my daily walk. The Cross
is the source of power. For the unbeliever, it is first the
power of God to salvation: "having made peace through the
blood of his cross."[2] It takes this power to transform a man
into a new creation. The Apostle Paul had experienced
this divine transformation. He who had persecuted Christians and taken great delight in ridiculing their faith; he
who thought at one time that the preaching of the Cross
was foolishness, had now experienced this power of God
personally.

This power in a person is for salvation, but it is also for
daily cleansing. "If we walk in the light, as he is in the
light, we have fellowship one with another, and the blood
of Jesus Christ his Son cleanseth us from all sin."[3] The
power of the Cross shows God's authority and right. "All
power is given unto me in heaven and earth."[4]

"Power in a person for a purpose." For what purpose, if
any, is a Christian to use this power? It is clearly indicated:
"Whereof I was made a minister, according to the gift of
the grace of God given unto me by the effectual working of

his power."[5] Surely we can clearly see that the purpose of the power of Christ's Cross is His service.

> Power in my person I ask anew today;
> Infilling, transforming, even as I pray.
> May the Cross resume its place
> As I look into Thy face,
> And Thy purpose be my purpose
> Now and every day.

[1] I Corinthians 1:17-18.
[2] Colossians 1:20.
[3] I John 1:7.
[4] Matthew 28:18.
[5] Ephesians 3:7.

       ❧   ❧   ❧

November 23

I CORINTHIANS 5–7
I CORINTHIANS 6

> Know ye not that your body is the temple of the Holy Ghost which is in you, which ye have of God, and ye are not your own? For ye are bought with a price: therefore glorify God in your body, and in your spirit, which are God's.[1]

TWO DEAR MISSIONARIES had served together on a dark continent. The years that had marked their service together were not easy and in their eyes the work appeared unfruitful. Eleven years had passed without a furlough because there were no replacements available. It is not surprising that one began to murmur somewhat and question God. To begin with, it was only a little doubt, now and then, and a few question marks. But "the beginning of doubt is the end of faith." Worry and doubt prevent the deep thought and meditation required by the Christian; they also hinder prayer, therefore are most dishonoring to our heavenly Father.

During those days of trying circumstances, the other missionary held fast. She clung to the verses that told her she was not her own but was bought with a price. She determined to glorify God. When the food supply ran low because of a shipping mix-up, she read again of Elijah and remembered the ravens which had fed him. Her body was a temple of the Holy Ghost, and she was certain that she and her companion would not be denied. The God of Elijah is also the God of those who trust Him today.

The months passed and the two went about their duties quite differently, one with a heavy heart, the other with a light heart; one depressed, the other encouraged in the Lord.

One day a package arrived containing some used books from home. One was about John Wesley. Amid the doubt and depression the fearful missionary was reading the book. One quotation rang in her heart. John Wesley had said, "I would as soon swear as fret." To the conservative missionary it was quite shocking. She was shaken. Then she began to think about the Lord, and of His provision in the past, His promises, and His protection. She thought of her friend who was carrying the burden for both, and she recognized her fretting was dishonoring and displeasing to the Lord. She confessed it to Him and, realizing that the temple within was cleansed, she set about her work again with new spirit and zest.

I can see myself at times in both of these people for, like a weather vane, we swing in one direction and then the other. Why should we not level off to a consistent, Christian walk? Our future is in God's hands. We should not worry but walk with Him day by day in obedient trust. Fulfill your part as a purchased one, knowing the Spirit is within, and your life is God-planned and God-sustained.

[1] I Corinthians 6:19-20.

❧ ❧ ❧

I Corinthians 8–10
I Corinthians 9

> For though I be free from all men, yet have I made
> myself servant unto all, that I might gain the more.
> . . . I am made all things to all men, that I might by all
> means save some. And this I do for the gospel's sake,
> that I might be partaker thereof with you.[1]

MANY TIMES, especially at a Bible conference or an evangelistic meeting, you will hear the question asked of a well-
known Christian, "What is your secret of winning so many
for Christ?" There are many answers. One was a challenge
to me, and as I have passed it on, others have testified to
blessing from it. It was original with Paul! "I am become
all things to all men, that I might by all means save some."
Paul's very life illustrated his passion to win men. As one
person testified, "For Paul, being a witness to Jesus Christ
was essential, other things were just important!" To fulfill
what he called a "universal obligation" he was weak to the
weak, Jew to the Jew, a man of rejoicing to those who rejoiced; but he also shed tears with those who wept. Think
of how Christ identified Himself with those to whom He
witnessed.

Remember Nicodemus, a ruler of the Jews? Christ knew
him and his intellectual need, and this was important; but
his spiritual need was basic. "Nicodemus, 'ye must be born
again.' "[2] Christ mingled with the publicans and sinners,
but He also spent time in the home of Mary and Martha.
He took time for blind Bartimaeus and rich Zacchaeus.
His heart of compassion reached to the thief on the cross as
He promised he would be with Him in Paradise.

I do not know what your circumstances are. Possibly
your life revolves around a city block or a great factory.
Others have much leisure time and considerable contact

with scores of people. Yet all have opportunity to be all things to win some.

In Spokane, Washington, I heard the testimony of a man who recently retired from selling vegetables at a large market. To the rich who bought, he had a special way of presenting the gospel with intellect which was God-given. To the poor, he would use himself as an illustration, pointing them with great simplicity to an understanding of Christ and His message. To the management, he first sought to be a good employee, and that made him eligible to be a witness. To the baggers he was a friend so that he could share His true Friend. "All things to all men"—and many were won! May this rich experience be ours, "for the gospel's sake."

[1] I Corinthians 9:19, 22-23.
[2] John 3:7.

❦ ❦ ❦

November 25

I Corinthians 11–13
I Corinthians 13

LOVE is the distinguishing feature of the Christian life. Many religions stress sacrifice but put little emphasis on love. It takes the love of God in a man's heart to make him a Christian. John wrote, "He that loveth not knoweth not God; for God is love."[1] Love helps us to see the good in the bad, it makes us willing to forgive and forget, it gives victory over bitterness, resentment, and jealousy.

Perfect love comes only through a life of daily surrender and faith. In chapter 12 Paul is speaking of other gifts, and he introduces today's reading with these words: "But you must earnestly continue to cultivate your higher spiritual gifts. And yet I will show you a way that is better by far."[2] Let this "better way" permeate your life in the realization that if God so loved us, we ought also to love one another."[3]

The Charles B. Williams Translation of the New Testament gives us the poem on love as follows:

> If I could speak the languages of men, of angels too,
> And have no love,
> I am only a rattling pan or a clashing cymbal.
> If I should have the gift of prophecy,
> And know all secret truths, and knowledge in its every form,
> And have such perfect faith that I could move mountains,
> But have no love, I am nothing.
> If I should dole out everything I have for charity,
> And give my body up to torture in mere boasting pride,
> But have no love, I get from it no good at all.
> Love is so patient and so kind;
> Love never boils with jealousy;
> It never boasts, is never puffed with pride;
> It does not act with rudeness, or insist upon its rights;
> It never gets provoked, it never harbors evil thoughts;
> Is never glad when wrong is done,
> But always glad when truth prevails;
> It bears up under anything,
> It exercises faith in everything,
> It keeps up hope in everything,
> It gives us power to endure in anything.
> Love never fails;
>
> .   .   .   .
>
> And so these three, faith, hope, and love, endure,
> But the greatest of them is love.[4]

[1] I John 4:8.
[2] I Corinthians 12:31, Charles B. Williams Translation.
[3] I John 4:11.
[4] I Corinthians 13:1-8, 13, Charles B. Williams Translation.

❧   ❧   ❧

I Corinthians 14–16
I Corinthians 15

> For I am the least of the apostles, that am not meet to
> be called an apostle, because I persecuted the church of
> God. But by the grace of God I am what I am; and his
> grace which was bestowed upon me was not in vain;
> but I laboured more abundantly than they all: yet not I,
> but the grace of God which was with me.[1]

THE APOSTLE PAUL found it important to identify himself
with the Corinthian Christians. In doing so he made a
statement which was a combination of self-reproach and
self-esteem: "I am what I am." It may seem we are taking
these few words out of context, yet here is a message, simple
and clear, for Christians.

"I am what I am." How important it is for a Christian
to see himself as he actually is. Paul believed himself to be
"the least of the apostles." In another of his books, Paul
warns a man "not to think of himself more highly than he
ought to think."[2]

There is danger in too much introspection, and many
have the tendency to belittle themselves beyond reason; yet
it is vital to make an honest evaluation. Just what are we?
Where do we stand? A wise person asked, "What have you
done with what you have and what you are?" Will you settle down and be content to be just what you are? No matter what our background may be, our culture, our previous
mistakes or problems, we can each be better, and we can
better utilize our talents and abilities for Him.

It is important to see ourselves as we are, and to strive
to improve, but it is even more important to see ourselves
with the plus factor, the added measure of the grace of God.
His grace truly is unmerited favor, and Paul well knew this
in writing, "I am what I am—by the grace of God." Never

think Paul had a high opinion of himself. He knew it was only because of the grace of God that he was what he was.

A desire to "be something for Christ" is the starting point. He then adds His grace, His strength, His power—and things begin to happen. Being someone for Christ has nothing to do with your social or economic background, as some would choose to believe. Becoming something for God requires a combination of our will and His making. It is illustrated in the Apostle Peter. Here was a man who had little background or culture, according to today's standards, but he met Christ and turned his life over to Him. The result: "Thou art Simon . . . thou shalt be called Cephas."[3] In other words, "I will make you something better."

William James put it like this: "We and God have business with each other; and in opening ourselves to His influence, our deepest destiny is fulfilled. It is not what we have or what we can do, but what we are receptive to that really counts."

"I am what I am." But are we what we ought to be? "God is able to make all grace abound toward you; that ye . . . may abound to every good work!"[4]

[1] I Corinthians 15:9-10.
[2] Romans 12:3.
[3] John 1:42.
[4] II Corinthians 9:8.

❧　❧　❧

II CORINTHIANS 1–4
II CORINTHIANS 3

> Ye are our epistle written in our hearts, known and read
> of all men. But we all, with open face beholding as in
> a glass the glory of the Lord, are changed into the same
> image from glory to glory, even as by the Spirit of the
> Lord.[1]

"THE BEAUTY OF HOLINESS" is a phrase often used to refer
to the Puritan Christians. The expression occurs frequently in their writings. Today we do not often hear about
holiness without someone expressing fear of the experience.
Yet "the beauty of holiness" is a soul beauty which should
characterize each child of God. It is simply and specifically
the beauty of Christ in us. If, as Paul writes, we who are
believers are "known and read of all men," is it not essential that our day-by-day walk radiate the winsomeness of
true holiness?

A present-day saint of the Lord was once described by
a close associate as "possessing the beauty of thought, word,
and deed." Beauty of thought, because her very thought
processes were centered about Christ. She took literally
the words of Paul when he urged the Philippians, "Whatsoever things are lovely, . . . think on these things."[2] Her
words were gracious, and even unbelievers took note of
this woman. One cannot but be reminded of our Lord, of
whom it was said that the multitude "wondered at the
gracious words which proceeded out of his mouth."[3] Even
the unbelievers proclaimed, "Never a man spake like this
man."[4]

This lady's actions portrayed "the beauty of holiness"
too. We have long known that actions are much more effective than words, but we, as followers of Christ, those "known
and read of man," must think of our actions as "the gospel
according to us!"

The growth of this spiritual grace comes through prayer and Bible study. The Scriptures clearly teach that "strength and beauty are in his sanctuary."[5] For some, spiritual grace comes through intense suffering and persecution. As a Puritan wrote, "Holiness is a healthy root producing healthy fruit from healthy soil." The more we look at our Saviour, the more we resemble Him, and the more we reflect Him, the more we are like Him, "with open face beholding as in a glass the glory of the Lord."

May God continue to work in each of our lives until each possesses "the beauty of holiness" for His glory.

[1] II Corinthians 3:2, 18.
[2] Philippians 4:8.
[3] Luke 4:22.
[4] John 7:46.
[5] Psalm 96:6.

❧   ❧   ❧

November 28

II Corinthians 5–7
II Corinthians 5

> For the love of Christ constraineth us; because we thus judge, that if one died for all, then were all dead: and that he died for all, that they which live should not henceforth live unto themselves, but unto him which died for them, and rose again. Now then we are ambassadors for Christ, as though God did beseech you by us: we pray you in Christ's stead, be ye reconciled to God.[1]

WHILE VISITING mission stations in South America, I heard a common greeting among the people in Colombia, which seemed to me most unusual and rather amusing. Rather than the expected "How are you?" the natives ask, "What have you done?" To one not accustomed to the salutation, it came as a shock. I had to stifle the rejoinder that what

I had done was strictly my own business. However, the usual reply is quite disarming: "Nothing worthwhile."

If the love of Christ truly constrains us, we shall stand with great joy before the presence of Christ some day to answer His question, "What have you done?" Unfortunately, if we have not taken our ambassadorship seriously, our lack of works will speak for itself in a resounding "Nothing worthwhile."

If for a moment we can indulge in what one theologian calls "sanctified scripturalizing," it might not be imprudent to imagine the Apostle Paul had spent some time deliberately considering in his mind before writing his statement in today's reading. "Because we thus judge, that if one died for all, then were all dead: and that he died for all, that they which live should not henceforth live unto themselves, but unto him which died for them, and rose again." To Paul there was but one conclusion: He who did this for us demands our full attention and devotion as Christians. It could be no other way. To Paul the opinions of the critics of his day were of no consequence. He was constrained by the love of Christ and by what Christ had accomplished for him on the cross.

Dear reader, it may do you good to ponder carefully what Christ has done for you. If you stood before Him today and He asked, after all He has accomplished for you, "What have you done?" only you could honestly evaluate what He already knows, whether your answer would be "Nothing" or "Something worthwhile." May there be no question as to what He demands: our devotion and loving service—something worthwhile.

[1]II Corinthians 5:14-15, 20.

🍀 🍀 🍀

II Corinthians 8–10
II Corinthians 8:9; 9:8

> For ye know the grace of our Lord Jesus Christ, that, though he was rich, yet for your sakes he became poor, that ye through his poverty might be rich. And God is able to make all grace abound toward you; that ye, always having all sufficiency in all things, may abound to every good work.[1]

"God's grace is like an ocean at full tide."[2] It is limitless and knows no bounds! Some seek to define grace: "unmerited favor," "mercy," "kindness." Another penned it like this: "Grace is God setting aside what man seeks to do of and for himself. God does it; and under grace God continues to do it."[3] Grace is available to you. "Therefore being justified by faith, we have peace with God through our Lord Jesus Christ: by whom also we have access by faith into this grace."[4]

Justification by faith alone is essential first. Peace then quickly follows, and grace is the sequel. Paul stressed grace and often ended his writings with the familiar words "The grace of our Lord Jesus Christ be with you." Recognizing this grace makes the nearness and dearness of our Lord real to us. Our affection for Him grows and we become more intimately acquainted with Him.

It is a growing knowledge of grace that the believer needs. "God is able to make all grace abound toward you." No need of ours is too great for His supply. He has promised to do "exceeding abundantly above all that we ask or think."[5] Too many of us live in spiritual poverty. We know we have received His gift of faith, but too often we rely instead on our own resources. How foolish, when the reservoir of grace is infinite and available!

Is there a physical problem, a temporal problem, or a difficult circumstance with which you have been wrestling alone? Admit your helplessness in full confession and rely on Him who promised, "My grace is sufficient for thee: for my strength is made perfect in weakness."[6]

In a country where food and the necessities of life were in short supply, a native Christian remarked triumphantly to her pastor, "Aren't you glad we know about something of which there is more than enough?" The two were discussing grace, and reveling in its abundance! Truly, there is "more than enough" for you too.

[1]II Corinthians 8:9; 9:8.
[2] F. B. Meyer.
[3]Norman B. Harrison.
[4]Romans 5:1-2.
[5]Ephesians 3:20.
[6]II Corinthians 12:9.

❧ ❧ ❧

November 30

II CORINTHIANS 11–13
II CORINTHIANS 11:22-23

> In weariness and painfulness, in watchings often, in hunger and thirst, in fastings often, in cold and nakedness. Beside those things that are without, that which cometh upon me daily, the care of all the churches. If I must needs glory, I will glory of the things which concern mine infirmities. He that glorieth, let him glory in the Lord.[1]

THE PRESIDENT of an Eastern university lay desperately ill. Pain racked his body and there was little prospect of relief. The man's son was deeply moved as he sat by his father's bedside. After a time he spoke. "Father, would to God I could take some of your pain in my body." The reply came from a truly great Christian. "I haven't a pain to spare!"

Surely the Apostle Paul is a biblical example of a man who suffered. We know he was persecuted, beaten, and stoned. Yet it was not in those things that he gloried. He unequivocally gloried in the Lord, and would have been quick to admit, "I haven't a pain to spare."

We are not exempt from suffering. Possibly we will not be called upon to bear the brands of suffering for Christ that the Apostle did, yet the Scriptures teach, "Yea, and all that will live godly in Christ Jesus shall suffer . . ."[2] "Unto you it is given in the behalf of Christ, not only to believe on him, but also to suffer for his sake."[3]

Suffering is a school where the secrets of strength are learned. It is here that Christ becomes manifest to us in ways we have not heretofore experienced. The Bible clearly speaks, and we have new understanding: "Though he were a Son, yet learned he obedience by the things which he suffered."[4]

Deeper understanding of any aspect of our lives, such as suffering, takes time. Furthermore it is often difficult for us to learn. The lessons become more bearable as we apply the sacred teachings by leaning harder and trusting more confidently. "The God of all grace . . . after that ye have suffered a while, make you perfect, stablish, strengthen, settle you."[5]

Dear friend, though your malady seems unceasing, some injustice hurts beyond human comprehension, grief darkens those long hours, you will do well to focus on the Saviour who suffered for you. Look up, give thanks, and admit, "I haven't a pain to spare!"

[1] II Corinthians 11:27-28, 30; I Corinthians 1:31.
[2] II Timothy 3:12.
[3] Philippians 1:29.
[4] Hebrews 5:8.
[5] I Peter 5:10.

❧   ❧   ❧

December

GALATIANS 1–3
GALATIANS 3

> I am crucified with Christ: nevertheless I live; yet not
> I, but Christ liveth in me: and the life which I now live
> in the flesh I live by the faith of the Son of God, who
> loved me, and gave himself for me.[1]

HERE IS AN ASTONISHING FACT that the gospel presents to the
believer: "Christ lives in me." Nothing parallels it. Few
begin to comprehend its meaning. The One who created
all things and who holds them together, lives in me. He
"who gave himself for our sins, that he might deliver us
from this present evil world"[2] has taken residence in my
heart. The thought—and far greater, the reality—should
bring me humbly before Him in praise and wonder.

Yet, how dedicated are we to this One who indwells us?
As I was teaching a class of youngsters this Galatian truth,
one of them thoughtfully responded by saying, "When it
comes to God living in my heart, I really think there's more
of me than He!" His English could have been improved,
but his childish confession was very apt. We adults have
the same problem: "more of me than He!"

Two facts, if kept constantly before us, will help reverse
the order. First, I must realize anew that Christ does live
in me. Recalling the price He paid to accomplish my redemption is important. Then, I must recognize that He
gave the Holy Spirit who dwells and works within me. This
makes the difference. This ends the struggle for supremacy.
Result? He will increase as I decrease.

The same child referred to above asked a few weeks later, "Have you ever tried to crowd yourself out of your heart?" He had been sincerely trying, in matters of school, playground, and the Boy Scouts, to let Christ be first. What a blessing if one so young can learn to give way to the indwelling Christ! He could not do it alone, but even in the sixth grade he could draw on supernatural resources.

Sometimes this very thing is called a mystery. Paul further clarifies: "Even the mystery which hath been hid from ages and from generations, but now is made manifest to his saints: to whom God would make known what is the riches of the glory of this mystery among the Gentiles; which is Christ in you, the hope of glory."[3]

[1]Galatians 2:20.
[2]Galatians 1:4.
[3]Colossians 1:26-27.

❧ ❧ ❧

December 2

GALATIANS 4–6
GALATIANS 5

> Ye did run well; who did hinder you that ye should not obey the truth?[1]

ONE COULD NEVER DESCRIBE the Apostle Paul as dull. His clarifications of spiritual truth are full of life and vivid illustrations. On occasion he included a spiritual metaphor.

In the book of Galatians he used four. Metaphors are colorful figures of speech. As implied comparisons they often graphically describe a concept.

The metaphor "hinder," scholars tell us, came from the Greek word *enkopto,* which means "to cut into." They explain that it was a term used in military operations. By breaking up roads or making bridges impassable, it was possible to impede the oncoming forces.

531

This illustration also applies to the army of God. A new soldier of the Cross is on the front lines. A fresh realization of the power of Christ in his life makes him ready for service. Then suddenly something happens. His Christian experience is cut into and he becomes one of those to whom Paul spoke: "Ye did run well; who did hinder you?"[1]

God cannot use a limping army. If ever physical fitness is essential it is so for the Christian. Our very senses must be at their best for our Captain's service.

Eyes to see the needs of those around us: "Look on the fields; for they are white already to harvest."[2] Ears to be tuned to Himself and not distracted or cut off from a sensitiveness to His voice. What if Samuel had been hindered? Instead, his spiritual hearing was alive as he quickly responded, "Speak, Lord; for thy servant heareth."[3] Hands and feet willing to work and run for Him. How easily they are hindered! We trip, even fall, and too readily become discouraged. Why is this so, when the Word promises renewal of strength, so that we may "mount up with wings as eagles . . . run, and not be weary . . . walk, and not faint"?[4]

Loss of appetite is a sure indication of ill health. Could it be we are hindered by our lack of feeding on the Word? "O taste and see that the Lord is good."[5]

May this simple truth cause us to check that no crippling defects are hindering our Christian walk. May clear vision, alert hearing, and perfect obedience cause each of us to run well.

[1] Galatians 5:7.
[2] John 4:35.
[3] I Samuel 3:9.
[4] Isaiah 40:31.
[5] Psalm 34:8.

❧ ❧ ❧

EPHESIANS 1–3
EPHESIANS 2

> Now unto him that is able to do exceeding abundantly
> above all that we ask or think, according to the power
> that worketh in us, unto him be glory in the church by
> Christ Jesus throughout all ages, world without end.
> Amen.[1]

SUNDAY AFTER SUNDAY the morning service would conclude
with this familiar benediction. To the youngsters, it was a
time to put away the multifold and scribbled church bulletin. To the junior set, it brought a feeling of "It's almost
over." Unfortunately, many adults also reached for gloves,
or buttoned coats. It was the same at every morning worship service. The benediction could be quoted from memory, but so often without heart appreciation.

One particular morning a young woman had come into
the sanctuary for her first visit to a Protestant church in
years. She clung to every word of each song. The prayers
pulled at her heart, and the sermon probed deep.

The minister talked about the first ten verses in Ephesians
2: "And you hath he quickened, who were dead in trespasses and sins." "Quickened," he explained, meant "being
made alive." "Wherein in times past ye walked according
to the course of this world, according to the prince of the
power of the air, the spirit that now worketh in the children
of disobedience." The minister explained that "the children of disobedience" includes all of us, since we are all
descendants of Adam and, when he sinned, we sinned with
him.

As he spoke the young woman reflected on the Christian
home in which she had been reared, on the teaching of godly parents, and then on her choice to turn aside from her
training and seek new horizons. Then her mind would
come back to the minister. He now was quoting, "But God,

who is rich in mercy, for his great love wherewith he loved us, even when we were dead in sins, hath quickened us together with Christ (by grace ye are saved)."

At that moment, though she was a stranger, there in the church pew the young lady asked God to forgive her past and cleanse her heart. At once she was changed. She explains, "Instantaneously I felt His forgiveness, experienced His riches of mercy and loving kindness. But it was the benediction that sent me out rejoicing. Christ had received me and now He promised to do 'exceeding abundantly above all that . . . [I] ask or think, according to the power that worketh in us.' I had already felt that power!"

To Him be the glory that this same power to do "exceeding abundantly" is ours for the asking!

[1] Ephesians 3:20-21.

❧ ❧ ❧

December 4

EPHESIANS 4–6
EPHESIANS 5

> Giving thanks always for all things unto God and the
> Father in the name of our Lord Jesus Christ.[1]

UNCHURCHED NEIGHBORS were invited to a lovely California home for afternoon coffee and to hear a Christian physician speak. One was seated on a beautiful new sofa, covered in elegant silk. For a moment she became distracted and her coffee spilled, staining the cushions. The hostess was quick to put the abashed woman at ease, assuring her that no damage was done. Then she looked up to God in silent thanks! How could she give thanks for a coffee stain which had ruined her new piece of furniture? It was easy for one who took God's word literally! It was also the beginning of reaching this lost soul for the Saviour. She could not forget the Christlike composure of her hostess. She was compelled to listen to the doctor, and opened her heart that day to his message.

Ingratitude is a true sin. In the book of Romans, Paul tells us that unthankfulness can lead to even greater sin. Speaking of the sinfulness of mankind through the centuries, he said, "Because that, when they knew God, they glorified him not as God, neither were thankful."[2] The chapter continues to tell of man's growing depravity and its results.

Thanklessness is often thoughtlessness, or possibly indifference. What Christian can be indifferent to God?

"Giving thanks always for all things" means just what it says. Some things may seem unjust or unnecessary or even not of the Lord, but they exist only to accomplish His best in a life. Charles G. Finney said, "A state of mind that sees God in everything is evidence of growth in grace and a thankful heart."

> O Lord, you've given so much to me—
> My blessings grow each day;
> But there is one request, You see:
> For this just now I pray.
>
> I knelt today with sense of need.
> For this I came apart
> That I may have in word and deed,
> Dear Lord, a grateful heart.
>
> Not grateful just on sunny days
> Or when my needs are met,
> But in all things to offer praise
> And never, Lord, forget.

"In every thing give thanks: for this is the will of God . . . concerning you."[3]

[1] Ephesians 5:20.
[2] Romans 1:21.
[3] I Thessalonians 5:18.

🦋 🦋 🦋

PHILIPPIANS 1–4
PHILIPPIANS 1

> And this I pray, that your love may abound yet more
> and more in knowledge and in all judgment; that ye
> may approve things that are excellent; that ye may be
> sincere and without offence till the day of Christ; being
> filled with the fruits of righteousness, which are by
> Jesus Christ, unto the glory and praise of God.[1]

READING THE BOOK of Philippians gives the reader a different view of its author, the Apostle Paul. His letter is to
dear friends and he writes intimately and informally. Yet
the letter covers many Christian principles and, as one man
describes it, it contains both the "art" and the "heart" of
Christian living.

In today's verse, "And this I pray, that your love may
abound yet more and more in knowledge . . .," Paul is
presenting to us a law of progress and daily growth. It was
not by accident that when he wrote he put love before
knowledge, for love is stronger than knowledge. True, each
has its place, but there is no question of order. Knowledge,
Paul previously contended, has the tendency to puff up,
but love without qualification edifies. Paul himself had
experienced that all the wisdom of the world does not bring
the love of Christ to one. Let us not forget that personal
love and affection for Jesus Christ constitute the first step,
and are basically fundamental in Christian living.

But this love must now abound in knowledge, a higher
knowledge. "That Christ may dwell in your hearts by faith;
that ye, being rooted and grounded in love, may be able to
comprehend with all saints what is the breadth, and length,
and depth, and height; and to know the love of Christ,
which passeth knowledge, that ye might be filled with all
the fulness of God."[2]

I remember hearing an old and wise Christian fervently

admonishing a young one in the faith. There were both affection and rebuke in her voice as she spoke. "If you sincerely love Him, you'll grow up in Him!" When we love someone, we have a great desire to know more about him. Our love provides an incentive for learning the deeper things of our beloved Lord. How else can we "approve things that are excellent"? Surely if Paul were writing to your church today, his prayer would remain the same. This generation desperately needs kindled hearts and enlightened minds.

> Enlighten my mind,
> Kindle my heart
> And for Thy glory
> Set me apart.
>
> Approving the excellent
> Without offense,
> Sincerely I'll seek Thee
> Every day hence.

[1]Philippians 1:9-11.
[2]Ephesians 3:17-19.

❧   ❧   ❧

December 6

COLOSSIANS 1–4
COLOSSIANS 4

> As ye have therefore received Christ Jesus the Lord, so walk ye in him: rooted and built up in him, and stablished in the faith, as ye have been taught, abounding therein with thanksgiving. For in him dwelleth all the fulness of the Godhead bodily. And ye are complete in him, which is the head of all principality and power.[1]

THE LATE Dr. Norman B. Harrison had a simple illustration which vividly illustrated what it is to be "complete in him."

He asked that someone bring him a glass of water. In-

537

variably it would be brought to him about two-thirds full. Holding it in his hand he would query, "Is this really a glass of water?" He would go on to show that two-thirds of the contents was water and one-third was air!

This shows us just how incomplete many of us are. "Completeness" means being what He intended us to be, filled to the brim with the power Christ has made available by His eternal Spirit.

"As ye have therefore received Christ Jesus the Lord, so walk ye in him." How complete a walk do we have before God and our fellowmen? Walking is a continual succession of steps—one after the other—as we walk toward a goal. It may be walking to work, or for some fresh air, but it has some definite purpose. Walking with and in Christ means being "rooted and built up in him, and stablished in the faith," making for practical spiritual completeness.

What are our spiritual proportions? A mixture of half self and half Christ? This is far from fullness.

Dr. Harrison would end his demonstration by taking a pitcher of water and filling the glass to the top. Then he would ask, "What happened?" It was evident that the air was gone and the glass was full of water.

As you walk and grow and abound, the element of self will be crowded out by Christ, and you will enter into the glorious reality of being "complete in him."

[1]Colossians 2:6-7, 9-10.

❧ ❧ ❧

I Thessalonians 1–5
I Thessalonians 4

> But as touching brotherly love ye need not that I write
> unto you: for ye yourselves are taught of God to love
> one another. And indeed ye do it toward all the
> brethren which are in all Macedonia: but we beseech
> you, brethren, that ye increase more and more; and that
> ye study to be quiet, and to do your own business, and to
> work with your own hands, as we command you; that
> ye may walk honestly toward them that are without, and
> that ye may have lack of nothing.[1]

IN DISCUSSING the believer's life, Paul used a phrase which
touches the uncommon in our busy, active daily lives:
"Study to be quiet." Circumstances seldom allow us silence.
Mothers with large families are so accustomed to noise that
their first expression of concern comes when there is stillness. Many folks come home from work and quickly turn on
the stereo or television. Anything for noise!

How does one go about studying to be quiet? We study
for final examinations, for a piano recital, to better con-
verse on world affairs, or to present a Sunday school lesson.
We study, yes, but not to be quiet.

This is not an easy admonition. Studying takes concentration. We must apply ourselves to this nugget of wisdom
to understand its wisdom and benefit. Studying to be quiet
takes real effort. In a quiet place we make an attempt, with
the distractions of life hovering close by. In stillness and
silence are found many of the deep secrets of our Christian
lives. There God speaks and makes clear that He wants
our devotion before He can use us in active service.

Remember when the disciples gathered about Jesus one
day, after they had all been out proclaiming the gospel?
Many were filled with enthusiasm. No doubt some had incidents they were anxious to relate to the Master. Others

wanted to discuss the people they had met. What was the Lord's reaction to their eager jostling and excited talk? "Come ye yourselves apart into a desert place, and rest a while."[2] Here they found refreshment and, most important, had time in the quietness to meet God.

"Study to be quiet" even in your time of prayer. God has not promised to hear our prayers for their beautiful phrasing, or length, or smoothness. The Psalmist learned this and wrote, "I will hear what God the Lord will speak: for he will speak peace unto his people."[3]

An old German woman had a hand-carved plaque which she hung on her closet door during her times of devotion. It was not out of necessity, for she lived alone. But its message had been her source of quietness and confidence before God: *Ruhe bitte,* "Silence Please." And in the stillness God spoke.

[1]I Thessalonians 4:9-12.
[2]Mark 6:31.
[3]Psalm 85:8.

❧   ❧   ❧

December 8

II Thessalonians 1–3
II Thessalonians 3

> Finally, brethren, pray for us, that the word of the Lord may have free course, and be glorified, even as it is with you: and that we may be delivered from unreasonable and wicked men: for all men have not faith. But the Lord is faithful, who shall stablish you, and keep you from evil.[1]

PARENTS with six active children were getting ready for their first vacation trip away as a family. The father compiled a list of duties that must be accomplished before departure and added a postscript: "You will finish faster if you will run."

We find a somewhat similar situation in chapter 3 of Paul's second letter to the Thessalonians. Paul asks his readers to pray "that the word of the Lord may have free course." In other words, "Let the gospel run!"

How prone we Christians are to be impatient about many things, but too seldom are we impatient enough to run with the gospel!

Dennis was a new Christian. He was excited about his faith in Christ and willing to run with the good news. Then he met one obstacle after another. The daily deterrents slowed his pace almost to a halt. One hindrance was a friend's disinterest, another was a relative's statement that he was bordering on fanaticism. These are what the Bible calls "unreasonable and wicked men." One evening when talking the situation over with the Lord, Dennis read this short second epistle to the Thessalonians. "For all men have not faith. But the Lord is faithful." Dennis was served with a new challenge. Was it not true that Jesus Christ had left instructions as to the conduct of the family of God? He told Christians how to live. He told them what their task was. And better still, He left His Spirit within them.

Dennis experienced some "divine impatience" and with new zeal he took up the banner of the Cross and set forth to "run" with the gospel. His words of reassurance came from Isaiah: "They shall run, and not be weary."[2] He rejoiced in the promise of the Lord, "Faithful is he that calleth you, who also will do it."[3]

[1] II Thessalonians 3:1-3 (also RSV).
[2] Isaiah 40:31.
[3] II Thessalonians 3:1-3.

❧ ❧ ❧

I Timothy 1–3
I Timothy 1

> Paul, an apostle of Jesus Christ by the commandment
> of God our Saviour, and Lord Jesus Christ, which is our
> hope; unto Timothy, my own son in the faith: Grace,
> mercy, and peace, from God our Father and Jesus
> Christ our Lord.[1]

OH, THE INEXPRESSIBLE JOY of spiritual parenthood! There
is no news that gladdens your heart as much as the news of
spiritual birth when you have helped to bring it about.
Your part may have seemed insignificant, like planting a
seed, or occasionally watering it, but there is great satisfaction in seeing the Lord grant the increase.

Timothy had been brought to Christ through the ministry of Paul. He was beloved by his spiritual father, who
acted as a good father should to protect his son in the faith.
He carefully nurtured him, prayed for him and, during
their absence from one another, wrote to him.

Some of the letters Paul wrote to Timothy make up the
two books that bear his spiritual son's name.

Reading these brief words of salutation always impart a
challenge to me, not just that my spiritual children will
grow in "grace, mercy, and peace" but also that the family
of God will be increased through their influence.

Todd was only eleven. He came faithfully to Sunday
school and often stayed for church with his parents. Some
of the stories and messages began to take root in his heart.
It happened one day on the playground. Tommy, a neighbor and good friend, displayed some bad sportsmanship,
and was called into the principal's office. Just before he
went, Todd yelled at Tommy, "I'm gonna pray for ya!"
After school, Todd waited for his friend. On the way home
he asked if the prayers had helped. Tommy said he thought
so because the principal had been "all right." Todd took

the opportunity to tell Tommy how the Lord can come into a "guy's" heart and make it clean. He could also be a "very present help in trouble"![2] (The verse was most appropriate on this occasion!) Tommy asked the Lord Jesus to come into his heart, and the next Sunday the boys were off to Sunday school together. Both learned a lot from their fifth grade teacher. When questioned by his mother as to his quick obedience at home, his willingness to help, and his diligent study of his quarterly, Todd's answer was quite unexpected: "You see, Mom, I have a son now. He looks to me!" Eleven may seem young for spiritual parenthood, but both boys are studying for the Christian ministry today.

We too, as spiritual parents or prospective spiritual parents, must assume the same responsibility. Your heart will be warmed and your joy overflow as you experience the joy of having your "own son in the faith."

[1] I Timothy 1:1-2.
[2] Psalm 46:1.

❧   ❧   ❧

December 10

I TIMOTHY 4–6
I TIMOTHY 6

Keep thyself pure.[1]

TO BE PURE in heart is a challenge and command that weaves a thread throughout the Old Testament as well as the New.

In Old Testament days there were many laws that dealt with purity. The penalties for breaking them were most severe and often resulted in death. Throughout the Psalms, David discussed purity. "Who shall ascend into the hill of the Lord? or who shall stand in his holy place? He that hath clean hands, and a pure heart."[2] He later prayed, "Create in me a clean heart."[3]

The New Testament continues the thread. In the Beatitudes we read, "Blessed are the pure in heart: for they shall see God."[4] Now we are told, "Keep thyself pure."

The command is impossible to keep, humanly speaking, but we are not called upon to rely on human resources. Through the supernatural work of Christ and His blood shed for us, we are cleansed. It is Jesus Christ who purifies our hearts. Just as Isaiah confessed he was unclean, and was made clean, so we can by honest admission of sin obtain His cleansing. "If we confess our sins, he is faithful and just to forgive us our sins, and to cleanse us from all unrighteousness."[5]

The believer still has a dual nature which causes constant combat in the heart. The old nature came from the first Adam, and the new one was imparted by the second Adam, or Christ. The continual struggle causes much defeat, and it is often encouraged by unconfessed iniquity in one's heart. God cannot tolerate sin, and one who cherishes it within must confess and be made right before experiencing the purity of heart that is characteristic of a Christian.

A mother desires that her child be outwardly clean. It is a frail comparison, but surely He who made us and bought us for Himself has every right to ask and expect inward and outward obedience. Through his devout apostle, He said, "Keep thyself pure."

[1] I Timothy 5:22.
[2] Psalm 24:3-4.
[3] Psalm 51:10.
[4] Matthew 5:8.
[5] I John 1:9.

❧　❧　❧

II Timothy 1–4
II Timothy 1

> Thou therefore, my son, be strong in the grace that is in
> Christ Jesus. And the things that thou hast heard of
> me among many witnesses, the same commit thou to
> faithful men, who shall be able to teach others also.
> Thou therefore endure hardness, as a good soldier of
> Jesus Christ.[1]

THERE ARE BIBLE SCHOLARS who believe that the second
epistle of Paul to Timothy, his spiritual son, was his last.
We know it was written toward the final period in the reign
of the Emperor Nero. If it is to be considered Paul's last
will and testament, it will be interesting to note the things
he emphasized.

One of the most familiar themes is that of being a faithful witness. It is followed by the challenge to "endure
hardness as a good soldier of Jesus Christ."

Possibly Paul was stressing endurance of hardness as a
means of fortifying Timothy's courage. Paul knew what it
was to suffer, and by imparting some of the building materials of his life to this much younger man, a stalwart, true
soldier might be trained.

Preparation for suffering does not always take place in the
life of a believer. Many collapse under its pressure because
they had no time to prepare. How well Paul knew of suffering with Christ. His intimacy with suffering did not
lessen the blows, but suffering for Christ's sake was for
Paul the only cause worth living and dying for. Suffering
alone has no merits, but suffering for Christ, enduring
hardness for Him, has rich rewards. "For unto you it is
given in the behalf of Christ . . . to suffer for his sake."[2]

Peter Marshall wrote, "It is better to fail in a cause that
will ultimately succeed, than to succeed in a cause that will
ultimately fail." Christians who are discouraged by suffering

for Christ may take strength from the reminder He gave: "I am Alpha and Omega, the beginning and the end."[3] He will reign forever. The good soldier prepares for all opportunities and eventualities, and the Christian soldier also prepares, knowing that if he suffers with Christ, he will also reign with Him. Here then, is purpose for life and for death.

Press on, be strong, endure. Victory in Christ is assured!

[1] II Timothy 2:1-3.
[2] Philippians 1:29.
[3] Revelation 22:13.

❧   ❧   ❧

December 12

TITUS 1–3
TITUS 2

> Who gave himself for us, that he might redeem us from all iniquity, and purify unto himself a peculiar people, zealous of good works.[1]

FOR CENTURIES there have been those who took delight in labeling Christians as "peculiar" people, implying that they were queer or eccentric, and no doubt the cause of Christ has suffered somewhat. There have been some Christians, sincere and devout, who felt satisfied that if the Bible mentioned "peculiar" people, then "peculiar" people they would be.

When I was a teen-ager this was clarified for me, and the truth continues to be a challenge. No teen-ager wants to be "peculiar," so I listened earnestly when this reference was fully explained to me. I learned that the meaning was "a people for his own possession,"[2] special rather than queer, those in whom God takes rare delight.

We have an illustration of this type of people in the Pilgrims. True, they were noncomformists in the eyes of fellow Europeans and were often called "peculiar." Yet, determined and dedicated, they came to the New World, not for gold but for God. They loved the Bible, those early Americans. The textbooks for their schools, such as the New England Primer, were nothing but the Scripture. Their outreach extended to the Indians, whom they taught to read and write, and many of whom they led to Christ. John Eliot translated the entire Bible into the language of the Massachusetts Indians.

Different? Yes, they were different, and the difference was that they were not faithless but believing. Their devotion was such that they sacrificed self, service, and convenience. Some willingly gave their lives that future generations might truly worship God freely.

If this is the "peculiar" people that we are called to be, "people for his own possession," God grant that we shall fulfill our sacred obligations. The results will be earthshaking.

[1]Titus 2:14.
[2]Titus 2:14, ASV.

❧ ❧ ❧

PHILEMON
PHILEMON

THE BOOK OF PHILEMON has been called "a masterpiece of Christian courtesy." In this short classic, written to Philemon, Paul intercedes on behalf of Onesimus, a runaway slave. In those days, slaves were considered property, not people. Paul explained to his friend that Onesimus had been set free from sin, in meeting Jesus Christ, and now he wanted to return to his former master.

"Receive him as myself," wrote Paul. "If he hath wronged thee, or oweth thee ought, put that on mine account."[1] Here is a vivid illustration of the term "imputation," which is one way of expressing the idea of charging or crediting an account. It appears only one other time in the New Testament.

On the surface, this is a simple, sweet story, but if the significance of crediting one with the righteousness of another is seen, it offers a profound message. In it we must see ourselves in the role of Onesimus—in slavery to sin. Our glorious atonement was made possible through Jesus Christ. "If the Son therefore shall make you free, ye shall be free indeed."[2] When God saves, He charges all the sinner's debts against his righteousness in Christ. We know that only God can justly declare a man righteous, and that the justification is by faith alone.

> Paul the Apostle in prison one day
> Wrote to a friend in a most tactful way.
> His letter gave thanks, he expressed love indeed,
> And with friend Philemon, he shared a need.
>
> A slave he had met (whom Christ had freed),
> And on behalf of this "son" he would plead.
> "Receive him, forgive him, I will repay.
> The debts that he owes, charge to me today."

The scene takes me back to a Cross on a hill,
Where a Father and Son in the solemnness still
Looked out on a world of men in sin,
Slaves and great debtors, with no peace within.

"Receive them, forgive them, I will repay,"
Said the Son to the Father that redemptive day.
And through His death God's great mercy was shown.
Today man is justified by faith alone!

[1]Philemon 17-18.
[2]John 8:36.

❧ ❧ ❧

December 14

HEBREWS 1–4
HEBREWS 4

> There remaineth therefore a rest to the people of God.
> For he that is entered into his rest, he also hath ceased
> from his own works, as God did from his. Let us labour
> therefore to enter into that rest, lest any man fall after
> the same example of unbelief.[1]

WE LIVE IN A DAY when the calendar is choked with activities. We barely complete a task before another urgently presses. We are surrounded by the intricacies and complexities that comprise modern living. The pace is so accelerated that there is little time for "rest."

The very sound of the word has a quieting effect. Yet do we comprehend its meaning? In the rush of today how much do we know of calmness and composure, of tranquility of heart and mind?

"Come unto me, all ye that labour and are heavy laden, and I will give you rest."[2] This verse illustrates a "given" rest. The order is simple: "Come . . . and I will give." This is the rest known by believers—rest from the pressure and guilt of sin.

"There remaineth therefore a rest to the people of God."

This has been described as a "found" rest, a rest of spirit which stems from a complete confidence in God. In this rest the Christian finds sufficiency, stability, and serenity.

The Psalmist wrote, "Therefore my heart is glad, and my glory rejoiceth: my flesh also shall rest in hope."[3] He was referring to the threefold being of man: heart, spirit, and flesh. Our emotions come from the heart, and our fellowship with God from the spirit. Yet David does not forget that the flesh, our physical being, shall "also rest [literally, 'permanently stay'] in hope," the hope of one day being resurrected and changed into His glorious image. Body, soul, and spirit are all included in God's loving care. Thus the Christian can truly experience God's rest.

Accept the rest that is yours in trusting Christ completely. Let your prayer ascend with David, "Return unto thy rest, O my soul; for the Lord hath dealt bountifully with thee."[4]

[1]Hebrews 4:9-11.
[2]Matthew 11:28.
[3]Psalm 16:9.
[4]Psalm 116:7.

❧　❧　❧

HEBREWS 5–8
HEBREWS 5

> Therefore leaving the principles of the doctrine of
> Christ, let us go on unto perfection; not laying again
> the foundation of repentance from dead works, and of
> faith toward God, of the doctrine of baptisms, and of
> laying on of hands, and of resurrection of the dead, and
> of eternal judgment. And this will we do, if God per-
> mit.[1]

WE MAY OBSERVE that highly educated and proficient people are seldom content with their knowledge. They constantly search on, delve deeper, and admit that the more
they learn the less they feel they know.

This may be contrasted with the experience of a Christian who seeks to digest the Word but is content with an
elementary understanding, and fails to seek the deeper
truths which are uncovered only through study.

The writer of Hebrews described this type of person in
chapter 5: "For when for the time ye ought to be teachers,
ye have need that one teach you again which be the first
principles of the oracles of God; and are become such as
have need of milk, and not of strong meat. For every one
that useth milk is unskilful in the word of righteousness:
for he is a babe. But strong meat belongeth to them that
are of full age, even those who by reason of use have their
senses exercised to discern both good and evil."[2]

A young seminary student expressed his feelings on this
complaint about the Hebrew converts. Said the student, "I
feel as if I were in a lineup, and God was judging me as to
my understanding of these precepts. I step out of the pene-
trating rays of His searching light and say, 'What lack I
yet?' I pray for strength and discernment to go on to perfection."

As we go on to perfection, the mysteries of the gospel begin to unfold.

"Press on," we are encouraged, "in knowledge and in holiness toward God. Walk in His light." Should Satan confront us with our failure, let us remember that if we are growing in grace, we are pleasing in God's sight. We all make mistakes and fail, but, as someone wrote so well, "Our failures, confessed honestly to Him, are as dust washed at the close of each day from the feet of one who is stepping heavenward." May we step onward to mature understanding, and be fed with meat instead of the milk of infancy.

[1]Hebrews 6:1-3.
[2]Hebrews 5:12-14.

❦ ❦ ❦

December 16

HEBREWS 9–10
HEBREWS 9

> Christ was once offered to bear the sins of many; and unto them that look for him shall he appear the second time without sin unto salvation.[1]

A SECOND-GRADE TEACHER was emphasizing to her pupils the importance of being ready for a visit by the principal of the school. Classes found in order would be rewarded. The children were to keep their desks clean and their books neat. Nothing was to be thrown on the floor so that the room would be tidy at any time for the special visitor. Each time the door would open in the front of the classroom, little expectant eyes would focus on the person entering. By the end of the afternoon, however, the youngsters were growing lax, and their anticipation was waning. An occasional kleenex slipped unnoticed to the floor, and books slid out of position. Impatience fostered whispers which muffled the sound of the back door opening.

In walked the principal. His presence startled the young ones who knew at once that their formerly orderly room was now not ready. They were saddened at the thought of missing the promised reward.

The lesson learned by the second graders is elementary, but we often learn from children. "Unto them that look for him shall he appear." Will we be ready?

We too are expecting Someone's arrival. For a time we make ready, and then the cares of the world, the preoccupations of life, and the business of the day put us in disarray and muffle the words that He spoke: "I will come again." Let us heed the admonition and keep ready.

> O blessed hope! Perhaps today—
> A moment more, and then—away!
> Caught up in clouds to be with Him,
> Beyond the reach of conflicts grim,
> Of disappointments, pain, and tears.
> O blessed hope! The rapture nears!
> Today, perhaps! We hail the dawn,
> Of heaven's glad, eternal morn;
> Above earth's turmoil, strife, and fear,
> Christ's "Lo, I come!" His children hear.
> All things declare the time's at hand!
> God's schedule will mature as planned.[2]

[1]Hebrews 9:28.
[2]Annie Lind-Woodworth.

❧   ❧   ❧

HEBREWS 11–13
HEBREWS 11

Jesus Christ the same yesterday, and to day, and for ever.[1]

THROUGHOUT HEBREWS the major theme has been the immutable Christ. He is unchangeable. There is great security in recognizing a changeless Christ in a very changeable world. "Thou, Lord, in the beginning hast laid the foundation of the earth; and the heavens are the works of thine hands: they shall perish; but thou remainest; and they all shall wax old as doth a garment; and as a vesture shalt thou fold them up, and they shall be changed: but thou art the same, and thy years shall not fail."[2]

"The same yesterday . . ." How far back does that go? David had a ready answer: "Lord, thou hast been our dwelling place in all generations. Before the mountains were brought forth, or ever thou hadst formed the earth and the world, even from everlasting to everlasting, thou art God."[3] His presence was as real yesterday as it is today. In the days of Abraham and in the days of the disciples, God was the same. He did not change during the time of the Reformation, nor in the centuries since.

"The same today . . ." As I rise to meet the new day, there is the assurance that today His mercies are as new as they were yesterday. We can say in confidence, "Great is thy faithfulness."[4] Whatever presents itself today, whether sorrow or problems or tasks beyond ourselves, His Spirit lives within us to guide us. Then why should we fear? He will sustain us today.

"Forever." Here is great anticipation. We may take heart from the past. Yesterday He led, today He leads, and forever He will go before. No matter what unknown territories we traverse, we need not fear. The One whose voice quieted the sea, who transformed lives by a word, who said,

"Come unto me,"[5] has also promised, "Lo, I am with you alway."[6] He met us yesterday, and He'll be there tomorrow. In this confidence we can rest today.

> The God of tomorrow foresees every need.
> Grant Him your future, He surely will lead.
> Yesterday's promises change not nor decay.
> Is the God of tomorrow your God today?

[1]Hebrews 13:8.
[2]Hebrews 1:10-12.
[3]Psalm 90:1-2.
[4]Lamentations 3:23.
[5]Matthew 11:28.
[6]Matthew 28:20.

❧ ❧ ❧

December 18

James 1–5
James 1

> Every good gift and every perfect gift is from above,
> and cometh down from the Father of lights, with whom
> is no variableness, neither shadow of turning.[1]

WITH THE HOLIDAYS rapidly approaching, we are preoccupied with the giving of gifts. Parents in particular are concerned about making their children happy. Everyone has the Christmas spirit.

The Christian is well aware that the Gift of gifts was given to us by the goodness of God. He became incarnate at Bethlehem. Each heart must be opened to receive the Son of God.

Truly our gift of eternal life is from "the Father of lights." Primary science tells us that in the physical world the sun is the father of light because it literally generates light. The moon and the planets only reflect the sun's rays. They have no light in themselves. God is the Christian's only source of light and life. In ourselves we have no light, but we can reflect light from Him.

The Psalmist wrote, "The entrance of thy words giveth light."[2] God is the source of knowledge, of wisdom, and of understanding. The light of God's Word fosters faith and purity in the Christian's life.

How sad that the Christian's light is sometimes dimmed by a "shadow of turning." Something comes between us and the Sun of Righteousness. It may cause only a partial eclipse, but anything between God and us cuts off the total reflection that should be ours. In Him, there is no shadow of turning.

I wonder how often, during the next several days, we will see packages piled high beneath decorated trees with sparkling lights. The season brings much outward merriment, but how sad it is that so few pause for inward meditation. This should be a time to let the true Gift of gifts surpass all else. It is not only our privilege but our sacred duty to share "the gift of God," which "is eternal life," with those around us.[3]

God gave us all that we have. Let us anew commit our grateful hearts to Him in deep desire to share the Gift from the Father of lights with the world.

[1]James 1:17.
[2]Psalm 119:130.
[3]Romans 6:23.

I Peter 1–5
I Peter 3

> Forasmuch as ye know that ye were not redeemed with corruptible things, as silver and gold . . . but with the precious blood of Christ.[1]

"Redemption for Christmas" was the sermon topic on a church bulletin board in a western city. To one particular passerby, whose Sunday schedule did not include church, the topic was intriguing. He purposed in his heart to attend, and he did.

The minister began the sermon by telling about the struggles for victory during World War II. With each victory there was fresh rejoicing because the enemy army had been driven back. How was this accomplished? It was not by jet aircraft in that war, nor by nuclear warheads. It was done by the shedding of blood of many thousands of military men from several nations.

Blood is a precious physical possession. Even the Old Testament spoke with reverence of blood: "The life of the flesh is in the blood."[2]

But what does this have to do with "Redemption for Christmas"? thought the newcomer to the church. He continued to listen. From the Bible the minister told of the way God first made us, "in his own image,"[3] and for His glory. However, man had a will of his own, and chose to be disobedient to his Maker. Adam, the first man, sinned. God was rich in mercy. He looked down from heaven on those whom He had made and moved to free them from bondage to sin and disobedience. How? By sending His Son, first to be born as a baby, and then to die for sin— to shed His blood. Through this sacrifice mankind could be redeemed. "Without shedding of blood is no remission."[4]

"Redemption for Christmas!" The message became clear to the listener. If Jesus Christ paid such a great price to bring man back to God, then He was worthy of faith and trust. *Henceforth,* thought the visitor at church, *I will live for Him who died for me!*

The blood of Christ cleanses from all sin. What a gift for Christmas! Forgiveness, cleansing, redemption!

[1] I Peter 1:18-19.
[2] Leviticus 17:11.
[3] Genesis 1:27.
[4] Hebrews 9:22.

❧ ❧ ❧

December 20

II Peter 1–3
II Peter 1

> His divine power hath given unto us all things that pertain unto life and godliness.[1]

A DAUGHTER who was writing home to her mother asked her to send some extra money for the Christmas holidays. "You'll never know how many debts I have incurred," wrote the young woman, "and I haven't started to buy presents!" Her letter had the added impact of this P.S.: "Send today as much as you can." It was signed, "Love, Judy."

Mother replied with a rather unusual note. "It is not possible for us to send the money that you need today. We are really sorry. Have a wonderful Christmas. Love, Mother." Mother's letter also contained a P.S. It simply read, "Turn the page." On the other side of the letter was another note. "I cannot send the money today, because I sent it yesterday!"

There was great relief in Judy's young heart. The needed resources were on the way, even before she had asked. This was real provision from one who really loved her.

At times we Christians find ourselves in this type of

dialogue with the One who forever loves us, our Heavenly Father. We pray, we plead, we beg that He will send those things which we need—and sometimes things which we just think we need! And the answer comes back as somewhat of a disappointment in the form of "No" or "Wait." Our hurt feelings resemble Judy's toward her mother until we turn that "sacred page" and experience great relief of heart and mind. "Now we have received . . . the spirit which is of God; that we might know the things that are freely given to us of God."[2] We have been asking for blessings which are already ours in Christ!

Even mature Christians may become childish when they start to doubt the Giver of all things. Life, in its fullest sense, and godliness are our rich inheritance in Christ. God grant that we will appropriate and radiate both, until others also enjoy their eternal riches in Him.

[1] II Peter 1:3.
[2] I Corinthians 2:12.

🍀 🍀 🍀

I John 1–2
I John 2

> I write unto you, fathers, because ye have known him
> that is from the beginning. I write unto you, young
> men, because ye have overcome the wicked one. I write
> unto you, little children, because ye have known the
> Father. I have written unto you, fathers, because ye
> have known him that is from the beginning. I have
> written unto you, young men, because ye are strong, and
> the word of God abideth in you, and ye have overcome
> the wicked one.[1]

THE FIRST EPISTLE OF JOHN has been called a heart-to-heart
talk. It is overflowing with expressions of love and advice
such as a father would use in admonishing his son. It is
said that a Christian can take his spiritual temperature by
the thermometer of First John.

I visited the home of a friend who has a six-year-old son.
On the wall of their kitchen were two yardsticks, one atop
the other. With a red pencil, the various dates and heights
of the boy had been recorded. While we were having some
coffee and conversation, in walked the proud youngster and
stood against the measure. "Show Sarah how I've grown,"
he said, with his head high and his shoulders back. He
had grown, and he was proud.

In the light of these chapters, we Christians can see just
how we measure up. Can we with great joy read these
pages and respond warmly, "How I've grown in the Lord"?
Or do our heights remain the same as to spiritual progress
as the years fly by?

There are three levels in the Christian experience. The
"little children" the apostle writes about feed on the milk
of the Word and rejoice mainly in sins forgiven. The
"young men," however, are not standing still, for they are
strong and shielding themselves from sin with the armor of

God. They will continue on in their knowledge, progressing to fatherhood.

None should stand still in their growth. The little children will graduate to meat, the young men will become more mature as they are guided by the Spirit, and the fathers will contribute much to the kingdom of God.

How sad it would have been if, in the kitchen of my friend, the measure of the past months had not shown growth in the eager, anxious child. It is even sadder if we Christians do not continually "grow in grace, and in the knowledge of our Lord."[2]

[1]I John 2:13-14.
[2]II Peter 3:18.

❧ ❧ ❧

December 22

I JOHN 3–5
I JOHN 5

> And we have known and believed the love that God hath to us. God is love; and he that dwelleth in love dwelleth in God, and God in him.[1]

"LOVE IS AN IMAGE OF GOD, and not a lifeless image, but the living essence of the divine nature which beams full of all goodness."[2] What love God had for us to send His Son to be born in Bethlehem; to lead Him to the cross to make provision for our eternal needs!

The love that a Christian should feel for the Lord has been described with four adjectives. Together they teach us ways in which we can obey the injunction "Love the Lord thy God with all thy heart."[3]

Love for Him must be filial. Truly He is our Father, and this is one of the glorious realities of Christian relationship. "For in him we live, and move, and have our being."[4] Imagine the sonship He has made possible: the joy of being a child of His and an heir with Him!

Love for God must be reverential. "He sent redemption unto his people: he hath commanded his covenant for ever: holy and reverend is his name."[5] "Serve God acceptably with reverence."[6]

Love for God must be grateful. God forbid that it should be said of us, "When they knew God, they glorified him not as God, neither were thankful."[7] We must continually "enter into his gates with thanksgiving, and into his courts with praise: be thankful unto him."[8] At Christmas, when we are careful to thank those who remember us, let us not forget to look up often and thank God for His unspeakable Gift.

Our love must be delightful to God. We sincerely delight in being with those we love. Time together enhances the relationship and separation brings regret. What of our times with the Lord? Are we regretful for the times He is crowded out of a busy holiday schedule? "Delight thyself also in the Lord!"[9] This reflects in every area of our lives. Do we delight in doing His will? At Christmas it is easy to do for those about us in the spirit of the season; but what of those days when the merriment passes, the bills come in, and there is someone in need? Do we delight our Lord by accepting the responsibility, or do we displease Him by delay or indifference?

"Beloved, if God so loved us, we ought also to love one another."[10] As Christians (and not just at Christmas), let us cultivate and practice our love for God. Let us exhibit love and share it, and may the spectrum of love be diffused in multitudes of little services done from our hearts for others for His sake.

[1] I John 4:16.
[2] Martin Luther.
[3] Mark 12:30.
[4] Acts 17:28.
[5] Psalm 111:9.
[6] Hebrews 12:28.
[7] Romans 1:21.
[8] Psalm 100:4.
[9] Psalm 37:4.
[10] I John 4:11.

❧   ❧   ❧

II JOHN
II JOHN

> Grace be with you, mercy, and peace, from God the
> Father, and from the Lord Jesus Christ, the Son of the
> Father, in truth and love.[1]

IN A SMALL FARMING COMMUNITY in Nebraska, a family were gathered for what seemed to be a meager Christmas celebration. The mother had been ill for sometime and the seven children had assumed the responsibility of the home. Their father was away working with a road crew to make as much money as possible to sustain his family.

The packages were opened. Some of the wrappings showed imagination. One gift was wrapped in wax paper with snow-scene etchings and fir-needle detail. It was evident that though little had been spent, great thoughtfulness was put into the simple gifts.

The oldest son had been a source of grief to the parents. He had been away at the State Reformatory. It was always difficult for him to determine the difference between truth and falsehood. As the stack of small packages diminished, an envelope addressed to the family was opened. In it was written the following:

> To all my family a very Merry Christmas. My packages
> will be missing from under the tree (that I should have
> cut for you), but I'm thinking about you there.

> This will be a significant Christmas for me. I have been
> going to a weekly Bible study and found out about
> Someone who could really help me. His name is Jesus
> Christ. He was born on Christmas Day. You won't
> know until I see you just how much He has done for
> me, but He is the reason I am sending you just two
> words for my present. It seems too simple, but through
> them my life has been changed. I'm coming home soon.

Enclosed in the envelope were pieces of cardboard, carefully lettered, each wrapped. On one was the word *love* and on the other, *truth*.

This son had been through many unpleasant experiences and had tasted the fruit of evil. But the gospel had transformed him and taught him the essential principles for right living—those expressed in this Second Epistle of John. Christ exemplified both truth and love, as He is their Source.

Let us pray with the Psalmist, "Send out thy light and thy truth: let them lead me."[2]

[1]II John 3.
[2]Psalm 43:3.

❧ ❧ ❧

December 24

III JOHN
III JOHN

> Beloved, I wish above all things that thou mayest prosper and be in health, even as thy soul prospereth. For I rejoiced greatly, when the brethren came and testified of the truth that is in thee, even as thou walkest in the truth.[1]

IT WAS CHRISTMAS EVE. A group of carolers were singing in the corridor of the General Hospital. The familiar words resounded down the halls and into the rooms of patients who would spend the holidays in bed.

A light lit up at the nurses' station, and a young woman responded to the call from Room 104. The patient's request was unusual: Could one of the lovely young people who were singing come in and visit with her for a few minutes? The nurse said she would ask. One who was not in a hurry to rush home to family festivities as the others were, agreed and, when the singing ended, made her way to Room 104.

The patient was middle-aged, and the medical evidence predicted that she would spend the rest of her days just as she was then—bedfast and hospitalized. The visitor was a picture of health, vivacious and eager and bright. They started to talk. The conversation centered around the Christmas season, and the patient was quick to come to her point. She related the joy that had been hers one Christmas when she had visited the Holy Land, where she could re-live the story the carolers had been singing. There, a score of years before, she had met Him who was born in the City of David, and He had become her Saviour. Since then it has been her desire to daily bear witness of what had happened to her through the transforming power of Christ.

The years passed and the two became friends. The young woman accepted Christ, and the patient was her true spiritual mother. Then the patient took a turn for the worse. At once the young woman sent flowers, and accompanying them was a card containing today's verse. It had been written some two thousand years ago by the Apostle John to a beloved friend, Gaius. Evidently the health of Gaius was poor, but John found an opportunity to send words of encouragement: "I wish you were as well in body as you are in soul."

What a supreme compliment to pay another believer, that his soul prospers above his health! God grant that our souls may prosper. Prayer appointments are always available with the Great Physician, who has promised that "they which do hunger and thirst after righteousness . . . shall be filled."[2]

[1] III John 2-3.
[2] Matthew 5:6.

꙳   ꙳   ꙳

JUDE
JUDE 24–25

> Now unto him that is able to keep you from falling, and
> to present you faultless before the presence of his glory
> with exceeding joy, to the only wise God our Saviour,
> be glory and majesty, dominion and power, both now
> and ever. Amen.[1]

THESE VERSES are an apt doxology for Christmas, one which
the great heavenly host could continually sing in praise of
fulfilled promise. God is able to keep us, and to present us
faultless because of His glory, majesty, dominion, and
power. This fact should cause our hearts to be raised in
devout affection toward our Lord. He causes us to be
not just blameless but faultless. There is a difference. As
long as man is on earth, he will have faults; but when
faults are confessed, they are laid on Christ who dealt with
them on Calvary. A carol long beloved takes on new significance: "Cast out our sin, and enter in, Be born in us
today."[2] He does this the day we experience rebirth. And
some day soon He will present us faultless before the Father.
"Praise God, from whom all blessings flow!"[3]

> "Now unto him"—This Christmas Day
> Present yourself to walk His way.
> Accept His gift, and He assures
> That life eternal is freely yours.
>
> "That is able to keep"—Oh, power divine.
> His keeping power today is mine.
> Power to present me faultless indeed
> To stand before God. 'Tis all I need.
>
> "The only wise God, our Saviour"—His birth
> Revealed to the world God's Gift of great worth.
> We offer glad homage, His glory we sing
> Who reigns all-triumphant, eternal, our King.

"Now and forever"—Established above,
A promise to keep—one made in great love.
"Amen and Amen"—So may it be!
His power and presence sustaining me.

Praise to His name this Christmas Day!
Thank God, in Him I have found the way.
With Christ in my heart, I can join that throng
In praise to God through word and song!

[1]Jude 24-25.
[2]"O Little Town of Bethlehem," Phillips Brooks.
[3]Thomas Ken.

❧   ❧   ❧

December 26

REVELATION 1–3
REVELATION 1

> The Revelation of Jesus Christ, which God gave unto
> him, to shew unto his servants things which must
> shortly come to pass; and he sent and signified it by his
> angel unto his servant John: who bare record of the
> word of God, and of the testimony of Jesus Christ, and
> of all things that he saw.[1]

GOD, WHO INSPIRED MEN to write the Holy Scriptures, entitled this book "The Revelation of Jesus Christ." This
book shows the unveiling of Jesus Christ. It gives us some
insight into details God wants us to know regarding the
future. A revelation uncovers, and much spiritual truth
is presented herein. Revelation has been called "a view
of the Lord's life on the other side of death where He acts
as Priest and is preparing to rule as King."

Christ's birth was in humility. His glory was hidden
then, but we know that some day we shall see Him as He
is. He will then be gloriously revealed, and the Christians
will be transformed, for we are told that we shall be like
Him.

Like Him, yes, but there will be a difference which one commentator on Revelation described. "He will be the Blesser, and we the blest: He the Giver, and we the receivers: He the Fountain, and we the vessels: He the uncreated Light, yea, and with His Father, the very Source itself of life and glory, and we as precious stones on which that divine effulgence is poured out. Wherever He is, this people and this church shall be with Him and abide in His unveiled presence."[2]

Revelation is a book of judgment. It is a book of instruction on things to come. The divisions are in verse two: first, the Word of God, which deals with the future, and then the testimony of Jesus Christ about the conditions of the churches.

A friend who had been fervently studying and laboring through this book expressed his feelings this way: "I felt as if the Spirit of God had allowed me to go behind the scenes onto a stage already set. The story that would take place was complicated and difficult to interpret. But my script of twenty-two chapters would guide me."

"Blessed is he that readeth, and they that hear the words of this prophecy, and keep those things which are written therein: for the time is at hand."[4]

[1]Revelation 1:1-2.
[2]F. B. Meyer.
[3]W. Lincoln.
[4]Revelation 1:3.

     ✄ ✄ ✄

> Behold, the Lion of the tribe of Juda, the Root of David, hath prevailed to open the book, and to loose the seven seals thereof. And I beheld, and, lo, in the midst of the throne . . . and in the midst of the elders, stood a Lamb as it had been slain.[1]

WHAT A CONTRAST between the Lion and the Lamb! One exempifies strength and majesty, the other meekness. In our revelation of Jesus Christ we see Him here portrayed in both roles.

Jonathan Edwards, the great American theologian of the eighteenth century, delved deeply into the things of God. He wrote, "There do meet in Jesus Christ infinite highness and infinite condescension. Christ, as he is God, is infinitely great and high above all. He is higher than the kings of the earth: for he is King of kings and Lord of lords. He is higher than the heavens, and higher than the highest angels of heaven. He is so high that he is infinitely above any need of us, above our reach that we cannot be profitable to him, and above our conceptions that we cannot comprehend him.

"Christ is one of infinite condescension. None are so low or inferior, but Christ's condescension is sufficient to take a gracious notice of them. He condescends not only to angels, humbling himself to behold the things that are done in heaven, but he also condescends to such poor creatures as men; and that not only so as to take notice of princes and great men, but of those that are of meanest rank and degree, the 'poor of the world.' He takes gracious note of little children. His condescension is sufficient to take a gracious notice of the most unworthy sinful creatures, those that have infinite ill deservings.

"His condescension is great enough to become their friend

569

... their companion, to unite their souls to him in spiritual marriage. It is great enough to take their nature upon him, to become one of them that he may be one with them. And what act of condescension can be greater?"

One stands back in awe. Jesus Christ, the Lamb of God, was slain for us. For those who accept Him He is the "strong Lion" of defense. The contrast is almost inconceivable, but He is like a lion only because of His willingness to first become the Lamb of God.

Revelation 5 continues: "Worthy is the Lamb that was slain to receive power, and riches, and wisdom, and strength, and honor, and glory, and blessing."[2]

[1]Revelation 5:5-6.
[2]Revelation 5:12.

❧ ❧ ❧

December 28

REVELATION 8–11
REVELATION 8

> And another angel came and stood at the altar, having a golden censer; and there was given unto him much incense, that he should offer it with the prayers of all saints upon the golden altar which was before the throne. And the smoke of the incense, which came with the prayers of the saints, ascended up before God out of the angel's hand. And the angel took the censer, and filled it with fire of the altar, and cast it into the earth.[1]

SAINTS ARE PRAYING PEOPLE! In today's reading we have evidence of this fact. Not just during the tribulation period described in our reading but at all times. Our hopes and fears should be expressed to the Father, and, where His will is made clear, we should seek to cultivate submission of heart as we diligently pray.

Our prayers rise like incense and are acceptable to God,

for they are proof of our faith in Christ's redemptive work on Calvary.

In Old Testament times, prayers for forgiveness were accepted on the basis of Christ's future sacrifice, of which the Paschal lamb was a type. After His resurrection, Christ ascended to the Father, where "he ever liveth to make intercession for" those who are trusting in His redeeming work on Calvary.[2] Thus our praying is never in vain, though at times it seems that the answer is delayed.

In this verse we also have the thought that prayer may be an oblation to God. Only prayer that is offered in Christ's name is acceptable to God. Believing, expectant prayer is pleasing to Him. It is always answered for God's glory and the Christian's good. Hence the Christian's confidence in God is strengthened and his gratitude to Him deepened.

Let these glorious facts encourage us to pray more, to pray without ceasing, in full realization that, as our prayers ascend, they are joined with those of Christians around the world. Together, these prayers ascend to God; the answers will descend just as surely. Let us wait with patience in full assurance that our God does all things well.

[1]Revelation 8:3-5.
[2]Hebrews 7:25.

❧ ❧ ❧

> And they overcame him by the blood of the Lamb, and
> by the word of their testimony; and they loved not their
> lives unto the death.[1]

"WHAT IS A MARTYR?" asked a little girl who was being told
the story of five young men who gave their lives for Christ
in Ecuador. "It is somebody who dies for a cause," another
answered. There was still a further thought. "A martyr is
not selfish!"

These three chapters in the book of Revelation form a
parenthesis which covers the Great Tribulation. Today's
verse is often referred to as "a song of martyrs."

Martyrdom for the cause of Christ is a true conquest of
the evil one. Those young men who endeavored to reach a
lost tribe, chose willingly to suffer the possible consequences
of death by a hostile group rather than live without giving
those Indians an opportunity to hear about the Lamb of
God who takes away the sin of the world. In the providence
of God they died, but their death was a victory.

Christmas is just over, but let us not forget that the
manger led to the cross. Christ shed His blood, but His
death was a victory. He overcame death and conquered the
evil one, and because of this, we now can triumph in Christ.
The beloved Charles Wesley expressed it like this:

> No condemnation now I dread;
> Jesus, and all in Him, is mine!
> Alive in Him, my living Head,
> And clothed in righteousness divine,
> Bold I approach the eternal throne,
> And claim the crown, through Christ my own.

Undeniably, ours is the victory of Christ, but victory places
a grave responsibility on those who truly will follow Christ.

Each must be a faithful, unselfish witness. "They overcame . . . by the word of their testimony." We must place our lives on the front lines of service, and love them not "unto the death."

John wrote some solemn words which should be prayerfully pondered as we face a new year. "He that loveth his life shall lose it; and he that hateth his life in this world shall keep it unto life eternal."[2]

[1]Revelation 12:11.
[2]John 12:25.

❧ ❧ ❧

December 30

REVELATION 15–19
REVELATION 19

. . . and worshipped God . . . saying, Amen; Alleluia.[1]

"AMEN SAYS, 'So be it,' Alleluia, 'I'm glad it is!'" It was an interesting and different idea for me and came from one who illustrated her definitions by her life.

The Christian says a mental amen as an act of submission in accepting the will of God. There are times when we pray for answers and seek direction. The outcome is not as we planned or prayed, but in what we call "obedience" we submit with an amen.

Some friends are laboring in a foreign field. They left with great anticipation and excitement to serve the Lord with gladness. On arrival they learned that their place of service and phase of ministry had been changed. Letters of protest came home asking, "Why? For what reason?" Yet each letter contained the desire for God's will. They had made a reluctant assent by "trusting it was God's will." One could easily see that there was little joy in their service.

Then one day the mail brought an air letter. It started with praise, continued in praise, and ended with an underlined hallelujah! The previous weeks had been difficult, but our missionary friends had progressed past the point of just "So be it," and stepped upward to the plane of "Alleluia, I'm glad it is!" Their exuberance reflected the Spirit of Christ who had taken possession. They delighted to do God's will and were honoring Him and edifying themselves by serving Him with joy.

More time passed, and this field saw an upsurge of Christian progress that had been unparalleled in the century. The missionaries now knew why they had been reassigned, and they were grateful for the lessons they had learned in the interim.

Another year is passing. Undoubtedly there are things you have misunderstood or thought unreasonable in the past months. A new year dawns with its mysteries and unknowns. As a Christian, it will be easy to accept what He sends with an amen. The true test, the real elixir of our spiritual life, comes by joyfully adding a resounding alleluia!

[1]Revelation 19:4.

❧ ❧ ❧

REVELATION 20–22
REVELATION 22

> I am Alpha and Omega, the beginning and the end, the
> first and the last.[1]

HAVE YOU EVER STOOD in a transportation terminal and
watched people saying good-bye? Sometimes you will see
a small group assembled. The one who is going away has
so much to say that he can barely bring himself to step on
that plane, and bid his final farewell. Then there are moments of tenderness, and one cannot help but glance at the
faces of those who remain. In their eyes is reflected the hope
that their loved one will have a good trip and, above all, a
safe return.

Such must have been John's state of mind as he completed the inspired closing portions of the book of the
Revelation. We find him expressing love. Here is his warm
assurance that the Lord will come back again. Yes, there
will be a time of separation, but each day will bring us
closer to that glorious day when the true loved One returns.

For many Christians this is not an easy book to study.
We are often prone to neglect it or skim over it. My prayer
is that each of you will have gleaned a new truth. It may
be just a glimpse into the glory that will come, a new view
of the Bride of Christ, or a better understanding of the
Lamb of God.

Christ is here described as "Alpha and Omega." How
significant at the end of the year to know that He is the
God of endings as well as of beginnings. We have read those
sacred words bequeathed to us: "Surely I come quickly."[2]

Our response should be, "Even so, come, Lord Jesus,"
for we are yearning for His return.

May God grant that as we wait we will walk in close
communion with Him, work so that the world will hear,

and daily experience the blessed reality of seeing and experiencing the glory of the Lord.

[1]Revelation 22:13.
[2]Revelation 22:20.